"TSAR AND GOD"

AND OTHER ESSAYS IN

RUSSIAN CULTURAL SEMIOTICS

CW01081275

Ars Rossica

Series Editor:
David Bethea
University of Wisconsin—Madison

ACADEMIC
STUDIES
PRESS

"Tsar and God" and Other Essays in Russian Cultural Semiotics

Boris Uspenskij
and
Victor Zhivov

Translated from Russian by Marcus C. Levitt,
David Budgen, and Liv Bliss

Edited by Marcus C. Levitt

Boston
2012

The publication of this book is supported by the Mikhail Prokhorov Foundation (translation program TRANSCRIPT).

 transcript

Library of Congress Cataloging-in-Publication Data:
A catalog record for this title is available from the Library of Congress.

ISBN 978-1-61811-804-2
ISBN 978-1-61811-124-1 (electronic)

Book design by Ivan Grave

Published by Academic Studies Press in 2012
28 Montfern Avenue
Brighton, MA 02135, USA
press@academicstudiespress.com
www.academicstudiespress.com

Table of Contents

TSAR AND GOD:
SEMIOTIC ASPECTS OF THE SACRALIZATION
OF THE MONARCH IN RUSSIA

B. A. Uspenskij and V. M. Zhivov

"I finally got the boys so worked up that they demanded to see the major. But earlier that morning I'd borrowed the rascal [a knife] from my neighbor and I took it and tucked it away, you know, just in case. The major comes over, all in a rage. He's coming. Well, don't fear, my boys, I say. But they were so afraid their hearts sank right down into their boots. The major ran in, drunk. 'Who's here! What's going on! I am tsar and God!'

"As soon as he said 'I am tsar and God!'—I came forward," continued Luchka, "with the knife in my sleeve.

"'No, your Excellency,' I say, moving closer and closer to him, "no, that's impossible, your Excellency,' I say, 'how can you be our tsar and God?'

"'Oh, so it's you, it's you,' screamed the major. 'The ringleader!'

"'No, I say, (moving nearer and nearer all the time), no, I say, your Excellency, as you yourself probably know, our God, who is all-powerful and omnipresent, is one, I say. And there is also only one tsar, who is put over us all by God Himself. He, your Excellency, I say, is the monarch. And you, your Excellency, I say, are only a major—our boss, your Excellency, by the tsar's grace, I say, and by your own deserts.'

"'Wh-at-t-t-t!' he clucked, unable to speak, choking with anger; he was so surprised.

"'That's how it is,' I say, and suddenly throw myself at him and stick the knife right into his stomach, all the way in. Neatly done. He started to move but his legs only jerked. I ditched the knife.

"'Look, I say, boys, lift him up now!'

"Here I'll make a short digression. Unfortunately, expressions like 'I am tsar and God' and many similar things were quite common among many of the commanding officers in the old days."

—F. M. Dostoevskii, *Notes from the House of the Dead,* chap. 8

The present study simultaneously belongs to literary studies and to social history, as well as to the history of culture and of political ideas. It concerns attitudes toward the tsar in Russia during various periods of Russian history, and the linguistic—and more generally speaking, semiotic—means by which these attitudes were manifested. Obviously, this is connected to the history of political views. At the same time, insofar as we are speaking of the sacralization of the monarch, a series of problems necessarily arise which, generally speaking, belong to the sphere of religious psychology. We would like to show how differing attitudes toward the tsar correlate with various stages of Russian political and cultural history; how diverse aspects of Russian cultural life converged around this question; and how in different periods the very same texts could be interpreted as having very different content, as they related to the interests of the particular historical period.

From a certain moment the attitude toward the monarch in Russia assumed a religious character. This feature of Russian religious consciousness struck foreigners strongly. Isaak Massa, for example, wrote that Russians "consider their tsar to be a supreme divinity"[1]; and other writers repeat this as well. Thus in the words of Henrik Sederberg, the Russians "consider the tsar almost as God,"[2] and Johann Georg Korb remarked that Muscovites "obey their Sovereign not so much as citizens as much as slaves, considering him more God than Sovereign."[3] But it was not only foreigners who testified to this. At the All-Russian Church Council of 1917-1918, the opinion was voiced that for the imperial period "one should not speak of Orthodoxy [*Pravoslavie*, literally, "correct glorifying"] but of glorifying the tsar (*ne o pravoslavii, a o tsareslavii*)."[4] The priestless Old Believers also characteristically declared that what differentiated their belief from Orthodoxy was that "there is no tsar in our religion."[5]

Such statements will not seem tendentious if we recall that M. N. Katkov, for example, wrote, "For the people that constitute the Orthodox Church the Russian tsar is an object not only of respect, to which any legitimate power has the right to expect, but also of a holy feeling by right of his significance in the economy of the Church."[6] Elsewhere, Katkov wrote, "The Russian tsar is not simply the head of state but the guardian and custodian of the eastern Apostolic Church which has renounced all secular powers and entrusted the tasks of its preservation and daily affairs to the Divinely Anointed One."[7] In the words of Pavel Florenskii, "in the consciousness of the Russian people autocracy is not a juridical right but a fact, manifested by God and God's mercy, and not a human convention, so that the tsar's autocracy belongs to the category not of political rights but of religious dogma; it belongs to the sphere of faith and is not derived from extra-religious principles that consider social or governmental utility."[8] "The truth of Orthodox tsars' autocracy . . . is raised in some sense to the level of a tenet of faith," explains the monarchist brochure *The Power of*

Autocracy According to Divine Teaching and the Russian Orthodox Church.[9] "Who does not know how we Russians look at our tsars and their children? Who has not felt that lofty feeling of ecstasy that overcomes Russians when they look upon the tsar or the tsar's son? Only Russians call their tsar 'the earthly God,'" wrote P. I. Mel`nikov-Pecherskii.[10]

How should we interpret these pronouncements? What is the origin of this tradition? Is it something ancient and indigenous or new to Russia? How did the deification of the monarch, something that so clearly suggests paganism, reconcile itself to a Christian outlook? These questions demand answers. Let us begin with chronology.

I. THE SACRALIZATION OF THE MONARCH IN THE CONTEXT OF HISTORICAL AND CULTURAL DEVELOPMENT

1. *Early Russian Notions of State Power and the Beginning of the Sacralization of the Monarch*

1.1. Russian religious and political thought developed under the direct influence of Byzantium. It was precisely from Byzantium that the idea of the parallelism of tsar and God was borrowed. However, this idea in and of itself in no way presumes the sacralization of the monarch. Sacralization involves not only comparing the monarch to God, but the monarch's acquisition of a special charisma, special gifts of grace due to which he begins to be seen as a supernatural being. The Byzantine texts that came to ancient Rus` in Church Slavonic translations say nothing about this kind of perception.

The parallelism of the monarch and God as "mortal" versus "imperishable" tsar came to Russia with the work of the sixth-century Byzantine writer Agapetos (Agapit), which was well known to early Russia writers.[11] In the twenty-first chapter of his work Agapetos states that in his perishable nature the tsar is like all people, but that in his power he is like God; from this association of the tsar's power with God's it is concluded that the tsar's power is not autonomous but God-given and therefore must be subordinated to God's moral law. This chapter was included in the early Russian anthology *Bee* (*Pchela*). In a copy of the fourteenth-fifteenth century the passage goes like this: "The tsar's fleshly nature is equal to that of all humans, yet in power of rank [he is] like God Almighty, because there is no one higher than him on earth, and it is proper for him not to be prideful, since he is mortal, and neither to become enraged, since he is like God and is honored for his divine nature (although he also partakes of mortal nature), and through this mortal nature he should learn to act toward everyone with simplicity."[12] The idea of a moral limitation on the tsar's power as a power derived from God is expressed here with complete clarity.[13]

Agapetos' juxtapositions are often encountered in early Russian writing. Thus in the Hypatian Chronicle in the story of Andrei Bogoliubskii's murder in 1175 we find an echo of his idea: "Although the tsar's earthly nature is like that of every man, the power of his rank is higher, like God;"[14] and the same words are found in the same place in the Laurentian and Pereiaslavl` Chronicles.[15] The same quotation is also found in Iosif Volotskii, both in a fragment of his epistle to the grand prince (which, generally speaking, represents an abbreviation of Agapetos' chapter)[16] and also in the sixteenth sermon of the *Enlightener* (*Prosvetitel`*).[17] In the *Enlightener* we find the monarch referred to directly as "the perishable (*tlennyi*) tsar." In proving that it is wicked to demand that God give account of the world's end, Joseph writes: "If you began to interrogate the earthly and fleshly tsar and to say: why didn't you do this the way I thought it should be done, or in the way I know; you would not have accepted bitter suffering, like an impudent, evil, proud and disobedient slave. And you dare to interrogate and to test the Tsar of tsars and Creator of everything . . ."[18]

In the Nikonian Chronicle Mikhail Tverskoi says to Baty: "To you, tsar, a mortal and perishable man, we give honor and obeisance as to one who has power, because the kingdom and the glory of this quickly perishing world is given you by God."[19] It is noteworthy that these words which one could also take as an echo of Agapetos' ideas are addressed to a non-Christian monarch; it is clear that the point in this case (as with the juxtaposition of a "mortal" and "imperishable" tsar) is connected to the notion of the divine sanction of all power,[20] the idea of the monarch's responsibility for what has been given into his care, but in no way concerning the ruler's special charisma.

Finally, Aleksei Mikhailovich (1629-1676) often referred to himself as a "perishable tsar" (*tlennyi tsar`*). For example, in documents addressed to V. B. Sheremet`ev he wrote: "You know yourself how the great Tsar, the eternal, was pleased to be with us (*izvolil byt` u nas*), the great sovereign and perishable tsar, you [know this], Vasilii Borisovich, [who are] not a boyar for nothing . . . Not simply did it please God that we, great sovereign and perishable tsar, render honor to you and for you accept it. . . . Thus [it should be], according to God's will and our command, [that of the] great sovereign and perishable tsar . . ."[21] We find the same expression in his epistles to the Trinity-Sergius Monastery of 1661 announcing his victory over the Poles.

Here he refers to himself in the following way: "Faithful and sinful slave of Christ . . . seated on the tsar's throne of this transient world and preserving . . . the scepter of the Russian kingdom and its borders by God's will, the perishable Tsar Aleksei."[22]

The above characterized attitude to the monarch expressed in the appellation "fleshly tsar" is also clearly stated in the forty-first sermon of Nikon of the Black Mountain's *Taktikon,* which was well known in Rus'. In particular, in the excerpt from John Chrysostom there is a specific distinction made between divinely-established power as a principle and God's sanction of a particular ruler: "It is said there is no power but of God, and you ask if every prince is appointed by God. Nothing is said about that and I would not speak about any particular prince. But we shall speak about the principle that power has to exist and that some have to possess it and others have to be possessed by it, so as not to move about randomly, here and there, like waves . . . so don't say that there are no princes not installed by God. In the same way, when a wise man says that a bride is betrothed to a groom by God, it means that the marriage was created by God but not that He necessarily unites everyone alive with a wife, since we see some people living in sinful and unlawful marriage with each other, and we do not ascribe it to God."[23] There is an ample number of occasions in the ancient tradition when the tsar is called "god." However, until a particular period this label only occurs in a special context. The most well known example is the statement of Iosif Volotskii who, addressing tsars in *The Enlightener* (sixteenth sermon), says: "You gods and sons of the Most High, beware that you not be sons of anger and do not die as human beings and take the place of a dog in hell. Tsars and princes, heed this, and fear the horror of the Most High: it was written for your salvation, do God's will, accept his grace, because God put you in His place on the throne."[24] This is how M. A. D'iakonov interprets this passage: "Tsars are not only servants of the divine who have been chosen and placed on the throne by God; they themselves are gods, like people only in nature, but in power like God Himself. This is no longer a theory of the divine derivation of tsarist power but the utter deification of the tsar's person."[25] D'iakonov's opinion is suggestive, but does not accurately correspond to the true state of affairs, as it is the result of a mistaken reading of the text.[26]

First of all, it is necessary to note that most of the passage cited from *The Enlightener* does not belong to Joseph himself. The same words are repeated with greater or lesser accuracy in other old Russian texts, all of which are based on one common source, the "Sermon of Our Holy Father Vasilii, Archbishop of Cesarea, On Judges and Rulers," a monument apparently of Russian derivation, sometimes ascribed to Metropolitan Kirill II (1224-1233). Here we read: "Heed, as it is written: you are gods and sons of the Almighty. Princes and all earthly judges are servants of God, about whom the Lord says, where I will be, there also will be my servant. Beware, and do not be the progeny of anger; being gods, do not die as human beings, and do not take the place of a dog in hell, as that is a place for the devil and for His angels, but not for you. For God Himself chose for you a place on earth and placed you up on the throne, giving you life and grace. Therefore be like fathers to the world; as it is written: princes of this world are truth."[27] With variations this text is reproduced in the *Scales of Righteousness* (*Merilo pravednoe*) and in Iosif Volotskii—both in *The Enlightener* and in the *Fourth Sermon on Punishments* (*Ob epitimiiakh*).[28]

Until a certain period—precisely, before the eighteenth century—calling the tsar "god" is only encountered in this context, in which it carries a special meaning. Just what is this? Significantly—and this has escaped the attention of commentators on Joseph's text and the other cited works—the phrase "you are gods and sons of the Most High" (*bogi este i synove Vyshiago*) is a quotation from the eighty-first psalm, line 6.[29] But if this is so, first of all, the given usage goes beyond the Russian tradition alone, and secondly, we can define rather clearly the specific meaning put into these words. There is no doubt that both the authors and readers of the given texts knew the biblical source and hence would have understood them in the sense in which they found them used in the Psalter. And this meaning is precisely defined in the *Explanatory Psalter* (*Tolkovyi Psaltyr`*), which Iosif Volotskii and the other authors also certainly knew. The issue concerned earthly judges whose power over human fates made them comparable to God,[30] i.e., a functional comparison of tsar and God concerning power and the right to judge and make decisions. Understandably, this interpretation of the Psalm made its citation natural in texts of a didactic and juridical character, a category to which all of the above-cited monuments belong; moreover, the very appearance of this quotation in monuments concerning law indicates that this very interpretation of the Psalm was in mind.[31]

Hence the fact that early Russian texts testify to calling the tsar "god" by no means signifies the identity of God and tsar or some kind of actual similarity between them. The issue only concerned a parallelism between them, and the parallel itself only served to underscore the infinite difference between the earthly tsar and Heavenly Tsar. Both the power of the prince and his right to judge thus do not appear absolute at all, but delegated by God with strict conditions whose violation would lead to the complete disidentification of ruler and God, to someone God would renounce, condemn and overthrow.[32]

The Florentine Union and fall of Byzantium, as a result of which Russia found itself the single Orthodox kingdom (not counting Georgia, which was suffering from feudal divisions and played no part in the political arena), introduced a new element into Russian religious and political thinking. Significantly, the fall of Constantinople (1453) almost coincided with Russia's final overthrow of Tatar overlordship (1480). These two events were connected in Rus`: at the same time as in Byzantium Islam triumphed over Orthodoxy, in Russia the opposite occurred—the victory of Orthodoxy over Islam. Thus Russia took the place of Byzantium and the Russian grand prince the place of the Byzantine basileus. This opened up new possibilities for a religious understanding of the Russian monarch.

The conception of Moscow as Third Rome defined the Russian grand prince as successor to the Byzantine emperor and at the same time put him in a position that had no direct precedent in the Byzantine model. The conception of Moscow as Third Rome was eschatological, and in this context the Russian monarch as head of the last Orthodox kingdom was endowed with a messianic role. In the *Epistle about the Sign of the Cross*, sometimes ascribed to the elder Filofei (Philotheus) of the Eleazarov (Yelizarov) Monastery, it says that "today's single holy Catholic apostolic eastern church shines more brightly than the sun in all the heavens, like Noah in the ark saved from the flood."[33] For all of the importance of the Byzantine emperor for Byzantine religious life he had no such messianic role. Christianity and empire existed in Byzantium as connected but independent spheres, so that Orthodoxy could be considered separately from the Orthodox empire.[34] For this reason transferring the status of the Byzantine emperor onto the Russian monarch necessarily led to rethinking its status.

Starting with Vasilii II (the Blind) who ruled during the fall of Constantinople, Russian rulers were more or less consistently called "tsars," that is, the way in which Byzantine emperors were referred to in Rus' (earlier such usage had merely been occasional).[35] In 1547 Ivan IV (the Terrible) became the crowned head of the kingdom, and the title of tsar, fixed by sacred rite, became an official attribute of the Russian monarch. In the Russian context this title had different connotations than in Byzantium. In Byzantium calling the emperor "basileus" (tsar) referred primarily to the imperial tradition; the Byzantine sovereign acted as legal successor to the Roman emperors. In Russia the title of the monarch referred primarily to the religious tradition, and to the texts in which God was called "tsar"; and in Russia the imperial tradition was not relevant.[36] Thus if in Byzantium the name tsar (basileus) was perceived as describing the office of supreme ruler (which metaphorically could be applied to God), in Russia the same title was perceived, in essence, as a proper name, as one of the divine names; in these circumstances, calling a person a tsar could take on mystical meaning.

In this context the evidence of Russian grammatical works that described the writing of sacred words using an abbreviation mark (*pod titlom*) is extremely indicative of what was happening. In principle, the same word could be written with a "titlo" above or without one depending on whether it signified a sacred object or not. According to the oldest tradition, the word "tsar" would be written with a "titlo" only if it referred to God: "[The name] of the heavenly King, the creator of all creations visible and invisible is only [to be written] with a titlo, while the earthly tsar, even if he is holy, is to be written syllable by syllable, without a titlo."[37] In other texts, however, this use of the "titlo" was extrapolated onto the names of pious tsars: "Do write [the name] of the Heavenly King and a holy tsar with a titlo, but [when naming] an unlawful tsar write out all of the syllables without a titlo."[38] Clearly, such extrapolation presumes incorporating a pious tsar into the religious tradition, transferring the attributes of the Heavenly Tsar onto him. In his travel notes of 1607 Captain Margeret described the Russians' special perception of the title of tsar. According to him, Russians believe that the word "tsar" was created by God and not by men; accordingly, the tsar's title sets him apart from all others that lack this divine nature.[39]

Thus having taken the place of the Byzantine basileus, the Russian tsar, in the opinion of his subordinates, as well as his own, acquired special charismatic power. One might presume that this perception developed gradually and was not universal. However, it is very clear that the first Russian tsar, Ivan the Terrible, believed that he himself unconditionally possessed such special charisma. It was precisely this perception that led Ivan to believe that his actions were not liable to human judgment. "For whom do you place as judge or ruler over me?" he asked Prince Kurbskii.[40] The tsar's acts are not subject to review or in need of justification, just like those of God; to his subordinates the tsar acts as God, and it is only in his relations with God Himself that his human nature manifests itself.

"Why do you not agree to suffer from me, stubborn ruler, and inherit the crown of life?" he asks Kurbskii, demanding from him the same unthinking obedience as that which God demands.[41] Kurbskii on the other hand does not share this view of the tsar's power. In Ivan's excesses Kurbskii sees his departure from the ideal of the just tsar and his transformation from a pious monarch into a "torturer." For Ivan, to the contrary, these excesses may serve as the mark of his charismatic exceptionalism. No canon of charismatic behavior existed, so that Ivan could interpret his new status as permission for complete license.[42]

This view of the tsar's power sharply contrasts with traditional views as presented in logically consistent form, for example, in Iosif Volotskii's seventh sermon from *The Enlightener*: "If there is a tsar ruling over people and that tsar is ruled by foul passions and sins, greed and anger, craft and falsehood, pride and frenzy, . . . lack of faith and blasphemy, such a tsar is not God's servant, but the devil's, not a tsar but a torturer . . . And you should not obey such a tsar or prince who leads you into dishonor and craftiness, even if he applies torture to you and threatens you with death."[43] Thus, in Joseph's opinion, one should only obey a just tsar, while opposition to an evil one is justified. A subject must decide him or herself whether or not the tsar is just or evil, guided by religious and moral criteria, and alter their behavior accordingly. Kurbskii apparently adheres to these traditional ideas.[44]

Calling the tsar "the righteous sun" (*pravednoe solntse*) which in liturgical texts refers only to Christ testifies to the developing sacralization of the tsar's power.[45] In any case, this label was used for the False Dmitrii; in the Barkulabovskii Chronicle it is said of him: "He is the true indisputable tsar, Dimitrii Ivanovich the righteous sun."[46] According to the testimony of Konrad Bussow, after the False Dmitrii's entrance into Moscow in 1605 the Muscovites fell down before him exclaiming (in his outlandish transcription): "Da Aspoidi, thy Aspodar Sdroby. Gott spare dich Herr gesund . . . Thy brabda solniska. Du biist die rehte Sohne," that is, "Let the Lord give you, sovereign, health. You are the righteous sun!"[47] Later (in 1656) Simeon Polotskii addressed Aleksei Mikhailovich the same way: "We greet thee (*Vitaem tia*) Orthodox tsar, righteous sun."[48]

At the same time we have evidence that this kind of sacralization was not universal. For those for whom this perception of the tsar was alien, the expression "righteous sun" when applied to the tsar or to any mortal individual in general sounded like blasphemy. We may conclude this from a special work that has come down to us in a seventeenth-century copy, apparently composed at that time, the "Opinion (*povest'*) about the chosen words about the righteous sun and about not heeding divine commandments, since people call each other righteous sun, flattering themselves."[49] Here we read:

> In ignorance and thoughtlessness many people apply words of grace to a mortal person in affectionate phrases. I will tell you about such as these, brothers; for people use flattering and affectionate words, and making a request they may say to one another: "righteous sun"! My soul is horrified at this human lack of understanding and my spirit quakes . . . because righteous

sun is god's name. Sinful and mortal people assume God's glory and . . . call each other by Christ's name . . . Understand this, beloved brethren; never call anyone righteous sun, not even the earthly tsar himself, [since] no one of earthly power can be called righteous sun; for this is God's name, not that of perishable man . . . And you, terrestrial rulers, learn from the Lord and serve Him with fear, and accept this teaching about this word and take special care not to call yourself "righteous sun," and do not order simple folk to call you "righteous sun" . . .

It is completely clear that this work opposes the sacralization of the monarch and applying sacred names to him.

Sacralization is also evident in depictions of the tsar which to a great degree recall those of saints. Thus, according to the testimony of Ivan Timofeev, Boris Godunov ordered his picture painted on a fresco with his name inscribed in the same way as saints' were: "He intended to create an adorned image of his likeness on the walls, and [to place] his name together with those of the saints."[50] In an analogous way depictions of Aleksei Mikhailovich were made later that contemporaries would interpret as his claim for holy status. In this connection Patriarch Nikon wrote: "And let us learn not to prescribe Divine glory prophesied by prophets and apostles to ourselves, nor to be painted freely amid the Divine mysteries of the Old and New Testaments, as it was done in the Bible printed in Moscow: the depiction of the tsar on an eagle and on a horse is indeed pride, ascribing to him prophesies prophesied about Christ."[51] Subsequently, a depiction of the reigning monarch could appear on the *panagia* [an image worn around the neck of Orthodox bishops], and here the raising of the tsar to sacred status is indisputable; in 1721 Ekaterina Alekseevna granted such a panagia with a portrait of Peter I (with a Crucifixion on the other side) to Feodosii Ianovskii.[52]

The conception of the tsar's special charismatic power fundamentally altered traditional notions, as the juxtaposition of just and unjust tsar now became that of genuine and false tsar. In this new context "just" may signify not "acting justly" but "correct," where correctness is defined as chosen by God. Thus the true tsar is determined not by behavior but by providence. At the same time the problem arises of distinguishing between true and false tsar, since it is not amenable to rational solution; if true tsars receive their power from God, then evil ones get theirs from the devil. Even the church rite of sacred anointment and crowning cannot confer grace on a false tsar, insofar as these are only visible actions, and in actuality it may be demons that crown and anoint at the bidding of the devil.[53]

Because of this the phenomenon of pretendership (*samozvanstvo*) or imposture also testifies to the sacralization of the tsar and the charismatic nature of his power. Pretendership appears in Russia when tsars appear, that is, after the establishment and stabilization of tsarist power; it is itself a claim for the sacred status of a tsar. The violation of the natural order of succession gave rise to the appearance of pretenders; in this situation the question naturally arose whether or not the true tsar was sitting on the throne, and thus created an opening for rival claimants to this power. Neither Boris Godunov nor Vasilii Shuiskii, for all the correctness of their ascensions, could be seen as authentic tsars,[54] and they themselves thus turn out to be a kind of pretender ("false tsars," "seeming tsars," etc.). The presence of a false tsar on the throne provokes the appearance of more false tsars, as there occurs a kind of competition between claimants, each of whom insists that he is the chosen one. However paradoxical it may be, such a way of thinking is based on the conviction that the only one who can judge who the genuine tsar is is not a person, but God. Pretendership is thus a fully natural and logically justified consequence of the sacralization of the tsar's power.

1.2. And so, with the assumption of the title of tsar, Russian monarchs began to be seen as endowed with special charismatic power. The sacralization of the monarch which we are observing here is far from a unique phenomenon. In particular, it was to some extent characteristic of both Byzantium and Western Europe.[55] However, neither in Byzantium nor in Western Europe was the sacralization of the monarch so directly connected to the problem of authenticity as it was in Russia. Although the character of monarchal charisma could be understood in different ways, charisma itself was ascribed to the status of the monarch, to his functions rather than to his natural qualities.

In Byzantium, ancient notions of the emperor as a god that had become part of the official cult of the Roman Empire were reworked in terms of Christianity. In their Christianized variant, these notions developed into a parallelism between the emperor and god, in the framework of which sacralization could occur, or be preserved. This sacralization did not fundamentally differ from the sacralizing of the clergy, which was based on a similar parallelism, according to which the higher clerics represented a living image (icon) of Christ. Thus, in Byzantium the emperor was perceived as part of the church hierarchy and could be perceived as a man of the church.[56] One could say that in the conditions of "symphony" between church and state as existed in Byzantium the sacralization of the tsar consisted in his participation in priesthood and priestly charisma; possibly, this derived to some extent from traditions of the Roman Empire, where the emperor functioned as *pontifex maximus* in the pagan hierarchy.[57]

In Western Europe, the sacralization of the monarch had other roots. It developed from magical notions about the leader on whom the well-being of the tribe depended. Upon Christianization, these notions transformed into the belief in the personal charismatic power of the king who possessed miraculous powers. The monarch was perceived as source of well-being, and in particular, it was thought that touching him would cure sickness or ensure a good harvest.[58] It is no accident that the canonization of monarchs was more characteristic of Western Europe than Byzantium; one may hypothesize that the most ancient Russian princely canonizations were oriented precisely on Western, first of all Western Slavic, models.

If in Byzantium and Western Europe sacralization of the monarch had definite traditions, in Russia it developed at a relatively late period as a result of the assumption of the title of tsar and rethinking the role of the ruler. The idea of the parallelism of tsar and God was assimilated from Byzantium; this was characteristic of both traditional and newly developed ideas about supreme power. On the other hand, similarity with the West was manifested in the understanding of the monarch's charismatic power as a personal gift. The tsar was seen as partaking in the divine as an individual, which defined his relations both to God and to man.

2. New Ideas about the Tsar in Connection with Foreign Cultural Influences: The Reconstruction of the Byzantine Model and Assimilation of Baroque Culture

2.1. As we have seen, the sacralization of the monarch in Russia began within the framework of the conception of Moscow as the Third Rome. This conception presumes a separation from external cultural influences almost by definition. And it is true that it arose from a negative attitude toward Greeks, insofar as Moscow became the Third Rome precisely because they were unable to maintain Constantinople as the Second Rome; having concluded an alliance with the Catholics (the Florentine Union), the Greeks betrayed Orthodoxy and were punished by the destruction of the empire. Hence it was natural for Russians to distance themselves from the Byzantine model; what was important was to preserve Orthodox traditions, not Greek cultural models. So if earlier Byzantium had taken on the role of teacher, and Rus` its pupil, now it could be thought that Russia became the teacher. Furthermore, the connection to Byzantium was defined not by cultural orientation but the fact of succession itself. The Russian tsar assumed the place of the Byzantine emperor, but

Russians derived their notions about the tsar's power from their own tradition which was only connected to Byzantium in its origin.

The political and religious ideology that was conditioned by the perception of Moscow as Third Rome may be defined as a theocratic eschatology: Moscow remains the only Orthodox kingdom, so the tsar's mission takes on a messianic character. Russia as the last outpost of Orthodoxy is juxtaposed to the rest of the world, and this conditions the negative attitude toward foreign cultural influences (to the extent that they are perceived as such). The purity of Orthodoxy is confined to the borders of the new Orthodox kingdom, which was alien to the task of universally spreading the faith; cultural isolationism is perceived as a condition for preserving its purity. The Russian state is itself taken to stand for the entire universe in an isomorphic relation and therefore has no need to spread or propagandize its ideas. Conversing with representatives of the Greek Church in 1649, Arsenii Sukhanov argued that:

> In Moscow they would even kick out the four patriarchs, just like the pope, if they weren't Orthodox . . . Indeed you Greeks can't do anything without your four patriarchs, because in Tsargrad [Constantinople] there was a pious tsar alone under the sun, and he appointed the four patriarchs and the pope in the first place; and those four patriarchs were in one kingdom under one tsar and the patriarchs gathered in councils at his royal pleasure. But today instead of that tsar there is a pious tsar in Moscow, the single pious tsar in the world—and God has glorified our Christian kingdom. And in this kingdom the sovereign tsar established a patriarch instead of a pope in the ruling city of Moscow . . . and instead of your four patriarchs he established four metropolitans in ruling capacity. So we can carry out God's law without your four patriarchs.[59]

This ideology underwent a basic transformation in the reign of Aleksei Mikhailovich. Moscow was confirmed as the Orthodox capital, but at this stage the conception of Moscow as Third Rome acquired not theocratic but political meaning. This presupposed a rejection of cultural isolationism and a return to the idea of a universal Orthodox empire. In consequence, the Byzantine cultural legacy again became relevant. Aleksei Mikhailovich strove in principle for a rebirth of the Byzantine Empire with its center in Moscow as a universal monarchy that would unite all of the Orthodox into a single state. The Russian tsar did not merely need to occupy the place of the Byzantine emperor but also to *become* him. For this new function, traditional Russian notions of kingship were clearly insufficient. The Russian tsar was conceived according to the Byzantine model, and this stimulated its active reconstruction. Russian traditions were seen as provincial and insufficient;

hence there was a new positive attitude toward Greeks, who were seen as carriers of the Byzantine cultural tradition.

The attempt to renew a universal Orthodox kingdom was realized first of all on a semiotic level. The Russian tsar tried to behave like a Byzantine emperor, and because of this Byzantine texts (texts in a broad semiotic sense) took on new life. One may say that they borrowed the text of imperial behavior which was supposed to give Russia new political status. From this point of view it is exceptionally indicative that both Aleksei Mikhailovich as well as his successor Fedor Alekseevich assumed the symbolic attributes of the Constantinopolitan basileus. Aleksei Mikhailovich ordered an orb and diadem from Constantinople to be made "following the image of [those belonging to] the pious Greek Tsar Constantine."[60] During the coronation of Tsar Fedor Alekseevich, he took communion at the altar according to the priests' rite, as Byzantine emperors did.[61] In this way the Russian tsar seemed to acquire a definite place in the church hierarchy, as it was with Byzantine emperors (see section I-1.2.1). Since the time of Aleksei Mikhailovich references to the tsar during the church service gradually broadened to include the entire reigning house.[62] Thus the church blessing was not only given to those who bore the burdens of rule but to those who were in one way or another connected to the sacred status of the monarch. It seems possible that in publishing the Law Code (*Ulozhenie*) of 1649 Aleksei Mikhailovich was also acting in the footsteps of the Byzantine emperors. For them lawgiving, including the publication of juridical codes, was one of the most important privileges of the supreme power, insofar as the emperor here acted as the formal source of the law and even, in Justinian's phrase, "the living law (*odushevlennyi zakon*)."[63] Lawgiving was a crucial mark of the emperor's worth, and it was precisely in this capacity that Aleksei Mikhailovich took over the practice.

The borrowing of new texts also presumes the borrowing of the new language in which they are written. Generally speaking, in order to identify Aleksei Mikhailovich as a Byzantine emperor one needs Byzantines who know all of the requisite symbolism. As far as Russia was concerned, one may say with assuredness that there were very few who were familiar with it, and that the majority of people could only read it using the old language.

What sort of message could be garnered from such a reading? As we already know (see section I-1.2.1), in Byzantium the sacralization of the monarch was marked by his connection to the church hierarchy. To Russians this was unfamiliar and could be interpreted as the infringement of the state on the church, as the monarch's usurpation of ecclesiastical power. This is because in the old cultural language this kind of sacralization was read as blasphemy.

Dressed in Greek robes and according himself the sacred status of a Byzantine emperor, Aleksei Mikhailovich was transformed in traditional Russian consciousness from an Orthodox tsar into Nebuchadnezzar, who compared himself to God, and into Manasseh, who made the church submit to him. This is what Archpriest Avvakum, in particular, wrote about him. He charged the tsar with breaking Orthodox traditions and with a contemptuous attitude toward Russian saints. "Our Russian saints were fools," he spoke, echoing the tsar, "they were illiterate!" Avvakum ascribed Nebuchadnezzar's blasphemous sentiments to him: "I am God! Who is my equal? The Heavenly One, really? He rules in heaven, and I on earth, His equal!" At the same time he compared the tsar to Manasseh, likening his ecclesiastical policies that led to the schism to the forced introduction of paganism, and he saw Aleksei Mikhailovich's behavior as the sacrilegious appropriation of church power: "In whose law does it say the tsar should control the church, change the dogmas, burn holy incense? His proper role is to look after it and protect it from the wolves that are destroying it, not to instruct it in how to keep the faith and how to make the sign of the cross. For this is not the tsar's affair, but that of the Orthodox hierarchs and true pastors . . . "[64]

Objections to the tsar's usurpation of church prerogatives in the second half of the seventeenth century did not only come from Old Believers. Avvakum's nemesis Patriarch Nikon criticized Aleksei Mikhailovich in similar terms, also charging him with improper claims on church power. From Nikon's point of view, the tsar was aiming at leadership of the church. He stated: "When is the tsar head of the church? Never, and the head of the church is Christ, as the apostle writes. The tsar is not, nor can he be head of the church, but is one of its members, and therefore can do nothing in the church more than the lowest rank of reader."[65] So accusations of this sort came from various opposing parties, and one must admit that Tsar Aleksei Mikhailovich actually did give reason for such reproofs, in many ways anticipating Peter I's church policies (see section II-2.1). These new aspects of the tsar's relations with the church merged in the cultural consciousness of the era with the growing sacralization of the monarch.

In the sphere of practical activity the tsar's new relations with the church were expressed predominantly in the establishment of the Monastery Office (*Monastyrskii prikaz*) which was supposed to administer church property and fulfill a series of administrative and judicial functions that were formerly under the jurisdiction of the church. This reform was carried out by the Law Code of 1649 (chapter 13), and elicited a sharply negative response from the clergy.[66] The establishment of the Monastery Office was clearly perceived as the tsar's infringement on the power that had formerly belonged to the pastors of the church.

A change in the formulas of certificates of ordination (*stavlenye gramoty*) given out upon elevation to the priesthood was also perceived as an infringement on church authority. These now included a declaration that the elevation was carried out "by order of the sovereign tsar." Protesting against this, Patriarch Nikon wrote to the tsar around 1663: "Your hand controls both all episcopal courts and property, and it is terrifying to say much less to endure if [it is true] what we hear, that bishops are installed and archimandrites and abbots are ordained by your order, and that in certificates of ordination you are given equal honor to the Holy Spirit, since it is written that [they are ordained] by the grace of the Holy Spirit and command of the great monarch. [As if] the Holy Spirit wouldn't be able to ordain without your order."[67] Likewise, arguing with the boyar Semen Streshnev, Nikon wrote: "You say, interlocutor, that our most gentle and most fortunate tsar entrusted Nikon with watching over the church's fate; it was not the tsar that entrusted Nikon with watching over the church's fate, but the grace of the Holy Spirit; but the tsar demeans and dishonors the grace of the Holy Spirit, and treats it as powerless, as if without his order this or that archimandrite, abbot or presbyter, cannot be ordained on the basis of the Holy Spirit's grace, but only by the command of the great monarch, as it is written [that one may] bury someone who's been strangled or killed, or [say] a prayer for a child born in sin—all by the monarch's order. The monarch does not respect the high clergy, but dishonors it in a way that is indescribable, [bringing] more dishonor than pagan tsars did."[68] It is clear from these quotes that the change in formulaic conventions was perceived as the tsar's appropriation of the high clergy's authority.

No less characteristic was Nikon's protest against Tsar Aleksei Mikhailovich's Law Code (*Ulozhenie*), which he similarly perceived as a claim on religious authority.[69] Nikon objects in particular to the formula: "the judgment of the sovereign Tsar and Grand Prince Aleksei Mikhailovich" (chapter 10, article 1). He argued that true judgment belongs to God alone; from this perspective, Aleksei Mikhailovich was misappropriating divine authority.[70] Thus according to Nikon tsarist power was being illegitimately sacralized. We should note that the given formula in the Law Code was traditional for Russian jurisprudence,[71] but in the context of the increasing sacralization of tsarist power it became semiotically significant.

Behind these semiotic changes that Aleksei Mikhailovich was introducing stood a profound transformation of notions about the nature of the tsar's power. If this power had originally been connected with the tsar's piety and justice (see section I-1.1), and then with his divine election, that is, with his charismatic nature (see section I-1.2), now its relationship to the Byzantine cultural model took precedence. From the point of view of these new notions, Russia's inclusion in the centuries'-old tradition of the Roman and Byzantine empires became fundamentally important. In this tradition the king's charisma took on more or less definite contours. If earlier it had been expressed in certain special powers, bestowed from above and inaccessible to simple mortals, now it was manifested in a definite norm of behavior; a certain canon of charismatic behavior replaces fortuitous charisma. In this canon the most semiotically significant are the relations between church and state; the tsar's new prerogatives in this area manifest his sacral status.

Understandably, older conceptions of the tsar's power continued to live on in the cultural consciousness of Russian society; they could interact variously with the orientation on Byzantine cultural models. At the same time these models themselves could be interpreted differently. All of this created the basis for new cultural conflicts. One should keep in mind that in Byzantium itself relations with the emperor were not without ambiguity;[72] thus the Byzantine theory of a symphony between church and state could be understood very differently in Russia. We may presume that the conflict between Aleksei Mikhailovich and Patriarch Nikon was based on opposing interpretations of the very same Byzantine ideas.[73] It is no less indicative that Patriarch Nikon, who apparently considered that Aleksei Mikhailovich's behavior deviated from the correct Byzantine model, condemned him in very traditional Russian terms, describing him as an unjust tsar.[74]

Aleksei Mikhailovich's early cultural reforms were defined by Byzantinization. Borrowed forms were torn from their original context in which their meaning had been defined by historically established interpretations. Transferred into a new cultural context, they took on new life, which could only have had indirect connection to their previous existence. Furthermore, new signs could also create new content; torn from their traditional signification they take on a meaning-generating function. This gives them stability and independence from passing cultural trends (e.g., fashion). This is exactly what happened in the case of Byzantinization. It might seem that in the Petrine era, a time of intensive westernization, it would have ceased, the more so since Peter's negative attitude toward Byzantium is well known.[75] However, this is not what happened. Byzantinization was not only compatible with Europeanization, but as concerns the sacralization of the tsar's power, it combined with Europeanization, forming a single whole. This combination had its origins in the pre-Petrine epoch.

2.2. Thus under Aleksei Mikhailovich a Byzantinizing of Russian culture took place. This process, generally speaking, was internal, insofar as Byzantium as such had not existed for a long time. The issue had to do with reconstructing the Byzantine tradition, and this led to a search for those who had preserved it (as opposed to those in Moscow who had repudiated it after the Union of Florence). This is why Greeks and Ruthenians who had preserved the connection with the Greek church became so important at this time. If at one time a part of the Russian church had rejected subordination to Constantinople, connecting preservation of the Orthodox tradition with its autocephaly, now attention turned to those in the church who had preserved that connection. The Ruthenian tradition thus played a key role in the combination of Byzantinization and Europeanization discussed above.

Indeed the Ruthenian cultural tradition simultaneously connected Muscovite Rus` with Constantinople (southwestern Rus` came under the jurisdiction of the Constantinopolitan patriarchate) and with Western Europe (southwestern Rus` was part of the Polish kingdom). Together with Greek cultural traditions came panegyric texts modeled on the Latino-Polish Baroque. Independent of origin, Greek or Western, the imported texts were inscribed into the Great Russian cultural tradition and here subjected to reinterpretation. The mechanisms of this reinterpretation were uniform and revolved around the same cultural disputes: if, for traditional consciousness, things both Byzantine and Western could be taken as new and blasphemous,[76] in the reformist, Kulturträger perception they both appeared as the means to transform Russia and to aid Russia's assimilation of universal cultural values. In relation to the monarch, both of these external traditions combined organically to create a certain resonance that led to the ever increasing sacralization of the tsar's power.

As a result, Byzantine and Western influence led to the creation of a new culture that contained features of both traditions. This new culture was juxtaposed to the traditional first of all in its attitude toward the sign and the ways of interpreting the new texts. Starting with the era of Aleksei Mikhailovich, semiotic behavior (and, in particular, linguistic activity) ceased to be homogeneous in Russia. Two attitudes toward the sign came into conflict: on the one hand, the sign as a convention, which was characteristic of southwest Russian learning (and which ultimately derived from Latino-Polish Baroque culture), that is, one which was based on Western sources of the new culture; and on the other, a view of the sign as non-conventional, characteristic of the Great Russian tradition.[77] Thus the very same texts could function in two keys, and what for some could represent a conventional figure of speech for others could suggest sacrilege. This conflict became more serious with time and became especially obvious in the Petrine period. When, for example, Feofan Prokopovich greeted Peter who had unexpectedly dropped in on one of his little nocturnal feasts with the words of the troparion "Behold the Bridegroom cometh at midnight!",[78] for some this was nothing more than a metaphorical image while for others it sounded like blasphemy.

Metaphorical usage is but one particular aspect of the Baroque attitude to the word; characteristic of the Baroque was not only play with words but play with meanings. In particular, in Baroque culture quotations are primarily used for ornamentation, and consequently the goal of a citation was by no means to be faithful to the main idea of the words; on the contrary, putting a quotation in an unexpected context to create a new resonance, a play with alien speech, was one of its most sophisticated rhetorical devices. Thus a Baroque author could seem externally similar to a medieval bookman or theologian but profoundly different in terms of his basic attitude to language.

A striking example of this attitude is from Prokopovich's treatise "On the Tsar's Power and Honor" (1718). In laying out his theory of tsarist power, Feofan writes:

> Let us also add to this teaching, like a crown, names or titles appropriate to high power, names that are not vain, as they are given by God Himself, which are the best adornment of kings, better than porphyry and diadems, better than all the most magnificent external paraphernalia and its glory, that all together demonstrate that such power comes from God Himself. What titles? What names? They call them God and Christ. The words of the Psalm are splendid: *I said, "You are 'gods;' you are all sons of the Most High;"*[79] for this is addressed to rulers. The Apostle Paul is in agreement with this: *Indeed there are many "gods" and many "lords."*[80] But even before both of these Moses referred to rulers the same way: *Thou shalt not revile the gods, nor curse the ruler of thy people.*[81] But what is the reason for such lofty names? The Lord Himself says in John the Evangelist that people to whom the word of God came are called gods.[82] What other word should be used? Was it not given by God as an admonition to them to uphold justice, as we read in the Psalm we cited? For the power given by God they are called gods, that is, God's deputies on earth. And Theodoret[83] says this well: *Since there is God the true judge, judgment is also entrusted to man; therefore they are called gods because in this they imitate God.*[84]

On the one hand, Feofan's reasoning is a typical example of a Baroque play on meanings, and on the other, it makes a clear political argument. The texts he cites do not make the point he derives from them, and Feofan of course was perfectly aware of this. Thus in the citation from the Epistle to the

Corinthians "gods" does not refer to rulers but to pagan idols, and hence cannot serve as exegesis of Psalm 81. Just as baseless is the reference to Theodoret's commentary, which was part of the Explanatory Psalter (Tolkovyi psaltyr`). According to Theodoret, the name "gods" is given to rulers and judges as a sign of their responsibility before God and not as a title meant to glorify them. This kind of free use of quotes was fully appropriate in the framework of Baroque culture and also consistently served the political aims of the given treatise; Baroque rhetoric was used as an instrument to sacralize the monarch. It apparently did not bother Feofan that his readers and listeners who were familiar with the New Testament and the Explanatory Psalter could not help but understand the quoted texts in quite a different way. This polemical challenge was also part of the Baroque play of meanings, although Baroque culture itself did not necessarily presume an opposition (as in the current case) between the "enlightened" adherents of Petrine ideology and the "ignorant masses" that held to traditional notions.

It is completely understandable that the traditional audience perceived reasoning like this in the context of its habitual language rather than via that which was being imposed on it, that is, it saw here a direct identification of the tsar with God, which it could only regard as sacrilege.[85] In the polemical Old Believer treatise "A Collection from Holy Writ About the Antichrist" it says of Peter: "And this false-Christ began to exalt himself beyond all so-called gods, that is, the anointed."[86] It is not difficult to take this as a response to Feofan Prokopovich's words quoted above, when Feofan calls Peter (as the anointed one) god and Christ, which the Old Believers took to be the realization of the prophesy that the antichrist would be revealed as one who will "exalt himself over everything that is called God or is worshiped, so that he sets himself up in God's temple, proclaiming himself to be God."[87]

We find another example of this sort of response to Baroque texts of an analogous political tendency in the anonymous Old Believer *Testimony of a Spiritual Son to a Spiritual Father* (1676) in which the death of Aleksei Mikhailovich is reported: "They did not expect this death, [as] their very own published books [called] him immortal. They have a new book—'Nikon's Sabre,' which they call 'The Spiritual Sword,' by the Chernigov Bishop Baranovich. And in the preface of the book there is a picture of the tsar, and tsaritsa, and all their offspring, cunningly done, in a picture. And right there they exalt him criminally, poor ones, saying 'You, sovereign tsar, reign here as long as the sun is in its orbit, and in the world to come reign without end'."[88] The reference is to the book by the Bishop of Chernigov Lazar Baranovich, "The Spiritual Sword"; on the second page of the preface is an engraving of Aleksei Mikhailovich and his family. The Old Believer's objection is evidently to Baranovich's words: "There is no end to the Kingdom and its tsar, indeed the Kingdom of Your Serene Majesty abides forever."[89]

Thus two traditions, the southwestern and Great Russian, clashed, but it is important that the collision took place on Great Russian soil. This created the potential for, one might say, the realization of the metaphor, that is, any Baroque image could begin to be perceived not as a convention but literally. Therefore the comparison of God and tsar could be interpreted in a direct and non-figurative sense, and not be dismissed as mere rhetoric. Two kinds of facts testify to this. On the one hand, there is the response to this practice as blasphemous, implying that the tsar's power was that of the antichrist (as in the examples cited above);[90] on the other there is the evidence of religious adoration of the monarch, about which we will speak below. Here we should also note that both of these perceptions were grounded in the same world-view.

II. THE SACRALIZATION OF THE MONARCH
AS A SEMIOTIC PROCESS

1. *Semiotic Attributes of the Monarch: Tsar and God*

1.1. The orientation on foreign cultural traditions had a clearly expressed semiotic character. In the process of borrowing, borrowed forms themselves take on a new function: namely, they indicate a connection with the corresponding cultural tradition. A German wearing a cloak means nothing, while a German cloak on a Russian is transformed into a symbol of adherence to European culture. In the sphere under investigation this sort of process acquires special significance. This is the case with a whole series of phenomena, in particular, with the various ways of naming and addressing the monarch. The Russian monarch could be addressed in the same way as a Byzantine basileus or as a European emperor. The primary function of these new denominations was to symbolize a corresponding cultural and political orientation, that is, to testify to the new status of the Russian monarch. In the cases when these titles were connected to the semantics of holiness, in the Russian cultural context they could be taken literally. This literalism could have two results: if taken in the positive sense, it could lead to the sacralization of the monarch's power, if in the negative, to the rejection of the entire state system, insofar as attributing sacred attributes to the tsar could be perceived as blasphemy. Naturally, this latter attitude could be seen as disloyalty and be persecuted by the state. Moreover, apologists for state power insisted on the appropriateness of sacral attributes, which made the external marks of sacralization a matter of state policy. Thus sacralization of the tsar turned into a state cult. As a result of this development, the history of these external attributes of the tsar's power was directly connected to the struggle between church and state and to associated ideological controversies. Hence the disputes that arose from these conflicts are especially significant, insofar as they expose the different types of semiosis that set the two opposing sides apart.

In the following section, we will examine the various attributes of the tsar's power that were connected in one way or another with the semantics of holiness, focusing particularly on linguistic behavior as most revealing in this respect. Our discussion naturally falls into two parts. First we will look at those attributes which are directly related to the tsar's personal charisma and then at those attributes of sacralization which depend on his perception as head of the church.

1.2. We will begin by analyzing the history of calling the tsar "holy." This epithet (*sviatoi*, ἅγιος) was part of the title of Byzantine emperors. This fact was more or less known in Russia, as evidenced both by the fact that this epithet was applied to Byzantine emperors in documents from Constantinopolitan patriarchs to Russian grand princes and metropolitans, and by fact that Russian grand princes and metropolitans themselves used the phrase in relation to the Byzantine emperor.[91] At the same time, neither before nor after the fall of Constantinople was this epithet used for Russian tsars and grand princes, neither by Russian tsars and grand princes themselves nor by Russian metropolitans and patriarchs.[92] On the other hand, after the fall of the Byzantine monarchy Greek hierarchs began to address Muscovite tsars and grand princes as "holy."[93] Addressing the Russian tsar in this way was characteristic not only for the sixteenth and seventeenth centuries but also for the eighteenth.[94] In particular, we may note that in the letters of the Eastern patriarchs of 1723 recognizing the establishment of Synodal administration, it says that the Synod was founded "by the holy Tsar of all Moskovia, Little and White Russia and ruler of all northern countries, Sovereign Peter Alekseevich, Emperor, beloved in the Holy Spirit and our most adored brother."[95]

The Greek hierarchs' form of address, however, did not influence Russians' usage until a particular moment. In this connection, it is quite characteristic that the epithet "holy," introduced into the tsar's titles by Patriarch Jeremiah in the Greek ordination rite for the first Russian patriarch, was omitted in the Russian adaptation of this rite used to ordain Patriarch Job.[96]

Under Aleksei Mikhailovich the monarch began to be called holy during the church service, which quickly provoked protest on the part of the Old Believer party. Archpriest Avvakum wrote indignantly: "Nowadays they [the Nikonians] do everything backwards (*vse nakos` da popereg*); go and call a living person holy to his face . . . In the commemoration of the dead it is printed: 'we will pray for the holy sovereign lord tsar.' How unfortunate for a man! But in the Paterikon (*Otechnik*) it is written: when, it says, you praise a person to his face, you give him over to Satan with a word. It is unheard of at any time that someone order himself to be called holy to his face, apart perhaps from Nebuchadnezzar of Babylon!"[97]

In the following period this usage spread. Thus in his testament Patriarch Ioakim wishes Tsars Ioann and Petr Alekseevich "to live in purity, in abstinence and in holiness, as befits holy anointed ones [or: "anointed saints," *pomazannikam sviatym*]."[98] Stefan Iavorskii speaks in 1703 of tsars as of "a holy clan of God's anointed."[99] A. A. Vinius characteristically addresses Peter I in a letter of March 9, 1709 in the following way: "I pray the Lord and Almighty God to preserve your holy person in health."[100] In the first version of V. P. Petrov's ode "On the Composition of a New Law Code" (1767) appear these lines:

> Great [was] the Lord in Peter the Great,
> Great he was in Elizabeth,
> [And] in Your holy Catherine,
> In the miracles She performed![101]

Subsequently, the epithet "holy" could be applied to anything relating to the tsar. Thus in 1801 Metropolitan Platon (Levshin) spoke of the "holy blood" of Empress Maria Fedorovna that flowed in Emperor Alexander's veins,[102] and in the 1810s Archbishop Avgustin (Vinogradskii), administrator of the Moscow diocese, refers to the "holy will" and "holy prayers" of the tsar.[103]

Notably, a phrase with the epithet "holy" ("*Gospodi sviatyi, bogovenchannyi tsariu*" [Holy Lord tsar, crowned by God]) was removed from the coronation rite for Tsar Fedor Alekseevich.[104] This phrase had been included in the coronation rite of Fedor Ioannovich, Mikhail Fedorovich, and Aleksei Mikhailovich.[105] In this context "holy" evidently signified the same thing as the final exclamation (*vozglas*) of the liturgical rite, "Holy of holies."[106] This refers to the holiness that is required of every believer in order to take the Eucharist. Just as believers who are preparing for communion are called "holy," insofar as they have been purified by confession and repentance, so too is the tsar when he takes communion as part of the coronation ritual. The elimination of the epithet was due to a change in the word's meaning. It was precisely because the tsar began to be called "holy" independent of context that it came to be connected with the special status of the tsar as the anointed one, so that its use before his consecration seemed improper. Thus the removal of the epithet from the coronation ritual by no means contradicted the general tendency to sacralize the monarch, but on the contrary, represented one of its special manifestations.

1.2.1. As we see, the tendency toward sacralization of the monarch was manifested not only in using sacred signs but also in their elimination. This was conditioned by the fact that the development of this sacralization caused certain elements of traditional practice to be associated with the cult of the tsar that had had no such associations before. Traditional practice itself could only exist insofar as this kind of association was impossible. Its new semiotic significance becomes an indicator of the changed attitude toward the tsar. Thus Fedor Alekseevich forbade comparison of himself with God in petitions to him. In an imperial ukase of June 8, 1680, it says that "In your petitions you write that he, the Great Lord, should *deign to be merciful, like God*, but writing this word in petitions is improper, and you should write of your affairs in petitions [rather, for example] *for the sake of the upcoming holiday and for the Sovereign's continuing health*."[107] We should keep in mind that the forbidden form of petition had existed long before Fedor Alekseevich (at least, already in the sixteenth century), but clearly had not been connected to the sacralization of the monarch, but rather indicated his duty to rule justly, like God, and to his responsibility before God. Doing away with the form was definitely connected to a change in this conception. In this case, under Fedor Alekseevich, the comparison of the tsar as a person (not as a ruler) to God was seen as too direct and could at this time still seem inappropriate. We see a very analogous train of thought a century and a half later in 1832 when an imperial directive was issued to remove portraits of the tsar and representatives of the ruling family from churches.[108] Apparently this directive was due to the fact that these portraits could be taken to be icons.[109] The very fear that such a misunderstanding might occur indicates the sacralized status of the monarch.

1.3. From these examples it may already be clear that calling the tsar "holy" was in a certain definite way connected to calling him the anointed one. Indeed, from the time of Aleksei Mikhailovich, the moment of anointing or consecration took on extreme importance for the perception of the monarch in Russia.[110] And it is characteristic that at least from the start of the eighteenth century the monarch could be called not only "the anointed one," but also "Christ." The word Christ in the meaning of "the anointed" is an obvious Grecicism,[111] and in this sense we may speak of the convergence of the Greek and Russian traditions. In the epistle of the Eastern Patriarchs to Aleksei Mikhailovich of 1663, loyalty to the tsar was presented as a requirement of the faith, in view of the fact that the tsar was named Christ (χριστός, that is, the anointed); hence it was impossible to be a Christian if one was not a loyal citizen. "Just as God's power in the heavens embraces everything, so too the tsar's power extends to all of his subjects. And just as an apostate from the faith is separated from the bosom of the Orthodox, so too those unfaithful to the tsar's authority are unworthy to be called Christian (ἀνάζιος ἡμίν δοκά ἀπό χριστού κεκλῆσθαι καί δνομάζεοθαι), for the tsar is God's anointed one (χριστός), with a scepter, and orb, and diadem from God."[112] Here it is quite clear how the Byzantinization of Russian culture proceeded in the matter under consideration.

Nevertheless, the use of the word "Christ" together with the older and more usual term "anointed" (*pomazannik*) fundamentally distinguishes the Russian situation from the Greek and lends the title of tsar as "Christ" a special connotation. Although in the sermon "On the Tsar's Power and Honor" (1718) Feofan Prokopovich defends the legitimacy of such usage, referring to the etymological meaning of Christ as "anointed,"[113] it is clear that he had in mind not merely etymology alone, but also the tsar's immediate likeness to Christ.[114] Evidence of this is the writing of the word "Christ" with a capital letter and also using a diacritic (*titlo*), as was done with sacred names. It should be stressed that in his justification for calling the tsar "Christ" Feofan not only bases himself on the etymology of the word, but sees the etymology itself as a manifestation of the objective connection between God the Word and the tsar; according to Feofan, being anointed was assimilated to Christ's nature from the beginning, and so "such a miraculous ceremony" is carried out "so as to create one great and glorious anointment with the Savior."[115] This juxtaposition of the tsar with Christ, going beyond mere etymology, appears quite unambiguously in texts dedicated to the victory of Poltava. Peter is called Christ, Mazepa is labeled Judas, and Peter's companions—apostles. Thus in the "Service of Gratitude . . . for the Great God-Given Victory . . . at Poltava," written in 1709 on Peter's order by Feofilakt Lopatinskii, and personally edited by the tsar himself,[116] it says (in the sedalen [kathisma] of the seventh voice of the morning service): "A second Judas appeared, a slave and flatterer, an irredeemable son appeared, a devil by nature and not a man, thrice an apostate, Mazepa, who abandoned the Lord Christ, his lord and benefactor, and attached himself to the evil one."[117] At the same time, it says here of Peter's fallen soldiers: "let them be honored as apostles, not yielding to Mazepa the second Judas, but giving their souls for their sovereign."[118] Correspondingly, in his "Laudatory Sermon on the Battle of Poltava" of 1717, Feofan Prokopovich bases his references to Mazepa as Judas precisely on the fact that Peter is "Christ": "O unexpected enemy! O pariah to your own mother! O new Judas! And no one should imagine that to call a traitor Judas is excessive indignation . . . The lawfully reigning monarch . . . is Christ the Lord . . . hence it is fitting to call Christ's betrayer Judas."[119]

Nonetheless, calling the tsar "Christ" was not limited to merely etymological considerations, but testifies to the fact of their basic proximity in the consciousness of that time. This is clear, in particular, from calling the monarch "Savior" (*Spas*). Thus in his sermon on Peter's birthday of May 30, 1709, Stefan Iavorskii said: "And about our monarch, what will I proclaim? I bring you great joy, for your Savior is born. Born for you, and not for himself. And what salvation is this? For our eyes have seen his salvation. Oh, great is the salvation of our earthly Savior—our fatherland unjustly stolen and for many years groaning to be free of the enemy yoke, our forefathers' subjects, like Israelites, truly in Egyptian bondage, to return again to their original state, to purify the province of Livonia and the Izhorian land of infidels."[120] The phrase "For our eyes have seen his salvation" is a paraphrase of Simeon's words addressed to Christ,[121] while the line "I bring you great joy, for your Savior is born" comes from Archangel Gabriel's speech to Mary.[122] Calling the tsar "Savior" (*Spas*) was evidently secondary in relation to calling him "Christ." The example clearly demonstrates that the etymological arguments cited to justify naming the monarch "Christ" were only a pretext for making a real association between tsar and Savior. Of course, this kind of title was perceived as blasphemy by the traditional Russian cultural consciousness. In this perspective, the etymological arguments were insignificant and rejected as irrelevant on principle, while the attempt to make the real association was the key issue. This kind of reaction is completely apparent in a whole series of Old Believer works. Thus in the "Epistle Against Reverence to the Tsar's Two-Headed Eagle and to the Four-Pointed Cross" (1789) the Russian tsar is compared to impious pagan kings who tortured Christians, and moreover, it is emphasized that unlike the Russian tsar, "these impious tsars did not openly call themselves Christ." From this it is concluded that the Russian monarch was not simply impious (according to the traditional theory of "righteous" and "impious" tsars) but a tsar-antichrist.[123] In another early nineteenth-century Old Believer work by Iakov Petrov of the Fedoseev sect that argued the impossibility of prayers for Nikonian monarchs, we read: "O God, preserve us from such darkening of the mind and absolute insanity, and clear deviation of praying to God for the antichrist. Reader, beware, lest we call on the name of the beast in daily prayer in the divine books instead of pious tsars. For he calls himself tsar, and god, and savior. This is absolute apostasy."[124] The mention of the tsar calling himself "god and savior" clearly refers to labeling the tsar "Christ," which is perceived as evidence of the tsar's nature as antichrist. In precisely the same way, in the Old Believer (Begunskii sect) work entitled "Epistle of Christians on the Notebooks Sent from Pomoria," the emperor (Peter I is the concrete one in mind) is characterized as "Satan's anointed, Jewish tsar, exalted above all other so-called gods and idols, a false Christ, dog from hell, two-headed snake, misappropriating for himself church and state power."[125] The expressions "false Christ" and "Satan's anointed" indubitably refer to the tradition we are examining of calling the tsar "Christ." In this context the reference to the tsar as "anointed" could also give offense when seen as suggesting the affinity with Christ.[126]

1.3.1. The tradition of calling the tsar "Christ" began to emerge in Great Russia at the very beginning of the eighteenth century. Characteristically, we first hear this label from an emigrant from south-western Russia, namely, Dimitrii Rostovskii, in his speech greeting Peter I of March, 1701.[127] "Even before we receive the opportunity to see Christ, the Heavenly Lord God, in the future age, and to delight in the sight of his most bright face; now in this age we are honored to see the most bright face of the Lord's Christ, Anointed of God, the earthly tsar, the Christian Orthodox Monarch, Your Most Bright Tsarist Majesty, and be filled with joy."[128] This tradition clearly took root in Great Russia and very soon after this we encounter this epithet not only in rhetorical works but also in letters to the tsar.[129] We may also note several precedents in Stefan Iavorskii. Thus in his "Sermon on the Victory over the Swedish King near Poltava in 1709" he exclaimed: "The victor Christ conquered the tribe of Judas through Christ our tsar."[130] And in the "Sermon of Thanksgiving on the Taking of the Swedish City Called Vyborg in 1710" he said: " . . . But the sun of the most holy Virgin and her son, Christ the Savior, began to shine and send rays of grace to Peter our Christ, strengthening him and defeating the Lion, the Swedish king, who could only find refuge in Turkey and not in his own place of rest."[131] In the "Sermon for the Week of Pentecost" we read: "O dove, Paraclete, who sends grace unto Christ your David, always show the same protective mercy for our Christ, your anointed one."[132]

It is understandable that such usage was especially characteristic of Feofan Prokopovich, who as we have seen, repeatedly defended the appropriateness of this epithet in the sermon "On the Tsar's Power and Honor" (1718),[133] the "Investigation of the Pontifex" (1721),[134] and in the speech on Catherine I's coronation day (1726).[135] Examples are numerous;[136] worthy of special attention is that this expression also figures in the "Spiritual Regulation," the juridicial act written by Prokopovich that remained in force over the church until 1917. Here we find that "perfidious people . . . do not hesitate to raise their hands agaist the Lord Christ."[137]

In this same period calling the tsar "Christ" also made its way into liturgical texts. We already cited such usage in the "Service of Thanksgiving for the Victory near Poltava," and we find here a whole series of similar examples. Thus in the sedalen (kathisma) of the fourth voice (*glas*) we read: "Lord send down strength to help us . . . and confuse them [our enemies]; bring your grace on Peter your Christ."[138] Characteristically, Old Believers considered this usage in liturgical books blasphemous. Ivan Pavlov wrote about the sedalen of the fourth mode from the service on the Poltava victory that "they called him [Peter] in print not only the antichrist, but Christ."[139]

In the following years of the eighteenth century the epithet we are examining occurred more rarely, insofar as the place of the anointed emperor was mostly occupied by empresses, whom calling "Christ" was somewhat awkward. However, not all writers considered this so. Thus the Tambov priest Ivanov called Catherine II "Christ" in a speech on her coronation day in 1786: "How humble, how far-seeing and how generous, is this, the one anointed and crowned today for the Russian kingdom, the Lord's Christ!"[140] At the same time, for lack of an emperor the heir to the thone could be called "Christ." Thus the court teacher, hieromonk Simon Todorskii (later Archbishop of Pskov) in his sermon on the birthday of Grand Prince Petr Fedorovich in 1743 said that "Christ, that is, the anointed to the Russian throne, comes from no other tribe but that of the seed of the Russian David, Peter the First."[141]

With Paul I's ascension this awkwardness disappeared and the tradition we are examining was renewed. Thus in the ode "The Triumphal Coronation and Consecration to the Kingdom of His Imperial Majesty Paul the First on April 5, 1797," V. P. Petrov spoke of Paul: "Do not touch him! He is the Lord's Christ!"[142] The reign of Alexander I offers abundant similar material. In the classic sermon of the Moscow Metropolitan Platon (Levshin) at Alexander I's coronation, it says: "Thus, seeing [Russia] everywhere protected and strengthened, we rejoice in You, Great Soverign, and exult, and hail you, and thank the Lord, for He came and brought salvation to his people, and raised high the horn of his Christ."[143]

Platon also calls Alexander I "Christ" in other places.[144] Platon's successor to the Moscow archbishop's pulpit, Avgustin (Vinogradskii) refers to Alexander I as "Christ" extraordinarily often. Thus in the "Sermon on the Occasion of the Taking of the French Capital by Allied Russian Troops," delivered on April 23, 1814, Avgustin exclaimed: "But what can we say about You, Comfort of Humanity, Savior of Europe, Glory of Russia? What can we say about You, the Lord's Christ, God's Friend, Desired Man! We can say nothing."[145] One could cite many such passages.[146] The well-known Kievan preacher, Archpriest Ioann Levanda, greeted Alexander in 1801 with the words: "Our eyes wanted to see an Angel, to see their Christ, God, who has mercy on us: they now see all this in you."[147]

Notably, when Levanda's sermons were reprinted in 1850 the spiritual censors eliminated this form of address as "deviating from the truth and approaching flattery."[148] Thus calling the tsar "Christ" could still seem inappropriate, as opposed to calling him "the anointed." We meet the same response in Metropolitan Filaret (Drozdov). In 1863 he sent the Synod a report about the book *Service to the Most Holy Mother of God Called Ease My Sorrow* (1862). Metropolitan Filaret's attention was drawn to a prayer to the God Mother in an appendix in which it says: "Strengthen unseen our true tsars, who have been honored with the awe-inspiring name of Your Only-Begotten Son . . . against the enemies who surround them." Filaret clearly associated these words with the tradition of calling the tsar "Christ" and wrote that "the *Only-Begotten Son* of the God Mother, who is also the Only-Begotten Son of God, is our Lord Jesus Christ alone, and no created being may be *honored with the awe-inspiring name of the Only-Begotten Son* of God the Father and the *Only-Begotten Son* of the God Mother. If the author of the prayer wanted to suggest the designation *Anointed of God*, he prevented such a meaning by using the expression *honored with the awe-inspiring name. Awe-inspiring* (*strashnyi*) rightly refers to God and the God Son, but the words *awe-inspiring name* are inappropriate in reference to someone anointed, which David does not even dare attribute to Saul."[149] It is clear from this that Filaret wanted to exclude any association between calling the tsar "Christ" with Jesus Christ, and to reject the very tradition of using this term of reference.

This is all the more indicative of the fact that this tradition did not disappear even at the end of the nineteenth century. Thus in the "Sermon on the Day of Coronation and Most Holy Consecration of His Majesty the Most Pious Sovereign Emperor Alexander Nikolaevich, All-Russian Autocrat," delivered by Archpriest of the Samara cathedral Ioann Khalkolivanov on August 26, 1871, after an unsuccessful attempt on the tsar's life, it says: "In the greatest days of Christ's passion, when true Christians grieved over their sins, this new Judas was planning evil against the anointed of God, the Lord Christ, and on the day of Christ's glorious resurrection, when everyone was rejoicing in the resurrected Savior, he rushed to bring death to our tsar, immortal in His glorious acts, our hope and joy!"[150]

Thus the given tradition applied to the entire Synodal period.[151] This was the natural result of the fact that the principle of sacralization of the monarch was part of the very basis for Synodal administration, and no particular limitations (like censors' restrictions) could diminish the influence either of the principle or of the texts that embodied it, which preserved their productive power, and which Synodal authority could not repudiate without harm to itself.

1.4. Calling the tsar "earthly god" is another example of Byzantine traditions that were echoed in the new period of Russian history. Similar to calling God the "Heavenly Tsar," the tsar could be referred to as "god on earth." The former designation occurs in liturgical texts (for example, in the prayer "Heavenly Tsar"), while the latter was an everyday commonplace. We know that this designation was possible in Byzantium. In the eleventh century "Advice and Tales of Kekaumenos [Cecaumenus]" in addressing the king it says: "My holy commander, God raised you to the kingly throne and by his mercy (αὐτο) made you, as they say, an earthly god, able to behave and act according to your desire. Therefore may your behavior and acts be filled with reason and truth, and may righteousness abide in your heart."[152] As is apparent, calling the king "earthly god" was usual linguistic practice in Byzantium of that time.[153]

This description of the tsar was also used in Russia, although we can't trace its source to Byzantium. At first it was found among foreigners, and in many cases one can't say for sure whether the phrase was used by Russians or comes from the foreign author himself. Thus in his pamphlet about Ivan the Terrible (1585) Paul Oderborn noted that for his subjects the tsar was both pope and earthly god: "Bey seinem Leben hielyen in sein Unterthanen nicht allein für einem irrdischen Gott, sondern auch für iren Kayser und Papst."[154] Isaac Massa, writing in 1612, remarked apropos of the Russian subjugation of Siberia that "with the help of several locals who had learned Russian from Russian peasants in their villages the Muscovites told the savages about their tsar, asserting that he was almost an earthly god [*dezelve by na eenen aertschen god te zijn*]."[155] In his "Politics" (1663-1666), Iurii Krizhanich compared the Russian tsar with "some God on earth" and calls him an "earthly god," referring to Psalm 81 (82): "Earthly god. The king is like some kind of god on earth. 'I said, You are gods and all sons of the Most High' (Psalm 81)."156 A letter from Patriarch Nikon to Aleksei Mikhailovich (apparently from 1663) also testifies to the use of the label. Addressing the tsar, Nikon says: "Woe to those who after death will be thrust into gehenna, who should fear, for those who today are exalted in this world and who are prideful, as if they were immortal and gods, are praised by the foolish, listening with pleasure to senseless words like 'you are an earthly god.' Holy Writ however teaches us that our God created everything in the heavens and on earth that He desired. Nebuchadnezzar, the king of Babylon, enjoyed this kind of foolish phrase, and lost his kingdom."157

As we see, the expression "earthly god" was known in Russia. However, evidence concerning its use derives from peripheral sources and are absent in the Russian manuscript tradition. On the other hand, it widely entered into Russian literature from the mid-eighteenth century. This could be explained by the fact that it had previously existed outside of the manuscript tradition, evidently as something specifically secular; subsequently, as Russian culture became more secularized, it became part of literature (of cultural texts). Simultaneously, by strength of the growing sacralization of the monarch, the phrase became a permanent part of the cult of the emperor. It took on an almost official character whose new significance was expressed with maximal clarity by E. V. Barsov who wrote in the introduction to his edition of the coronation ritual: "The supreme power, so exalted by the Church, is considered 'holy' before the face of the people and the tsar's ideal image is elevated to the significance of 'earthly god' in the people's consciousness."158

In the eighteenth century, one of the earliest examples of the use of this phrase is in a letter from Stefan Iavorskii to Peter I of April 14, 1714: "More than the forgiveness of guilt, what kind of virtue can there be that is more worthy of your tsarist preeminence? For in this way you, earthly gods, resemble the heavenly God Himself."159 In a story by A. K. Nartov about Peter I it says: "We who had the good fortune to be close to this monarch will die faithful to him, and our burning love for this earthly god will only be buried with ourselves."160 From the mid-eighteenth century, the expression "earthly god" became completely standard, making its way into religious literature as well. Thus in 1750 the prefect of the Kievan Spiritual Academy Manassiia Maksimovich said in the "Sermon on the Choice of a Hetman in Glukhov" (although not speaking of the tsar but about Hetman Kirill Razumovskii): "All . . . republics, magistrates, administrations, from the richest to the smallest, are under the supreme power . . . Divine Providence has established this for us, having placed His deputies, earthly gods, among us."161 S. Naryshkin wrote in his "Epistle to Catherine II" in 1762: "We call earthly tsars gods," and further, addressing

Catherine directly: "You are an earthly God, and ours, O You, Catherine!."[162]
A similar comparison was subsequently used widely by G. R. Derzhavin,
though here one can trace the ongoing connection to Psalm 81 (82) (which
is also present, by the way, in Naryshkin). In a variant of his "Epistle to
I. I. Shuvalov" (1777) Derzhavin writes:

> Pillars of the fatherland! This is your one goal,
> Although you carry thunder with manifest strides,
> Although you secretly conclude peace with earthly gods.[163]

In the poem "To Rulers and Judges" (1787) we read:

> Almightly God arose, and judges
> The earthly gods in their assembly.[164]

In the poem "Providence" (1794) Derzhavin writes:

> With the majesty of an earthly god
> Catherine, casting a glance . . . [165]

In the poem "Desires" (1797) he says:

> I by no means seek
> To be close to earthly gods
> And I in no way want
> To be exalted higher . . . [166]

Finally, in the ode "To the New Year, 1798" we read:

> We see shattered thrones
> And the earthly gods fallen from them.[167]

V. P. Petrov expresses himself the same way in a letter to Catherine II of
December 3, 1793, speaking of putting his hopes on "the earthly god, so that
[she] would deign to restore divine mercy to me."[168] And Karamzin in his
"Ode on the Occasion of the Inhabitants of Moscow Taking the Oath . . . to
Paul I . . . " (1796) causes the rivers and thunder to exclaim: "O Paul! You are
our earthly god!"[169] In "Treatise on the Fruits of Christ's Coming to Earth"
(1806), Bishop Feofilakt (Rusanov) asks: "Are governments more burdened and

overwhelmed where the Sovereign is considered an earthly god? Or where they see in him only the right of the stronger?"[170]

Together with the expression "earthly god," in the eighteenth century one often encounters the synonymic combination "earthly deity" (zemnoe bozhestvo) referring to the tsar in the same function. Thus in his first inscription to a statue of Peter (1750) Lomonosov writes that "Russia honors [Peter] as an earthly deity."[171] Precisely the same title of "all-Russian earthly deity" was subsequently applied to Catherine II, as in A. Perepechin's poem "Heartfelt Feeling of the Most Genuine Zeal, Dedicated With Reverence to the All-Russian Earthly Deity Catherine the Second . . . " (St. Petersburg, 1793): "All villages, lands, cities and the thriving peoples in them sing a song to the all-Russian earthly deity Catherine the Second." Petrov also calls Catherine "earthly deity" in his ode "On Composing a New Law Code" (1782):

> *Thus it pleases Catherine;*
> *The Earthly Deity orders it . . .* [172]

Characteristically, A. S. Pishkevich uses this phrase not in a panegyric text but in his everyday writing about the empress: "Zorich . . . was about to attract the gaze of this earthly deity,"[173] referring to Catherine II. Given the wide use of this phrase in eighteenth-century poetry, it is natural that one encounters a variety of paraphrases of it. Thus, for example, in his ode "On Concluding Peace with the Ottoman Porte" (1775), Petrov calls Catherine "Deity of the earthly dale" (*Bozhestvo zemnogo dola*).[174] N. P. Nikolev gives an even more expressive paraphrase in his ode "On the Taking of Warsaw, 1794," in which a juxtaposition of Heavenly God and earthly god uniquely metamorphozises into a contrast between a general and particular God:

> *Tsar—valor! Particular God of the world!*
> *You will not insult the general God . . .*
> *(Tsar—doblest`! chastnyi mira Bog! /*
> *Ty obshchu Bogu ne sogrubish` . . . . . .).*[175]

One could cite many similar examples.[176]

It is completely natural that calling the tsar "earthly god" provoked sharp opposition from those who did not accept the official ideology. Thus in 1834 in Petersburg, "under interrogation the peasant Abram Egorov testified that in an Assembly of [the sectarian] Skoptsy, when he called the Sovereign Emperor 'earthly God,' using the expression consecrated in Rus`, the deviants answered him with a wild wail that 'he is an earthly ***!'"[177] It is curious too that in the notes to his fourth satire, Kantemir condemns the practice of calling a military commander "god" (he apparently had the emperor in mind, considering the etymological meaning of the corresponding Latin word), noting that Romulus and Remus had been "deified due to the people's superstition."[178]

1.5. The traditions of denominating the monarch described above arose within the context of relating him to liturgical texts, which developed widely starting from the Petrine period. Using liturgical texts for this purpose naturally presumes applying attributes of God to the tsar, and these cases themselves thus testify to the sacralization of the monarch. This tendency, it seems, was not only cultivated by Peter's entourage but was directly encouraged by the tsar himself. Thus Tsarevich Aleksei Petrovich testified under torture that his teacher, N. K. Viazemskii, told him that: "Stepan Beliaev and his chorus sing before your father [that] if god wants, he overcomes the laws of nature, and similar verses; and they keep singing, gesturing to your father; and he likes being compared to God."[179] Applying liturgical references to the tsar became a common occurrence. We will cite several examples. A. A. Vinius had the habit of addressing Peter I with the words: "I pray, do not bring your slave to judgment."[180] These words coincide with those from a prayer from the matins service ("Hear me, Lord, in your truth, and do not bring your slave to judgment") which derives from the second verse of Psalm 142 (143). Under suspicion for conspiring with Tsarevich Aleksei, Prince Ia. F. Dolgorukii wrote to Peter in February 1718: "Today I am forced to disturb the most precious ears of your majesty with my unworthy wail: I call on you, O God, for you will answer me; lower your ear, Lord, and deign to hear the voice of your slave, crying out to you on the day of my misfortune!"[181]

In his celebrated sermon on the burial of boyar A. S. Shein (1700), Stefan Iavorskii addressed the tsar in the name of the deceased, putting into his mouth the last words to God of St. Simeon the God-Receiver: "Now dismiss your slave, Lord, in peace: For my eyes have seen your salvation, which you have prepared in the sight of all people."[182] Peter was delighted with the sermon, and this played a decisive role in Iavorskii's career.[183]

The well known Petrine figure A. A. Kurbatov, in congratulating Peter on his military successes, used the form of the akathist hymn, as a result of which all greetings and praise of the monarch took on the character of prayers.[184] This was the case of his congratulations to Peter on the taking of Narva in 1704:

Rejoice, most glorious tsar, for today people belonging to God and expecting deliverance revive hope through you and choose a better lot. . . . Rejoice, God's follower who takes on the appearance of a slave , for the Lord is with you. . . . Rejoice, our most joyous tsar, strong as adamant . . . Rejoice, our most merciful sovereign, filled with worthy zeal and truth . . . Rejoice, anointed of God, in the appointed measure . . . [185]

His congratulations on the Poltava victory of 1709 was structured on the same model:

Rejoice, for your tsar's heart is forever in God's hands; rejoice, for you are fulfilling the commandment of God's Word, pledging your soul for your servants; rejoice, for your godlike humility lays low those who boast of might; rejoice, for thanks to this humility the armaments of your rule not only have brought glory, but terrified the universe; rejoice, for by your effective and wise bravery your troops have been purified like gold in a crucible; rejoice, for those foreign lips that belittled Russia have not only been silenced, but made to tremble; rejoice that, with God's help, there is hope of fulfilling your immemorial desire to gain the Varangian [Baltic] Sea; rejoice, that all-merciful God is bringing all of your good beginnings to realization, thanks to your humility; rejoice that henceforth, thanks to this same humility and your unswerving trust in Him, all of your good intentions will come to fruition through his omnipotence.[186]

Kurbatov was not alone in delivering this kind of panegyric; see, for example, the greetings to Peter from St. Petersburg typography workers when he returned from abroad in 1717, which was also structured on the model of the akathist hymn.[187] A song in the Poltava cycle indicates that this kind of salutation was common:

> Rejoice, two-headed Russian eagle. . . .
> On this [victory], we offer "rejoicings" to you,
> And pray God for your well-being.[188]

In the foreword to his "Notes on the History of Peter," P. N. Krekshin addresses him: "Our Father (*Otche nash*), Peter the Great! You brought us from unbeing into being . . . Before you everyone called us last, but today they call us the first."[189] To what extent such quotation of holy texts in reference to the tsar was usual may be seen by the fact that the Metropolitan of St. Petersburg and Novgorod Amvrosii (Podobedov), addressing a petition to Alexander I asking that he be kept on the Novgorod pulpit, began his letter of March 16, 1818, with the words of the Psalm: "All-Merciful Sovereign! Do not abandon me in my old age . . . "[190]

Thus one could address the tsar in the same way as God, and Metropolitan Platon (Levshin) justified this practice in his "Speech on the Arrival of His Imperial Majesty [Alexander I] in the Reigning City of Moscow, On his Entry into the Uspenskii Sobor," delivered on September 8, 1801, a week before his coronation. Platon said:

> The Holy Spirit proclaims and commands us: *Lift up your heads, O you gates; be lifted up, you ancient doors, that the King of glory may come in.* [Psalm 23 (24)]. This was said about the great spiritual Tsar, the Lord Jesus Christ, so that we, trapped by sin, would open the gates of our hearts to him, and make a dwelling place for him in our soul. But why should we not take these words to refer to ourselves, and to Your sacred Person, most pious Monarch! You bear the image of the Heavenly Tsar; we contemplate His unseen glory in Your visible glory, and this temple is the image of our hearts, for the external Church images the inner one. The doors of this [external] temple are open to you, but so that our inner temple will open to your coming, we hurry to open the gates of this [inner] temple with the keys of our heart. So descend, Tsar of glory! The gates of the inner and outer temple are lifted up. The path is free. Descend to the divine altar, to God, rejoicing in Your youth. Fall before the feet of the Tsar of tsars. Come in here and together with Yourself lead the most august persons, the one blessed with carrying You in her womb, the other, companion in the holiness of Your bed—and with them also lead all of Your sacred blood. Come in here! And we, preceding and following You, will sing Glory to God in the highest! [Luke 2: 6].[191]

Alexander I's objection to this way of addressing him is noteworthy. In an order to the Synod of October 27, 1815, he wrote that "During my last trip through the provinces in speeches delivered by clergymen I was unfortunate to hear excessive praise of myself that would have been be appropriate for God alone."[192] Another example is Catherine II's disapproval of the reference to her as a "deity" in a letter to E. R. Dashkova, who had sent her a draft of her encomium to be presented at the Russian Academy: "Also cross out 'as a beneficent Deity'—such an apotheosis doesn't conform to the Christian religion, and I am afraid that I do not have the right to sainthood, insofar as I have imposed various restrictions on church property."[193]

1.5.1. This series of examples could be interpreted simply as the playful citation of sacred texts, so characteristic of the Baroque and post-Baroque traditions. In the context of the growing sacralization of the monarch it is impossible to distinguish such playfulness from actual deification; they are not only interwoven in our interpretation but in reality itself. It is significant in this connection that together with prayerful addresses to the monarch actual church prayers could serve as panegyrics. In a letter of March 17, 1884, to K. P. Pobedonostsev, N. I. Il'minskii drew special attention to this. He wrote that "the eighteenth century introduced much that was alien, secular, obsessive and servile into the ecclesiastical sphere," and as an example he cited the service to Saints Zachary and Elizabeth:

> The Menalogion under September 5 lists the "ancient service for the holy prophet Zachary, father of the honored John the Baptist" transcribed from Greek. After this comes: "Another service for the same holy prophet Zachary and for the holy righteous Elizabeth" . . . We began to celebrate our Patron Saints' day [in a church dedicated to the two saints] according to this "other service." In church I always stand next to the reader. The kontakion hymn amazed me: "As a full moon, you received the light of truth from the Messiah, from the ideal (*myslennyi*) sun" and so on. I imagined a portrait of Elizaveta Petrovna, full and roundfaced—*a full moon*. I suspected that this service had been written during Elizaveta Petrovna's reign; I read and explored carefully and found this expression in two troparia of the ninth ode of the canon: "And entreat the most gracious Lord to save the souls of your namesake and of all who extol you." "Pray to the most gracious one and the namesake [i.e., the Empress Elizabeth, celebrating her saint's day]." Since there is [another] service in honor of Zachary, this "other service" is only so to speak a supplement, and in it Elizabeth is glorified almost exclusively, and Zachary only rarely mentioned. The service is composed as for any holiday: there are paremii and a song of praise with which, instead of a selected psalm, words from Zachary's song have been very aptly added: Blessed is the Lord . . . for He visits and brings deliverance to His people. It is natural that people felt relieved and elated after the transition from the epoch of "Bironovshchina" to that of the entirely Russian monarch Elizaveta Petrovna, but everything has a limit, and to bring one's obviously earthly interests into the church, and more subtly and cleverly than sincerely and piously, seems improper. In the presence of Elizaveta Petrovna it seems that all of these seeming praises of St. Elizabeth, mother of John the Baptist, were meant for her, her namesake.[194]

This protest against the cult of the tsar expressed in a letter to the Ober-Procuror of the Synod was for that time exceptionally bold and could have been interpreted as rebellion. Il'minskii understood this very well. At the beginning of the letter he wrote: "Written February 2; having reread it, I am sending it off on February 29, 1884. I beg your indulgence and trust. I have read everything again, made three deep bows, and decided to send it off. God's blessing! The morning of March 17, 1884."[195]

2. Semiotic Attributes of the Monarch:
The Tsar and the Patriarch

2.1. As noted above (sections 1-2.1), those processes of sacralizing the monarch that were originally conditioned by the Byzantinization of Russian culture under Aleksei Mikhailovich by no means ended during the period of turning to Western models. Moreover, in the eighteenth century, during the epoch of the active Europeanizing of Russian culture, these processes reached a crescendo. Under Peter I the sacralization of the monarch not only did not abate, but on the contrary, sharply intensified. If for the earlier period (the second half of the seventeenth century) one may speak of the relative similarity of the Russian and Byzantine situations, in the eighteenth the Russian cultural situation markedly differed from the Byzantine—precisely in the greater sacralization of the monarch. It is at this time that the relation to the monarch that characterized the entire imperial period of Russian history, and about which we spoke at the start of this study, definitively took shape.

What changed under Peter? What were the origins of this new attitude toward the monarch in the Petrine and post-Petrine periods? The answer is simple: the tsar began to be perceived as the head of the church, and this had the direct result of associating him with God. The Byzantine perception of the monarch and his having been awarded a place in the church hierarchy perfectly interacted with Protestant notions about the monarch as head of the church that Peter was promoting.[196] A vivid example of this concurrence is Feofan Prokopovich's "Investigation of the Pontifex" (*Rozysk o pontifekse*) (1721) in which the Protestant idea of the monarch's priority in church administration was casuistically supported precisely on the grounds of Byzantine precedent.

In practice this was manifested in the abolition of the patriarchate and in assigning the monarch a series of prerogatives that had formerly belonged to the patriarch. In this the Russian situation was fundamentally different from the Byzantine insofar as the "symphonic" reciprocity of spiritual and secular powers (however it may have operated in practice) was replaced by the single and all-encompassing authority of the secular principle. We should keep in mind that in its time the need to establish the patriarchate in Russia had been motivated precisely by the Russian monarch's assumption of tsarist power, since the title of tsar presumed that where there was a tsar there had to be a patriarch.[197] Calling the tsar and patriarch a "god-chosen, holy and divinely wise double" (*dvoitsa*), an "eternally abiding pair" (*dvoitsa*), and a "divinely-chosen duo" (*sugubitsa*) in the Nikonian service book is an exceptionally expressive example of this.[198] After the fall of Byzantium and Moscow's assumption of the function of Constantinople (as the Third Rome—see section 1-1.2), the Russian monarch became the head of the Orthodox ecumene and thus took the place of the Byzantine basileus (or "tsar" as he was called in Russia). Accordingly, the first hierarch of the Russian church in some sense also replaced the Constantinopolitan patriarch and should therefore receive that title.[199] One of the reasons for ordaining a Moscow patriarch was that the tsar, in the words of the eastern patriarchs, "alone . . . is a great tsar on earth, as well as Orthodox."[200] Priesthood and kingship, according to Justinian's sixth Novella,[201] should develop harmonious relations and therefore be of equal honor.[202]

At the same time, under Peter the opposite idea took root—that having a tsar (emperor) not only does not presume the presence of a patriarch, but excludes the possibility, insofar as any independent ecclesiastical rule was perceived as an encroachment on the tsar's autocratic power.[203] Hence the former conception became the subject of constant attack on the part of adherents of the Petrine reforms. Thus, for example, Feofan Prokopovich wrote in the "Spiritual Regulation" that "the simple folk do not know how the religious power differs from the Autocratic, but, amazed by the great honor and glory of the Supreme pastor, think that such a ruler is a second Sovereign, equal to the Autocrat or even greater than he, and that the spiritual order is different and greater than that of the state . . . Thus simple hearts are [so] corrupted by this opinion that in some situations they may not look at their Autocrat as the Supreme pastor."[204]

No less indicative in this context is the organizing of the All-Jesting and All-Drunken Council whose activities spanned practically the whole of Peter's reign.[205] The main goal of this establishment was undoubtedly to discredit religious authority and to challenge the traditional respect that it enjoyed in Russia. At the same time it parodied the principle of symphonic unity between the spiritual and secular authorities, the principle of "doubling" (*dvoitsa*) that Patriarch Nikon had advocated. A "prince-caesar" headed the assembly together with a "prince-pope" who could also be called the "all-jesting and all-drunken patriarch"—a parodic double that was juxtaposed to Peter's real and undivided power. In line with this conception the patriarchate was replaced by the Spiritual College and, later, the Synod (Feofan's words cited above provided the basis for this reform); and the monarch was proclaimed the "ultimate judge" (*krainii sudiia*) of this body in 1721.[206] This was directly reflected in the functioning of the church administration, whose court of last appeal was precisely the monarch. In the manifesto establishing the Synod Peter openly referred to his responsibility to reform the ecclesiastical order,[207] which meant the monarch's direct intervention in the life of the church. In particular, bishops were to be appointed by imperial decree,[208] while in the post-Petrine period the practice became established for the Synod to nominate three candidates from whom the emperor made the final choice.[209] This procedure transformed traditional practice which had been for a council of bishops to propose three candidates from which the patriarch made the choice.[210] Obviously the Synod was taking the function of the council upon itself, with the emperor in the role of the patriarch. Virtually every aspect of Church life was subject to imperial decrees.[211] Finally, any changes in the rules governing the Synod itself could only be carried out with the emperor's consent.[212] In general, the Synod functioned as nothing less than as an auxiliary organ of autocratic power, whose principle was later spelled out in the Fundamental Laws in the following formula: "In ecclesiastical administration the autocratic power acts through the Most Holy Governing Synod, which was established by [this power]."[213] Peter still did not call himself the head of the church, although he was factually in charge of it; notably, foreign contemporaries unanimously recognized him as in this capacity, and in particular could suppose that he was president of the Spiritual College (Synod).[214] This opinion had indisputable basis: thus the Synod itself, in 1721, defending its independence from the Senate, asserted that "today the spiritual administration under His Tsarist Majesty's distinguished and benevolent supervision has not been established on the model of patriarchal administration, but has its own special form, and does not consist in one person, and does not carry out its duties under its own name, but by means of supremely powerful decrees from His Tsarist Majesty, who as the Most Pious monarch, following the example of the ancient Christian tsars, has presented himself to this Holy Synod as Supreme President and Judge."[215] V. N. Tatishchev considered that Peter had "left presiding [*predsedanie*] over the Synod to himself,"[216] which N. M. Karamzin also described in his "Memoir on Ancient and Modern Russia": "Peter declared himself head of the church, having destroyed the patriarchate as dangerous for unlimited autocracy."[217] In this context A. K. Nartov's story is very indicative. According to this, Peter "became head of the church in his state and once, describing the struggle between Nikon and his father Aleksei Mikhailovich, commented: 'It was time to curb the elder's power, which didn't belong to him. God is pleased for me to attend to the citizenry and the clergy, and I am both sovereign and patriarch for them; they have forgotten that in ancient times these were united'."[218]

One may presume that Peter did not call himself head of the church because according to his lights the administration of the church was a natural prerogative of autocratic power.[219] Moreover, after the Petrine period the sacralization of the monarch grew, as did the monarchs' conviction of their special charisma, and it was apparently with this charisma that they connected their function as head of the church. And in accordance with this new consciousness they indeed began to call themselves this. Catherine II was the first to call herself head of the church, although still in private correspondence with foreigners.[220] Then in 1797 Paul formally legalized this title in the Act on Succession to the Throne in which it says that "Russian sovereigns are the head of the Church;"[221] moreover, here the formulation is presented as something well known, made in the context of an argument that Russian monarchs must be Orthodox. Thereafter it was used in the Fundamental Laws.[222]

If for one part of Russian society the notion of the tsar's special charisma justified the subordination of the church to the tsar as its head, for another— in particular, the Old Believers—the subordination of the church to the tsar threw the church's own charismatic status into doubt. Old Believer monk Pavel stated (in 1846) that "the Old Believers accepted clergy and simple people from the Great Russian church until the era of Emperor Peter I in the third rank [as those who renounce heresy], and thereafter and until now accept people from there as second rank [through Chrismation as well as from churches without a legal clergy]." The particular reason for this change consisted in the fact that Peter, "having usurped spiritual power, put an end to the existence of the Moscow patriarchate, and wanted to be head of the people and head of the church."[223]

The belief in the charismatic basis of the monarch's function as head of the church may also be seen in the perception of the monarch as a priest. In the words of Joseph de Maistre, among the Russians "it is precisely the emperor who is the patriarch, so there is nothing surprising in the fact that Paul I had the fantasy of officiating at a mass."[224] Fedor Golovkin also testified to Paul's desire right after his coronation "in his capacity of head of the church" to officiate over the liturgy; similarly, Paul wanted to be spiritual confessor to his family and ministers,[225] although the Synod talked him out of it, objecting that "the canon of the Orthodox Church forbids a priest to carry out the sacraments if he's been married for a second time."[226] Grivel likewise reports that Paul expressed the wish of leading the Easter service, referring to the fact that he was the head of the Russian church, which made the clergy subordinate to him; Grivel believed that it was precisely this incident that led the Synod to tell him that a cleric married for a second time could not lead services.[227] Thus at least in words the Synod recognized the emperor as a priest. Accordingly, in his ode "Russia's Well-Being, Established by her Great Autocrat Paul I" (*Blagodenstvie Rossii, ustroiaemoe velikim eia samoderzhtsem Pavlom Pervym*) of 1797 Zhukovskii calls Paul "bishop, pastor and hierarch" (*vladykoi, pastyrem i ierarkhom*), putting the following words into Russia's mouth:

> *This is Paul, my guardian angel,*
> *A model, an ornament of crowned heads;*
> *My protection, my shield and joy,*
> *Bishop, pastor and hierarch.*[228]

This perception of the tsar as priest led to the paradoxical rethinking of the Byzantine theory of the "symphony" between church and state. Thus at the All-Russian Church Council of 1917-1918 the idea was expressed that "until this time in Russia, tsarist rule combined 'kingdom' and 'priesthood' [*tsarstvo i sviashchenstvo*]."[229] And as a matter of fact, uniting the functions of head of state and head of church seemed natural, so that when in 1905 the idea arose of reviving the patriarchate, Nicholas II quickly nominated himself for patriarch: "speaking with a deputation of hierarchs who were lobbying to convene an All-Russian Council to select a patriarch, the Sovereign wanted to know who they had in mind for the patriarchal throne, and upon learning that they had no one, he asked if the hierarchs would agree to the Sovereign Emperor putting forward his own candidacy. The deputation fell silent in confusion."[230]

The perception of the tsar as church representative was also reflected in the semiotics of behavior. Thus members of the clergy had to kiss the tsar's hand (as did other subjects), at the same time as tsars (as opposed to laymen) did not kiss clergymen's hands. The kissing of hands was the accepted response to receiving a blessing, but blessings were given by the elder to the younger, so that the kissing of hands testified to hierarchical subordination. The fact that members of the clergy kissed the tsar's hand, but not the reverse, apparently testifies to their relationship to him precisely as head of the church.[231] When Alexander I kissed the hand of a priest in the village of Dubrovskii after he was brought a cross it was seen as something completely extraordinary. "The priest was so struck by this act of the pious Christian tsar that until his very death he spoke of no one else but Alexander and kissed his hand, which had been touched by the imperial lips."[232] Such behavior was apparently usual for the pious Alexander,[233] but nevertheless was a deviation from the norm of tsarist behavior. Hence when Alexander met with the Iur`ev Archimandrite Fotii, he kissed his hand after obtaining his blessing.[234] However, when later Fotii blessed Nicholas I and extended his hand to be kissed, the emperor ordered him to be sent to Petersburg to learn proper decorum.[235] In N. K. Shil`der's words, Fotii "was so flustered that he forgot about all of the rituals rendered in such cases to the head of the state and church."[236] No less significant, when bishops entered the imperial palace they had to abandon their crozier staffs.[237] The significance of this fact becomes clear if we keep in mind that according to the decision of the Council of 1675 high church officials had to leave their staffs behind when officiating together with the patriarch.[238] Abandoning the staff clearly signaled hierarchical dependence. In this context the instructions given to Patriarch Job who was to meet with the patriarch of Constantinople, Jeremiah, and receive his blessing in 1589 are significant. He was ordered to give up his staff if Jeremiah did the same, but in the opposite case not to give it up for any reason; it is perfectly clear that this would have been seen as a sign of the Moscow patriarch's subordination.[239]

2.2. As we have seen, with the abolition of the patriarchate the monarch assimilated the patriarch's functions, and this directly influenced his image. In particular, the special charismatic power that was attributed to the monarch as head of the church might have been connected to the special charismatic status of the patriarch in pre-Petrine times; this special charisma, as distinguished from that of the episcopate, was defined by the fact that the patriarch's enthronement service involved a special consecration (chirotony or cheirotonia) that was unknown outside of the Russian church.[240] This helps explain the perception of the monarch as living image of God.[241]

As the visible head of the Church, the patriarch represents the image of Christ as its invisible Head. In principle, this relates to any ruling church hierarch as leader of a self-sufficient ecclesiastical community; in Russia, however, in light of his special ordination, the patriarch possessed not only administrative but also charismatic priority over other bishops. Hence the patriarch also justifiably took first place in being perceived as God's image. Patriarch Nikon declared that "the Patriarch [acquires] the image of Christ, the city Bishops the image of the twelve Apostles, and rural Bishops the image of the seventy Apostles"[242]; and that "the patriarch is the living image of Christ and in his spirit, acts and words embodies the truth [zhivopisuia istinu]."[243] After the patriarch ceased being head of the church this divine image became associated mainly with the tsar. When in the mid-nineteenth century a regimental chaplain taught that "the earthly tsar is the visible head of the Church,"[244] he clearly had in mind that the tsar was the image of Christ, that is, the image of God. Calling the tsar the image of God may be connected to the Byzantinization of Russian culture (see section II). Indeed, in Byzantium, together with the doctrine of the patriarch as image of God, the idea was also expressed that the emperor too was God's image.

Thus in a panegyric speech to Constantine by Eusebius of Caesarea it says that the king is "the image of the only tsar of all [the universe]" (εἰκὼν ἑνὸός τοῦ παμβασιλέως).[245] Similarly, an anonymous twelfth-century text asserts that "The earthly kingdom is a shining image of the Kingdom of God, and the emperor himself is the image of God."[246] It should be noted that if the doctrine of the patriarch as image of God was generally accepted in Byzantium, the ascription of analogous merit to the emperor merely remained the opinion of particular individuals.[247]

Occasionally, this opinion could also be voiced in Russia when Byzantine sources were cited. Perhaps the first example of this occurs in Maksim Grek who testified not to the Russian but the Byzantine tradition, although he thus brought the idea to the attention of Russian readers. In his Epistle to Ivan the Terrible (c. 1545),[248] Maksim wrote: "The tsar is none other than the living and visible, that is, animated image of the Heavenly Tsar Himself; as one of the Greek philosophers said to a certain tsar: Confident of [the divine] kingdom, be worthy of it, because the tsar is God's animated image, that is, His living image."[249] Metropolitan Filipp (Kolychev) also spoke of the tsar as God's image when he denounced Ivan the Terrible, denying him blessing as a ruler who had perverted this image: "Because, tsar, you are esteemed God's image, but have been impressed [i.e., perverted] by an earthly touch";[250] this was a citation from Agapetos[251] and was fully compatible with ancient Russian theories of the tsar's power (see section I, 1.1) which juxtaposed just and unjust tsars. The Patriarch of Jerusalem Dositheus also connected the tsar's righteousness with being "the image of God" in a letter to Tsar Fedor Alekseevich of June 27, 1679: "The tsar worries and grieves, and prays and keeps vigil, and inquires, reads, and studies, and appreciates the good of all of his officials, and may he truly be 'the image of God' and the blessed habitation of the greatly praised Trinity."[252] Be that as it may, all indications are that right up to the eighteenth century there was no appreciable tradition of calling the tsar "the image of God." In this connection it is characteristic that Nikon made a special protest against calling the tsar the "likeness of God" (*podobnik Bozhii*), pointing out that this title was only appropriate for a bishop.[253] Calling the monarch "the image of God" only became widespread from the reign of Peter the Great. If there was an echo of the earlier tradition, then from this period it took on a fundamentally different meaning. As early as 1701 Dimitrii Rostovskii called the tsar "the living image of Christ," and referred to him as "Christ" at the same time, directly connecting this title to the tsar's dominating position in the Church. Thus in the salutary speech to Peter of 1701 cited above (section II, 1.3.1) he said:

The countenance and dignity of the Christian tsar on earth is the living image and likeness of Christ the Tsar living in heaven. Just as a human being is image and likeness of God by virtue of his soul, so Christ of the Lord [on earth], the Divine Annointed, in his royal dignity is the image and likeness of Christ the Lord. The heavenly Christ the Lord presides over the triumphant church. Christ of the Lord on earth by grace and mercy of the heavenly Christ is first leader of the militant church . . . And since the dignity of the Christian tsar on earth is the image and likeness of Christ, the heavenly Tsar, the majesty of [the earthly] Christ of the Lord has some mystical likeness to the majesty of [the heavenly] Christ the Lord.[254]

Official triumphant odes and sermons reflect the perception of the tsar as image of God with special vibrance. Thus, in Lomonosov's ode on Elizabeth's arrival of 1742, God addresses the empress with the words:

> *The peoples honor my image in You,*
> *And the spirit streaming from Me.*[255]

In another instance (the ode on Elizabeth's birthday in 1757) God speaks of Elizabeth: "I myself appeared in Her person."[256] Similarly, in Sumarokov's ode on Catherine's name day of 1766, God addresses the empress with the summons "be My Image on the earth."[257] This sort of address, from God to the empress, becomes a standard cliché of high poetry. For example, V. I. Maikov in his "Ode on the Occasion of the Choice of Deputies for Composing a New Law Code in 1767" writes:

> *God manifests His image to us in her*
> *And through her amazes all of us*
> *How wise and great He is.*[258]

In the same way God says to Paul in V. P. Petrov's poem "Russia's Lament and Consolation, to His Imperial Majesty Paul I" (1796): "Everyone knows this, that You are My true image."[259] In Petrov's ode "On His Imperial Majesty Paul I's Triumphal Entry into Moscow" of 1797 we find an entire dialogue between Paul and God in which Paul says to Him that "Yes, [I am] Your image, I agree with Your desires;" and God says to Paul,

> *Arise, My Son! Stand high in spirit!*
> *The God in whom You believe is with You,*
> *Arise and, my image, shine forth under the sun!*[260]

In the same poem an angel also addresses Paul:

> *Here the delicate Alexander, and there*
> *Constantine holds*
> *Your Holy frame,*
> *—These are your angels, closest to the throne,*
> *You are Divine, and they carry Your image forth.*[261]

Petrov also calls Catherine II "the image of Divinity."[262] No less characteristic was Derzhavin's use of this motif, to which he gave unique justification:

> *The tsar is the bond of opinion, the cause of all action,*
> *And the humble power of the one father—*
> *Pattern of the Living God.*[263]

He addresses Alexander I correspondingly in the poem "The Voice of St. Petersburg Society" of 1805:

> *The mirror of the heavens, in which*
> *We see the clear gleam of the Divinity,*
> *Oh, beautiful angel of our days,*
> *The image of the Benificent Essence.*[264]

It is precisely the image of God that Derzhavin honors in the monarch; cf. the drafts to his poem "The Drunk and Sober Philosopher" of 1789:

> *I wanted to become a grandee*
> *And to serve in the presence of tsars,*
> *To zealously honor the image of God in them*
> *And to tell them only the truth.*[265]

What was characteristic of the ode was also typical of the sermon. In 1801 Metropolitan Platon addressed Alexander I, "You who bear the image of the Heavenly Tsar."[266] And Archbishop Avgustin expresses the same idea in general terms in his "Speech on the Coronation Day of Emperor Alexander I" of 1809: "The tsars on earth are the image of the heavenly Tsar."[267] Analogous expressions also characterize the sermons of Feofilakt Rusanov. Thus, in his "Speech on Reading the Royal Manifesto of War Against the French" (1806) he said that "for every loyal subject the Sovereign is not merely a most holy figure, but the image on earth of the Divinity itself."[268] Similarly, in the "Speech on the Taking of Paris," delivered on May 3, 1814, he asserted that "the Christian people honors its Sovereign as the Annointed of God, and in him hails the image of Divinity itself."[269] Likewise, the Petersburg Metropolitan Mikhail asserted that "the tsar is by the blessing of God like the great sun, like His image."[270] Even in the twentieth century we may come across statements like "our tsar is the image of the Heavenly Tsar."[271] The cited examples by no means exhaust the great many other similar expressions of this idea.[272] Basing himself on this rhetorical tradition but completely ignoring its Baroque, metaphorical character (that is, perceiving it as direct evidence of Russian religious consciousness) N. V. Gogol` wrote: "Our poets penetrated the supreme significance of the monarch, realizing that he must, finally, entirely become pure love, and it will thus become clear to everyone why the sovereign is the image of God, which our whole land, by the way, recognizes by intuition . . . It has been our poets, and not lawgivers, who have grasped the supreme significance of the monarch, and they have heard with trepidation God's will to establish it [power] in Russia in its legitimate form—and this is the reason that their tones become biblical every time the word 'tsar' flies from their lips."[273] The idea that the monarch "must become pure love" evidently derives from the Gospel notion of God as love[274]; here this interpretation also defines the perception of the monarch as the image of God.

If at first the perception of the monarch as the image of God derived from literary sources, we may surmise that it gradually became a fact of religious consciousness. The incident that Catherine II describes in a letter to N. I. Panin of May 26, 1767, is indicative: "In one place along the route peasants brought candles to be put in front of me, but they were sent away."[275] Apparently the peasants thought of Catherine as a living icon. In his memoirs V. A. Rotkirkh testifies to the same attitude. Here some soldiers, responding to a greeting from Nicholas I, crossed themselves devoutly "as if church bells had summoned them to Matins;" later, travelling by rail with Alexander II, the same author had the opportunity to observe how railway workers greeted the tsar's train by the trackmen's huts: "the railway men and their entire households crossed themselves and bowed down to the earth to their earthly god."[276]

2.3. That the perception of the monarch as the image of God was connected with the disbanding of the patriarchate and the transferring of the patriarch's functions to the tsar is clearly illustrated by the history of addressing the monarch with the words "Blessed is he who comes in the name of the Lord! . . . ," that is, with the words addressed to Christ on Palm Sunday (the

Lord's Entry into Jerusalem). They come from the Gospels[277] and are repeated during the holiday service.

After the victory of Poltava Peter was greeted in Moscow on December 21, 1709, with the singing of "Blessed is he who comes in the name of the Lord, Hosanna in the highest, the Lord God has appeared to us..." as the tsar was met by children dressed in short white sticharions bringing "incense and branches." Similarly, when Peter visited the Spasskii Monastery he was met with the singing of "Hosanna in the highest..." and the symbolism was underscored by the fact that Peter wore a crown of thorns.[278] When Peter returned to Moscow in triumph on December 18, 1722, after the Persian campaign he was greeted with a speech by Feofan Prokopovich in the name of the Synod. It began: "Blessed is he who comes in the name of the Lord! What can we who are greeting you say that is more appropriate than this, valiant man, our most majestic Monarch?" And it concluded: "Come then quickly, rejoicing, run like a giant, going from strength to strength, from glory to glory, whence the destinies of the Almighty take you, led by the Lord's right hand, whence our precursor Jesus has gone, always and everywhere blessed, coming in the name of the Lord."[279]

Subsequently this type of greeting became a tradition. In blessing Emperor Alexander for the struggle against Napoleon, and sending him an icon of St. Sergius of Radonezh, Mertropolitan Platon wrote to him: "Most gracious Sovereign Emperor! The first capital city, Moscow, the New Jerusalem, takes its Christ like a mother into the embrace of its zealous sons, and through the rising haze foreseeing the brilliant glory of your Power sings in ecstasy: Hosanna, blessed is he who comes!"[280] When Alexander I returned to Russia, to Petersburg, after his victory over Napoleon, Archbishop Avgustin gave a speech in the Uspenskii Cathedral in Moscow on December 5, 1815. Addressing Russia, he exclaimed: "Your sons in victorious laurels proclaim in triumph: Hosanna, blessed is he who comes in the name of the Lord!"[281] And later, when Alexander himself attended the cathedral, on the day of Assumption, August 15, 1816, Avgustin greeted him with the words: "To you, conqueror of wickedness and falsehood, we shout: Hosanna in the Highest, blessed is he who comes in the name of the Lord!"[282]

It is characteristic that this same greeting became firmly associated with imperial coronations, that is, the emperor's ascension to the throne was connected to proclaiming Christ king of Jerusalem. For example, the Tambov priest Ivanov, who gave a speech dedicated to the opening of popular schools on Catherine II's coronation day in 1786 (which we quoted above), asserted that the empress is God's "true genuine image." He exclaimed in conclusion:

"How humble, how far-sighted, and how generous is this, the one anointed and crowned today for the Russian kingdom, the Lord's Christ! And so, may your entrance into the Russian capital to rule be peaceful, our farsighted one! Blessed be you forever who comes in the name of the Lord. Amen."[283] In this connection it is quite characteristic that Paul I specially timed his arrival into Moscow for his coronation to coincide with Lazarus (Palm) Saturday and the coronation itself to take place on Easter Sunday.[284] In this way Paul equated his entry into Moscow with Christ's entry into Jerusalem, as Messiah, Tsar and Redeemer, and his coronation to the ultimate glorification of Christ as the enthroned redeemer of mankind. In his sermon at the celebration the Kievan Archpriest Ioann Levanda asked: "Is He [Christ] not sharing the glory of His resurrection with our rightful Monarch?"[285] In his ode dedicated to the event Nikolev wrote:

> *The bowing palm branches rejoice!*
> *Christ has risen . . . and indeed they are crowning*
> *The successor to his holiness!*
> *Hosanna! Tsar coming by right,*
> *To the glory of the Lord's Name,*
> *He is the image of the very God.*[286]

In his ode "On the Triumphal Entry of His Imperial Majesty Paul I into Moscow on March 28, 1797," Petrov responded to the coronation in an analogous way:

> *Above the gates inscriptions everywhere shine:*
> *O You, beloved Man,*
> *Hope of countless souls,*
> *Merciful yesterday and forgiving today!*
> *Blessed are You who comes in the name of the Lord!*[287]

Similarly, Metropolitan Platon, greeting Alexander I who had attended the Uspenskii Cathedral a week before his coronation, proclaimed in the already cited speech: "Enter! And we, preceding and following You, sing out: 'Blessed is he who comes in the name of the Lord!'"[288] And in the "Song on the Supreme Visit . . . After the Holy Coronation and Annointing" that was presented to Nicholas I at the Moscow Spiritual Academy in 1826 we read:

> *Blessed be He on His great path*
> *Who comes in the name of God!*[289]

This tradition did not die out even in the later period. Thus in the official organ of the Synod, the *Church Herald* (Tserkovnyi Vestnik), it was said of Nicholas II's arrival in Moscow for his coronation on May 6, 1896: "If not with its lips, then with its heart all Moscow, and then all Russia, exclaimed: 'Blessed is he who comes in the name of the Lord!'"[290] Even later the Archpriest Petr Mirtov proclaimed in his sermon on the coronation day of Nicholas II: "Blessed is the Tsar and Autocrat of All Russia who comes in the name of the Lord."[291]

The emergence of this tradition was undoubtedly connected with the ritual "procession on a donkey" (*shestvie na osliati*),* abolished under Peter, which the patriarch used to perform in Moscow on Palm Sunday, celebrating the Lord's entry into Jerusalem.[292] In this procession the patriarch rode on a horse which the tsar led by the bridle; during the joint reign of Peter and Ioann the two tsars had led the steed from both sides. The patriarch would be greeted by young boys who scattered cloths and branches along his route and sang: "Blessed is he who comes in the name of the Lord! Hosanna in the Highest," etc. The ceremony was also carried out during the installation of patriarchs and metropolitans, which was apparently meant to symbolize the fact that they were deputies of Christ in their respective posts; in Moscow the tsar led the horse, and elsewhere the city head.[293] During the procession, the patriarch mystically personified Christ entering Jerusalem and was perceived as His living icon. A letter from Patriarch Nikon to Tsar Aleksei Mikhailovich of March 30, 1659, when he had already lost his leading position in the Russian church, eloquently testifies to this. The occasion for the letter was the news Nikon had received that Metropolitan Pitirim whom he had left as his *locum tenens* had performed the ceremony in Moscow on Palm Sunday, March 27, 1659. Nikon says that when he had carried out the ritual on Palm Sunday (*Nedelia vaii*) it had been frightening for him, the patriarch, to assume the place of Christ; he makes it clear that the issue was precisely about the patriarch representing a living icon of Christ, an image of God.[294] But that the ritual had been performed in Moscow by a simple metropolitan, and not a patriarch, Nikon describes as "spiritual adultery" and as an assault on the patriarch's charisma; the culprit should be prohibited from carrying out episcopal duties. Metropolitan Pitirim's repeat of the ritual in 1660 and 1661 was one reason that Nikon anathematized him in 1662.[295] In the cathedral of the Voskresenskii Monastery (New Jeruslaem) it was triumphantly proclaimed that "to Pitirim, who without the blessing of his spiritual father for the last three years assumed the role of the patriarch of all Russia and even that of Christ himself, and thus

---

*   *Translator's note*: In practice this was actually a horse whose ears were tied back.

committed the crime of spiritual adultery, . . . anathema."²⁹⁶ Later, responding to Semen Streshnev's questions, Nikon described the event in a somewhat different light. In his "Objection or Ruin of the Humble Nikon, by God's Grace Patriarch, Against the Questions of Boyar Simeon Streshnev," written between December 1663 and January 1665,²⁹⁷ we read: "And that the sovereign tsar led the Metropolitan of Krutitsk on a horse, [it is] as the sovereign tsar wishes; whoever he seats [on a horse] and leads—it's his choice."²⁹⁸ Here Nikon seems to be avoiding condemnation of the tsar, who had taken part in the ceremony with Metropolitan Pitirim, and at the same time denies their action any religious significance: without the patriarch, the procession becomes merely walking a horse with a rider. It can only assume sacred character when the patriarch takes part, because he alone has the authority to personify Christ on earth.

Significantly, the Council of 1678 assigned the right to conduct the "procession on a donkey" exclusively to the patriarch, whereas before that time the ceremony could be performed in diocesan centers where the local bishop would ride and the local civic leader lead the horse. In the Council's decision it says:

> Such was the decision delivered: let this act as having nothing against the church or rules of the sainted apostles and holy fathers be performed in honor of Christ our Lord and for the piety of godly monarchs only in the royal city of Moscow, in the presence of the scepter-bearer, let it be performed personally by the patriarch, and not by any other hierarchs and not at all during a period between patriarchs, since it is not appropriate for the lower hierarchy to perform an act hardly permissible even for the patriarch. Let no bishop in any town anywhere in the entire Great Russian state dare to mount an ass and ride it in memory of the Lord's entry into the city of Jerusalem.²⁹⁹

This is motivated by the fact that the ritual of "riding an ass" had only recently arisen in dioceases and that it was thought to demean imperial dignity:

> [O]n the other hand it does not look very proper; for what was permitted for the piety of sovereigns has begun to be considered incorrectly as unchangeable law. Here in the royal and blessed city of Moscow during the period without a patriarch some bishops also used to perform this act, and in other cities they dare to do this when the one taking the tsar's part is led on an ass by someone of no high rank. [This decision is taken] in order to guard his [the tsar's] honor and since this act is not approved by church rules and never existed or exists in any Christian state.³⁰⁰

It is worthy of note that while Nikon had protested against anyone other than the patriarch riding the donkey, led by the tsar, the fathers of the 1678

Council were concerned that the tsar not do the leading. In the period between patriarchs, before the selection of Patriarch Ioakim, this role in the ceremony had still been performed by the tsar (on Palm Sunday, April 12, 1674) with Ioakim, still metropolitan of Novgorod, riding[301]; the validity of the ritual was still dependent on the tsar's participation. For the earlier period, however, the patriarch had been the main participant. According to the testimony of Martin Ver,[302] when in 1611, because of the troubles of the interregnum, the military leaders called off the triumphal appearance of the patriarch on Palm Sunday, "the mob . . . loudly grumbled and preferred death to tolerating this outrage; so it was necessary to carry out the people's will; instead of the tsar, the most important grandee of Moscow, Andrei Godunov, took the bridle." Thus the efficacy of the ceremony was defined primarily by the participation of the patriarch, while the tsar's place could be taken by a substitute.

With the greater sacralization of the tsar's power and the struggle to completely subordinate the church to the state, the ritual of "procession on a donkey" began to be perceived as emphasizing the greatness of the patriarch and at the same time belittling the power of the tsar. This is exactly the way Peter I saw it. An episode which Archpriest Petr Alekseev of the Moscow Arkhangel`skii Cathedral related in a letter to Paul I is representative. At a name-day party at a navy captain's house, an officer asked Peter, "Honored tsar, what was the reason that your father, Tsar Aleksei Mikhailovich, got so angry at Patriarch Nikon that he condemned him and sent him into exile?" Peter answered that Nikon "got it into his head that he was higher than the tsar himself, and people also tried to persuade him of this noxious idea, especially in public ceremonies."[303] Petr Alekseev accompanied this story with the following commentary:

Is it not a kind of papist pride to subordinate a divinely crowned tsar to his equerries, that is, on Holy Week, in imitation of the inimitable Christ's entry into Jerusalem, for the patriarch, with great pomp, riding around the Kremlin on a court donkey, to force the autocrat to lead this beast of burden around by the bit in view of innumerable spectators? And after carrying out this sumptuous ceremony, the patriarch gave the all-Russian sovereign a hundred rubles, as if to be given out as charity, but in actuality, shameful to say, as a reward for his services leading him around. In his minority the Emperor Peter the Great himself was subjected to this indignity when he held the reins of [Patriarch] Ioakim's donkey together with his brother Tsar Ioann Alekseevich at just such a Palm Sunday ceremony. But later this practice that had been newly introduced into the church was completely abandoned, by order of the same great monarch.[304]

The anecdote "On the Repeal of the Procession on Holy Week," transcribed by I. I. Golikov from Peter the Great's own words, also describes the "procession on a donkey" as a ritual that demeans "the majesty of the tsarist rank."[305] Such a view of the "procession on a donkey" had some real basis insofar as the ritual did express the humility of monarchial power before the spiritual principle; as the fathers of the 1678 Council emphasized,

> [O]ur most pious Autocrats have the good will to show the Orthodox folk an image of humility and free subordination to the Lord Jesus, because in accepting this most self-effacing custom of seating the patriarch on a donkey in memory of the Lord's entry into Jerusalem they humble their high tsarist stature and with their scepter-bearing hands deign to hold the donkey's reins and lead it to the cathedral, serving Christ the Lord; this is a praiseworthy deed, for many will be moved by such humility of the earthly tsar before the Heavenly Tsar, and they will experience . . . a profound saving humility, and from the treasures of their heart give forth a warm cry to Christ the Lord, singing out with devout lips, "Hosanna in the Highest, blessed be He who comes in the name of the Lord, the Tsar of Israel."[306]

In accord with this, in an anonymous Protestant work of 1725 dedicated to Peter's activities[307] it is noted that the "procession on a donkey" signified an honor which the tsar bestowed on the patriarch, and connected its abolition to the fact that Peter, having disbanded the patriarchate, assimilated the highest authority in the church to himself.[308] G.-F. Bassevich testified to the fact that the tsar considered this ritual demeaning and also saw the reason for its elimination in the fact that "Petr Alekseevich did not want to recognize anyone as head of the church except himself."[309] Thus the patriarch was rendered the honor which, according to Peter and his associates, belonged exclusively to the ruling monarch. In his speech "On the Tsar's Power and Honor" delivered in Petersburg on Palm Sunday, April 6, 1718, Feofan Prokopovich justified the argument that this honor should go to the tsar and not a church hierarch. Having described Christ's entry into Jerusalem, he said: "Do we not see here what reverence is due the tsar? Does it not behoove us, and will we indeed be silent about how we subjects should evaluate the supreme power? And how far resistance to this duty has appeared at the present time? [the reference is to the case of Tsarevich Aleksei]. Let no one think that our intention is to compare the earthly tsar to the heavenly one; let us not be so senseless; neither did the Jews who met Jesus know that he was the heavenly tsar."[310] Further, Feofan, with the help of very convoluted exegesis, demonstrates that the Jews who were awaiting the Messiah were waiting precisely for the supreme head of an earthly kingdom, and from this he concludes that kings should be rendered that honor whose prototype was the greeting which the Jews gave to Jesus when he entered Jerusalem. This reasoning is fully characteristic of the casuistry with which Feofan endeavored to justify the actual sacralization of tsarist power and the debasing of religious authority, by presenting them as the appropriate realization of biblical and patristic commandments.

Thus for Peter the "procession on a donkey" ritual symbolized the power of the patriarch, and because of this a limitation on his own imperial power. Therefore its abolition under Patriarch Adrian (from 1697) signified the fall of the patriarch's power. The abolition of the patriarchate itself, which, according to contemporaries, Peter decided on right after the patriarch's death in 1700, soon followed. Hence the "procession on a donkey" was itself an important symbolic act, but it became even more significant from the fact that the tsar introduced a just as symbolic blasphemous ritual in its place, one which served to recall the abolished ceremony and the vanquished patriarchate. In his diary of 1721, F. V. Berkhgol`ts reports: "In former times in Moscow, every year on Palm Sunday a special procession took place in which the patriarch rode on horseback and the tsar led his horse by the reins through the whole city. In place of all this now there is a completely different ceremony: on this day the prince-pope and his cardinals [a reference to the mock patriarch of the All-Joking, All-Drunken Synod, P. I. Buturlin, and his mock bishops] ride through the whole city and make visits riding on oxen and donkeys, or in sleighs drawn by pigs, bears or goats."[311]

The victory over the patriarchate, however, meant not only the abrogation of patriarchal power, but also its assimilation by the monarch. And together with the fact that the tsar took on the administrative functions of the patriarch he also appropriated elements of patriarchal behavior, first of all the role of living icon of Christ.[312] It was precisely from this that the tradition arose of greeting the tsar with the words "Blessed be He who comes in the name of the Lord."[313]

2.4. We have spent so much space on interpreting the importance of addressing the tsar with the words "Blessed be He who comes in the name of the Lord" primarily because this example shows very clearly how concretely historical events of the Petrine era furthered the sacralization of the monarch. At the same time, it is worth noting that with time the given greeting became associated with a particular semantic context, that of ascending the throne. The development of this kind of connection is familiar in many other cases; starting with the Petrine period it became acceptable to relate liturgical texts to the tsar as long as their use was sanctioned by circumstances.

Still one more tradition of using a sacred image became associated with ascension to the throne, and that was calling the tsarist throne "Favor" (Tabor), thus equating the tsar with the transfigured Christ.* Thus in a sermon on Alexander I's ascension day delivered in the Kazan Cathedral on March 12, 1821, Archimandrite Neofit said: "When God's all-active right hand brought him to the throne, as onto some kind of Tabor, to transfigure His humility into the glory of tsarist majesty, it seems, the voice of the Heavenly Father secretly but perceptibly proclaimed to the sons of Russia: I have Chosen this one as my son, and I will be to him as a Father; and I will strengthen His Kingdom forever [1 Chronicles 28:6-7]."[314] The very well known preacher, Kherson Archbishop Innokentii (Borisov), expressed himself in very similar terms:

> Why do our most devout sovereigns ascend the throne? So that from its height they will be closer to heaven, to more constantly and freely commune in spirit with the One in Whose hand lies the fate of peoples and kings. Even pagans know that the well-being of kingdoms does not only depend on the arbitrariness and exertions of men, and Christians more so, who believe that the Most High controls the kingdom of men [Daniel 4:22] and that the rulers of men, for all their greatness, are but servants [Romans 13:4] of the Heavenly Sovereign. This is why there must be an unceasing, vital communion between the heavenly and earthly tsar for the good of the people. Where does this take place? Must it really be amid crowds of people? Amid the clamor of prejudice and passion? Amid the dust and whirlwind of daily cares? Before the eyes of anyone and everyone? Moses ascends Mount Sinai to speak with God and to receive his law [Exodus 19:20]; Elijah is raised up to Mount Horeb to contemplate God's glory [1 Kings 19:11 (3 Kings 19, Russian Bible)]; the Son of God Himself hears a voice calling him His beloved Son on the silent peak of Tabor [Matthew 17:5]. For the peoples too there must be a continuous Tabor on which the will of the heavenly Lawgiver can be discerned, where the light of God's glory is reflected on the face of the crowned representatives of the people. This Sinai, this Tabor—is the tsar's throne.[315]

In a similar way, succession to the throne is equated with Christ's arrival in the Heavenly Kingdom, and the one who is expected to be seen on the throne is addressed with the plea to "Remember me, Lord, when you come into your kingdom," which the judicious thief addressed to crucified Christ.[316] A half a year before Elizabeth's ascension, the new Metropolitan of Tobol'sk Arsenii Matseevich who had been appointed under Anna Leopol'dovna paid

---

*   *Translator's note:* See Matthew 17:1-9, Mark 9:2-8, Luke 9:28-36, and 2 Peter 1:16-18; Mount Tabor is not mentioned, and only became associated with the scene by Origen and later theologians.

her a visit, and upon bidding farewell to the tsarevna, said to her: "Remember me, sovereign, as soon as you come into your kingdom."[317] Pushkin's great grandfather Abram (Petr) Petrovich Hannibal (Gannibal), who had to hide out in the country before the coup of 1741 that brought Elizabeth to the throne, addressed the very same words to her. Pushkin relates in "The Start of an Autobiography": "Minikh saved Hannibal by sending him off secretly to an Estonian village where he lived for around ten years in constant agitation. . . . When Empress Elizabeth ascended the throne, Hannibal wrote her the words from the Gospel: 'Remember me when you have come into your kingdom.' Elizabeth immediately called him to court."[318] A similar appeal was made to Paul when he was heir to the throne. "Once Paul was riding on horseback with his adjutant Kutlubitskii along Meshchanskaia Street in Petersburg. They passed some convicts, and Paul ordered that they be given alms. 'Remember me, Lord, when you come into your kingdom,' said one of the prisoners, Prokhor Matveev. Paul ordered his name written down, and carried the note with him, transferring it from pocket to pocket every day. After Paul ascended to the throne, Prokhor Matveev was freed."[319]

In an analogous way the tsar's arrival was equated with Christ's and the image of "the Bridegroom that cometh at midnight." We already cited the story of how Feofan Prokopovich greeted the tsar who had arrived at a nocturnal feast with the words of the troparion "Behold the Bridegroom cometh at midnight!"[320] Much later, Moscow Metropolitan Filaret (Drozdov) used the same imagery when alerting the head of the Trinity-Sergiev Monastery Archimandrite Antonii of an upcoming visit of the emperor. In a letter of July 22, 1832, Filaret wrote Antonii that soon "the Sovereign Emperor's procession may happen along the route to the lavra [monastery]," and he expressed the hope that "if the Groom comes at midnight not everyone will be dozing."[321] The same image, with the same semantic motivation, occurs in Filaret's writing more than once; see his letter to Antonii of October 26, 1831 and August 17, 1836.[322]

2.5. Thus, various events in the life of the tsar were perceived in terms of the earthly life of Christ, and for this reason they could also be incorporated into the liturgical practice of the Orthodox Church (in a similar way as Christ's life on earth is the basic theme of the Christian liturgy). It is precisely this that explains the opportunistic use of Gospel imagery for the monarch, illustrated above; in a similar way, as we have seen, this or that phrase from the Gospels came to be used in troparions. The events of the tsar's life began to be celebrated in church, marked by a ceremonial service and usually a sermon (which also provided an opportunity to make use of material from the Gospels, fitted to the occasion). Thus arose the notion of "high triumphal days" (*vysokotorzhestvennye dni*), that is, church holidays dedicated to the tsar's birthday, saint's day, day of ascension and coronation. These became official church holidays which were duly noted in church calendars; the failure of priests to observe them was considered serious misconduct that entailed mandatory ecclesiastical punishment.[323] Furthermore, there were even attempts to create special church prayer services for these days. A project for one was proposed by the priest Razumovskii in the 1830s. We may judge the nature of his proposed service by the following canticle (sixth tone):

> Glory to God in the highest, peace on earth, and in the Russian kingdom goodwill; for from the root of the prophet Tsar David, chosen by God, and from the flesh of the most pure Virgin Mary, came shining forth to us Christ, Savior of the world; thus from the root of Prince Vladimir, equal to the apostles, and from the flesh of a noble and most Christian line, and from holy tsarist blood our Emperor Nicholas came shining forth to us, Nicholas, the true image of Jesus Christ, crowned and annointed monarch of the church and of the Russian kingdom, heir to God's kingdom, placeholder of Christ's throne and acting Savior of the fatherland. Glory to God in the highest, peace in the church militant, goodwill in the Russian kingdom.[324]

Just as in the church holidays dedicated to the Mother of God and individual saints were celebrated together with the Lord's feast days, so too in the imperial cult that arose in the eighteenth century not only events in the emperor's life were celebrated but also those of the empress and the heir to the throne, and in general, members of the ruling house; high triumphal days included the birthdays and saints' days of all of the grand princes and princesses and their children.[325] They too were mentioned in the litany and their names were printed on the covers of liturgical books. Notably, on high triumphal days it was forbidden to hold funerals or conduct the service for the dead[326]—just as it was forbidden on Sunday holidays, on Holy Week, Passion Week, and so on.[327] Characteristically, associating this kind of "tsarist" holiday with church holidays had already elicited protest from Patriarch Nikon. He condemned the article in the Law Code of 1649 in which the birthday of the tsar and members of his family were declared days off together with church holidays. He wrote: "And what about the tsar? It appears to be a holiday on the sovereign tsar's birthday and similarly on the tsaritsa's and their children's. Are those holidays? Is it a sacrament, if it is only sensual and human? And in everything the human is likened to the divine, only it is preferred to the divine."[328]

And so the process of sacralization extended to the entire imperial family as the high triumphal days with their pomp and rewards became a special system of religious veneration for the tsar and the imperial household. This struck foreigners very strongly. K. Masson wrote, for example, in his "Notes" that "beyond the fifty-two Sundays Russians celebrate sixty three holidays out of which twenty five are dedicated to a special cult of the goddess Catherine [the Great] and her family."[329] The sacralizing of the monarch and the reigning house was reflected in both religious oratory and in odic poetry. Thus Metropolitan Platon, in the above cited speech on Alexander I's arrival in Moscow in 1801, spoke of "all the sacred blood" of the emperor, by which he meant the tsar's house.[330] Nikolev, addressing Paul I, proclaimed: "Your entire family is heavenly,"[331] and Petrov, in his ode "On the Celebration of Peace" of 1793, wrote of Catherine's grandchildren:

> *All are of a Divine breed,*
> *And an assembly of virtues.*[332]

In his poem "On the Grand Princes Nikolai Pavlovich and Mikhail Pavlovich's Departure from Petersburg for the Army" of 1814 Derzhavin calls the grand princes "from the race of gods,"[333] and in his poem "The Russian Amphytrite's Procession Down the Volkhov [River]" of 1810, dedicated to Grand Princess Ekaterina Pavlovna's trip from Tver` to Petersburg, the imperial family that is awaiting her arrival is described in the following words:

> *I see the family so blessed,*
> *Brothers, sisters—a divine assembly.*[334]

Thus the sacralization of the monarch became a fact of church life and of the religious life of the Russian people. Sacralization affected diverse spheres—government administration, national historical consciousness, church services, religious education (from sermons to the teaching of scripture) and spiritual life itself. Moreover, the tsar's sacralization began to take on the status of confessional dogma. Veneration of the tsar became equated with venerating the saints, and in this way the cult of the tsar became almost a necessary condition of religiosity. We find eloquent testimony to this in the monarchist brochure "Autocratic Power," in which it is precisely the status of the imperial cult as dogma that is emphasized: "The truth of the autocracy of Orthodox tsars, that is, their ordination and affirmation on the thrones of kingdoms by God Himself, is so sacred that in the spirit of church doctrine and statute it is elevated to the level of a dogma of faith whose violation or rejection is accompanied by excommunication."[335] In the rite of anathematization, carried out during the Week of Orthodoxy, among the list of main doctrinal heresies, during the imperial period was added (as no. 11): "To those who think that Orthodox tsars are elevated to the throne not by God's special benevolence toward them, and that at their anointment the grace of the Holy Spirit for the transmission of this great calling does not stream into them, so that rebellion and betrayal is raised against them—anathema."[336]

III. THE CIVIL CULT OF THE MONARCH IN THE SYSTEM OF BAROQUE CULTURE

1. *The Cult of the Monarch and the Problem of Confessional Consciousness*

1.1. During Peter's reign panegyrical literature moved from the court, where it had been the property of a narrow circle, out onto the streets, where it became an extremely important instrument for the ideological reeducation of society. Here literature was organically combined with spectacle (triumphs, fireworks, masquerades, etc.), the goal of which was to underscore the unlimited nature of autocratic power. This kind of ceremony as a means of mass propaganda was an indispensable part of the cultural transformation of new imperial Russia, and was repeated year in and year out throughout the eighteenth century; panegyric events became state undertakings. In the words of G. A. Gukovskii, "the sphere to which art and ideas were applied was first of all the court, which played the role of political and cultural center . . . as a temple of the monarchy and as a theater in which a magnificent spectacle was played out, whose main idea was a demonstration of the might, greatness, and unearthly character of the earthly power . . . The triumphal ode, the panegyric speech ('word') were the most noticeable types of official literary creation that lived not so much in books as in the ceremonial of official celebrations."[337] The magnification of the monarch was carried out most of all by reference to religious imagery; exalting the emperor above people, panegyrists placed him alongside God. This religious imagery could refer both to Christian as well as classical pagan traditions, which here combined freely, subordinate to the laws of multilayered semantics that characterizes Baroque culture in general.[338] In the context of Baroque culture, with its play of meanings and basic metaphorical quality (see section I-2.2), this kind of panegyrical ceremony generally speaking nevertheless testifies to an actual sacralization of the monarch. These celebrations suppose a different mechanism of understanding in which the question of reality per se becomes illegitimate. In this sense panegyrical celebrations have no semblance to church rituals, for which a play of meanings is alien and which hence presuppose a direct, non-metaphorical understanding. The creators of the first panegyrical celebrations were careful to underscore just this difference between this kind of ceremony and church activities.

In 1704, on the occasion of the conquest of Livonia, a triumphal entrance into Moscow was arranged for Peter. The prefect of the Moscow Slavonic-Greek-Latin Academy Iosif Turoboiskii, who composed a description of the triumph, specially explained that the given ceremony did not have religious significance but was a particular kind of civic event: "This is not a temple or a church, created in the name of some saint, but something political, that is, civic, praise for those who labor for the safety of the fatherland." At the same time Turoboiskii emphasized the metaphorical nature of the imagery that was used and insisted on the necessity and validity of the metaphorical approach to meaning. "You also know, dear reader, how common it is for someone desirous of wisdom to imagine a thing in some strange way. Thus lovers of wisdom depict the truth as a yardstick, wisdom as a clear-seeing eye, courage as a pillar, restraint as a bridle, and so on forever. This should not be seen as some kind of mayhem or the arrogance of vaporous reason, because we see the same thing in divine writings."[339] In this way a special civil cult of the monarch was created that was inscribed into the Baroque culture of the Petrine era.

Even though, as we have seen, there were voices that called for approaching such texts metaphorically, there is reason to believe that they were not always perceived in this way. Turoboiskii in particular himself mentions this when he bids the reader not to follow the "ignoramuses" (*neveglasy*) and what he sees as their traditional opinions; "Because you, pious reader, will not be surprised by what we have written, nor be jealous of the uninformed who know nothing and have seen nothing, but who like a turtle in its shell never ventures out, and as soon as it sees something new is shocked and belches out various unholy claptrap."[340] One suspects that these "ignoramuses" did not take his advice about metaphorical interpretation but understood texts literally and saw in the triumph a blasphemous attempt at deification of the tsar. In the context of the growing sacralization of the monarch such a perception actually had some basis. Because of this, it became impossible to separate religion from the civil cult of the monarch. On the contrary, panegyrical texts were read literally and served as an additional source of the very same sacralization.

Thus we see how two perceptions of the sign—conventional and non-conventional (see section I-2.2)—clashed when the civil cult of the monarch was established by imperial Russian state policy. The non-conventional view of the sign led to the expansion of the civil cult in the religious sphere, although in this case the sacralization of the monarch in one form or another could come into conflict with religious attitudes. However obligatory and widespread the Baroque tradition of verbal glorification of the monarch may have been, the Great Russian cultural context in which this tradition existed made it impossible to completely renounce the possibility of interpreting these verbal expressions literally, and this very possibility, as soon as it became evident, could not help but lead to perplexity and confusion. Significantly, even in the representatives of Baroque culture one may trace successive attempts to avoid conflict with Christian religious consciousness and to exclude the very possibility of improper interpretation. We will see below the problems that arise in this connection, how the panegyrical tradition came into conflict with confessional awareness and what compromises were reached in order to avoid this conflict. We will limit ourselves to odic poetry of the eighteenth century. As is well known, the triumphal ode was an integral part of the civil cult of the monarch. As part of secular festivities, it served as functional equivalent of panegyrical sermons in religious ceremonies, which was reflected in their constant interaction.[341] The ode's connection to the sermon made the problems which it posed to traditional religious consciousness especially vital.

1.2. In this respect, Lomonosov's works are especially indicative. One must keep in mind that panegyric glorification of the monarch using sacral imagery was exceptionally characteristic of odes, and in this Lomonosov was the founder of the entire tradition. Thus in his ode on the day of Elizabeth's ascension to the throne of 1746, Lomonosov compared the court coup of 1741 that brought Elizabeth to power with the biblical story of creation:

> *Now our wounded people*
> *Were dwelling in most miserable night.*
> *But God, looking to the ends of the universe,*
> *Raised his gaze to the midnight land,*
> *Glanced at Russia with tender eye,*
> *And seeing the profound gloom,*
> *With authority spake: "Let there be light!"*
> *And there was! O Master of creation!*
> *Again you are Creator of light for us*
> *Having brought Elizabeth to the throne.*[342]

In his 1752 ascension ode to Elizabeth, Lomonosov just as boldly compared Peter's birth to that of Christ, addressing to Peter's mother, Natal`ia Kirillovna, Archangel Gabriel's words to Mary:

> *And you, blessed among women,*
> *Through whom brave Aleksei*
> *Gave us an incomparable Monarch*
> *That revealed the light for all of Russia.*[343]

In another place (Elizabeth's ascension ode of 1748) Lomonsov addresses Elizabeth herself as "blessed among women."[344]

In the ode of 1742 on Elizabeth's arrival in Petersburg from Moscow, Lomonosov puts an entire tirade in the mouth of God the Father, addressed to the empress:

> *"Be blessed forever,"*
> *Proclaims the Ancient of Days to Her,*
> *"And all the people with you,*
> *That I entrusted to Your power.*
> *. . .*
> *In You the peoples revere my image*
> *And the spirit that poured from Me . . . ."*[345]

In the ode on the arrival of Petr Fedorovich of 1742 Lomonosov speaks of Elizabeth:

> *And eternity stands before Her,*
> *Unfolding the book of all the ages . . .* [346]

Of course, the "unfolded book" (*razgnutaia kniga*) is a symbol of divine revelations about the future.[347]

Nonetheless, one may state that Lomonosov puts the most explicit cases of Baroque identification of God and tsar into an ambiguous context. In cases in which the sacralization of the monarch is not realized by paralleling poetic and biblical texts, but by directly designating the monarch as "God" or some similar word, Lomonosov consciously distances the corresponding texts from the Christian tradition. Elements of biblical imagery that might give rise to sacralization that was unacceptable for Christian consciousness are surrounded by pagan images, and by this means the cult of the emperor is given a neutral pagan rationale that is fully fitting within a Baroque cultural framework. It seems clear that this was a fully conscious decision on Lomonosov's part; the pagan context obviates the conflict between Baroque texts and religious consciousness. Thus, in the ode on Petr Fedorovich's name day of 1743, Lomonosov says of Peter I:

> *He is God, he was your God, Russia,*
> *In you he took on fleshly limbs,*
> *Having descended to you from mountain heights.*[348]

For traditional consciousness these words were blasphemous by themselves, and indeed the Old Believers saw in these lines another indication that Peter was the antichrist.[349] However, Lomonosov is not speaking here in his own voice, but puts these words into the mouth of Mars, who is addressing Minerva; in this way the given passage involves an equation with pagan rather than Christian divinity despite the association with Christ's taking on human flesh suggested in the last lines.

Even more typical of Lomonosov is another device for removing the contradiction between sacralization of the monarch and Christianity: avoiding the word "God," Lomonosov regularly calls the empress "goddess." This is a term Lomonosov can call Catherine I,[350] Anna Ioannovna,[351] Elizabeth,[352] and Catherine II.[353] The same word used for the regent Anna Leopol'dovna,[354] Tsarevna Anna Petrovna (Elizabeth's sister),[355] and the Austrian Empress Maria Theresa.[356] This kind of denomination effectively took sacralization beyond the bounds of Christianity and directly correlated with Lomonosov's use of pagan goddesses' names for empresses, e.g., Minerva (Pallada) or Diana.[357] In other cases Lomonosov can call the monarch—Peter or Elizabeth—"Divinity." In the ode of thanks to Elizabeth of 1751, the Egyptian pyramids and walls of Semiramis are juxtaposed to the buildings which the empress erected in Tsarskoe Selo:

> *Human beings created you—*
> *Here a divinity creates.*
> *(Variant: "Here Divinity itself creates.")*

And after this:

> *With magnificent tops*
> *The temples mount to the heavens;*
> *From them Elizabeth shines at us*
> *With most luminous eyes.*[358]

That a pagan divinity is being described is quite obvious, insofar as these words are put into the mouth of a nymph who personifies the river Slavena (*Slavianka*) which flows in Tsarskoe Selo. Nonetheless the given device (translation onto the plane of pagan mythology) did not achieve the desired result—the cited lines provoked a determined protest by Trediakovskii, who would not accept such equivocation. In his report to the academic chancellery of September 17, 1750, Trediakovskii indignantly referred to Lomonosov's "false idea" "that the Egyptian pyramids were built over many centuries by human beings while Tsarskoe Selo was built by a divinity."[359]

Lomonosov also uses the word "Divinity" for Peter; see his first inscription to a statue of Peter (1750): "Russia reveres [him] as an earthly divinity."[360] Initially he had written that "Russia reveres [him] as a domestic divinity," but apparently Lomonosov did not like the overly direct association to pagan penates (hearth gods), a comparison which might have demeaned the emperor's status.

The Baroque use of Biblicisms in service of sacralization of the monarch was so common for Lomonosov that he did not always manage to translate sacred terminology into pagan very successfully. Hence arise paradoxical combinations of pagan and Christian terminology. Thus in the already cited ode on Elizabeth's arrival in Petersburg from Moscow of 1742 Lomonosov writes about God the Father (using the specifically Old Testament phrase "Ancient of Days" [*Vetkhii den`mi*]), placing Him on the pagan Olympus:

> *Sacred terror overcomes my mind!*
> *The all-powerful Olympus opened the door.*
> *All creation attends with great terror,*
> *Seeing the Daughter of great Monarchs,*
> *Chosen by all true hearts,*
> *Crowned by the hand of the All-High,*
> *Standing before His face,*
> *Whom He in his light*
> *Looks to with generous praise,*
> *Confirms the covenant and consoles.*
> *"Be blessed forever,"*
> *Proclaims the Ancient of Days to Her . . . .*[361]

Just as the Christian divinity can turn up on pagan Olympus, so a goddess that is unmistakably pagan can be found in the biblical paradise. Thus, in the ode on the marriage of Petr Fedorovich and Ekaterina Alekseevna of 1745, Lomonosov says:

Is this not a sacred garden I see,
Planted by the All-High in Eden,
Where the first marriage was legitimized?
The Goddess enters the chamber in glory,
[And] leads in the most gracious couple . . . [362]

1.3. What we observe in Lomonosov is typical for the mid-eighteenth century. Indeed, we find the same tactics and the very same devices in Sumarokov, at the same time as his literary position may radically differ from that of Lomonosov. For Sumarokov, as for Lomonosov, the use of sacred imagery for the monarch is characteristic. For example, in his speech on the birthday of Pavel Petrovich of 1761 he applies the archangel's words to Mary to Catherine: "Rejoice, Catherine! Blessed be you among women and blessed be the fruits of Your womb!"[363] Remarkably, just like Lomonosov as seen above, in his ode to Peter's victory Sumarokov also addresses the same words to Peter's mother:

What a blessed time that was
When Great Peter was born!
Blessed be the womb
By which he was brought into the world.[364]

In the poem "The Russian Bethlehem" Sumarokov writes:

The Russian Bethlehem: village of Kolomenskoe
Which brought Peter into the world.[365]

Like Lomonosov, Sumarokov puts praise of the empress into the mouth of God the Father ("the All-High"). In his ode on Catherine's birthday of 1764, God addresses Russia with the following words:

Heed what the All-High proclaims,
And what God doth say to you:
I decided to reveal beauty,
Catherine, to nature.
And I watered her with my dew,
To reveal the likeness of Divinity;
With Her hellish malice will be banished,
Truth will arise from the grave,
And the age of paradise will return . . . [366]

Together with this we find in Sumarokov the same device of translating sacral terms into the language of pagan mythology as seen in Lomonosov. Like Lomonosov, Sumarokov avoids calling the empress God and instead calls Catherine II "goddess,"[367] at the same time he identifies her as Pallada, Minerva, and Thetis.[368] Incidentally, Sumarokov doesn't differentiate among gods and tsars by gender, so that he may call Elizabeth Zeus,[369] and Peter Pallada.[370] We also find in Sumarokov the use of Biblicisms justified by being placed in the mouths of pagan divinities. In the ode dedicated to Catherine's ascension to the throne in 1762, Sumarokov sees in her a resurrected Peter, but here he speaks through the god Pluto:

> *Pluto cries: Great Peter*
> *Has arisen from the grave, and evil falls,*
> *Hell now loses its sway . . .* [371]

1.4. The things that we have observed in Lomonosov and Sumarokov take on a somewhat a different character in their epigones. At the same time, if, as we have seen, Lomonsov's system was rather precise (as he consciously avoided calling the tsar God or related words directly, without special motivation), in his followers this system was destroyed, and the sacralization of the monarch did not require any special motivation. It should be kept in mind that the odic language of later poets was to a significant extent composed of stock phrases taken precisely from Lomonosov, taking them out of the original context that justified their use. Thus if Lomonosov, as noted, calls Peter God ("He is God, he was your God, Russia"), discreetly putting these lines into the lips of a pagan god, N. P. Nikolev could use the same words without any equivocation:

> *She . . . She is your God, Russia.*[372]

In another case Nikolev can write about Catherine's two natures, divine and human, in this likening her to the hypostases of God the Word:

> *Where Catherine's Divinity*
> *Is at one with her humanity!*[373]

In the very same way, V. P. Petrov freely attributed names of God to the tsar, which in some cases may be seen as references to Lomonosov's poetry. Thus addressing Catherine Petrov writes:

You are God, You are God, not a person . . . [374]

In the "People's Love" Petrov says of Peter: "This God inspired me with new strength."[375] Petrov also refers to Paul in similar terms:

Today her [Russia's] soul strives for Him,
For her Savior and her God.[376]

Remarkably, Petrov also refers to Grand Prince Alexander Pavlovich—the future emperor—this way, which evidently reflected Catherine's desire to see him as heir to the throne. In the ode on Alexander's birth of 1777 Petrov writes: "Although he is an infant, he's a god [or: he is god]."[377] This reference is even more eloquent in the ode dedicated to the peace with Turkey (1793), which coincided with the marriage of Alexander and Elizaveta Alekseevna:

O young and beautiful God!
Enter, blessed, the bridal chamber,
Your palace is Russia's Eden.[378]

In poets like Petrov and Nikolev, we also find the empress called "goddess,"[379] and also Pallada, Minerva, Themis, Astreia, etc.[380] However, in contrast to Lomonosov these titles were not a conscious poetic device but mere clichés.

We will cite an even more characteristic example from the poem "The Action and Glory of the Creating Spirit" (*Deistvie i slava zizhdushchago dukha*), signed "S. B."[381] Here it says of Peter I:

The future generation will remember what this new god
Brought to life, and [think] what more he could have done.
This divine image we see in Catherine.
It is so majestic in this northern goddess
That embracing near half the world with her might
It transfigures everything, giving it a new appearance.

Here, very diverse elements of the tradition we have been examining come together: Peter is called a god, Catherine a goddess, and at the same time Catherine is seen as a divine image of God—of Peter; all of which connects with calling tsars the divine image (see section II-2.2), and at the same time reflects the odic tradition according to which each successive monarch resurrects Peter I.

1.5. Derzhavin occupies a special place here. A whole series of his texts would have us see in him a follower of Lomonosov when, in using sacral terminology for the monarch, the poet gives the context a clearly non-Christian character. Thus, in the cycle of odes dedicated to Catherine as "Felitsa" ("Felitsa," "Gratitude to Felitsa," "A Murza's Vision"), Derzhavin writes of Catherine as a divinity but puts the words in the mouth of a Tatar murza: "My god, my angel in the flesh"[382] or:

> To you alone is it appropriate, Tsarevna,
> To create light from the dark.[383]

Derzhavin repeats the same device in the ode "To the Tsarevich Khlor," addressed to Alexander I in the name of an Indian Brahmin.[384] Following Lomonosov Derzhavin often calls the empress a goddess,[385] as well as Minerva, Astrea, and Themis.[386] Similarly, he calls Alexander Apollo.[387] Continuing in the same vein, he calls Catherine "the god of love,"[388] and Alexander—"god of greatness"[389] or "god of love, all-powerful Lel`*."[390]At the same time, Derzhavin may also directly call a monarch God without any justifying motivation. Here Derzhavin follows the practice of Lomonosov's epigones. He may thus call Alexander I "tsar of glory,"[391] that is, the same way Christ is referred to in liturgical texts (possibly, under the influence of the above-cited speech by Metropolitan Platon—see section II-1.5). Derzhavin writes of Alexander's birth: "Be it known, some god is born"; characteristically, he prefers this line to an earlier variant—"Be it known, a demigod is born."[392] Of Peter I he writes:

> The mind of the most wise can't grasp it,
> Is it not God in him descended from heaven?[393]

Of Catherine we read:

> "O, how great," proclaims a crowd of people
> "Is God in the one who rules over us!"[394]

He also calls Grand Prince Pavel Petrovich and his wife Natal`ia Alekseevna, as well as the Grand Princes Nikolai and Mikhail Pavlovich, gods.[395] These

---

*   *Translator's note: Lel`*—allegedly an ancient pagan Slavic god of love, first asserted by eighteenth-century Russian poets, apparently on the basis of similar-sounding words in the chorus of wedding songs.

examples indicate that by the end of the eighteenth century it became automatic to call members of the ruling family gods.[396] This testimony is all the more eloquent insofar as Derzhavin—as we will see below—was conscious of the growing problem of confessional conscience. Following the odic clichés that had become standard by the end of the century, Derzhavin also demonstrates the utmost mixing of Christian and pagan terminology. Thus, describing the recently deceased Grand Princess Alexandra Pavlovna, he writes: "The goddess now rests in God."[397] Of the Empress Maria Fedorovna he says: "Goddess of widows and orphans,"[398] where the expression "widows and orphans" clearly refers back to ecclesiastical books. In the same way he can write about "the Parnassus Eden"[399] and put a commandment about happiness into Themis' mouth.[400]

1.6. The material we have analyzed shows what difficulties eighteenth-century literature ran up against due to the contradiction between religious consciousness and poetic devices connected with sacralizing the monarch. The very fact that the authors tried very hard, with various degrees of consistency and depending on the period, to translate this sacralization into terms of pagan mythology shows that these attempts to resolve the conflict were quite deliberate. But there is even more obvious evidence about just how much this problem was consciously perceived. Thus in the ode "To the Victories of Sovereign Emperor Peter the Great" Sumarokov wrote of Peter:

> *O most wise Divinity!*
> *From the start of the first age*
> *Nature has not seen*
> *Such a Person.*

These lines contain a clear juxtaposition of Peter and Christ; Peter is the first after Christ, and this is a clear hint at his likeness to God. However, Sumarokov immediately finds it necessary to make a significant qualification; immediately after this he says:

> *It is not proper in Christianity*
> *To consider created things Gods;*
> *But if such a tsar had existed*
> *Even during paganism*
> *His fame would only have spread,*

The entire universe, amazed
By his marvelous deeds.
Glory with incessant horn
Would not proclaim as tsar, but as God,
The man who had ascended the throne.[401]

In essence, we see here the same device of translation into the plane of classical mythology, but it is interesting at the same time that Sumarokov immediately takes a step in the direction of Christian sacralization—by means of equivocation, given here in extremely explicit form. Sumarokov repeats the same idea in the inscription "To an Image of Peter the Great, Emperor of All Russia" of 1760, which, by the way, is a rather exact translation of Nikolai Motonis:[402]

Peter, the number of your good deeds is very great!
If in an ancient age
Such a person as you had appeared
Would the people have called You Father and Great?
You'd have been called a god.[403]

Nevertheless, Lomonosov and Derzhavin specially justify the sacralization of the monarch in relation to Peter I, declaring directly that this does not contradict the Orthodox faith. Significantly, in this case Lomonosov recalls pagan cults, but in distinction from Sumarokov asserts that a cult of Peter is appropriate not only for paganism but also for Christianity. Thus he writes in his fourth inscription to a statue of Peter the Great (1750):

Divine honor was given by the ignorance of the ages
[Variant: Divine honor given by the Greeks]
To sculpted images, erected in ancient times
To heroes for their glorious campaigns,
And subsequent peoples honored their sacrifice—
Something that the correct faith [i.e., Orthodoxy] always rejects.
But you will be forgiven, you later descendants,
When hearing of Peter's famed deeds,
You will place an altar before this Heroic image
                                    (variant: sculpted image)[404]
Long ago we endorsed you with our example.
Amazed by His deeds that exceeded human strength
[We] did not believe that He was a mortal,
But during His life already considered Him as God.[405]

Derzhavin in his "Ode on Greatness" (1774) writes:

> *If people, with human weaknesses,*
> *Cannot be gods,*
> *A person must still compare*
> *Himself and his deeds to them.*
> *Why strive for a starry throne?*
> *Only to behold Peter the Great—*
> *He who can possess his spirit*
> *Will be like the gods.*[406]

In the just cited examples, the authors' justifications for celebrating Peter I could be connected to the kind of canonization of the tsar that was characteristic of Petersburg culture.[407] However, this problem of justification cannot be reduced to Peter's personality, just as sacralization, which grew more extensive year after year, cannot be reduced to Peter's influence.

The same Derzhavin writes, addressing Catherine in the ode "Providence,"

> *O gracious one! If creation*
> *May be likened to the Creator,*
> *Those great tsars*
> *Have a right to this above all others*
> *When from their thrones*
> *They terrify malice with thunder,*
> *Rain down fair blessings,*
> *Raise from death to life.*
> *And you, today generous to an orphan*
> *Are even more like Divinity.*[408]

No individual justifications, however, could completely resolve the problem. In this regard it is particularly characteristic that Derzhavin, evidently feeling dissatisfied with the usual arguments, came up with an entire theory that reconciled sacralization with Orthodox consciousness.[409] From this perspective on the conscious recognition of the difficulties involved in sacralization, poetic expressions of sacralization most often appear as linguistic clichés that essentially extra-literary processes imposed on poetry.

2. *The Preservation of the Baroque Tradition in the Religious Milieu*

2.1. With the passage of time the Baroque tradition in Russia faded away completely, and texts which earlier were meant to be interpreted in ludic terms and within a Baroque framework began to be taken more and more seriously and literally. This process also directly affected the sacralization of the monarch, indeed the very disappearance of the Baroque tradition in fact led to an ever increasing sacralization of the tsar. This intensification of sacralization outside of the Baroque tradition was especially strong during the Napoleonic invasion of 1812, when Biblical symbolism was applied on a scale heretofore unseen in Russia, and historical events were perceived in terms of an apocalyptic battle between Christ and Antichrist. It should be kept in mind, however, that the Baroque tradition held on tenaciously in the religious milieu.[410] Therefore, the disappearance of Baroque culture and texts should not be seen as their absolute elimination but as a sharp curtailing of their sphere of action. In general, the functioning of Baroque culture presumes a certain type—and a relatively high level—of education, including knowledge of rhetoric, classical mythology, and a whole series of standard texts. In the eighteenth century this type of education spread, in principle, to both the secular and religious milieu, while in the nineteenth century clear social limitations began to appear. If secular culture rejected the Baroque, the religious estate, on the strength of its characteristic conservatism, preserved the Baroque attitude toward texts to a significant degree. Characteristically, it was precisely at the start of the nineteenth century that a final rift took place between secular and religious literatures; in particular, the ode, whose poetics were diretly connected to sermons (see section III-1.1), ceased its existence as a genre, while Baroque mechanisms continued to act in the sermon.[411] This rift was naturally connected with the differentiation of the secular and religious language that was taking place at the time, that is, with the differentiation between secular and religious literature and the isolation of "seminary language" as a special dialect.

The social limitedness of the Baroque that increased from the later eighteenth century caused its very representatives (the clergy) to perceive Baroque language as coexisting with the languages of other cultures. Earlier, the Baroque understanding of the word seemed to be the only possible one, universal and obvious, while other views seemed beyond the sphere of culture and were therefore ignored. Now, however, carriers of the Baroque tradition could take account of other readings of the corresponding cultural texts insofar as the non-Baroque system of values (first of all, secular aristocratic culture) had also achieved a certain cultural prestige. In particular, the attention of the clergy could be drawn to two types of reception of the Baroque in the non-Baroque milieu: the literal understanding of Baroque texts that led to the complete deification of the monarch, or the tradition of consistently rejecting any kind of play with sacred images. At the same time, the intensification of the real—not Baroque or ludic—sacralization of the monarch also led to increased conflict between the sacralization of the monarch and Christian consciousness. For this reason, against the background of the sacralizing process that was plainly sustained by the clergy, we may from time to time observe the religious authorities' desire to partially limit this process.

This desire could be realized both in the purely semiotic sphere as well as in real-life practice. We presented a series of examples of this above. Thus, Metropolitan Filaret (Drozdov) expressed his dissatisfaction with the tradition of calling the monarch "Christ," evidently apprehensive of identifying the emperor with the Heavenly Tsar (see section II-1.3). He also protested against carrying out a religious procession around the statue of Peter I,[412] and also against having the imperial coat of arms depicted as being supported by Archangels Michael and Gabriel, arguing that this was "the subordination of the idea of the holy to the civic idea."[413] It is no less telling that Archpriest Ioann Levanda's greeting to Emperor Alexander, cited above (see section II-1.3.1), in which he saw in him an angel, Christ, and God, was eliminated fifty years later (1850) by the religious censors when Levanda's sermons were being reissued, as "deviating from the truth and approaching flattery."[414] The religious censorship banned the order of service for "high triumphal days" that had been proposed by Razumovskii (discussed above, see section II-2 5), and from time to time removed particular expressions that testified to the imperial cult.[415] On March 5, 1865, the same Metropolitan Filaret wrote to the Archimandrite Antonii, hegumen of the Trinity-St. Sergius Lavra: "The respected professor Shevyrev did not hesitate to compare the blowing up of Sevastopol [in the Crimean War] with the earthquake during Christ's passion. What confusion! And if we use the Hebrew word, we should say: what a Babylon, not only in the West but here at home."[416] Filaret's reaction to Feofan Prokopovich's "Investigation of the Pontifex" (*Rozysk o pontifekse*) (1721), with which he only became acquainted in 1849, is extremely indicative. Filaret wrote: "The book . . . assumes something unusual in the very need to write it. It puts the pagan pontifex and Christian bishop on one level and reasons about the pagan pontifex more precisely and penetratingly than about the Christian bishop. At times he writes about the pagan pontifex in a Christian way, how, for example, the pontifex Trajan *gave his blessing* (page 7); sometimes he refers to a Christian bishop in a pagan way, for example, how *the people may call sovereigns bishops*, because *the famous Greek poet Homer calls the Trojan sovereign Hector a bishop* (page 13)."[417] This suggests how Baroque mythology was perceived in the middle of the nineteenth century.

All of these instances relate to the sphere of language and, more generally, to the semiotics of behavior. However, they find their equivalence in their attempts to limit the sacralization of the monarch as a phenomenon. In this regard Metropolitan Filaret's position is intriguing. Thus when in 1835 Nicholas I appointed the heir Alexander Nikolaevich (the future Alexander II) a member of the Synod, Filaret (together with other church leaders) protested against it,[418] and when greeting him, they asked him when he had been ordained, making the point that the heir was a layman and had no charisma which would confer on him the right to join the Synod.[419] After the death of Nicholas I, when the possibility arose for some actions independent of the government, Filaret succeeded in limiting the celebration of "high triumphal days" and military victories.[420] In the same way he sent the Ober-Procuror of the Synod a memorandum "On the Necessity of Abridging the Exaltation of Imperial Names of the Most August Family in Divine Services," in which he referred to Greek and ancient Russian practice; Filaret's proposed abridgement was approved by Alexander II.[421] One may find analogous examples among the activities of other religious leaders. Thus the Synodal authorities gave orders to put Feofan Prokopovich's odious "Investigation of the Pontifex" under seal.[422] The religious censors sometimes criticized the fact that the emperor (governmental power) was referred to as the lawgiver in the properly ecclesiastical domain.[423] Such examples could be multiplied.

Nonetheless, these facts do not indicate basic changes in the status quo. Thus Metropolitan Filaret, who fought against various manifestations of the sacralization of the monarch, nevertheless remained a representative of Baroque culture and himself occasionally used its sacralizing language. This was even more characteristic of other representatives of the clergy. Hence we may speak here only of particular objections against this or that Baroque device within a tradition that was itself Baroque. The same goes for other noted instances of limiting sacralization on the part of religious authorities, which stand out on the background of the further development of sacralization. The same Metropolitan Filaret who, as we have seen, advocated relative restraint and caution in this regard, in other cases defended the emperor's cult. He was thus extremely unhappy that Old Believers and Uniates did not mention the emperor in their church services and considered such commemoration one of the required conditions for the reunification of the Uniate with the Orthodox church;[424] the Old Believers, in his opinion, required police prosecution.[425]

Commemoration of the tsar for Filaret thus acquired doctrinal status. Hence even in those cases when a problem with sacralization of the monarch was felt, the position of the church authorities remained internally inconsistent and this could not have been otherwise given its system of governance. The church's system of governance was obviously non-canonical, but at the same time the church's hierarchy not only had no possibility of changing it, but such change would have led to undermining the very basis of that hierarchy's existence, that is, to its self-destruction.[426]

In this respect the clergy's attitude toward oaths in the name of God, which were part of the pledge of allegiance to the emperor, is exceptionally significant. This form of oath, which was introduced by Peter I and Feofan Prokopovich for political reasons,[427] was certainly non-canonical and directly contradicted the Gospels (Matthew 5:34).[428] Nevertheless, throughout practically the entire Synodal period the clergy defended oaths in the name of God. In particular, Filaret laid out the teaching about oaths in his "Extensive Catechism"; this doctrine was omitted as non-canonical in the Greek translation of this catechesis that came out in Constantinople in the 1850s, and it is extremely noteworthy that Filaret registered a strong protest against this change; he clearly considered it an essential part of the Synodal order (and, consequently, that the Greeks were casting doubt on the divine approbation of the Russian church).[429] "The contemporary governmental position of the church in Russia, rooted in Peter's church reform," wrote one of the most authoritative church historians of the Synodal period in 1916, "has always obliged and obliges the clergy to defend and justify not only the given governmental order, irrespective of its moral qualities, but also the events and phenomena that follow from it."[430] These words also apply to the oath in God's name and also, to a lesser extent, to all of the other manifestations of the cult of the emperor (the sacralization of the monarch).

In one way or another, the clergy preserved the Baroque tradition, despite its complete disappearance from secular culture, and the preservation of this tradition was supported by the entire structure of state life into which the church was entirely subsumed. Therefore the differences between religious and secular culture could manifest themselves as a conflict between Baroque and non-Baroque traditions. Notably, representatives of secular culture were at times more sensitive to confessional issues connected to the sacralization of the monarch than were representatives of the religious estate.[431] M. P. Pogodin's correspondence with the famous preacher Innokentii (Borisov) may serve as an illustration of this conflict between religious Baroque and secular non-Baroque culture. The correspondence began over one of Innokentii's sermons published in the December, 1856, issue of "Christian Reading," which had been delivered in the Odessa cathedral, and which responded to Alexander II's recent coronation. In it the emperor's conversation with Innokentii about Sevastopol* was likened to a conversation of Christ with Moses and Elijah about Golgotha on Mount Tabor:

> On the morning of the wedding day, when everyone around the throne declared [him to be] God's Anointed one, and all of Russia, in the person of its representatives, hurried with greetings before the face of the Autocrat and His Spouse—receiving these, and me as well, as one of the Church leaders, as a pastor of this country, what do you think He deigned to prophesy about to me? About the fact that this was the last day of our southern [city of] Sevastopol. . . . Tell me yourselves, wasn't this like the time when the God-man [i.e., Christ] amid the glory of Tabor once conversed with Moses and Elijah about Golgotha (Luke 9:31), which was then still ahead of Him, though now—for us—it is past?[432]

This comparison upset Pogodin and his colleagues, who thought it was blasphemous. Innokentii responded to this objection in a letter to Pogodin on January 17, 1857: "It's strange and surprising that you keep howling about some sort of blasphemy: where is it? I don't see it even it now. Neither did the censors see blasphemy, nor did other good people, no one did. The Petersburg Academy didn't see it, and published it in 'Christian Reading'; the Holy Synod didn't see it, because it also saw the sermon before publication. And then your Moscow alone cries blasphemy! . . . So take a closer look yourselves at what offends you and it will seem different to you."[433] Pogodin wrote in reply on January 26, 1857: "As you will, the comparison is impermissible, and disturbs the soul! I do not understand how habit may blind such a highly intelligent person as you to such an extent. Christ, Golgotha—who and what may be compared to Christ and Golgotha? Believe me, even now the blood is rushing to my head. And what is it you say about censorship? Is this really a matter for censorship? It's a matter of inner feeling which tells us when to stop. But for you habit acted here. Glinka took God as his chum, said Krylov, so he'd go ahead and summon God to be godfather to his children. Only habit might justify this expression. Filaret himself says this sometimes. In cases such as yours juggling with words plays a role, and you don't remember at these moments whom they refer to. In general, who may be compared to Christ? But in this

---

*   *Translator's note:* After a prolonged siege the fall of Sevastopol led to Russia's loss in the Crimean War.

particular case there's nothing to say . . . I called this comparison blasphemous not in the sense of heresy; this adjective only meant that it was impermissible, reprehensible . . . Feeling, pious feeling is offended by your comparison."[434]

This exchange is curious in many respects. First of all, it is indicative that a layman senses confessional problems arising from such word use more sharply than a man of the cloth. In the second place, it is curious that Pogodin considers this kind of usage characteristic of clergymen like Innokentii Borisov and Filaret Drozdov. Thirdly, it is evident that Baroque traditions in the religious sphere continued. Finally, the correspondence suggests that problems arising from the sacralization of the monarch continued to persist for Orthodox religious consciousness insofar as sacralization could not be organically harmonized with it.

IV. CONCLUSIONS

We have examined the process of the sacralization of the monarch in Russia in its diverse semiotic manifestations. Understandably, in this process both political as well as cultural factors played a role. The material presented shows how difficult it is to draw a line between the two. Political collisions emerge as cultural ones, and at the same time the formation of new cultural languages may have a fully obvious political underpinning. In diverse historical periods, the sacralization of the monarch in Russia has always been connected, directly or indirectly, with external cultural factors. External models may give the impulse for new developments or be the object of conscious orientation. In both cases, however, an external cultural tradition is refracted through the prism of traditional cultural consciousness. As a result, the reading of texts from an alien tradition turns into the creation of texts that are fundamentally new.

The political preconditions for the sacralization of the monarch were twofold. On the one hand, this was the transference of the functions of the Byzantine basileius onto the tsar of Moscow that could be realized both in the conception of Moscow as the Third Rome, which was contrasted to Byzantium, and in the later Byzantanization of the Russian state and ecclesiastical life, beginning in the reign of Aleksei Mikhailovich. On the other hand, this was the tsar's assimilation of the functions of head of the church, beginning with the reign of Peter I. The very combination of these two essentially contradictory tendencies only became possible in the conditions of Baroque culture, insofar as texts that were authoritative for cultural consciousness could be reconceptualized in various ways within a single Baroque framework.

The cultural and semiotic precondition for the sacralization of the monarch consisted of the ability of those who spoke the traditional cultural language to read new texts. Thus, in particular the title of tsar, which the grand prince adopted as a result of assimilating the functions of the Byzantine basileius (tsar), acquired distinctly expressed religious connotations in Russia, insofar as for traditional cultural consciousness this word was associated primarily with Christ. In a similar way, the reading of Baroque texts by a non-Baroque audience could condition the later sacralization of the monarch, that is, produce literalist interpretations of what at first had only carried a conditional, figurative, ludic meaning. For this reason, Baroque texts relating to the tsar were perceived by some as blasphemy and gave others an impetus to actual veneration.

Sacralization of the monarch pertained to the whole Synodal era, and during this entire period it continually came into conflict with traditional religious consciousness. Such conflict was unavoidable in principle insofar as the sacralization of the monarch became part of the state mechanism itself, and in particular, of the Synodal system.

Translated by Marcus C. Levitt

NOTES

1   Isaak Massa, *Kratkoe izvestie o Moskovii v nachale XVII v.* (Moscow, 1937), 68.

2   Henrik Sederberg, "Zametki o religii i nravakh russkogo naroda," *Chteniia v Obshchestve istorii i drevnostei rossiiskikh pri Moskovskom universitete* 2 (1873): 37.

3   Johann Georg Korb, *Dnevnik puteshestviia v Moskoviiu* (1698 i 1699 g.) (St. Petersburg, 1906), 217. G. David's report is also significant. The Russians, he wrote, believe that "when God dies, his place will be taken either by St. Nicholas or the tsar." See: Georgius David, *Status modernus Magnae Russiae seu Moscoviae* (1690) (London, Hague, Paris, 1965), 115; B. A. Uspenskii, *Filologicheskie razyskaniia v oblasti slavianskikh drevnostei (Relikty iazychestva v vostochnoslavianskom kul`te Nikolaia Mirlikiiskogo)* (Moscow, 1982), 38ff.

4   *Sviashchennyi Sobor Pravoslavnoi Rossiiskoi Tserkvi. Deianiia* (Moscow-Petrogard, 1918), kn. II, vyp. 2, 351.

5   A. F. Belousov, *Literaturnoe nasledie Drevnei Rusi v narodnoi slovesnosti russkikh starozhilov Pribaltiki.* Candidate Thesis (Tartu University, 1980), 148.

6   M. N. Katkov, *O samoderzhavii i konstitutsii* (Moscow, 1905), 13.

7   Ibid., 14.

8   P. Florenskii, *Okolo Khomiakova (kriticheskie zametki)* (Sergiev Posad, 1916), 26. S. N. Bulgakov writes about the evolution of his attitude toward the tsar, which turns out to be connected with his return to Orthodoxy:

> by means of some sort of inner act [or] understanding , the strength for which Orthodoxy gave to me, my relationship to the tsar's power changed, [as well as] my

attitude toward it. I became, in the vulgar street expression, tsarist. I understood that the tsar's power in its essence is the highest kind of power, not in its own name, but in God's . . . I felt that the tsar also bore this power like Christ's cross, and that obedience to Him could also be Christ's cross and in His name. In my soul, the idea of holy tsarist power burned like a bright star, and by the light of this idea features of Russian history were lit up and began to sparkle in a new way, like precious stones; where before I had only seen emptiness, falsehood, Asiatic barbarism, now shone the divine idea of God's mercy, and not the human dispensation. (S. Bulgakov, *Avtobiograficheskie zametki* [Paris, 1946], 81-82; cf. 86.)

As evident, religious veneration of the tsar was not alien to members of the Russian "religious Renaissance," and in their view the sacralization of the monarch was an essential part of Orthodox doctrine that would have to be accommodated in any religious renewal.

9   *Vlast` Samoderzhavnaia po ucheniiu slova Bozhiia i Pravoslavnoi Russkoi tserkvi* (Moscow, 1906), 19.

10 P. I. Mel`nikov (Andrei Pecherskii), *Polnoe sobranie sochinenii* (St. Petersburg, 1897-1898), vol. XII, 367.
    Attacks on autocracy in anti-religious (but not anti-monarchist) arguments from late 1917 to early 1918 testify that autocracy could be perceived as a confessional rather than juridical fact. Thus in a program of anti-religious lectures read in the winter of 1917-1918 among the attacks on church doctrine and sacraments was included the thesis: "The dying out of god-tsars: the resurrection of Humanity" (Deianiia, *Sviashchennyi Sobor Pravoslavnoi Rossiiskoi Tserkvi*, kn. VI, vyp. 1, 30, 33). This perception becomes understandable in the context of statements like that of N. S. Suvorov, a well-known canonist: "the bulwark of the Orthodox Church in Russia can only be Imperial power, with whose fall no most holy patriarch will be able to save the Russian Orthodox Church from disintegration" (*Zhurnaly i protokoly zasedanii Vysochaishe uchrezhdennogo Predsobornogo Prisutstviia* [St. Petersburg, 1906], vol. I, 203).

11 See on him: V. Val`denberg, *Drevnerusskie ucheniia o predelakh tsarskoi vlasti* (Petrograd, 1916); I. A. Shevchenko, "Byzantine Source of Muscovite Ideology," *Harvard Slavic Studies* 2 (1954).

12 V. Semenov, *Drevniaia russkaia Pchela po pergamennomu spisku* (St. Petersburg, 1893), 111-112.

13 The juxtaposition of supreme and Divine power, indicating the responsibility of the monarch, is present in the first chapter of Agapetos, which was also cited by a series of Russian authors (see I.A. Shevchenko, "Byzantine Source of Muscovite Ideology," *Harvard Slavic Studies* 2 [1954]). Thus in an excerpt of an epistle of Iosif Volotskii to the Grand Prince (*Poslaniia Iosifa Volotskogo* [Moscow, Leningrad, 1959], 183-184) we read: "Because, sovereign, in the likeness of the heavenly power the heavenly tsar gave to you the scepter of the earthly kingdom of power in order to teach men, to preserve the truth, and to drive demonic temptations from us." With insignificant differences, this same quotation is repeated in the epistle of the Novgorod Archbishop Feodosii (*Dopolnenie k Aktam istoricheskim, sobrannym i izdannym Arkheograficheskoiu kommissieiu* [St. Petersburg, 1846-1875], vol. I, no. 4, 56).
    The extent to which Agapetos influenced religious literature may be seen by the fact that his formulations were repeated even in the second half of the nineteenth century (although they could be interpreted in a sense that was far from the original).

Thus in the Sermon on the day of ascension to the throne of 1865, the Samara priest
I. Khalkolivanov said: "The tsar, although of one nature as we, and having the same
bodily composition, yet He, being God's Anointed, is the divine deputy on earth in
regard to the people over whom God has entrusted him power . . . " (I. Khalkolivanov,
Slova i poucheniia na vse nedeli v godu (Samara, 1873), vol. II, 183).

14   *Polnoe sobranie russkikh letopisei* (St. Petersburg, Petrograd, Leningrad, Moscow, 1841-
1989), vol. II, 592.

15   Ibid., vol. I, 370.

16   *Poslaniia Iosifa Volotskogo* (Moscow, Leningrad, 1959), 184; also see: I. A. Shevchenko,
"Byzantine Source of Muscovite Ideology."

17   Iosif Volotskii, *Prosvetitel`* (Kazan, 1855), 602.

18   Ibid., 420.

19   *Polnoe sobranie russkikh letopisei,* vol. X, 131.

20   Rom 13:1.

21   *Zapiski Otdeleniia russkoi i slavianskoi arkheologii imp. Russkogo arkheologicheskogo
obshchestva* (St. Petersburg, 1861), vol. II, 751, 753.

22   *Akty, sobrannye v bibliotekakh i arkhivakh Rossiiskoi imperii Arkheograficheskoi ekspeditsieiu
imp. Akademii nauk* (St. Petersburg, 1836), vol. IV, no. 127, 172.

23   *Kniga prepodobnogo i bogonosnogo otsa nashego Nikona, igumena Chernyia gory* (Pochaev,
1795), 1, 306.

24   Iosif Volotskii, *Prosvetitel`*, 602.

25   M. A. D`iakonov, *Vlast` moskovskikh gosudarei. Ocherki iz istorii politicheskikh idei drevnei
Rusi do kontsa XVI v.* (St. Petersburg, 1889), 99.

26   V. Val`denberg, *Drevnerusskie ucheniia o predelakh tsarskoi vlasti*, 210-211; V. Val`denberg,
"Poniatie o tirane v drevnerusskoi literature v sravnenii s zapadnoi," *Izvestiia po
russkomu iazyku i slovesnosti* III, 1 (1929).

27   "Opredeleniia Moskovskogo Sobora 1675 g.," *Pravoslavnyi sobesednik* 1 (1864): 370.

28   On the first see: M. N. Tikhomirov, *Merilo pravednoe po rukopisi XIV veka* (Moscow, 1961),
27; Nikolai Kostomarov, ed., *Pamiatniki starinnoi russkoi literatury, izdavaemye grafom
Grigoriem Kushelevym-Bezborodko* (St. Petersburg, 1860-1862), vol. IV, 184; and on the
latter: S. Smirnov, *Materialy dlia istorii drevnerussoi pokaiannoi distsipliny* (Moscow, 1913),
230, 231.

29   Psalm 82 in the Western Psalter.

30   It is precisely this kind of exegesis that is presented in commentaries on the Psalter
(Tolkovye Psaltyri) which usually contain the commentaries of Athanasius the Great
(of Alexandria) or Theodoret of Cyrrhus (see in particular V. Pogorelov, "Chudovskaia
Psaltyŕ XI veka" in *Pamiatniki staroslavianskogo iazyka* [St. Petersburg, 1910], vol. III,
192-193). For the commentaries, see: J.P. Migne, ed., *Patrologiae cursus completis. Series
graeca* (Paris, 1857-1864), 364d-365b; vol. LXXX, 1528b-1529b.
In the patristic literature there also exists another tradition of exegesis of this Psalm
connected with the idea of the deification of saints, which sees them transfigured
"into gods by grace" (see V.M. Zhivov, "'Mistagogiia' Maksima Ispovednika i razvitie
vizantiiskoi teorii obraza." In *Khudozhestvennyi iazyk srednevekov`ia* [Moscow, 1982],
123; on calling saints "gods" see Vasilii [Krivoshein], Arkhiepiskop, *Prepodobnyi
Simeon Novyi Bogoslov [949-1022]* [Paris, 1980], 37, 99, 106, 157, 166, 177, 188, 201, etc.). It
is interesting to note that Patriarch Germanos (Germanus) of Constantinople (early
eighth century), in an epistle to Thomas of Claudiopolis, writes: " . . . we do not let

any of the holy men be called god, although . . . God gave this name to those who pleased Him, as it is written in the holy book of Psalms [Ps 81 (82): 1-6]" (D. Mansi, ed., *Sacrorum consiliorum nova et amplissima collection* [Venice and Florence, 1759-1798], vol. XIII, 121-124). It may be supposed that in Byzantium the two exegetic traditions opposed one another and belonged to two different ideological trends. In Russia, the second exegetical tradition attracted little interest. In Russia one may find saints being called "gods," but as a rule this is for different reasons; here icons could be called "gods," and therefore saints could be named the same way (for example, "Nikola—god of barge haulers," and so on; see B.A. Uspenskij, "Filologicheskie razyskaniia v oblasti slavianskikh drevnostei" in *Relikty iazychestva v vostochnoslavianskom kul`te Nikolaia Mirlikiiskogo* [Moscow, 1982], 10, 118-119).

31   The "Sermon of Vasilii Velikii" (Basil the Great) is directly connected to the "Sermon of Jesus son of Sirach on Ungracious Princes Who Judge Untruly," which is textologically related to it, and which was included in several Kormchie books (nomocanons) and Prologues (miscellanies) (see, for example, *Kormchii* in RGADA, f. 181, d. 576; RNB, QII, d. 46). In the opinion of V. Val`denberg (V. Val`denberg, *Drevnerusskie ucheniia o predelakh tsarskoi vlasti* [Petrograd, 1916], 129), this work was the source for the "Sermon of Vasilii Velikii." The monarch is not called "god" here, although it does say that "every true tsar or prince has an angelic or sacerdotal rank" (RGADA, f. 181, d. 576, ll. 454-455 verso); the word "true" (pravdivyi) here means "righteous" (pravednyi), "living according to truth, in accord with Divine commandments." For us it is important that here the same context pertains as above, that is, the issue is the monarch's responsibility before God (primarily for righteous judgments), which defines the specific connections between them. It is characteristic that both sermons were cited in this way by Iosif Volotskii (see "Chetvertoe poslanie ob epitimiakh" in S. Smirnov, *Materialy dlia istorii drevnerussoi pokaiannoi distsipliny* [Moscow, 1913], prilozhenie, 230-231).

32   M. Cherniavsky (1961, 32), considering the old Russian period, asserts that "basically, in Russian popular tradition and in Russian political theology, all princes were seen as saints, through actions or in their being, mediators between God and their people in life and in death, and in that sense true images of Christ." This statement is to a large degree based on the unmotivated veneration (from the perspective of the Christian canon of saintliness) of many Russian princes as saints. If we agree that a prince was more or less automatically accepted as holy, this would mean that he acted as a necessary mediator between God and man and in this way—according to old Russian religious and political views—possessed a special charisma. Such an assumption, however, cannot withstand criticism. Indeed, those sources on whose basis we may judge the the sixteenth century (E. Golubinskii, *Istoriia kanonizatsii sviatykh v Russkoi Tserkvi* [Moscow, 1903], 309f) sooner testify to retrospective sacralization, that is, to the spread of the cult of the monarch taking place in Russia at that time. Thus these sources cannot provide evidence of the religious and political views of the oldest period, but reflect later changes in social and religious consciousness.

33   A. L. Gol`dberg, "Tri poslamiia Filofeia (Opyt tekstologicheskogo analiza)," *Trudy otdela drevnerusskoi literatury* XXIV (1974): 87; V. Zhmakin, "Odin iz literaturnykh pamiatnikov XVII v.," *Zhurnal Ministerstva narodnogo prosveshcheniia* 221 (1882): 245.

34   J. Meyendorff, "Introduction à l'etude de Grégoire Palamas," *Patristica sorboniensa* 3 (1959): 158-159.

35   Wladimir Vodoff, "Remarques sur la valeur du term 'tsar' appliqué aux princes Russes avant le milieu du XV siècle," *Oxford Slavonic Papers* 11 (1978): 1-41.

36   The well-known dynastic legend about Riurik's descent from Prus, brother of Emperor Augustus, claims a direct connection between the rulers of Moscow and imperial Rome (R.P. Dmitrieva, *Skazanie o kniaz`iakh Vladimirskikh* [Moscow-Leningrad, 1955]). This legend arose approximately at the time of the notion of "Moscow—Third Rome" and may be seen as its secular, political and dynastic, complement. Although this legend was used in sixteenth century diplomatic relations as proof of the legitimacy of the tsar's title, and possibly also in internal political struggles, its importance for the religious and political consciousness of the era remained peripheral; there could be no comparison here with the significance of the Roman connection for Byzantium.

37   I. V. Iagich, ed., *Codex slovenicus rerum grammaticarum. Rassuzhdeniia iuzhnoslavianskoi i russkoi stariny o tserkovnoslavianskom i russkom iazyke* (St. Petersburg, 1885-1895), 437.

38   Ibid., 436, 454, 459; RGB, Tikhonrav. 336, ll. 15 verso-16.

39   *Rossiia nachala XVII v. Zapiski kapitana Marzhereta* (Moscow, 1982), 56-57, 148-149; N. Ustrialov, *Skazaniia sovremennikov o Dmitrii Samozvantse* (St. Petersburg, 1859), part I, 254.

40   *Perepiska Ivana Groznogo s Andreem Kurbskim* (Leningrad, 1979), 19.

41   Ibid., 14.

42   A. M. Panchenko, B. A. Uspenskii, "Ivan Groznyi i Petr Velikii: kontseptsii pervogo monarkha," *Trudy Otdela drenerusskoi literatury* XXXVII (1983). Ivan the Terrible's stated opinion that a church may only be erected over the tomb of a tsar (just as over the tomb of a saint) testifies to his view of the special sacral status of the tsar. In his epistle to the Kirillo-Belozerskii Monastery Ivan protests against the building of a church over the grave of Prince Vorotynskii, who was not a tsar and not venerated as a saint: "... it is arrogance and an example of inordinate praise to venerate someone like a tsar by [erecting a] church and [honoring him with] a sepulcher and pall" (Ivan Groznyi, *Poslaniia Ivana Groznogo* [Moscow, 1951], 173). On the sacral character of the epithet "groznyi," see A.M. Panchenko, B.A. Uspenskii, "Ivan Groznyi i Petr Velikii," 70-71.

43   Iosif Volotskii, *Prosvetitel`*, 324-325.

44   B. Norretranders, *The Shaping of Czardom under Ivan Groznyi* (Copenhagen, 1964), 45.

45   See, for example, the troparion (*tropar*) on the Birth of Christ, on Candelmas (*Sretenie*), the fourth and fifth song of the Paschal canon, etc.

46   N. T. Voitovich, *Barkalabauska letapis* (Minsk, 1977), 198.

47   Konrad Bussov, *Moskovskaia khronika: 1564-1613* (Moscow, Leningrad, 1961), 109.

48   I. Tatarskii, *Simeon Polotskii (ego zhizn` i deiatel`nost`). Opyt issledovaniia iz istorii prosveshcheniia i vnutrennei tserkovnoi zhizni vo vtoruiu polovinu XVII veka* (Moscow, 1886).

49   *Letopisi russkoi literatury i drevnosti* (Moscow, 1859-1863), vol. V, part III, 90-93.

50   *Russkaia istoricheskaia biblioteka, izdavaemaia Arkheograficheskoiu komissieiu* (St. Petersburg, Petrograd, Leningrad, 1872-1927), vol. XIII, 313.

51   *Zapiski Otdeleniia russkoi i slavianskoi arkheologii Imperatorskogo Russkogo arkheologicheskogo obshchestva*, vol. II, 464, 460.

52   I. A. Chistovich, *Feofan Prokopovich i ego vremia* (St. Petersburg, 1868), 84, 86. 10. Of course, only depictions of a tsar during his life are relevant in this regard. Posthumous images of this sort are a more or less common phenomenon. These Byzantine notions were possibly reflected in the "Sermon of Jesus son of Sirach" mentioned in note 31, in which it speaks of the "angelic or sacerdotal rank" of the true tsar.

In Byzantium this charismatic perception of the emperor was manifested in a series of imperial court ceremonies, in the emperor's relations with the clergy, in church rituals connected with the emperor, in his titles, and so on. Although in Byzantium itself these external marks of the emperor's charisma could be interpreted in different ways by various parties, the main mass of information available to the Russians (both oral and from books) convinced them that the head of the Orthodox empire was endowed with special spiritual powers and privileges.

It is curious to note that a series of these external marks of the emperor's charisma developed not as a result of the transfer of church ceremonies onto the emperor but due to a reverse process: the development of church ritual in the fourth and fifth centuries to a large degree consisted in transferring ceremonies and practices of the emperor's court into the church (see: L. Bréhier, P. Battifol, *Les Survivances du culte imperial romain* (Paris, 1920); A. Grabar, "L'empereur dans l'art Byzantine." *Publications de la Faculté des lettres de l'Université se Strasbourg* 75 [1936]). However, the memory of this in Byzantium had been lost quite early and was all the less relevant for Russia.

53   See Ivan Timofeev's *Chronicle (Vremennik)* in *Russkaia istoricheskaia biblioteka*, vol. XIII, 373; V. Val`denberg, "Poniatie o tirane v drevnerusskoi literature i sravnenii s zapadnoi," 223-224.

54   See, for example, Timofeev's *Chronicle* in *Russkaia istoricheskaia biblioteka*, vol. XIII, 326, 389.

55   A. Gasquet, *De l'autorité imperial en matière religieuse à Byzance* (Paris, 1879); G. Podskalsky, *Byzantinische Reichseschatologie* (München, 1972); E. H. Kantorowicz, *The King's Two Bodies* (Princeton, 1957).

56   Consider the notion of the emperor as an "external bishop," as in calling Byzantine emperor Leo III "bishop and tsar" in the so-called second epistle of Pope Gregory II in D. Mansi, ed., *Sacrorum consiliorum nova et amplissima collection* (Venice and Florence, 1759-1798), vol. XII, 979; or the emperor's assumption of a series of functions in the church ritual—see A. Gasquet, *De l'autorité imperial en matière religieuse à Byzance*, 52-60 and P. Dabin, "Le sacerdoce royal des fidèles dans la taradition ancienne et modern," *Museum Lessianum. Section théologique* 48 (1950): 126-128; in the last work the author indicates several echoes of these Byzantine ideas in the West.

57   Despite all of this, it is necessary to note that the ideas under discussion did not come together into a system of views that would unite Russian society. This ideology remained only one of several tendencies in religious and political thought. However, it was manifested clearly in Ivan the Terrible's reign, but was connected here with a whole series of particular issues and led to the splintering of Russian society that was expressed with full clarity in the Time of Troubles. Understandably, this later period did not facilitate the development of theocratic ideas, and it is indicative that at its end the idea of an elected tsar won out; cf. the constraints on electing the Polish prince Vladislav as Russian tsar as formulated by Russian envoys in 1610.

58   Marc Bloch, *Feudal Society* (London, 1965), vol. II, 379-388; Marc Bloch, "Les ropios thaumaturges: etude sur le caractère surnaturel attribué à la puissance royale, particulièrement en France et en Angleterre," *Publications de la Faculté des letters de l'Université de Strasbourg* 19 (1924); F. Barlow, "The King's Evil," in *The English Historical Review* 95 (1980): 374.

59   S. Belokurov, *Arsenii Sukhanov* (Moscow, 1891-1892), 85-87.

60   E. V. Barsov, *Drevnerusskie pamiatniki sviashchennogo venchaniia tsarei na tsarstvo v sviazi s grecheskimi ikh originalami. S istoricheskim ocherkom chinov tsarskogo venchaniia v sviazi s razvitiem idei tsaria na Rusi* (Moscow, 1883), 138.

61   Naturally, changes to the coronation rite that developed during his father's reign only applied to his coronation and should not be retroactively attributed to that of Aleksei Mikhailovich himself. See K. Popov, "Chin sviashchennogo koronovaniia (istoricheskii ocherk obrazovaniia china)," *Bogoslovskii vestnik* II (1896): 191; V. Savva, *Moskovskie tsari i vizantiiskie vasilevsy. K voprosu o vliianii Vizantii na obrazovanie idei tsarskoi vlasti moskovskikh gosudarei* (Kharkov, 1901), 147.

62   *Pis`ma mitr. Moskovskogo Filareta k namestniku Sviato-Troitskiia Sergievy lavry arkhimandritu Antoniiu* (Moscow, 1877-1881), vol. IV, 339-340, 342; *Sobranie mnenii i otzyvov Filareta, mitr. Moskovskogo i Kolomenskogo, po uchebnym i tserkovno-gosudarstvennym voprosam* (Moscow, 1885-1888), dop. tom, 444-450.

63   *Corpus juris civilis* (Berlin, 1903-1904), vol. III, 507.

64   *Russkaia istoricheskaia biblioteka*, vol. XXXIX, 466-469.

65   N. F. Kapterev, *Patriarkh Nikon i tsar` Aleksei Mikhailovich* (Sergiev Posad, 1909-1912), vol. II, 188.

66   For example, see Patriarch Nikon's protests in his letters to the Eastern Patriarchs in RGB, f. 178, d. 9427, l. 110; RGADA, f. XXVII, d. 140, ch. VII, l. 93; ch. VIII, ll. 15-17 verso, 53-56, 91 verso-94, 127-130; and in his "Objection or Ruin" (*Vozrazhenie ili razorenie*), the twenty-sixth question and answer, in RGB, f. 178, d. 9427, l. 291ff.

     After the Council of 1666-1667, judicial functions were removed from the Monastery Office (Monastyrskii prikaz) and returned to the church authorities; this was evidently the tsar's payment for the clergy's agreement to depose Patriarch Nikon. After Aleksei Mikhailovich's death on December 19, 1677, the Monastery Office was closed; one may assume that the young tsar (Fedor Alekseevich) acted here under pressure from the church. On January 24, 1701, after the death of Patriarch Adrian, Peter I again instituted a Monastery Office, which was one of his first steps in taking away the independence of church administration.

67   *Zapiski Otdeleniia russkoi i slavianskoi arkheologii Imperatorskogo Russkogo arkheologicheskogo obshchestva*, vol. II, 521, 546.

68   Ibid., 188-189.

69   Ibid., 430-432; V. M. Zhivov, "Istoriia russkogo prava kak lingvosemioticheskaia problema" in *Semiotics and the History of Culture. In Honor of J. Lotman* (Columbus, OH, 1988); V. M. Undol'skii, "Otzyv patriarkha Nikona ob ulozhenii tsaria Alekseia Mikhailovicha," *Russkii arkhiv* 2 (1886).

70   *Zapiski Otdeleniia russkoi i slavianskoi arkheologii Imperatorskogo Russkogo arkheologicheskogo obshchestva*, vol. II, 428, 430, 434.

71   *Pravda russkaia* (Moscow-Leningrad, 1940-1963), vol. I, 104, 117, 122; *Sudebniki XV-XVI vekov* (Moscow-Leningrad, 1952), 141.

72   Together with representations of the charismatic status of the emperor in patriotic literature one may find very rare instructions for the basileus on his status as a layman, for example, in St. Ambrosius of Milan or St. Maximus the Confessor. See J. P. Migne, ed., *Patrologiae cursus completis. Series latina* (Paris, 1857-1864), vol. XVI, 1041, 1038-1039, 1061; J. P. Migne, ed., *Patrologiae cursus completis. Series graeca*, vol. LXXXII, 1232-1237; vol. XC, 92, 116-117, 145-148; Theodoreti, *Eccl Historia V*, 17.

73   See on this conflict: N. F. Kapterev, *Patriarkh Nikon i tsar` Aleksei Mikhailovich*; M. V. Zyzykin, *Patriarkh Nikon: ego gosudarstvennye i kanonicheskie idei* (Warsaw, 1931-1939); and sections II-2.3.

74   Thus, responding to the boyar S. Streshnev, Nikon writes (the twenty-seventh question and answer): "Tell me, o interlocutor, what must be done according to the holy rules

with one who calls our most majestic tsar a torturer and dares call [him] an unjust abuser and predator? Answer: Why do you write anonymously, 'one who calls our most majestic tsar a torturer.' If you are speaking about us, it is not we alone who profess this, but all creation sympathizes and sighs with us over the fierce sorrows that we suffered, as has been shown above ... And the tsar's injustice and lack of mercy is clear to everyone." See RGB, f. 178, d. 9427, l. 454.

75 See, for example, the Spiritual Regulation (*Dukhovnyi Reglament*) in P. V. Verkhovskoi, *Uchrezhdenie Dukhovnoi Kollegii i Dukhovnyi Reglament* (Rostov-na-Donu, 1916), vol. II, 32 (first pagination); vol. I, 89, 183, 283-284, 368.

76 A paean to Petr Mogila may serve as a typical example of the Ruthenian panegyric style that must have been perceived as blasphemous by the Great Russian audience. Its author asks why Mogila's birth did not occur on the same day as Christ's (Mogila was born on December 21). The question is resolved like this: "Petr Mogila should have been born on the same day as Christ, but the applause of the luminaries themselves could not suffice for both of them together. The earth was not in condition to [sufficiently] marvel at these two great miracles of nature. The heavens did not want to have double joy; they divided it up for several days and decided to have Petr born a few days before Christmas so that having experienced and commended their hymns to the first, they could sing them to the second; they decided, however, that Petr should be born not long before Christ so that Petr and Christ could accept the heavenly applause appropriate for each." See S. Golubev, *Kievskii mitropolit Petr Mogila i ego spodvizhniki* (Kiev, 1883-1898), vol. I, 7, 19.

77 V. M. Zhivov, B. A. Uspenskii, "Metamorfozy antichnogo iazychestva v istotii russkoi kul`tury XVII-XVIII vv." in *Antichnost` v kul`ture i iskusstve posleduiushchikh vekov* (Moscow, 1984).

78 I. I. Golikov, *Anekdoty, kasaiushchiesia do Gosudaria Imperatora Petra Velikogo* (Moscow, 1807), 422-23; *Rasskazy Nartova o Petre Velikom* (St. Petersburg, 1891), 73.

79 Psalm 81:6 (Psalm 82:6 in the Western Psalter).

80 1 Corinthians 8:5.

81 Exodus 22:28.

82 John 10:34-35; Jesus here explains the meaning of the line cited from Psalm 81 (82).

83 Theodoret of Cyrrhus's commentary on Psalm 82. See J. P. Migne, ed., *Patrologiae cursus completis. Series graeca*, vol. 80, 1528C.

84 Feofan Prokopovich, *Arkhiepiskopa Velikogo Novagrada i Velikikh Luk, Sviateishago Pravitel`stvuiushchego Sinoda Vitse prezidenta, a potom pervenstvuiushchego Chlena Slova i rechi pouchitel`nyia, pokhval`nyia i pozdravitel`nyia* (St. Petersburg, 1760-1768), part I, 251. 17. The same idea but without such detailed argumentation is repeated by Feofan in the *Investigation of the Pontifex* (1721): "For the Christian law in holy writings more than any other human laws gives power to the highest authorities, and shows them to be quite inviolable, untouchable, and subject to no one's judgment other than God's. And therefore they adorn them with most glorious and exceptional names, calling them divine Christs and Gods." See Feofan Prokopovich, *Rozysk istoricheskii, koikh radi vin, i v iazykovom razume byli i naritsalis` imperatory rimstii, kak iazychestii, tak i khristianstii, pontifeksami ili arkhiereiami mnogobozhnogo zakona* (St. Petersburg, 1721), 37. Here Feofan gives a curious linguistic basis for applying sacred names to the tsar. See Feofan Prokopovich, *Rozysk istoricheskii*, 23-24. On the fact that tsars "are honored with partaking in divine titles is not due to human flattery but from God Himself who judges truly irrespective of person," Feofan also speaks in the sermon on the coronation

of Catherine I in 1726, referring to the same Psalm 81 (82). See Feofan Prokopovich, *Arkhiepiskopa Velikogo Novagrada i Velikikh Luk*, part II, 176-178.

[85] The figurative arts of the Petrine era offer the same possibility of such a dual reading, based on the collision of the two traditions. In this regard Aleksei Zubov's etching of 1717 is very indicative; here "the tsar is depicted in the center in armor and porphyry, above him the word God in an aureole." See P. P. Pekarskii, *Istoriia imp. Akademii nauk v Peterburge* (St. Petersburg, 1870-1873), vol. II, 386. The word "God" here indicates the invisible God; this image derives from the iconography of the Dutch "Piscator Bible" (see A. S. Retkovskaia, "O poiavlenii i razvitii kompozitsii 'Otechestvo' v russkom iskusstve XIV-XVI vekov" in *Drevnerusskoe iskusstvo XV—nachala XVI veka* (Moscow, 1963), 258), but to the Russian viewer, brought up on icons (the more so since secular painting had only recently appeared in Russia), this inscription must have been perceived as a title (*titlo*), that is, relating to the name of the person depicted below it.

[86] V. Kel'siev, *Sbornik pravitel`stvennykh svedenii o raskol`nikakh* (London 1860-1862), vol. II, 248.

[87] 2 Thessalonians 2:4.

[88] N. Bubnov, N. Demkova, "Vnov' naidennoe poslanie iz Moskvy v Pustozersk 'Vozveshchenie ot syna dukhovnago ottsu dukhovnomu' i otvet protopopa Avvakuma (1767 g.)," *Trudy otdela drevnerusskoi literatury* 36 (1981): 144.

[89] Lazar` Baranovich, *Mech dukhovnyi ezhe est` glagol bozhii* (Kiev, 1666), 10 verso.

[90] There are many examples of this sort of reaction, such as the composition by Ivan Pavlov published by Pekarskii in his article "Voluntary Sufferer for Making the Sign of the Cross with Two Fingers." See P. P. Pekarskii, *Istoricheskie bumagi, sobrannye K.I. Arsen`evym* (St. Petersburg, 1872), 114-132.

[91] See *Russkaia istoricheskaia biblioteka*, vol. VI, 421, 523, 529, 534-536, 540, 558, 576-578, 583, 584; V. Savva, *Moskovskie tsari i vizantiiskie vasilevsy*, 68-69.

[92] It is curious to note that in this and many other issues the southern Slavs (first of all those living in Greek cultural centers) tended much more spontaneously toward the Byzantine tradition than the Russians. Thus in the Serbian typicon of the Holy Laura of St. Sabba (in Jerusalem) we read in the Polychronion (*mnogoletie*): "May many years be granted to our pious and God's anointed, holy Tsar Stephen." This refers to the Serbian King Stephen Urosh (Uroš) III who reigned at the time the typicon was written, and who died in 1371. See A. Dmitrievskii, *Opisanie liturgicheskikh rukopisei, khraniashchikhsia v bibliotekakh pravoslavnogo Vostoka* (Petrograd, 1917), vol. III, part II, 464-465, 469.

[93] See V. Savva, *Moskovskie tsari i vizantiiskie vasilevsy*, 70-71; there are many examples here.

[94] See for example the documents and letters of the patriarchs of Jerusalem and other bishops in N. F. Kapterev, "Snosheniia Ierusalimskikh patriarkhov s russkim pravitel`stvom," *Pravoslavnyi Palestinskii sbornik* 43 (1895), 17, 18, 102, 109, 118, 136, 169, 178, 247, 259, 284, 304, 348, 350, 374, 377, 420, 421, 424, 436; *Pis`ma i bumagi imperatora Petra Velikogo* (St. Petersburg-Moscow, 1887-1977), vol. II, 718, vol. VII, 483.

[95] *Polnoe sobranie postanovlenii i rasporiazhenii po vedomstvu pravoslavnogo ispovedaniia* (St. Petersburg-Petrograd, 1869-1916), vol. III, no. 1115, 161.

[96] The change evidently concerned the exclamations in the Greek rite of enthronement that announced the choice of patriarch: "Our soverign and holy autocrat and tsar, and the divine ... council invite your Most Holiness to the Highest Throne of the Constantinopolitan patriarchate." See V. Savva, *Moskovskie tsari i vizantiiskie vasilevsy*, 70-71.

[97] Avvakum's commentary on Psalm 44 in *Russkaia istoricheskaia biblioteka*, vol. XXXIX, 465-466.

[98] N. G. Ustrialov, *Istoriia tsarstvovaniia Petra Velikogo* (St. Petersburg, 1858-1859), vol. II, 471.

[99] *Propovedi blazhennyia pamiati Stefana Iavorskogo* (Moscow, 1804-1805), vol. II, 154.

[100] *Pis'ma i bumagi imperatora Petra Velikogo*, vol. IX, 631.

[101] V. P. Petrov, *Oda imperatritse Ekaterine Alekseevne vo iz'iavlenie chuvstvitel'neishiia synov rossiiskikh radosti i iskrenneishego blagodareniia, vozbuzhdennogo v serdtsakh ikh manifestom o izbranii deputatov k sochineniiu proekta novogo ulozheniia* (Moscow, 1767), 2 verso.

[102] Platon (Levshin), *Rech' Gosudariu Imperatoru Aleksandru Pavlovichu po sovershenii koronovaniia* (Moscow, 1801), 4 verso.

[103] Avgustin (Vinogradskii), *Rech' pred nachatiem blagodarstvennogo molebstviia po sluchaiu vozvrashcheniia Aleksandra I v Rossiiu* (Moscow, 1815), 6; Avgustin (Vinogradskii), *Rech' Ego Imp. Velichestvu Aleksandru Pervomu po sluchaiu pribytiia v Sviato Troitskuiu Sergievu Lavru* (Moscow, 1816), 5.

[104] *Drevniaia rossiiskaia vivliofika* (Moscow, 1788-1791), vol. VII, 357.

[105] Ibid., 288; *Sobranie gosudarstvennykh gramot i dogovorov, khraniashchikhsia v gosudarstvennoi kollegii inostrannykh del* (Moscow, 1813-1894), vol. II, 83, vol. III, 84.

[106] It is important to emphasize that the exclamations "Holy of holies" and "Holy lord, tsar anointed by God" were directly connected to the rules for the tsar's coronation. See A. Ia. Shpakov, *Gosudarstvo i tserkov' v ikh vzaimnykh otnosheniiakh v Moskovskom gosudarstve. Tsarstvovanie Fedora Ioanovicha. Uchrezhdenie patriarshestva v Rossii* (Odessa, 1912), appendix II, 120-121.

[107] *Sobranie gosudarstvennykh gramot i dogovorov,* vol. IV, 375-76; some phrases have been left out.

[108] *Perepiska Filareta mitropolita Moskovskogo s S. D. Nechaevym* (St. Petersburg, 1895), 85-86.

[109] An actual case of revering the emperor's portrait as an icon was recorded in I. I. Golikov, *Anekdoty*, 532-535.

[110] This specific view receives a deliberate theological justification: "According to [Russian] Orthodox theologians, anointing, combined with coronation, is a special sacrament: the tsar is not initiated into the religious hierarchy as it was with the Byzantine emperor and does not assume the authority of performing the rite or of teaching, but does receive the authority and wisdom to perform the highest governmental role in both church and state." See F. V. Brokgauz, I. A. Efron, eds., *Entsiklopedicheskii slovar'* (St. Petersburg, 1890-1904), vol. XXXI, 320-321; Kataev, N. *O sviashchennom venchanii i pomazanii tsarei na tsarstvo* (St. Petersburg, 1847). In a sermon on Emperor Paul's coronation, Metropolitan Evgenii (Bolkhovitinov) called the coronation ceremony and anointing the tsar "a God-given sacrament." See Leskov, N. S. "Tsarskaia koronatsiia," *Istoricheskii vestnik*, (1881) vol 5: 284. This point of view, by the way, was not alien to Byzantium, where some saw in the coronation τὸ τῆς βασιλείας μυστήριον. See K. Popov, "Chin sviashceennogo koronovaniia," 68. Whatever the particular differences from Byzantium, the very conferral of exceptional meaning on anointment clearly had Byzantine roots. Byzantium developed the doctrine that anointing the king not only accorded the emperor God-given gifts but also freed him from sin. See Ibid., 67.

[111] Maksim Grek uses the word "khristos" as a Grecicism in the meaning "anointed one." This word appears as a gloss to "anointed" (*pomazannyi*) several times in the manuscript of a Lectionary Psalter (*Sledovannaia Psaltyr'*) from the late fifteenth century. See glosses to Psalms 104(105):15, 131(132):10 and to the fourth song of Prophet

Avvakum, verse 13 in RGB, Troitsk. 315, ll. 134 verso, 161, 181. In Maksim's collection of corrections to the Psalter we find the following commentary to the given usage: "*И вознесетъ рогъ ха* [with diacritic] *своего.* Com[mentary]: in Greek, *khristi,* in Russian it is called *anointed (pomazanii).*" See Ibid., Troitsk. 201, l. 481. Of course, for Maksim this was a purely linguistic correction that had no political significance. (Note that when Maksim corrected the Lectionary Psalter, in the 1540s, in Russia the tsar was not yet "anointed for the kingdom").

112 *Sobranie gosudarstvennykh gramot i dogovorov,* vol. IV, 88. In a Church Slavonic translation contemporary to the epistle, this place reads: "God is in heaven and in everything, and it is the same on earth—God is also in those who are below the tsar's rank and eminence, and just as those who deny faith in God are deprived of the assembly of the faithful , in a similar way those who don't keep faith in the tsar's rank but surreptitiously show themselves false to him are unworthy of to be called Christians because he [the tsar] is God's anointed, having the crown and diadem and strength in himself." See Ibid. Another contemporary translation published by Gibbenet renders the text even less precisely. See N. Gibbenet, *Istoricheskoe issledovanie dela patriarkha Nikona* (St. Petersburg, 1882-1884), vol. II, 672-673.

113 Feofan Prokopovich, *Arkhiepiskopa Velikogo Novagrada i Velikikh Luk,* part I, 252.

114 The etymology of the word *khristos* was also fully obvious to those of conservative views, i.e. for that "ignorant throng" whom Feofan Prokopovich and his cohort strove to enlighten. Archpriest Avvakum wrote in his commentary on Psalm 44: "Christ . . . was anointed by the Father from on high by the Holy Spirit and filled with grace and truth. For this reason he was called Christ, or the anointed, or tsar." See *Russkaia istoricheskaia biblioteka,* vol. XXXIX, 459; also, see Feofan's exegesis of the same psalm concerning the same issue in Feofan Prokopovich, *Rassuzhdenie o knize Solomonovoi, narekaemoi Pesni Pesnei* (Moscow, 1774), 23-25. It is remarkable that Avvakum connects the kingly dignity of Christ precisely with anointing, however, he concludes from this that Christ may be called "tsar," but not at all that a tsar may be called "Christ." Here we clearly see the difference in attitude toward verbal signs that we discussed above (section I-2.2).

115 Ibid., 25-26. This idea also has a Byzantine source. Feofan could have borrowed it from Eusebius' "Church History" which he undoubtedly knew well. Eusebius writes: "And tsars too, by God's determination, were anointed by prophets and through this became prefigurations of Christ, because they bore on themselves the image of the imperial and supreme power of the single and true Christ, the Word of God that reigns over all." See J. P. Migne, ed., *Patrologiae cursus completis. Series graeca,* vol. XX, 72; Evsevii Pamfil, *Sochineniia, perevedennye s grecheskogo pri SPb. Duhovoi Akademii* (St. Petersburg, 1850-1858), vol. I, 15; Hist. Eccl. I, 3.

116 P. P. Pekarskii, *Nauka i literatura v Rossii pri Petre Velikom* (St. Petersburg, 1862), vol. 2, 202.

117 Feofilakt Lopatinskii, *Sluzhba blagodarstvennaia, Bogu v Troitse sviatoi slavimomu o velikoi Bogom darovannoi pobede, nad sveiskim korolem Karolom 12, i voinstvom ego. Sodeiannoi pod Poltavoiu, v leto 1709* (Moscow, 1709), 16 verso; *Mineia Iiun`* (Moscow, 1766), 237 verso.

118 Feofilakt Lopatinskii, *Sluzhba blagodarstvennaia,* 19 verso; *Mineia Iiun`,* 239 verso.

119 Feofan Prokopovich, *Arkhiepiskopa Velikogo Novagrada i Velikikh Luk,* vol. I, 155.

120 P. Morozov, *Feofan Prokopovich kak pisatel`* (St. Petersburg, 1880), 83-84.

121 Luke 2:30.

122 Luke 2:10-11.

123 Ia. S. Gur`ianova, "Neizvestnyi pamiatnik staroobriadcheskoi polemiki kontsa XVII—nachala XIX v. ob imperatorskoi vlasti" in *Drevnerusskaia rukopisnaia kniga i ee bytovanie v Sibiri* (Novosibirsk, 1982), 85.

124 Ia. S. Gur`ianova, "Staroobriadcheskie sochineniia XVIII—nachala XIX v. o dogmate nemoleniia za gosudaria v fedoseevskom soglasii" in *Issledovaniia po istorii obschestvennogo soznaniia epokhi feodalizma v Rossii* (Novosibirsk, 1984), 84-85; Ia. S. Gur`ianova, "Staroobriadcheskie sochineniia XVIII—nachala XIX v. o dogmate nemoleniia za gosudaria" in *Rukopisnaia traditsiia XVI-XIX vv. na vostoke Rossii* (Novosibirsk, 1983), 81.

125 Ibid., 75.

126 The Old Believer tract "Collection About the Antichrist from Holy Writ" cited above says of Peter I that "this false Christ began to exalt himself above all so-called gods." See V. Kel`siev, *Sbornik* vol. II, 248. This work evidently was the source for the Beguny tract also cited above.

127 On the circumstances surrounding the speech, see I. A. Shliapkin, *Sv. Dimitrii Rostovskii i ego vremia (1651-1709 gg.)* (St. Petersburg, 1891), 277.

128 Dimitrii Rostovskii, *Sobranie raznykh pouchitel`nykh slov i drugikh sochinenii* (Moscow, 1786), vol. I, 1.

129 For example, in the letter of Vasilii Rzhevskii to Peter I of September 4, 1704, congratulating him on the victory at Narva: "And I the last slave of you, my Christ, praise God the lord of all, in songs of prayer." See RGADA, f. 9, otd. II, op. 3, d. 1, l. 212.

130 *Propovedi blazhennyia pamiati Stefana Iavorskogo*, vol. III, 242.

131 Ibid., 253.

132 Ibid., vol. I, 167.

133 Feofan Prokopovich, *Arkhiepiskopa Velikogo Novagrada i Velikikh Luk*, vol. I, 252.

134 Feofan Prokopovich, *Rozysk istoricheskii*, 37.

135 Feofan Prokopovich, *Arkhiepiskopa Velikogo Novagrada i Velikikh Luk*, vol. II, 178-179.

136 See in particular Ibid., vol. I, 31, 217, 253, 267-268; vol. II, 63; P. V. Verkhovskoi, *Uchrezhdenie*, vol. II, 157 (first pagination).

137 *Dukhovnyi Reglament Vsepresvetleishego derzhavneishego gosudaria Petra Pervogo, imperatora i samoderzhtsa vserossiiskogo* (Moscow, 1904), 17. The expression the "Lord's Christ" (*Khristos Gospoden`*) was commonly applied to the tsar. One should not conclude, however, that this phrase was specific for the tsar as anointed sovereign; in liturgical texts Jesus Christ could also be called the "Lord's Christ." For example,in the stichera for Candelmas: "What does the old man Symeon see, who cries out to you; Now you let your slave, O Lord, see the Lord's Christ in the arms of the virgin." See *Stikhirar` prazdnichnyi* (mid-twelfth century) in RNB, Sof. 384, l. 41.

138 Feofilakt Lopatinskii, *Sluzhba blagodarstvennaia*, 18 verso; *Mineia Iiun`*, 238 verso. See also the stichera of the Small Vespers, first mode: "You have glorified your Christ, and all of the Orthodox" in Ibid., 231-231 verso and Feofilakt Lopatinskii, *Sluzhba blagodarstvennaia*, 1.

139 P. P. Pekarskii, *Istoricheskie bumagi*, 124.

140 G. R. Derzhavin, *Sochineniia* (St. Petersburg, 1864-1883), vol. IX, 134. In 1757 the Siberian priest Petr Khomiakov was accused of blasphemy because "in front of many guests, for no apparent cause or reason among various conversations made the following statement: 'May God give Christ health, [because] we, sinners, in Christ [our] God receive salvation and remission of our sins.' During the investigation Khomiakov explained that he had had in mind not Jesus Christ but Empress Elizaveta Petrovna

[Elizabeth]. 'In conversations I incidentally used the expression, God give Christ health, to mean that the Lord God would give the anointed one, our All-merciful Sovereign Empress Elizaveta Petrovna, problem-free prosperity.'" The investigators were apparently satisfied with this answer. See N. D. Zol`nikova, *Soslovnye problemy vo vzaimootnosheniiakh tserkvi i gosudarstva v Sibiri (XVIII v.)* (Novosibirsk, 1981). See also note 278 below.

141   Simon Todorskii, *Slovo v vysochaishee prisutstvie eia sviashchenneishago imperatorskago velichestva blagochestiveishiia samoderzhavneishiia velikiia gosudaryni nasheia Elisavety Petrovny imperatritsy vseia Rossii, v vysokotorzhestvennyi den` rozhdeniia ego Imp. Vyso-chestva Petra Fedorovicha. Propovedannoe Ego Imp. Vysochestva pridvornym uchitelem Iero-monakhom Simonom Todorskim v pridvornoi tserkve v Sanktpeterburge fevralia 10 dnia 1743 goda* (St. Petersburg, 1743), 12; G. A. Voskresenskii, *Pridvornaia i akademicheskaia propoved` v Rossii poltorasta let nazad* (Moscow, 1894), 78). In the same sermon Simon Todorskii compares Petr Fedorovich's arrival in Russia from Holstein to Christ's return to Israel from Egypt: "God spoke with inner inspiration in the heart of magnanimous Elizabeth: Get up, Mother, take the child, take your beloved Nephew to the land of Israel, since some who sought for the child's soul have died and others were exiled." See Simon Todorskii, *Slovo v vysochaishee prisutstvie*, 16. The preacher is paraphrasing Matthew 2:20.

142   V. Petrov, *Sochineniia* (St. Petersburg, 1809), part II, 239. See also 1 Chronicles 16:22.

143   Platon (Levshin), *Rech` Gosudariu Imperatoru*, 4 verso.

144   I. M. Snegirev, *Zhizn` moskovskogo mitropolita Platona* (Moscow, 1856), part II, 42.

145   Avgustin (Vinogradskii), *Sochineniia* (St. Petersburg, 1856), 112.

146   See Ibid., 8, 21, 31, 41, 64, 95; Avgustin (Vinogradskii), *Slovo pred nachatiem molebstviia po sluchaiu pobedy u Laona* (Moscow, 1814), 3; Avgustin (Vinogradskii), *Slovo v prazdnik Rozhdestva Iisusa Khrista* (Moscow, 1814), 4, 11; Avgustin (Vinogradskii), *Rech` Aleksandru Pervomu po vysochashem Ego Velichetva pribytii v Moskvu* (Moscow, 1817), 3.

147   A. Kotovich, *Dukhovnaia tsenzura v Rossii (1799-1855 gg.)* (St. Petersburg, 1909), 466. See also references to Paul I and Alexander I as "Christ" in *Slova i rechi Ioanna Levandy, protoiereia Kievo-Sofiiskogo Sobora* (St. Petersburg, 1821), part II, 208-209, 251.

148   A. Kotovich, *Dukhovnaia tsenzura*, 466.

149   *Sobranie mnenii i otzyvov Filareta*, vol. V, 392. The quoted prayer was written by Ephrem the Syrian and taken by the publishers of the "Service for the Most Holy God Mother" from the Russian translation of his works, which Filaret didn't realize. See Efrem Sirin, *Tvoreniia* (Moscow, 1848-1853), vol. VIII, 113, and the Latin translation in Efrem, *Sancti patris nostri Ephraemi Syri opera*, ed. D. A. B. Caillau (Paris, 1842), vol. VIII, 287. For us it is not so important what Ephrem had in mind but how this text was perceived on Russian soil.

150   I. Khalkolivanov, *Slova i poucheniia*, vol. II, 212-213.

151   It is indicative that Mikhail Bakunin, speaking of the tsar as an ideal of the Russian people, calls the emperor "the Russian Christ" in *Narodnoe delo: Romanov, Pugachev, ili Pestel`* (1917), 42. There is clearly confusion here between calling the tsar "Christ" and the expression "the Russian God" as a description of the national idea.

152   *Sovety i rasskazy Kekavmena. Sochinenie vizantiiskogo polkovodtsa XI v.* (Moscow, 1972), 275; V. Vasil`evskii, "Sovety i rasskazy vizantiiskogo boiarina XI veka," *Zhurnal Ministerstva narodnogo prosveshcheniia*, June-August (1881): 316.

153   This usage was most likely based on the doctrine of human deification, widespread in Byzantium, according to which a saintly life could make a person "a god by grace"

(on the calling saints "gods" in Byzantine literature see note 13). The "Advice and Tales of Kekaumenos [Kekavmen]" includes a simplified reflection of this doctrine. "Moreover, I consider that all people, the basileiuses, and the archons, and those who earn their daily bread, are children of one man—Adam.... Indeed if he wants, a person, as a rational creature, himself may become a god by means of divine grace (χάριτι θεοῦ)." See Ibid., 345; *Sovety i rasskazy Kekavmena*, 287. It was evidently also thought that people have a special responsibility for this power, so that righteous behavior making them "gods by grace" was understood as an obligation. In the beginning of this work there is also an exhortation in which the following is addressed to a rich man: "Help the needy in all things, since a rich man is god to the poor, because he does good deeds for him." See Ibid., 121; V. Vasil`evskii, "Sovety i rasskazy," 254. However, one can also find examples of calling the tsar "god" in Byzantine literature as a direct expression of his deification. Thus a writer from the end of the fourth century, speaking of the oath "by God and Christ and the Holy Spirit, and the emperor as well," remarks that one must honor the emperor "as the visible and corporal God [*tamquam praesenti et corporali Deo*]." See F. R. Vegetius, *Epitoma rei militaris* (Leipzig, 1885), 38.

[154] P. Oderbornius, *Wunderbare, Erschreckliche, Unerhörte Geschichte, und warhaffte Historien: Nemlich, Des nechst gewesenen Großfürsten in der Moschkaw, Joan Basilidis, (auff jre Sprach Iwan Basilowitz genandt) Leben* (Hörlitz, 1588), 3.

[155] M. P. Alekseev, *Sibir` v izvestiiakh zapadnoevropeiskikh puteshestvennikov i pisatelei* (Irkutsk, 1932), 252.

[156] Iurii Krilsanich, *Politika* (Moscow, 1965), 206.

[157] *Zapiski Otdeleniia russkoi i slavianskoi arkheologii*, vol. II, 552-553; see the same comparison of Aleksei Mikhailovich and Nebuchadnezzar by Archpriest Avvakum cited above (section I-2.1). It is possible that an indirect reflection of this phrase was calling the tsar "Man God" in Lazar Baranovich's "Trumpets of Homiletic Words" (*Truby sloves propovednykh*). Speaking of the birth of a son to Aleksei Mikhailovich he writes: "Joy to Aleksei Man of God, for he begat a Man God." See Lazar` Baranovich, *Truby sloves propovednykh* (Kiev, 1674), 16). We may assume that here too Baranovich was playing on the juxtaposition of the God-man (a common title for Jesus) and man-god (as description of the future tsar), a juxtaposition that is analogous to the heavenly and earthly tsar, god of heaven and god of earth, etc.

[158] E. V. Barsov, *Drevnerusskie pamiatniki*, iv.

[159] I. A. Chistovich, *Feofan Prokopovich*, 66.

[160] *Rasskazy Nartova*, 69.

[161] S. I. Maslov, "Pereizdanie propovedi Georgiia Konisskogo i Manassii Maksimovicha," *Chteniia v istoricheskom obshchestve Nestora Letopistsa* I-II (1909): 87.

[162] S. Naryshkin, *Epistola Ekaterine II, imperatritse vserosiiskoi, podnesennaia vsepoddaneishim rabom Semenom Naryshkinym* (St. Petersburg, 1762).

[163] G. R. Derzhavin, *Sochineniia*, vol. I, 53. He has in mind that the pillars of the fatherland, i.e., grandees, have one goal—the well-being of the people, whatever means they must resort to for its realization, including public threats and secret councils with earthly gods, i.e., tsars.

[164] Ibid., 109. 35. This poem is a paraphrase of Psalm 81 (82). It is all the more characteristic since Derzhavin, deviating from the original text, calls rulers not "gods" (as in the psalm) but "earthly gods."

[165] Ibid., 565.

166   Ibid., vol. II, 102.

167   Ibid., 147.

168   I. A. Shliapkin, "V. P. Petrov, ´karmannyi´ stikhotvorets Ekateriny II (1736-1799)," *Istoricheskii vestnik* 11 (1885), 401.

169   N. M. Karamzin, *Polnoe sobranie stikhotvorenii* (Moscow-Leningrad, 1966), 189.

170   Feofilakt Rusanov, *Razsuzhdenie o plodakh prishestviia Khristova na zemliu, otnosite`no k pol`zam chelovecheskikh obshchezhitii* (Moscow, 1806), 15. Compare the use of this phrase in an ironic or negative sense in V. G. Belinskii's "Letter to Gogol'" of 1847 in V. G. Belinskii, *Sobranie sochinenii* (Moscow, 1948), vol. III, 711; and also by A. K. Tolstoi in "Song on Potok the Warrior" in A. K. Tolstoi, *Polnoe sobranie sochinenii* (St. Petersburg, 1907-1908), vol. I, 298, 299.

171   M. V. Lomonosov, *Polnoe sobranie sochinenii* (Moscow-Leningrad, 1950-1959), vol. VIII, 285.

172   V. Petrov, *Sochineniia*, vol. I, 31.

173   A. S. Pishkevich, *Zhizn` A. S. Pishkevicha, im samim napisannaia, 1764-1805.* (1885), 28.

174   V. Petrov, *Sochineniia*, vol. I, 89.

175   N. P. Nikolev, *Tvoreniia* (Moscow, 1795-1798), part II, 248.

176   We find an echo of this tradition in A. A. Bestuzhev's letter to Ia. N. Tolstoi of March 3, 1824: "The Duchess of Wittenberg died yesterday on my watch, and I saw what an impression this made on people who consider themselves gods . . . " See *Russkaia starina*, November (1889): 375-377.

177   V. Kel`siev, *Sbornik*, vol. III, 232; the obscene noun seems especially expressive in the mouths of Skoptsy (Castrates)!

178   A. D. Kantemir, *Sochineniia, pis`ma i izbrannye perevody* (St. Petersburg, 1867-1868), vol. I, 260, 273. The title "earthly god" could be transferred from the tsar onto other officials who appear as little tsars in their domains. Thus in the satirical "Petition to God from Crimean Soldiers" it says:

> *Adam labored and served the one God,*
> *Why have so many little earthly gods (bozhki) appeared . . .*

And further:

> *Save us from the power of the little earthly gods*
> *And let us not fall into the tyranny of their power.*

(G. Gukovskii, "Soldatskie stikhi XVIII veka."
Literaturnoe nasledstvo 9-10 [1933], 126)

Cf. in this connection the characteristic comments of an Old Believer, a Runner (Begun), about landowners (1851): "Will these gods remain much longer?" (K. V. Chistov, *Russkie narodnye sotsial'no-utopicheskie legendy* (Moscow, 1967), 244). In both cases the plural (bozhki, bogi) apparently indicates a connection with pagan idols. The expression "earthly god" could thus describe someone with unlimited power. An episode related by M. A. Dmitriev is representative. A landowner, Major Ivashev, stumbled onto a tent in the Syzran uezd in which the bishop of Kazan was serving vespers. The tent fell, and so did he, the bishop ran out, saw the man lying on the ground, and without bothering to figure out what had happened, ordered him to be flogged. Ivashev then galloped off to the village (Ivashevka) and warned that "the bishop is coming, mighty angry, so angry that he flogged him! By early morning all of the gentlewomen of Ivashevka had gathered by the village gates to meet the bishop and when he arrived they fell face down on the ground with loud wails, through which could be heard: 'Little father, earthly god! Don't destroy us'" (M. A. Dmitriev, *Melochi iz zapasa moei pamiati* [Moscow, 1869], 127).

179 S. M. Solov`ev, *Istoriia Rossii* (Moscow, 1962-1966), vol. IX, 186.

180 See letters from Vinius of April 29, 1701 in *Pis`ma i bumagi imperatora Petra Velikogo*, vol. I, 852, and of November 16, 1706 in Ibid., vol. V, 718.

181 N. G. Ustrialov, *Istoriia tsarstvovaniia Petra Velikogo*, vol. VI, 493, 197; see also Psalms 16:6 (17:6)], 30:3 (31:3).

182 I. Chistovich, "Neizdannye propovedi Stefana Iavorskogo," *Khristianskoe chtenie* 1-2 (1867): 139; see also Luke 2:29-31.

183 J. Cracraft, *The Church Reform of Peter the Great* (London, 1971), 123. We will cite one characteristic passage: "That same sweet song he sings for you, o illustrious and never overpowered monarch, when you pass away: Now you let your servant go in peace, my Lord, according to your word. My eyes have seen your salvation, which you prepared for all humans, sparing your tsarist health that is more precious than all treasures, to protect your ardent devotion and all of us. My eyes have seen salvation, which you prepared, bringing down the strong walls of Azov, Kizirm, Tartar and other fortresses. My eyes have seen the salvation which you prepared, passing through and illuminating the entire universe, your face like the sun. I have enjoyed seeing all that and I came, says the defunct, and now you let your servant rest in peace."

184 One should keep in mind that in the Petrine period only two akathyst prayers were accepted in Great Russia: to the God Mother and to "the Sweetest Jesus." A multitude of akathyst prayers appeared in Great Russia during the Synodal period.

185 RGADA, f. 9, otd. II, o. 3, d. 3, ll. 75-75 verso.

186 *Pis`ma i bumagi imperatora Petra Velikogo*, vol. IX, vyp. 2, 1063-1064; also with unmentioned abridgement in S. M. Solov`ev, *Istoriia Rossii*, vol. VIII, 277; see also Ibid., 335; *Pis`ma i bumagi imperatora Petra Velikogo*, vol. X, 648.

187 P. P. Pekarskii, *Istoriia imp. Akademii nauk*, vol. II, 392.

188 A. V. Pozdneev, "Russkaia patrioticheskaia pesnia v pervoi chetverti XVIII veka" in *Issledovaniia i materialy po drevnerusskoi literature* (Moscow, 1961), 351.

189 I. Porfir`ev, *Istoriia russkoi slovestnosti*, vol II: 1, p. 90.

190 I. A. Chistovich, "Rukovodiashchie deiateli dukhovnogo prosveshcheniia v Rossii v pervoi polovine tekushchego stoletiia" in *Komissiia Dukhovnykh uchilishch* (St. Petersburg, 1894), 183; see also Psalm 70:9 (71:9).

191 I. M. Snegirev, *Zhizn` moskovskogo mitropolita Platona*, part II, 114-115.

192 *Sbornik Russkogo istoricheskogo obshchestva* (St. Petersburg, Petrograd, 1867-1916), vol. CXIII, part 1, 416. As a typological parallel with Byzantium one may recall the protest of Emperor Theodosius, who in a letter to Caesarea refused to accept honors appropriate only to God; see A. Gasquet, *De l'autorité imperial*, 43.

193 E. R. Dashkova, *Memoirs of the Princess Daschkaw, lady of honor to Catherine II empress of all the Russias, written by herself, comprising letters of the empress and other correspondence* (London, 1840), vol. II, 95. We note in this connection A. V. Nikitenko's diary entry of January 3, 1834, concerning the book by V. N. Olin, *A Picture of Eight Years: Russia 1825—1834*, that he reviewed as censor, a book which glorified Nicholas' reign. "A censor finds himself at a spiritual impasse in such cases—one can't ban such books but it's uncomfortable to approve them. Fortunately, this time the Sovereign himself clarified

the matter. I had passed the book, however, having cut several things, for example, the place where the author called Nicholas a god. The Sovereign still did not like the unrestrained praise and charged a minister to explain to the censors that in future they should not allow such works. My thanks to him!" See A. V. Nikitenko, *Dnevnik v trekh tomakh* (Moscow, 1955), vol. I, 131-132.

[194] N. I. Il`minskii, *Pis`ma* (Kazan, 1895), 78-80.

[195] Ibid., 78.

[196] The Protestant approach to the monarch (*Landsherr*) as the highest instance of religious administration became evident under Peter, in particular, in the fact that the tsar also acted as the head of the Protestant communities in Russia. See I. Smolitsch, *Geschichte der russischen Kirche, 1700-1917* (Leiden, 1964), 131-132.

[197] See the doctrine of the Epanagoge that the emperor and patriarch are like body and soul in Zachariae von Lingenthal, *Collectio librorum juris graeco-romani ineditorum. Ecloga Leonis et Constantini, Epanagoge Basilii Leonis et Alexandri* (Leipzig, 1852), 68; see also V. Sokol`skii, "O kharaktere i znachenii epanagogi. Ocherk iz istorii vizantiiskogo prava," *Vizantiiskii vremennik* 1 (1894): 29, 31-33, 37-38, 43-45.

[198] *Sluzhebnik* (Moscow, 1656), 21, 22, 34, 40.

[199] On the new status of the monarch as reason for instituting the patriarchate, see A. Ia. Shpakov, *Gosudarstvo i tserkov`*, xi, 219.

[200] *Kormchaia* (Moscow, 1653), 22, 15.

[201] *Corpus juris civilis*, vol. III, 35-36; see the citations from it in the Nikonian service book—*Sluzhebnik,* 2, 14-15.

[202] In this regard the projects that preceded the choice of a Moscow patriarch to transfer the oecumenical Constantinoplitan pulpit to Vladimir, whence Patriarch Jeremiah was to move, are characteristic. See N. F. Kapterev, *Kharakter otnoshenii Rossii k pravoslavnomu Vostoku v XVI i XVII stolietiakh* (1914), 43; A. Ia. Shpakov, *Gosudarstvo i tserkov`*, 291-295; prilozhenie 1, 117-121.

[203] The extent to which this perception had become rooted in cultural consciousness is apparent from the fact that when in 1915 the annexation of Constantinople by Russia seemed imminent, there were discussions in Petrograd about abolishing the pulpit of the patriarch of Constantinople and establishing a Metropolitan there who would be subordinate to the Synod. See *Sviashchennyi Sobor Pravoslavnoi Rossiiskoi Tserkvi*, vol. II, vyp. 2, 342.

[204] *Dukhovnyi Reglament*, 16. Recall that this text remained in juridicial force right up to 1917. Feofan clearly hints here at the Catholic position in which the clergy makes up "a state within a state" and he attributes this situation to Russia, thus justifying the reformation being undertaken there. See the attack on this casuistic device of Feofan's by Markell Rodyshevskii in P. V. Verkhovskoi, *Uchrezhdenie Dukhovnoi Kollegii*, vol. II, 131, 133 (second pagination). Feofan's words about the fact that the people consider the patriarch "the second Sovereign" apparently refer to Patriarch Nikon, who, like the tsar, was called Great Sovereign. On this title see *Polnoe sobranie zakonov Rossiiskoi imperii. Sobranoe pervoe* (St. Petersburg, 1830), vol. I, 8, 124, 333; for Nikon's statements on this, see *Zapiski Otdeleniia russkoi i slavianskoi arkheologii*, vol. II, 515. Is is significant that Nikon had assimilated several points of Catholic doctrine concerning secular and religious authority, something that his contemporaries noted. See N. Gibbenet, *Istoricheskoe issledovanie*, part II, 78. Feofan purposefully attributes the same papist claims to Nikon's successors in the patriarchal pulpit.

205 The first reports on the Council are from 1692. See P. Gordon, *Dnevnik* (Moscow, 1892), part II, 360; R Wittram, *Peter I, Czar und Kaiser. Zur Geschichte Peters des Grossen in seiner Zeit* (Göttingen, 1964), vol. I, 106f.

206 See the oath of members of the Spiritual College and then the Synod in P. V. Verkhovskoi, *Uchrezhdenie Dukhovnoi Kollegii*, vol. II, 11f (first pagination); this oath was only abolished in 1901; see Ibid., 8. It is worth noting that the words about the "Supreme Judge" were added to the text of the oath by Feofan Prokopovich with his own hand. Later, Arsenii Matseevich, already a member of the Synod, refused to take the oath on the grounds that only Christ can serve as the supreme judge of the church. See M. S. Popov, *Arsenii Matseevich i ego delo* (St. Petersburg, 1912), 97, 390, 430.

207 P. V. Verkhovskoi, *Uchrezhdenie Dukhovnoi Kollegii*, vol. II, 6 (first pagination).

208 As noted (section I-2.1), under Aleksei Mikhailovich there appeared a formula in the bishops' certificates of ordination according to which the ordination was made "by order of the Sovereign tsar," although this did not change the traditional practice of ordaining bishops, that is, the tsar only confirmed the decision made by the religious authorities. The situation changed completely in the eighteenth century when the emperor's choice became the official procedure.

209 I. Smolitsch, *Geschichte der russischen Kirche,* 171, 126. This practice creates the illusion of the church's relative independence, however even this was not observed consistently. Thus in 1819 Alexander I ordered Archimandrite Innokentii (Smirnov) to be bishop of Orenburg. Characteristically, this provoked an objection from Petersburg Metropolitan Mikhail (Desnitskii), who in the presence of members of the Synod drew the attention of the Minister of Religious Affairs and Popular Education, Prince A. N. Golitsyn, to the fact "that for the first time a bishop was appointed directly by the emperor, without Synodal election and contrary to church procedure." See *Starina i novizna* XV (1911): 182-183; I. A. Chistovich, "Rukovodiashchie deiateli," 200.

210 *Russkaia istoricheskaia biblioteka,* vol. VI, 442-443; for the late seventeenth century see GIM, Sin. 344, ll. 7-8 verso.

211 Right down to giving permission to tonsure monks, see *Vnutrennii byt Russkogo gosudarstva c 17-go dekabria 1740 g. po 25-e noiabria 1741 g., po dokumentam, khraniaschimsia v Mosovskom Arkhivr Ministerstva Iustitsii* (Moscow, 1880-1886), vol. I, 53-54, 70.

212 *Dukhovnyi Reglament*, 6.

213 *Svod zakonov Rossiiskoi Imperii* (St. Petersburg, 1892), vol. I, part 1, art. 43, 10; see also J. Meyendorf, "Russian Bishops and Church Reform in 1905," *Russian Orthodoxy Under the Old Regime* (Minneapolis, 1978), 170-171.

214 See P. V. Verkhovskoi, *Uchrezhdenie Dukhovnoi Kollegii*, vol. I, iv, v, vii, xi, xii-xiv, xli, xlii, xliv, lvi.

215 *Polnoe sobranie postanovlenii i rasporiazhenii*, vol. I, no. 112, 157.

216 V. N. Tatishchev, *Istoriia rossiiskaia s samykh drevneishikh vremen* (Moscow-St. Petersburg, 1768-1848), vol. I, 574.

217 N. M. Karamzin, *Zapiska o drevnei i novoi Rossii* (St. Petersburg, 1914), 29; A. N. Pypin, *Istoricheskie ocherki. Obshchestvennoe dvizhenie v Rossii pri Aleksandre I* (St. Petersburg, 1900), 491. According to the exceptionally precise formulation of the Decembrist M. A. Fon-Vizin: "By means of the abolition of the patriarchate and establishment of the Synod Peter unconditionally subordinated the church to his arbitrary rule [*proizvol*]. He appreciated the so-called territorial system of reformation, according to which every powerful sovereign was declared a natural bishop and head of the

church on his land. Peter, while he did not formally proclaim himself the head of the Orthodox Greco-Russian Church, according to the formula of the oath of allegiance for members of the Synod and high clergy upon their appointment, in essence did become its head; the Synod became one of many administrative departments and came to depend unconditionally on the tsar's arbitrary rule. A worldly and purely military bureaucrat under the strange title of Ober-Procuror of the Most Holy Ruling Synod acts in name of the soverign with complete power in the church's council and rules the clergy with complete power." See M. A. Fon-Vizin, *Zapiski ochevidtsa smutnykh vremen tsarstvovanii Pavla I, Aleksandra I i Nikolaia I* (Leipzig, 1859), 22-23; *Obshchestvennoe dvizhenie v Rossii v pervuiu polovinu XIX veka . . . Stat`i i materialy.* (St. Petersburg, 1905), vol 1, 112.

[218] *Rasskazy Nartova*, 72. Nartov was a contemporary of Peter's but it is difficult to date his stories precisely.

[219] Peter's view of the extent of his autocratic power is clearly manifested in the his ukase establishing the Synod (January 25, 1721): "We were afraid to be ungrateful to the All-High, having received divine assistance from him in reforming the military as well as the civil order, but having neglected as yet to reform the religious order." See P. V. Verkhovskoi, *Uchrezhdenie Dukhovnoi Kollegii*, vol. II, 6 (first pagination). It is completely obvious that Peter in no way separates his activities administering the church from those involving civil administration. The unified nature of his administrative activity is reflected in the fact that even before the establishment of the Synod both civil and religious administration were under control of the Senate, which by the ukase of March 2, 1711, had been granted the full scope of tsarist power. See I. Smolitsch, *Geschichte der russischen Kirche*, 81-83; *Polnoe sobranie zakonov*, vol. IV, no. 2328, 634-635. It is clear that even if Peter had believed in the special charismatic status of the tsar's authority, he could only transfer administrative power to the Senate but not charisma; consequently, Peter did not connect his function as head of the church with charisma.

[220] In correspondence with the Austrian Emperor Joseph II Catherine calls herself head of the Greek church and Joseph head of the Western European church. See P. V. Verkhovskoi, *Uchrezhdenie Dukhovnoi Kollegii*, vol. I, lvi. The Christian world thus found itself split into two halves: at the head of one stood the Holy Roman Emperor, living in Vienna, and at the head of the other the "head of the Greek church," living in Petersburg.

[221] *Polnoe sobranie zakonov*, vol. XXIV, no. 17910, 588.

[222] *Svod zakonov*, vol. I, part. 1, art. 42, 10. The "Project for Basic Laws of the Russian Empire" by G. A. Rosenkampf (1804) states: "The emperor is the supreme ruler of the entire state and head of the Church." See I. Smolitsch, *Geschichte der russischen Kirche*, 144. In the "State Charter [*ustavnaia gramota*] of the Russian Empire" by N. N. Novosil`tsev (1819), article 20 states: "As the supreme head of the Orthodox Greek-Russian church, the sovereign consecrates all ranks of the religious hierarchy." See N. K. Shil`der, *Imperator Aleksandr Pervyi. Ego zhizn` i tsarstvovavnie* (St. Petersburg, 1904-1905), vol. IV, 501. Hence A. S. Shishkov, addressing the emperor in a letter of May 22, 1824, calls him "head of the Church and the Fatherland." See A. S. Shishkov, "Zapiski admirala A. S. Shishkova," *Chteniia Obshchestva istorii i drevnostei rossiiskikh* 3 (1868), 4.

[223] N. Subbotin, *Istoriia Belokrinitskoi ierarkhii* (Moscow, 1874), 459.

[224] Joseph Marie de Maistre, Fidèle de Grivel, *Religion et moeurs des russes* (Paris, 1879), 5.

[225] Pavel performed the duties of a confessor as "magister" of the Maltese Order; the same Golovkin reports that "Commander Litta publicly confessed his sins, and the great magister accepted this repentence with tears of compassion." See F. Golovkin, *Dvor i tsarstvovanie Pavla I* (Moscow 1912), 188.

[226] Ibid., 158.

[227] Joseph Marie de Maistre, Fidèle de Grivel, *Religion et moeurs des russes*, 99-100. Evidence that Paul I conducted the liturgy may be found in S. N. Marin's "Parody of Lomonosov's Ode [Based on] Selections from Job," in which Marin substitutes a monologue by Paul for Lomonosov's monologue by God:

> *Was not my generosity clear*
> *When I ordered heads to roll?*
> *Have you never had the wish*
> *To shake a bit of incense in church*
> *Dressed in holy vestments,*
> *To fancy oneself jester to the world*
> *Serving mass in place of a priest?*
> *Is this idea really foolish?*

See S. N. Marin, "Polnoe sobranie sochinenii," *Letopisi Gos. literaturnogo muzeia* 10 (1948): 176, 177.

[228] V. A. Zhukovskii, *Polnoe sobranie sochinenii* (St. Petersburg, 1902), vol. I, 1. This kind of perception might have already arisen in the middle of the previous century. Thus Lomonosov in his "Speech in Praise of Peter the Great" of 1755 writes of Peter: "He awaited the divine service not only as a listener but as the highest ranking [church] official [*chinonachal'nik*] himself." M. V. Lomonosov, *Polnoe sobranie sochinenii*, vol. VIII, 606.

[229] *Sviashchennyi Sobor Pravoslavnoi Rossiiskoi Tserkvi*, vol. II, kn. 2, 198.

[230] N. D. Zhevakhov, *Vospominania* (Nowy Sad, 1928), vol. II, 385-388. The same Prince Zhevakhov writes in his memoirs that Emperor Nicholas "in 1905 asked Petersburg Metropolitan Antonii Vadkovskii for his blessing to abdicate the throne in favor of his son, and to take monastic vows." See Ibid. It is possible that these two reports are connected; if so, one might suspect that Nicholas had in mind the example of Patrarch Filaret who had run the government together with his son, Mikhail Fedorovich. In any case, between these two functions—head of the state and head of the church— Nicholas preferred the second. It is curious to juxtapose this episode with the report of the French envoy to Russia de La Vie concerning rumors circulating in Petersburg that Peter wanted to declare Tsarevich Aleksei patriarch. See *Sbornik Russkogo istoricheskogo obshchestva*, vol. XXXIV, 321. La Vie considered these rumors unfounded insofar as in that case the tsar would have had to kiss his son's hand and call him "father."

[231] The old practice—apparently until the time of Aleksei Mikhailovich—consisted of the tsar kissing the hand of the priest blessing him and the priest kissing the hand of the tsar; see the testimony of Pavel Aleppskii in *Puteshestvie antiokhiiskogo patriarkha Makariia v Rossiiu v polovine XVII veka, opisannoe ego synom arkhidiakonom Pavlom Aleppskim* (Moscow, 1896-1900), vyp. III, 95f; vyp. IV, 170; and Archpriest Avvakum in *Russkaia istoricheskaia biblioteka*, vol. XXXIX, 44, 194. See also N. F. Kapterev, "Snosheniia Ierusalimskikh patriarkhov," 135-136; I. Rotar, "Epifanii Slavinetskii, literaturnyi deiatel' XVII veka," *Kievskaia starina* (1901): 20. Patriarch Nikon speaks of this same practice in his "Objection or Ruin" (see *Zapiski Otdeleniia russkoi i slavianskoi arkheologii*, vol. II, 492-493):

The Boyar [Semen Streshnev] said to the patriarch: you give your hand to anyone to kiss, like the tsar does, and that's not good, he says. And the patriarch said: who made you speak, was it the tsar or you on your own? And the boyar said: the sovereign ordered me to speak. And the patriarch: so why does the tsar himself kiss the hands of priests whom we consecrated, and, coming for blessing, himself bend his head; it surprises us why the tsar compels bishops and priests to kiss his hands when he is not a bishop or a priest; if he, the sovereign, for his overweening pride considers the priesthood lower than the kingship, he will then learn the difference between the kingship and the priesthood when we will be examined by the authentic Judge, Christ our God.

In 1711 Peter I could still kiss Stefan Iavorskii's hand. See *Zapiski Iusta Iulia, datskogo poslannika pri Petre Velikom* (Moscow, 1900), 293. Later this custom ceased, and one may presume that this was connected with the reorganization of church administration, when the tsar became head of the church. This changed temporarily during the reign of Alexander I who in 1801 issued a special instruction that priests should not kiss the hands of the monarch or members of the royal family when giving blessing. See *Russkaia starina* XIV (December 1883): 730.

[232]   P. I. Mel`nikov (Andrei Pecherskii), *Polnoe sobranie sochinenii*, vol. XII, 365-366.

[233]   See for example N. K. Shil`der, *Imperator Aleksandr Pervyi*, vol. IV, 58; *Rasskazy babushki. Iz vospomimamii piati pokolenii. Zapisannye i sobrannye ee vnukom D. Blagovo* (St. Petersburg, 1885), 395.

[234]   Fotii (Spasskii), "Avtobiografiia Iur`evskogo arkhimandrita Fotiia," *Russkaia starina* 2 (1895): 208.

[235]   V. F. Chizh, "Psikhologiia fanatizma (Fotii Spasskii)," *Voprosy filosofii i psikhologii* I-II (1905): 185.

[236]   N. K. Shil`der, *Imperator Nikolai Pervyi. Ego zhizn` i tsrstvovavnie* (St. Petersburg, 1903), vol. II, 700.

[237]   *Sviashchennyi Sobor Pravoslavnoi Rossiiskoi Tserkvi*, vol. III, 8.

[238]   "Opredeleniia Moskovskogo Sobora 1675 g.," 440-441.

[239]   A. Ia. Shpakov, *Gosudarstvo i tserkov`*, prilozhenie, II, 170.

[240]   M. V. Zyzykin, *Patriarkh Nikon*, part II, 172-173.

[241]   In this connection it is indicative that in the popular imagination the fact that Peter headed the church after having taken the place of the patriarch could be directly connected with his deification. Thus in an Old Believer document entitled *The Tiumen Wanderer*, it relates how Peter, having shaved off his beard, killed the patriarch with his staff and "went into the Faceted Chamber [in the Kremlin], pulled out his sword of steel, and struck the table with it: 'I am your tsar, patriarch, your God,' he repeated three times." See I. K. Piatnitskii, *Sekta Strannikov i ee znachenie v staroobriadchestve* (St. Petersburg, 1912), 110. This story derives from an anecdote which we have in A. K. Nartov's transcription: "His imperial majesty, present at a gathering of church leaders, noting the strong desire of some to choose a [new] patriarch, which had repeatedly been proposed by the clergy, with one hand pulled from his pocket the "Spiritual Regulation" that he had prepared for just such an occasion and said to them threateningly: 'You ask for a patriarch: here's a spiritual patriarch for you, but for those who disagree with this (with his other hand he pulled a dagger from its sheath and banged it on the table), here's a steel patriarch!' Then he got up and left. After this the petition to choose a patriarch was abandoned and the Most Holy Synod was

established." See *Rasskazy Nartova*, 71; *Podlinnye anekdoty Petra Velikogo slyshannye iz ust znatnykh osob v Moskve i Sanktpeterburge, izdannye v svet Iakovom fon Shchtelinom* (Moscow, 1787), 352-354. Characteristically, the Old Believer reworking presents Peter as not only wanting to usurp the dignity of the patriarch, but also that of God. This perception had very ancient roots. In early Christianity the bishop represented the image of Christ himself for his church. Ignatius of Antioch compared bishops to Christ and the presbyters who helped him run the church to the apostles. See A. Shmeman, *Istoricheskii put` pravoslaviia* (New York, 1954), 50-51. This doctrine was also developed later by the Byzantine church fathers. The later Greek tradition also specified the sense in which a bishop represents an image of God, in opposition to all other people who are the "image and likeness" of God by virtue of creation (cf. Genesis 1: 26) and in contrast to a priest who manifests Christ during the liturgy. Thus Paisios Ligarides writes: "A bishop is in Christ's image when in his diocese, but not when they [bishops] gather around their head, the Patriarch, to whom they are subordinate." See M. V. Zyzykin, *Patriarkh Nikon*, part II, 188. Hence the bishop's assumption of Christ's image is directly connected to his running the church, in which the bishop acts as a mediator between God and men, as Patriarch Nikon wrote, extending this function of the bishop to a cosmic scale: "Between God and human nature stands the bishop." See RGB, f. 178, d. 9427, l. 206. In exactly the same way the tradition of calling the bishop the image of God was characteristic in Rus` from most ancient times. Thus in the Russian supplement to a letter of Loukas Chrysoberges (twelfth century) it says: "When you celebrate a prelate, you celebrate Christ: for he assumes the image of Christ and occupies Christ's throne." See *Russkaia istoricheskaia biblioteka*, vol. VI, 76. Metropolitan Kirill II (thirteenth century) wrote in his epistle to Novgorodians that "we are heirs to the apostles, having Christ's image and possessing His power." See *Polnoe sobranie russkikh letopisei*, vol. X, 149. In his epistle on adhering to the church council's verdict of 1504 Iosif Volotskii taught: "For divine law orders bodily obedience to both tsar and to bishop, as well as all other proper tribute, spiritual or not; to the bishop both bodily and spiritual, as successor to the apostles and one who bears the lord's image." See N. A. Kazakova and Ia. S. Lur'e, *Antifeodal'nye ereticheskie dvizheniia na Rusi XIV-nachala XVI veka* (1905), 509. This tradition was fully alive in Russia even at the end of the seventeenth century. Thus Archbishop Afanasii Kholmogorskii in his "Spiritual Exhortation" (*Uvet dukhovnyi*) speaks of "bishops who bear the image of Jesus Christ the Savior." See *Uvet dukhovnyi* (Moscow, 1682), 246. Proving the necessity of obedience to the church, he refers to "all bishops [who] assume the image of Christ, all pious tsars [who] adorn thrones with their justice." See Ibid., 14 verso; note the precise differentiation between the status of bishops and tsars.

[242] M. V. Zyzykin, *Patriarkh Nikon*, part II, 187.

[243] *Zapiski Otdeleniia russkoi i slavianskoi arkheologii*, vol. II, 481; see also N. F. Kapterev, *Patriarkh Nikon*, vol. II, 185. The last passage from Nikon is a precise quotation from the Epanagogue, chapter 2, section (*titul*) 3: Πατριάρχης ἐστὶν εἰκὼν ζῶσα χριστοῦ καὶ ἔμψυχος, δι ἔργων καὶ λόγων χαρακτηρίζουσα τὴν ἀλήθειαν. See Zachariae von Lingenthal, *Collectio librorum juris*, 67. Sections 2 and 3 of the Epanagogue went into Leunclavius' *Jus Graeco-Romanorum*, specially translated for Nikon by Epifanii Slavinetskii. See A. Engel'man, *Ob uchenoi obrabotkie greko-rimskago prava*. (St. Petersburg, 1857), 27; V. Sokol'skii, "O kharaktere i znachenii epanagogi," 50; G. V. Vernadsky, "Die kirchlich-politische Lehre der Epanagoge und ihr Einfluss auf das russische Leben im XVII Jahrhundert," *Byzantinisch-Neugriechische Jahrbücher* 1/2 (1928): 127, 139.

[244] A. Kotovich, *Dukhovnaia tsenzura v Rossii*, 465. It is remarkable that the religious censor found this expression unacceptable, arguing that "The Orthodox tsar believes that the Orthodox Church has only an invisible Head and not a visible one." See Ibid. Insofar as the definition of the tsar as "head of the church" was officially legitimized, the word combination "visible head of the church" might have provoked objection for its overly direct equation of the tsar and Christ. This kind of censorship was the result of church authorities' vacillations concerning the sacralization of the tsar, about which we will speak below (see section III-2).

[245] J. P. Migne, ed., *Patrologiae cursus completis. Series graeca*, vol. XX, 1357a.

[246] A. Gasquet, *De l'autorité imperial*, 39.

[247] G. V. Vernadsky, "Die kirchlich-politische Lehre der Epanagoge," 120.

[248] A. Ivanov, *Literaturnoe nasledie Maksima Greka; kharakteristika, atributsii, bibliografiia* (Leningrad, 1969), 149.

[249] Maksim Grek, *Sochineniia* (Kazan, 1859-1862), part II, 350.

[250] V. Skol'skii, *Uchastie russkogo dukhovenstva i monashestva v razvitii edinoderzhaviia i samo-derzhaviia v Moskovskom gosudarstve v kontse XV i pervoi polovine XVI v.* (Kiev, 1902), 198.

[251] I. A. Shevchenko, "Byzantine Source of Muscovite Ideology," 172; see also J. P. Migne, ed., *Patrologiae cursus completis. Series graeca*, vol. LXXXVI, 1172.

[252] N. F. Kapterev, "Snosheniia Ierusalimskikh patriarkhov," 239. Ivan Timofeev's *Chronicle* (*Vremennik*) may serve as indirect evidence of the possibility of perceiving the tsar as an icon. Here writes of the False Dmitrii: "Even before, [when he still was] outside the borders of the Russian land, everyone willingly obeyed him, bowing to this veritable idol as the tsar." See *Russkaia istoricheskaia biblioteka*, vol. XIII, 367. Similarly, he writes of the second False Dmitrii: "Those who had come to him, while knowing that he was the false tsar, still bowed to him as to an idol." See Ibid., 413. To all appearances, here a just tsar, as an icon, is being contrasted to a pretender as a false icon or idol (see section I-1.2).

[253] M. V. Zyzykin, *Patriarkh Nikon*, part II, 14.

[254] Dimitrii Rostovskii, *Sobranie raznykh pouchitel`nykh slov*, vol. I, 1 verso-2.

[255] M. V. Lomonosov, *Polnoe sobranie sochinenii*, vol. VIII, 85.

[256] Ibid., 637.

[257] A. P. Sumarokov, *Polnoe sobranie vsekh sochinenii v stikhakh i proze* (Moscow, 1787), part II, 75.

[258] V. Maikov, *Izbrannye proizvedeniia* (Moscow-Leningrad, 1966), 200.

[259] V. Petrov, *Sochineniia*, part II, 204.

[260] Ibid., 233-237.

[261] Ibid. 242.

[262] Ibid., part I, 107; part II, 130.

[263] G. R. Derzhavin, *Sochineniia*, vol. II, 295.

[264] Ibid., 574.

[265] Ibid., vol. I, 264. If for Derzhavin the tsar was a living icon, then an unjust tsar (that is, a false one) was not an icon but an idol. Thus in the "Ode on Nobility" (*Oda na znatnost`*) of 1774 he writes:

> Heed, princes of the whole universe:
> Without virtue you are statues!

—that is, idols. See Ibid., vol. III, 295. And in the "Epistle to I. I. Shuvalov" of 1777 he writes the same thing:

> Oh, pitiful demigod is one who vainly bears his rank:
> He is nothing before the throne, and on the throne—an idol.

See Ibid., vol. I, 55.

266 I. M. Snegirev, *Zhizn` moskovskogo mitropolita Platona*, part II, 114.

267 Avgustin (Vinogradskii), *Sochineniia*, 21.

268 *Slovo po prochtenii vysochaishego manifesta o voine protiv frantsuzov, govorenoe v gradskoi Georgievskoi tserkvi, chto za lavkami, preosv. Feofilaktom, ep. Kaluzhskim i Borovskim Dekabria 2 dnia, 1806 goda* (Moscow, 1806), 8.

269 I. A. Chistovich, "Rukovodiashchie deiateli dukhovnogo prosveshcheniia v Rossii," 83.

270 Mikhail Desnitskii, *Besedy, v raznykh mestakh i v raznyia vremena govorennyia... pokoinym Mikhailom, Mitropolitom Novgorodskim, Sanktpeterburgskim...* (St. Petersburg, 1823), vol. V, 254.

271 *Vlast` Samoderzhavnaia*, 25.

272 Note also that in the "Opinion of the Reverends Innokentii and Gavriil and the Hieromonk Platon on Catherine II's Instruction" of 1766 it says: "Confessing in all sincerity, as we are obliged to the All-seeing God and to the Monarch who bears His image on earth, we cannot help but declare that of this type of jurisprudence this composition is the most perfect." See I. M. Snegirev, *Zhizn` moskovskogo mitropolita Platona*, part II, 117. Even earlier, in a letter to the tsar of November 12, 1740, addressing Ioann Antonovich, Trediakovskii wrote of "the most generous god whose true image and perfect likeness here on earth is your imperial highness." *Pis`ma russkikh pisatelei XVIII veka* (Leningrad, 1980), 49.

273 N. V. Gogol`, *Polnoe sobranie sochinenii* (Moscow-Leningrad, 1937-1952), vol. VIII, 255-256.

274 1 John 4:8, 16.

275 S. M. Solov`ev, *Istoriia Rossii*, vol. XIV, 52.

276 *Russkaia starina* (April 1889): 52.

277 Matthew 21:9; Mark 11:9-10; Luke 19:38; John 12:13.

278 See P. P. Pekarskii, *Istoricheskie bumagi*, 123-124; E. Shmurlo, *Petr Velikii v otsenke sovremennikov i potomstva* (St. Petersburg, 1912), vyp. I, 18; I. I. Golikov, *Anekdoty*, xi, 364. The song in the Poltava cycle concludes with the words: "Hosanna, Hosanna, Hosanna in the highest! Blessed is he who comes in the name of the Lord! Hosanna, Hosanna!" See A. V. Pozdneev, "Russkaia patrioticheskaia pesnia," 352.

279 Feofan Prokopovich, *Arkhiepiskopa Velikogo Novagrada i Velikikh Luk*, vol. II, 99, 101.

280 I. M. Snegirev, *Zhizn` moskovskogo mitropolita Platona*, part II, 42. It is interesting to note that Leo Tolstoy, who sought the most striking material for the history of Russian society during the Napoleonic invasion, cited this letter by Metropolitan Platon in *War and Peace*—Prince Vasilii reads it in Anna Pavlovna Scherer's salon. See L. N. Tolstoi, *Polnoe sobranie khudozhestvennykh proizvedenii* (Moscow-Leningrad, 1928-1930), vol. VII, 8.

281 Avgustin (Vinogradskii), *Rech` pred nachatiem blagodarstvennogo molebstviia*, 5.

282 Avgustin (Vinogradskii), *Rech` Ego Imp. Velichestvu Aleksandru Pervomu*, 5; N. K. Shil'der, *Imperator Aleksandr Pervyi*, vol. I, 72.

283 G. R. Derzhavin, *Sochineniia*, vol. IX, 134. See also note 135 above.

284 N. K. Shil`der, *Imperator Pavel I. Istoriko-biograficheskii ocherk* (St. Petersburg, 1901), 342-344.

285 *Slova i rechi Ioanna Levandy*, part II, 190-191.

286 N. P. Nikolev, *Oda Ego Imp. Velichestvu Pavlu Pervomu na den` vsevozhdelennogo Ego pribytiia v Moskvu dlia sviashchennogo miropomazaniia 1797 goda* (Moscow, 1797), 6.

287 V. Petrov, *Sochineniia*, part II, 215-216.

288 I. M. Snegirev, *Zhizn` moskovskogo mitropolita Platona*, part II, 115.

289 S. Smirnov, *Istoriia Moskovskoi dukhovnoi akademii do eia preobrazovaniia (1814-1870)* (Moscow, 1879), 623.

290 *Tserkovnyi vestnik* 19 (1896): 621.

291 P. Mirtov, "Sviashchennye osnovy tsarskoi vlasti," *Pribavlenie k Tserkovnym vedomostiam, izdavaemym sv. Sinodom* 21 (May 21, 1911): 837.

292 On this ritual see K. Nikol`skii, *O sluzhbakh russkoi tserkvi, byvshikh v prezhnikh bogosluzhebnykh knigakh* (St. Petersburg, 1885), 45-97; *Puteshestvie antiokhiiskogo patriarkha Makariia*, vyp. III, 174-180; V. Savva, *Moskovskie tsari i vizantiiskie vasilevsy*, 158-175.

293 K. Nikol`skii, *O sluzhbakh russkoi tserkvi*, 1-40.

294 An incident is recorded, however, that a bishop ordered that he be greeted on Palm Sunday "with icons and lamps and with candles and branches," asserting that "you are greeting Christ." Characteristically, very soon after (in 1659) a complaint was made against him, and the religious authorities condemned this kind of behavior. See I. Rumiantsev, *Nikita Konstantinov Dobrynin ("Pustosviat"). Istoriko-kriticheskii ocherk* (Sergiev Posad, 1916), prilozhenie, 24, 30, 41, 44, 50, 66, 78, 81.

295 M. V. Zyzykin, *Patriarkh Nikon*, part II, 212-213, 372; N. F. Kapterev, *Patriarkh Nikon*, vol. I, 410.

296 M. V. Zyzykin, *Patriarkh Nikon*, part II, 185.

297 V. M. Undol`skii, "Otzyv patriarkha Nikona," 616.

298 RGB, f. 178, d. 9427, l. 259.

299 *Akty, sobrannye v bibliotekakh i arkhivakh*, vol. IV, no. 223, 309; *Drevniaia rossiiskaia vivliofika*, part VI, 360-361.

300 Ibid.

301 *Starina i novizna* XV (1911): 177-178 (second pagination).

302 N. Ustrialov, *Skazaniia sovremennikov o Dmitrii Samozvantse*, part I, 137.

303 This story seems reliable as Petr Alekseev notes precisely how he got it, and that was via Senator Ivan Ivanovich Kozlov, son of Ivan Polikarpovich Kozlov, who had been procurator of the Admiralty College under Peter, and who was a witness of the scene.

304 P. Alekseev, "Rasskaz Petra Velikogo o patriarkhe Nikone. Vsepoddanneishee pis`mo Alekseeva k imp. Pavlu Petrovichu," *Russkii arkhiv* 8-9 (1863): 698-699. When we consider that in pre-Petrine times the rank of equerry that the tsar voluntarily assumed indicated the monarch's necessary respect for the spiritual ideal, we can see very clearly how radically the relation between religious and secular authority had changed, and how secular power illicitly exalted itself, setting itself free of visible marks of the ruler's piety. Thus in the narrative about the Donation of Constantine that went into the supplement to the "Kormchaia" (*nomokanon*) of 1653 (the Nikonian Kormchaia) it is related that Emperor Constantine the Great offers Pope Sylvester imperial clothing and crown. Pope Sylvester refuses the latter, "not wanting to wear a crown of gold." Then Emperor Constantine tells him: "We shall place the crown of white color symbolizing the Ressurection of the Lord on his (Sylvester's) head with our own hands, and hold the reins of the horse with our hands, having given ourselves to him as an equerry to honor the blessed Peter, and we command that all bishops in their processions [carry out] this rite and custom, following the example of our kingship." Quoted in an Old Believer republication (Warsaw, 1785), second pagination, folio 8-9 verso. This episode from the narrative of the Donation of Constantine is cited with insignificant

variations in Metropolitan Makarii's epistle to Ivan the Terrible. See *Letopisi russkoi literatury i drevnosti*, vol. V, 130. According to an anonymous English witness who was serving in the Moscow court in 1557-1558, Ivan "recognizes the Metropolitan as higher than himself, because he says that 'the Metropolitan is the spiritual deputy of God, but I the tsar am only temporary.'" According to the author, this is manifested in particular by the fact that the tsar "leads the Metropolitan's horse on Palm Sunday." See S. M. Seredonin, ed., *Izvestiia anglichan o Rossii XVI v.* (*Chensler, Randol`f, Baus*) (Moscow, 1884), 22-23. Patriarch Nikon also cites this passage from the tale of the Donation of Constantine, describing the relations that should obtain between tsar and patriarch in the twenty-sixth answer of his "Objection or Ruin." See RGB, f. 178, d. 9427, l. 243, Hence when Peter I banned the "Palm ceremony," he responded to the current view that he would have been rendering the patriarch the homage which the first Christian emperor, equal to the apostles, Constantine the Great, had ordained be given to prelates. Peter was probably acquainted with the story of the Donation of Constantine as well as with the related Tale of the White Cowl. See I. Smolitsch, *Geschichte der russischen Kirche*, 401. Analogous logic was also applied to abolishing the "procession on a donkey" insofar as both the metropolitan's white cowl and the tsar assuming the role of an equerry would have testified to the monarch's humility before the spiritual principle.

[305] I. I. Golikov, *Anekdoty*, 55-58.

[306] *Akty, sobrannye v bibliotekakh i arkhivakh*, vol. IV, no. 223, 308-309; *Drevniaia rossiiskaia vivliofika*, part VI, 359-360.

[307] *Curieuse Nachncht von der itzigen Religion Ihro Käyserlichen Majestät in Russland Petri Alexiewiz, und seines grossen Reiches, dass dieselbe itzo nach Evangelisch-Lutherischen Grund-Sätzen eingerichtet sey* ([s.p.], 1725).

[308] "Dieser Patriarch hat unter andern am grünen Donnerstag einen Emzug in die Stadt Moscau, nach dem Exempel unsers Heylandes, auf emem Esel zu halten pflegen, da ihm denn der Czaar und Regent von Russland den Esel am Zaum führen, und dabey zu Fusze gehen müssen, um dadurch das grosse Ansehen und die Autorität des Patriarchen anzudeuten . . . Denn, nachdem der letzte Patriarch verstorben, hat Ihro Majest auch die am Grünen-Donnerstage gewöhnhche Ceremonien nicht mehr gelten lassen, keinen Patriarchen an seine Stelle aufs neue eingesetzet, sondern nach der Art Protestirender Fürsten, sich selbsten vor den obersten Bischoff seines Landes erkläret." See P. V. Verkhovskoi, *Uchrezhdenie Dukhovnoi Kollegii*, vol. I, viii-ix. The author of the cited work mistakenly relates the "procession on a donkey" to Holy Thursday rather than Palm Sunday.

[309] *Zapiski o Rossii pri Petre Velikom, izvlechennye iz bumag grafa Bassevicha* (Moscow, 1866), 81-82.

[310] Feofan Prokopovich, *Arkhiepiskopa Velikogo Novagrada i Velikikh Luk*, part I, 238.

[311] *Dnevnik kamer-iunkera F. V. Berkhgol`tsa. 1721-1725* (Moscow, 1902-1903), part I, 118-119. In her "Antidote" Catherine II later wrote about the "procession on a donkey" as a rite that demeans the tsar's rank. According to P. Alekseev, she, like Peter I, connected Nikon's deposition with it, as evidence of his "unbounded pretensions." See *Os`mnadtsatyi vek* IV (1869): 384.

[312] N. Makarov's story about a landowner from Chukhloma may be seen as an example of imitating the tsar's order, a peculiar type of "playing at tsar": "From a multitude of cynical and blasphemous pranks I will tell of one, known then in the Chukhloma district under the name of 'Entry into Jerusalem.' He once gathered

his field and house serfs of both sexes, and even children, and lined them up in two rows between his estate and the nearest village, for a length of several hundred feet. He ordered each person to take a palm frond in their hand, and he himself, seated on an old nag, rode by slowly from the village to his estate between the rows of his subordinates, who waved their palm branches at him." See N. Makarov, *Moi semidesiatiletnie vospominaniia i s tem vmeste moia polnaia predsmertnaia ispoved`* (St. Petersburg, 1881-1882), part I, 28.

313 Nevertheless, we know of an instance when a similar salutation to the tsar came from the Patriarch of Jerusalem. In a letter to Peter of September 28, 1709, Patriarch Chrysanthos, describing the desire of eastern Christians to be freed from Turkish rule by the Russian tsar, hopes "that they would accept their Orthodox liberator in their lands and would praise and exclaim in unison, Blessed be He who comes in the name of the Lord, king of Israel." See *Pis`ma i bumagi imperatora Petra Velikogo*, vol. V, 632. We should not assume that the Russian tradition examined above derived from similar Greek texts, which could only play a secondary role.

314 Neofit, *Slovo na Vysokotorzhestvennyi den` vosshestviia na Vserossiiskii Prestol Ego Imp. Velichestva Imperatora Aleksandra Pavlovicha* (St. Petersburg, 1821), 2-3.

315 Cited from V. M. Skvortsov, ed., *Tserkovnyi sovet i Gosudarstvennyi Razum. Opyt tserkovno-politicheskoi khrestomatii* (St. Petersburg, 1912), 64. We should keep in mind that in Biblical typology Moses on Sinai was prototype of Christ on Tabor. See, for example, Canon of the Transfiguration, song 8. The equation of the tsar's throne and Sinai (which apparently suggests the divine inspiration of the monarch's law-giving—on which see V. M. Zhivov, "Istoriia russkogo prava," note 82) also had a tradition. Thus V. Petrov addressed Catherine:

> We look at the place of the mirror,
> At Your, Monarch's, law.
> Almost all rulers under the sun
> Are great, in some measure;
> You are God among them, Sinai is Your throne!

See V. Petrov, *Sochineniia*, part I, 167. We see the same expressions in Petrov's ode on the "Triumphal Coronation and Consecration to the Kingdom of His Imperial Majesty Paul I":

> His soul is a paradise of goodness,
> His throne Sinai,
> Without thunder giving
> The Law to the house seething with children . . .

See Ibid., part II, 229. Typically, in the ode Pavel is compared to Moses descending from Sinai. See Ibid., 244. The same complex of associations may be seen, although less obviously, in Derzhavin. See, for example, G. R. Derzhavin, *Sochineniia*, vol. I, 274-275.

316 Luke 23:42.

317 M. S. Popov, *Arsenii Matseevich*, 57.

318 A. S. Pushkin, *Polnoe sobranie sochinenii* (Moscow-Leningrad, 1937-1949), vol. XII, 312-313.

319 V. V. Andreev, *Predstaviteli vlasti v Rossii posle Petra I* (St. Petersburg, 1871), 265-266.

320 I. I. Golikov, *Anekdoty*, 422-423; *Rasskazy Nartova o Petre Velikom*, 73.

321 *Pis`ma mitr. Moskovskogo Filareta*, vol. I, 38.

322 Ibid., 21, 214.

[323] "High triumphal (imperial) days" first appeared under Peter, apparently due to Protestant influence, and immediately gave rise to cases against priests who did not celebrate a triumphal mass on them; see, for example, the case of Archimandrite Aleksandr Lampadchik in 1719 in G. V. Esipov, *Raskoll`nich`i dela XVIII veka* (St. Petersburg, 1861-1863), vol. I, 134; N. B. Golikova, *Politicheskie protsessy pri Petre I po materialam Preobrazhenskogo prikaza* (Moscow, 1957), 154; and other similar cases in N. D. Zol`nikova, *Soslovnye problemy*, 152f, 167.

[324] See A. Kotovich, *Dukhovnaia tsenzura*, 209.

[325] Even the non-Orthodox confessional affiliation of members of the royal family did not prevent such celebration. Thus during the regency of Anna Leopol`dovna the birthday and name day of Duke Anton Ul`rikh, the ruler's spouse, were church holidays, even though he was Protestant. We should keep in mind that Protestants do not venerate saints, and therefore do not celebrate saints' days, so that when Duke Anton Ul`rikh became father of the emperor he had to find an Orthodox patron saint—St. Anthony the Roman. Further, when Anton Ul`rikh died in exile, in Kholmogory, he was refused a church burial, in accordance with Orthodox rules. See *Vnutrennii byt Russkogo gosudarstva*, kn. I, 81, 550, 554. Juxtaposing these two facts, we see that under pressure from the imperial cult the Orhodox Church was forced to celebrate the birth and saint's day of a person who according to Orthodox canons was a heretic.

[326] *Sobranie mnenii i otzyvov Filareta*, dopoln. tom, 174, 517-518.

[327] K. Nikol`skii, *Posobie k izucheniiu ustava bogosluzheniia pravoslavnoi tserkvi* (St. Petersburg, 1874), 736.

[328] *Zapiski Otdeleniia russkoi i slavianskoi arkheologii*, vol. II, 431; RGB, f. 178, d. 9427, l. 348 verso.

[329] Masson, *Mémoirs secrets sur la Russie* (Paris, 1802), vol. 2, 91. Masson notes that on these days they most likely sang "Te Deam" rather than "Te Deum" at court. See Ibid. This witticism probably derives from Voltaire's letters to Catherine. In one of them, on October 17, 1769, he had written: "Je supplie Votre Majesté imperiale de lui ordonner . . . d'assister à mon *Te Deum*, où plutôt à mon *Te Deam*." See F. M. A. Voltaire, *Oeuvres complètes* (Paris, 1877-1885), vol. XLVI, 476. In another (of October 30, 1769) he also made word play of the first words of the "Te Deum," congratulating Catherine on the victory at Khotin. He wrote: "Je chantais *Te* Catharinam *laudamus, te* dominam *confitemur*. L'ange Gabriel m'avait donc instruit de la déroute entière de l'armée ottomane, de la prise de Choczin." See Ibid., 481. Thus Voltaire proposes instead of the usual prayer formula "We praise You, God" to sing "We praise You, Catherine" and "You, mistress, we worship."

[330] I. M. Snegirev, *Zhizn` moskovskogo mitropolita Platona*, part II, 115.

[331] N. P. Nikolev, *Oda Ego Imp. Velichestvu Pavlu Pervomu*, 9.

[332] V. Petrov, *Sochineniia*, part II, 126.

[333] G. R. Derzhavin, *Sochineniia*, vol. III, 190.

[334] Ibid., 41.

[335] *Vlast` Samoderzhavnaia*, 19.

[336] It is curious to note that after the Petrine era enemies of the tsar could be seen as enemies of Christ, subject to excommunication from the church. It was on this very basis that Mazepa was excommunicated (*Polnoe sobranie zakonov*, vol. IV, no. 2213), as well as Stepan Glebov (*Polnoe sobranie postanovlenii i rasporiazhenii*, vol. I, no. 179) and Pugachev (*Polnoe sobranie zakonov*, vol. XX, no. 14233). During Catherine I's reign opponents of the "Charter Concerning the Inheritance of the Throne" were officially anathematized. See P. Morozov, *Feofan Prokopovich*, 305.

337   G. Gukovskii, *Ocherki po istorii russkoi literatury XVIII veka. Dvorianskaia fronda v literature 1750-1760-kh godov* (Moscow-Leningrad, 1936), 13.

338   See V. M. Zhivov, B. A. Uspenskii, "Metamorfozy antichnogo iazychestva," 221f.

339   V. P. Grebeniuk, ed., *Panegiricheskaia literatura petrovskogo vremeni* (Moscow, 1979), 155-156.

340   Ibid., 156.

341   V. M. Zhivov, "Koshchunstvennaia poeziia v sisteme russkoi kul`tury kontsa XVIII—nachala XIX v.," *Uchenye zapiski Tartusskogo gosudarstvennogo universiteta* 546 (1981): 65-70.

342   M. V. Lomonosov, *Polnoe sobranie sochinenii*, vol. VIII, 140.

343   Ibid., 504. See also Lomonosov on Peter in his "Speech of Praise": "If it were possible to find any person like God in our understanding apart from Peter the Great, I can't imagine it." See Ibid., 611.

344   Ibid., 225.

345   Ibid., 84-85.

346   Ibid., 66.

347   See Revelation 10:2; Revelation 20:12.

348   M. V. Lomonosov, *Polnoe sobranie sochinenii*, vol. VIII, 199.

349   V. Kel'siev, *Sbornik pravitel'stvennykh svedenii o raskol'nikakh*, vyp. II, 256.

350   M. V. Lomonosov, *Polnoe sobranie sochinenii*, vol. VIII, 773, 789.

351   Ibid., 30.

352   Ibid., 96, 97, 127, 139, 144, 210, 215, 221, 224, 274, 279, 281, 288, 291, 367, 396, 398, 404, 561, 566, 640, 642, 645, 653, 691, 693, 744, 745, 755, 773.

353   Ibid., 774, 777, 789, 793, 796, 799, 801, 810.

354   Ibid. 41.

355   Ibid., 633.

356   Ibid., 635.

357   See Ibid., 74, 194, 394, 502, 532, 692, 744, 749, 780, 801, 810.

358   Ibid., 399.

359   P. P. Pekarskii, *Istoriia imp. Akademii nauk*, vol. II, 150.

360   M. V. Lomonosov, *Polnoe sobranie sochinenii*, vol. VIII, 285.

361   Ibid., 84. See in the subsequent odic tradition the image of a divine voice calling through an open heavenly door. See E. Greshischeva, "Khvalebnaia oda v russkoi literature XVIII v." in V. V. Sipovskii, ed., *M. V. Lomonosov* (St. Petersburg, 1911), 116-118. This tradition was then reflected in sermons as well. See Avgustin (Vinogradskii), *Sochineniia*, 30, 115.

     A characteristic protest against combining the Greek Olympus with the Biblical Ancient of Days may be found in the anonymous "Note on the Slavonic Language and on Russian Secular Speech" (*Russkii vestnik* 7 (1811): 64), whose author was probably S. N. Glinka. "In the same ode by Lomonosov in which Olympus opens a holy door we also see the Ancient of Days. . . . It seems to me that such an opposition spoils the clarity and purity of the style." See V. M. Zhivov, B. A. Uspenskii, "Metamorfozy antichnogo iazychestva," 274.

362   M. V. Lomonosov, *Polnoe sobranie sochinenii*, vol. VIII, 127.

363   A. P. Sumarokov, *Polnoe sobranie vsekh sochinenii*, part II, 241.

364   Ibid., part II, 9.

365   Ibid., part VI, 302-303.

366   Ibid., part II, 63.

367 Ibid., part I, 272, 273; part II, 43, 55, 79, 86, 93, 102, 229, 253.

368 Ibid., part I, 279, 283; part II, 8, 46, 62, 69, 95, 100, 108, 119, 229.

369 Ibid., part II, 21.

370 Ibid., 87.

371 Ibid., 41.

372 N. P. Nikolev, *Tvoreniia*, part II, 239.

373 Ibid., 236.

374 V. Petrov, *Sochineniia*, part II, 159. See also Ibid., 128 on Catherine: "She is All God."

375 Ibid., part 154.

376 Ibid., part II, 207.

377 Ibid., part I, 157.

378 Ibid., part II, 134.

379 See Ibid., part I, 50, 89, 91,151, 152; part II, 123, 124, 132, 139, 149, 174; part III, 227, 265, 340; N. P. Nikolev, *Tvoreniia*, part II, 82, 112, 276, 277; see also poetry of Ermil Kostrov in *Poety XVIII veka* (Leningrad, 1972), vol. II, 130, 134, 136, 137, 140, 142, 147.

380 See Ibid., 142,147, 157; N. P. Nikolev, *Tvoreniia*, part II, 41, 42, 59, 92, 109, 121, 281; V. Petrov, *Sochineniia*, part I, 5, 14, 18, 26, 58, 68, 76, 122, 205, 225; part II, 45; part III, 228, 263, 268, 328.

381 S. B., "Deistvie i slava zizhdushchago dukha," *Sobesednik liubitelei rossiiskogo slova* 12 (1784): 6.

382 G. R. Derzhavin, *Sochineniia*, vol. I, 166.

383 Ibid., 140.

384 Ibid., vol. II, 405-412.

385 Ibid., vol. I, 96, 101, 163; vol. II, 585, 606, 659, 662, 693, 695, 696; vol. III, 245, 260, 389. In one instance Derzhavin addresses Catherine with the momentous question: "Who are you? goddess or priestess?" See Ibid., vol. I, 165.

386 Ibid., 18, 52, 176, 424, 545, 740; vol. III, 240, 251, 298, 371.

387 Ibid., vol. II, 380-381; vol. III, 522.

388 Ibid., vol. I, 310.

389 Ibid., vol. III, 179.

390 Ibid., vol. II, 378.

391 Ibid., vol. III, 216.

392 Ibid., vol. I, 83.

393 Ibid., 34.

394 Ibid., vol. III, 243.

395 Ibid., 190, 261.

396 See in this connection the parodic play on this name in the poem "The Dream Vision That I Had on June 4, 1794," written in the early nineteenth century:

> The celebration was so exceedingly great
> That I'm not able to describe it;
> Enlightened, even wildly so,
> I would be happy to include her [Catherine—Felitsa] among the gods!

See G. Gukovskii, V. Orlov, "Podpol`naia poeziia 1770-1800-kh godov," *Literaturnoe nasledstvo* 9-10 (1933): 83.

397 G. R. Derzhavin, *Sochineniia*, vol. II, 585.

398 Ibid., 606.

399 Ibid., vol. I, 52.

400 Ibid., vol. II, 522.

401 A. P. Sumarokov, *Polnoe sobranie vsekh sochinenii*, part II, 3-4.

402 The corresponding lines from Motonis go like this: "Te bene tamn meritum non Magnum Petre vocassent, / Nec patriae Patrem saecula prisca, Deum." N. Motonis, "In effigiem Petri magni Imperatoris totius Rossiae," *Prazdnoe vremia v pol`zu uptreblennoe* XXXII (1760): 259.

403 A. P. Sumarokov, *Polnoe sobranie vsekh sochinenii*, part I, 260. A. A. Rzhevskii gets out of this situation somewhat differently in his ode to Peter the Great of 1761, in which Peter is also compared to Christ. Rzhevskii describes how Russia had dwelt "in darkness," when God sent her a "savior" in the person of Peter; here there is a clear reference to Christ's arrival as presented in John 1:5. Then comes the remarkable reservation:

> While one can't consider you God,
> It is no lie that you were sent to us
> By holy will of the most high!

See *Poety XVIII veka*, vol. I, 245, 247. As we see, Rzhevskii resorts to a different solution, although he is just as clearly aware of the problem.

404 The source for this semantic move (pagans who would consider Peter a god) was apparently Feofan Prokopovich's "Sermon in Praise of Peter's Blessed Memory" (1725). Compare: "And if such a boy had appeared to the ancient Romans who were blinded by pagan superstition they would all have believed in truth that he was born from Mars" in Feofan Prokopovich, *Arkhiepiskopa Velikogo Novagrada i Velikikh Luk*, part II, 140. One of Simon Todorskii's sermons of 1745 suggests that Feofan's sermon gave rise to a certain tradition: "One may truly say of Great Catherine what was once said of Great Peter, that if this Monarch had been born at the time of pagan, godless polytheism, in their superstition they would have imagined that one of their goddesses had assumed human flesh." See *Bozhie osobennoe blagoslovenie imzhe vsegda blagoslovil bog i nyne blagoslavliaet Vsepresvetleishii dome Petra Velikogo pervago Imperatora vseia Rossii v den` vysochaishago brakosochetaniia Ego Imp. Vysochestva Petra Fedorovicha c Eia Imp. Vysochestvom Ekaterinoiu Aleksievnoiu. Propovedannoe Simonom Episkopom Pskovskim i Narvskim 1745 goda Avgusta 4 dnia* (St. Petersburg, 1745), 10. In Lomonosov this semantic move is used more than once. In the "Ode on the Arrival of Elizaveta Petrovna in Moscow from St. Petersburg" of 1742 he writes:

> Had ancient ages known
> Your generosity and beauty
> They would have worshiped
> Your beautiful image in a temple with sacrifices.

See M. V. Lomonosov, *Polnoe sobranie sochinenii*, vol. VIII, 101.

405 M. V. Lomonosov, *Polnoe sobranie sochinenii*, vol. VIII, 285-286.

406 G. R. Derzhavin, *Sochineniia*, vol. III, 291-292.

407 One could cite a whole series of facts testifying to the special cult of Peter the Great and his veneration as a holy person. There are cases of the religious veneration of Peter's portrait as an icon, complete with lighting candles, genuflections and prayers. See the story about the invalid Kirillov in I. I. Golikov, *Anekdoty*, 532-535. In his sermon on the birthday of Grand Prince Petr Fedorovich of 1743, Simon Todorskii calls Peter I "*vsepresvetleishii pravednik*" (very most serene righteous one). See G. A. Voskresenskii,

Pridvornaia i akademicheskaia propoved`*, 77. In his well-known sermon on the Chesme victory, delivered in the Peter-Paul Cathedral before Peter's burial chamber, the future Moscow Metropolitan Platon Levshin referred to Peter's "blessed relics" and his "divine spirit." See I. M. Snegirev, *Zhizn` moskovskogo mitropolita Platona, part I, 137, 139. P. I. Chelishchev, travelling in the Russian north in 1791, set up a big wooden cross in Kholmogory on the place where Peter disembarked with the inscription: "Put off thy shoe from off thy foot; for the foot of Peter the Great, Father of the Fatherland, touched the place where thou standest, and is therefore holy." See P. I. Chelishchev, "Puteshestvie po Severu Rossii v 1791 godu," *Pamiatniki drevnei pis`mennosti i iskusstva* 85 (1886): 121, and illustration on the same page. The deification of Peter is underscored by the fact that the inscription is a quotation from the Bible—the words that the Lord speaks to Moses when he summons him to devotion in a place illuminated by the divine presence in Exodus 3:5; Joshua 5:15; Acts 7:33. In his diary of July 31, 1830, P. A. Viazemskii cited the words of a certain Captain Sushchov, commander of the ship "Emperor Alexander": "What Christ was for Christians, Peter the Great was for Russians." See P. Viazemskii, *Polnoe sobranie sochinenii* (St. Petersburg, 1878-1896), vol. IX, 135. No less indicative is Nicholas I's resolution about M. P. Pogodin's tragedy "Peter I" on December 22, 1831: "The person of Emperor Peter the Great must be the object of devotion and love for every Russian; to put him on the stage would almost be the violation of something sacred, and is therefore completely improper. I forbid publication." See *Russkaia starina* 2 (1903): 315-316; *Starina i novizna* VII (1904): 161-162; Peter must not be presented on stage just as an icon or cleric must not be represented. This religious veneration is one of the profound themes of Pushkin's "Bronze Horseman": Evgenii's rebellion against Peter amounts to an attempt to overthrow something sacred, and his insanity—that of one who challenges God. For Evgenii Peter changes from a god, a "wonder-working builder," into "an idol on a bronze steed," "a haughty statue." All of these expressions are quite meaningful, and it is characteristic that they were all marked by Nicholas I as inadmissible in reference to depicting Peter. See T. Zenger, "Nikolai I—redaktor Pushkina," *Literaturnoe nasledstvo* 16-18 (1934), 522. In the framework of the civil cult a special religious attitude also formed toward Falconet's statue of Peter. See on this V. M. Zhivov, B. A. Uspenskii, "Metamorfozy antichnogo iazychestva," 228-230. A. F. Merzliakov's inscription "To the Monument of Peter the Great in Petersburg" was polemically directed at this issue:

> *He is flying on a blazing steed, like some god;*
> *His gaze embraces everything, he commands with a gesture.*
> *The snake of enmity, perfidy, dies, trampled,*
> *The soulless cliff takes on shape and life,*
> *And Russians would have been brought to perfection right then,*
> > *at the start of the new age,*
> *Had death not said to Peter: "Stop! You are not god—no further!"*

See A. F. Merzliakov, *Stikhotvoreniia* (Leningrad, 1958), 259-260.

[408] G. R. Derzhavin, *Sochineniia*, vol. I, 563-569. We encounter similar justifications in the poetry of Petrov and Nikolev analyzed above. Thus in Petrov's letter "To the High Title of Great Catherine, Accorded Her Majesty, Most Wise Mother of the Fatherland, in 1767," he wrote:

But what saith She? God alone is most wise,
Is it for me to assume God's name and honor?
Let Him make me wise, and act through me.

See V. Petrov, *Sochineniia*, part III, 13-14. Nikolev wrote of the very same Catherine:

Not God . . . but a human on the throne,
A human—in the most holy sense,
Born to defend her near ones,
Born to make the age happy

. . . .

Not God, but in Her we see the Creator.

See N. P. Nikolev, *Tvoreniia*, part II, 29.

In reference to such epigones, however, the question arises whether these justifications represent evidence of a conscious attitude toward the issue of sacralization or if they were merely a continuation of the tradition of similar justifications established by Lomonosov and Sumarokov, and thus merely one of the more refined methods of praising the monarch.

[409]   Notably, this theory derives in many ways from interpretations of Psalm 81 (82) and to a great extent recalls old Russian teaching about power. Derzhavin evidently assimilated the idea of juxtaposing righteous and unjust tsars from ancient Russian writings as well as the notion of limiting power by means of moral laws and of fair judgement as the necessary basis for correct rule. See G. R. Derzhavin, *Sochineniia*, vol. VII, 630; vol. VI, 415; vol. II, 220-222; vol. III, 58, 663. However, Derzhavin combines these ideas with his own. He does not reject the sacralization of the monarch, so characteristic for post-Petrine Russia, but makes it a consequence of the tsar's righteousness; sacralization would be unforgiveable if it were applied to a ruler without discrimination. It is justified, however, when addressed to a tsar who rules according to the law and the commandments, and when the tsar is in God's image. Derzhavin evidently resolved the conflict between the deification of the monarch and Christian religious consciousness—so characteristic for all eighteenth-century Russian culture—within this framework.

[410]   See V. M. Zhivov, B. A. Uspenskii, "Metamorfozy antichnogo iazychestva," 230-234.

[411]   True, in the nineteenth century there were also attempts to limit Baroque influence in sermons. Voices were heard in favor of making sermons less eloquent and more instructive. See the example of Archimandrite Innokentii Smirnov in V. Zhmakin, *Inookentii, episkop penzenskii i saratovskii. Biogr. ocherk* (St. Petersburg, 1885), 67. To a significant extent ancient mythology disappeared from sermons, and was considered inappropriate for religious literature. See, for example, *Pis`ma mitr. Moskovskogo Filareta*, vol. III, 62-63, 109; Filaret, *Pis`ma Moskovskogo metropolitan Filareta k pokoinomu arkhiepiskopu tverskomu Alekseiiu, 1843-1867* (1883), 110. There were also other manifestations of this tendency, which nevertheless only limited the continuing vitality of the Baroque tradition.

[412]   *Sobranie mnenii i otzyvov Filareta*, vol. IV, 332-333; V. M. Zhivov, B. A. Uspenskii, "Metamorfozy antichnogo iazychestva," 229-230.

[413]   *Sobranie mnenii i otzyvov Filareta*, vol. IV, 75.

[414]   A. Kotovich, *Dukhovnaia tsenzura*, 466.

415 Ibid., 84, 441, 442, 465.

416 *Pis`ma mitr. Moskovskogo Filareta*, vol. III, 392.

417 *Sobranie mnenii i otzyvov Filareta*, vol. III, 311.

418 I. Smolitsch, *Geschichte der russischen Kirche*, 164.

419 R. L. Nicholas, "Filaret," in *Modern Encyclopedia of Soviet and Russian History* (New York, 1979), vol. II, 123. This forced the heir to refrain from attending meetings of the body.

420 *Sobranie mnenii i otzyvov Filareta*, vol. V, 163-164; dopoln. tom, 517-581.

421 Ibid., 444-450; vol. IV, 339-340.

422 Ibid., vol. III, 311.

423 Ibid., vol. IV, 28-29; A. Kotovich, *Dukhovnaia tsenzura*, 289, 353.

424 *Mneniia, otzyvy i pis`ma Filareta, mitr. Moskovskogo i Kolomenskogo, po raznym voprosam* (Moscow, 1905), 22-24.

425 *Sobranie mnenii i otzyvov Filareta*, vol. IV, 297-301, 469; vol. III, 107-108, 512.

426 Characteristically, when the Rumanian Gospodar Alexander Cusa carried out a reform of church administration similar to that which Peter I had put into place in his era, it led to a rift between the Rumanian Church and the patriarch of Constantinople, and Metropolitan Filaret, like the entire Russian Synod, while condemning the Rumanians, was at the same time forced to justify the canonicity of the Russian church administration and to distinguish it from that of the Rumanian Church. See F. Kurganov, *Nabroski i ocherki iz noveishei istorii Rumynskoi tserkvi* (Kazan, 1899),170-171, 216-223, 336-346. Moreover, the Rumanian Gospodar directly cited Peter I's example and the juridicial status of the contemporary Russian Synod (see Ibid., 451, 475-458), and the response by members of the Synod, including Filaret's, seemed like sophistic self-defense, an attempt to hide from themselves, and from society, the conflict between Christian consciousness and the growing sacralization of the monarch, involving the increasing subordination of church to state. See Ibid., 493-496, 496-506; *Sobranie mnenii i otzyvov Filareta*, vol. V, 807-808, 834-839. Curiously, for all of the attempts to present the Russian situation as consonant with church norms, acknowledgement of the noncanonical establishment of this institution slipped into the Russian Synod's response. See F. Kurganov, *Nabroski i ocherki*, 459. Just as characteristic of the Russians' sophistry was Filaret's statement that the spiritual college "which Peter took from the Protestant . . . divine providence and the spirit of the church turned into the Most Holy Synod." See *Sobranie mnenii i otzyvov Filareta*, vol. IV, 145; by "the Protestant" Filaret meant G. F. Leibniz, who had proposed extending the collegial system to administer ecclesiastical matters.

427 Feofan offered a special defense of it in his "Treatise on Oaths and Pledges" (*Rassuzhdenie o prisiage i kliatve*). See Feofan Prokopovich, *Arkhiepiskopa Velikogo Novagrada i Velikikh Luk*, part IV, 243-265.

428 See Markell Rodyshevskii's protest against this kind of oath in P. V. Verkhovskoi, *Uchrezhdenie Dukhovnoi Kollegii*, vol. II, 91(second pagination).

429 See *Mneniia, otzyvy i pis`ma Filareta*, 190.

430 P. V. Verkhovskoi, *Uchrezhdenie Dukhovnoi Kollegii*, vol. I, 643.

431 See this overt protest against the sacralization of the monarch in Aleksei Tolstoi's "Song on Potok the Warrior":

> *Preserve us, Lord, from the earthly god!*
> *Writ sternly commands us*
> *To recognize only the heavenly God!*

A. K. Tolstoi, *Polnoe sobranie sochinenii*, vol. I, 299. True, Tolstoi is writing here about Muscovite Rus' and he characteristically attributes sacralization of the tsar to Tatar influence.

⁴³² Innokentii, "Slovo, proiznesennoe v Odesskom kafedral`nom sobore... po vozvrashche-nii iz Moskvy posle prisutstviia tam pri sviashcheneishem koronovanii ikh Imp. Velichestv," *Khristianskoe chtenie* (1856), 450; ellipsis in the original. The expression "last day" hints at Innokentii's book "The Last Days of Jesus Christ's Earthly Life," i.e., it specifically denotes Golgotha.

⁴³³ N. I. Barsukov, *Zhizn` i trudy M. P. Pogodina* (St. Petersburg, 1888-1910), kn. XV, 132.

⁴³⁴ *Pis`ma raznykh lits znamenitomu arkhiepiskopu Innokentiiu Borisovu* (Moscow, 1885), 17. Pogodin's letter was also published with some insignificant differences from the cited text by Barsukov (see N. I. Barsukov, *Zhizn` i trudy*, kn. XV, 134-135); Barsukov's publication seems less correct. The words Pogodin cites by Krylov on Glinka should be juxtaposed to the analogous statement by Pushkin in his letter to Pletnev of January 7, 1831:

> Poor Glinka works like a hired hand, but nothing worthwhile comes of it. It seems to me that he has gone off his head, mad from grief. Whom did he take the notion to ask to be godparent of his child! Just imagine into what kind of a position he will put the priest and the deacon, the godmother, the midwife, and the godfather himself, whom they will make renounce the devil, spit, blow, unite to Christ, and do other such stuff. Nashchokin assures us that everybody was spoiled by the late tsar, who stood godfather to everybody's children. Even now I can't get over Glinka's audacity.

A. S. Pushkin, *Polnoe sobranie sochinenii*, vol. XIV, 141; translation adapted from J. T. Shaw, trans., *The Letters of Alexander Pushkin* (Bloomington, 1967), 452. Pushkin has in mind F. N. Glinka's poem "Poverty and Consolation," in which there occur the lines: "Will God give children? . . . —Well, so what—Let him be our *godfather!*" See F. N. Glinka, *Izbrannye proizvedeniia* (Leningrad, 1957), 408. This incident indirectly reveals the association between God and monarch; it was the fact that Emperor Alexander baptized children that, as P. V. Nashchokin suggested, made it possible to conceive of God in the corresponding role.

TSAR AND PRETENDER:
SAMOZVANCHESTVO OR ROYAL IMPOSTURE IN RUSSIA AS A CULTURAL-HISTORICAL PHENOMENON

B. A. Uspenskij

1. Although *samozvanchestvo,* or royal imposture, is not an exclusively Russian phenomenon, in no other country has it been so frequent, or played such a significant role in the history of people and state.[1] To write the history of Russia and avoid the question of royal imposture is impossible: in the words of Kliuchevskii, "royal imposture in Russia, ever since the first False Dmitrii* made his appearance, became a chronic malady of the state from that moment on; almost until the end of the eighteenth century, hardly a single reign passed without a pretender."[2] From the beginning of the seventeenth century and even up to the middle of the nineteenth, it would be hard to point to more than two or three decades in which a pretender did not put himself forward, and indeed, in some periods, pretenders can be counted by the dozen.[3]

The root-causes of this phenomenon have not yet been fully explained. For the most part scholars have attempted to solve the question of royal imposture by reference to either a social or a political perspective: on the social level it is seen as a specific and persistent form of anti-feudalism, and on the political level as a struggle for power. Neither of these approaches, however, elucidates the *specific* nature of royal imposture as a cultural phenomenon: as we shall see below, royal imposture in the broader sense of the term is by no means invariably linked to social movements, nor does it necessarily involve a struggle for political power. If we are to grasp the essence of royal imposture, we clearly have to uncover those cultural mechanisms which precondition the phenomenon, i.e., to examine in a historical light the ideological

---

* Claiming to be Dmitrii, the youngest son of Ivan the Terrible, who had in fact been murdered in 1591, the False Dmitrii marched on Moscow in 1605 and held the throne for less than a year.

conceptions of Russian society. An important step in this direction was taken by K. V. Chistov, who has convincingly demonstrated the connection between royal imposture and the utopian legend of the Tsar-Deliverer; indeed, Chistov sees royal imposture as a realization of this legend.[4] While wholly accepting Chistov's conclusions, we should point out, however, that his explanation is not exhaustive. This approach, in fact, explains not so much the appearance of pretenders, as the social reaction to it, i.e. the response and support which they enjoyed among the populace; in addition, it highlights an important aspect of the phenomenon, namely *belief* in the pretender. Moreover, the question of royal imposture cannot be explained without delving further into the psychology of the pretenders themselves, i.e. into the whole complex of notions which directly motivated their actions. In this paper we shall attempt to show that it was *religious* notions which lay at the root of this psychology; in other words, we shall examine the religious aspect of royal imposture as a phenomenon of Russian culture.

2. It is quite clear that the psychology of royal imposture is directly connected with the question of attitude to the Tsar, i.e. the special way in which royal power was understood. Pretenders made their appearance in Russia only after there were Tsars, i.e. after the establishment and stabilization of royal power (no instances of pretenders claiming a *princely* throne are known). Moreover, the special nature of the attitude to the Tsar is determined by the understanding of royal power as being sacred, having a divine nature. It might even be suggested that royal imposture, as a typically Russian phenomenon, is connected precisely with the process of sacralization of the monarchy (which in turn is connected with the Byzantinization of monarchic power). Furthermore, the appearance of pretenders may actually be evidence of the start of the process of the sacralization of the monarch;[5] it is perhaps no accident that the first pretender appeared in Russia soon after the rite of anointing was added to the accession ceremony (along with that of crowning). Anointing confers, as it were, a special charismatic status on the Tsar: as the anointed one, the Tsar is likened to Christ (Greek: *christos,* "the anointed one") and consequently, from the beginning of the eighteenth century, could even be called "Christ."[6]

We should remember that the word "tsar" in early Russia was regarded as a sacred word and has the same feature of non-conventionality in relation to the linguistic sign that all sacred lexis has in general; by the same token, the act of calling oneself Tsar can in no way be viewed as a purely arbitrary act of will.[7] Captain Margeret writes in his notes in 1607:

Now, concerning the title which they take, they think that there is none more solemn than the one they have, "Tzar." They call the Roman Emperor *"Tsisar,"* deriving it from Caesar; other sovereigns they call *"kroll,"* following the example of the Poles; the Persian suzerain they call *"Kisel Bacha"* and the Turkish, *"Veliqui Ospodartursk,"* I.e. the Great Lord of Turkey . . . According to them, the word Tzar is to be found in the Holy Scriptures. For wherever mention is made of David, or Solomon, or other kings, they are called "Zar David" and "Zar Solomon" . . . For this reason they maintain that the name of Tzar which it once pleased God to confer on David, Solomon and other rulers of Judah and Israel is the most authentic, and that the words "Tsisar" or "Kroll" are merely a human invention and acquired by feats of arms.[8]

In this way the name Tsar is acknowledged to be a creation not of man, but of God; consequently the title of Tsar is seen as distinct from all other titles in as much as it is of divine nature. Even more important is the fact that this word is applied to God Himself: in liturgical texts God is often called "Tsar," and hence the characteristic parallelism, bequeathed to Christian religious consciousness, as it were from the earliest times, between Tsar and God,[9] a parallelism which finds expression in such paired phrases as *Nebesnyi* Tsar (King of Heaven—referring to God) and *zemnoi* Tsar (Earthly Tsar—referring to the Tsar); *Netlennyi* Tsar (Incorruptible Tsar, i.e. God) and *tlennyi* Tsar (Corruptible Tsar, i.e. the Tsar).[10] Cf. also the naming of the Tsar as *zemnoi bog* (Earthly God), which is attested to in Russian from the sixteenth century onwards.[11]

In such conditions as these the very fact of calling oneself Tsar—irrespective of the fact of wielding actual power or not—has an undeniably religious aspect to it, and either way betokens a claim to possess sacred qualities. It is typical that the False Dmitrii was called, like Christ, *"pravednoe solntse"* (sun of righteousness);[12] the Barkulabovskii chronicle speaks of him thus: "for he is assuredly the true Tsar of the East, Dmitrii Ivanovich, the sun of righteousness."[13] This is, as far as we know, the first case of such a title being applied to a Tsar.[14] In this sense, arbitrarily to proclaim oneself Tsar may be compared with proclaiming oneself saint, a custom found, for example, among the Russian sects of the *khlysty* (the flagellants) and the *skoptsy* (the castrates). Indeed, in certain cases these two tendencies coincide: the well-known Kondratii Selivanov, whom the *skoptsy* saw as the incarnation of Christ, was at the same time believed to be the Emperor Peter III.[15]* According to the teaching of the *skoptsy*, "in the beginning was the Lord Sabaoth, then Jesus

---

* Peter III (Petr Fedorovich) reigned from 1761-1762. He was overthrown and succeeded by his wife Catherine the Great.

Christ, and now the Lord and Father, Petr Feodorovich, God of Gods and Tsar of Tsars."[16] Similarly Akulina Ivanovna, "mother of God" to the *skoptsy,* was acknowledged to be both Mother of God and the Empress Elizabeth Petrovna,* and accordingly the mother of Kondratii Selivanov, since he was Tsar and God[17]; another "mother of God" to the *skoptsy,* Anna Sofonovna, considered herself to be the Grand Duchess Anna Feodorovna, the wife of the heir to the throne, the Tsarevich Constantine Pavlovich.[18]** In general, along with the pretenders who took the name of a Tsar, there were in Russia also pretenders who took the name of a saint, or who claimed to have special powers from on high; in a sense these are phenomena of the same order. Thus, for example, in the first half of the eighteenth century there appeared in Siberia a self-styled Prophet Elijah[19] (we should, incidentally, note in this connection that Kondratii Selivanov, whom we discussed above, was also at times called the Prophet Elijah).[20] At the end of the seventeenth century, Kuz`ma Kosoi (El`chenin), who led one of the Old Believer movements in the Don country, proclaimed himself "pope"[21] and maintained that he had to place Tsar Mikhail on the throne;[22] what is more, he acknowledged Mikhail to be God Himself.[23] According to other sources, he considered himself to be Tsar Mikhail, i.e. both Tsar and God together.[24] Self-styled Tsar Mikhails, as well as people who thought it their mission to put a Tsar Mikhail on the throne, have turned up in Russia at later dates too, right up to our own times.

3. The notion that royal power is established by God accounts for the distinction made in those days, and in particular in the seventeenth century, between "righteous" (*pravednyi*) and unrighteous" (*nepravednyi*) Tsars: *pravednyi* signifies not "just" (*spravedlivyi*) , but "the right one" (*pravil`nyi*). Thus Ivan Timofeev distinguishes in his *Chronicle* between Tsars who are genuine ("most true," "most original," Tsars "by nature") and those who are Tsars in outward appearance only ("unreal," who "make an assault" on tsardom "by means of pretence").[25] Neither usurpation of the throne, nor even legitimate accession to the throne through the rite of coronation, is sufficient to make a man Tsar. It is not conduct, but *predestination* which marks the true Tsar; so a Tsar may be a tyrant (as, for example, Ivan the Terrible) yet this in no way means that he is not in his rightful place. A distinction is therefore drawn between Tsars by the grace of God and Tsars by act of will, only the former being acknowledged as

---

* The Empress Elizabeth, who reigned from 1741-1761, was the daughter of Peter the Great and aunt of Peter III.

** Brother of Alexander I. He renounced his claim to the throne.

true Tsars; in other words, a distinction is made between the non-conventional and the conventional senses of the word *tsar*. The False Dmitrii, then, in contrast to Ivan the Terrible, is not, from Ivan Timofeev's point of view, a Tsar at all: although he was legitimately enthroned, he is in fact only a *samotsar`*, a *"self-styled Tsar."*[26] Similarly Boris Godunov,* according to the same author, "imposed himself on us ... by his own volition,"[27] and so Ivan Timofeev does not recognize him as Tsar; and he has the same attitude towards Vasilii Shuiskii.[28]**

On the other hand, Tsar Mikhail Fedorovich,*** as Avraamii Palitsyn emphasizes in his *Tale,***** "was chosen not by men, but in truth by God";[29] and moreover he does not understand this in the sense that God's will guided Mikhail Fedorovich's election in the Assembly of the Land, but rather that he was destined by God even before his birth and anointed from his mother's womb.[30] The Assembly of the Land simply divined, as it were, his predestination.[31] (It should be noted, by the way, that the early Russian scribes provide no practical indications whatsoever on how to distinguish a true Tsar from a false one.)

Similarly in the *Epistle to the Ugra* by the Archbishop of Rostov, Vassian (Rylo), dated 1480 and addressed to Ivan III, the author sees the Tatar Khan (Akhmat) as a false Tsar. He calls him a pretender and usurper who "captured our land like a robber, and ruled over it *although he was neither a Tsar nor descended from Tsars,*" and contrasts him with Ivan, who is the true Tsar, "the sovereign-ruler confirmed by God":

> And yet what prophet prophesied and what apostle or prelate taught this man, so unpleasing to God, this wicked man who *calls himself Tsar* to submit to you, the great Christian Tsar of all Russian lands?[32]

It must be borne in mind that during the period of Tatar rule the Khan was called "Tsar" in Russia, yet now this Tsar is called a *pretender* (we shall return to this question later). Cf. also a similar formulation in the denunciatory epistle from the clergy, headed by Iona (the future Metropolitan), to Prince Dmitrii Shemiaka in 1447, appealing to him to submit to Prince Vasilii the Blind:

---

*   Reigned 1598-1605.

**   Vasilii IV, a boyar who held the throne from 1606-1610.

*** Tsar Mikhail, the first of the Romanov dynasty, was elected Tsar in 1613. The Assembly of the Land was abolished by Peter the Great.

**** Avraamii Palitsyn (1555-1627) completed his *Skazanie* in 1620.

Lord, we must dare to say this: will you be overcome by spiritual blindness through your infatuation with what is temporal and ephemeral, and the totally illusory honour and glory of being prince and ruler: that is, to hear yourself addressed by the title of Prince and yet not to have it bestowed by God?[33]

In this case too, self-styled power (power by outward appearance only) is contrasted with God-given power (power by inner nature), and power conferred on oneself with power conferred by God; it is worth noting in this connection that it was precisely Vasilii the Blind who was the first of the early Russian princes more or less consistently to call himself "Tsar" and "autocrat" (*samoderzhets*).[34] Indeed, it is Metropolitan Iona[35] himself who calls him Tsar, and who is probably the author of the epistle of 1447 quoted above; thus, in this instance too, the point at issue is royal power by divine election.

If true Tsars receive power from God, then false Tsars receive it from the Devil.[36] Even the church rite of sacred coronation and anointing do not confer grace on a false Tsar, for these actions are no more than outward appearances; in reality the false Tsar is crowned and anointed by demons acting on the orders of the Devil himself.[37] It follows therefore that if the real Tsar may be likened to Christ (see above) and perceived as an image of God, a living icon,[38] then a pretender may be regarded as a false icon, i.e. an *idol.* Ivan Timofeev in his *Chronicle* writes of the False Dmitrii:

All obey this man who dwells beyond the borders of the Russian land; all willingly submit to him *though he is an idol, and pay homage to him as to a Tsar.*[39]

Thus the Tsar as icon is seen in opposition to the pretender as idol.

4. The idea of a true Tsar's being divinely preordained, of his being marked by divine election, is clearly apparent in the exceptionally persistent notion of special "royal signs," usually the cross, the eagle (i.e. the Tsar's coat of arms) or the sun-signs which are supposed to be found on the Tsar's body and which attest to his elective status. This belief has played an important part in the mythology of royal imposture: according to numerous historical and folklore sources it was precisely by virtue of these "royal signs" that the most diverse pretenders—for example, the False Dmitrii, Timofei Ankudinov,* Emel`ian Pugachev** and others—demonstrated their royal descent and their right to

---

*   Claiming to be the son of Vasilii Shuiskii (Vasilii IV), he was executed in 1653.

**   Emel`ian Pugachev (1726-1775) was the leader of the most widespread and serious popular revolt under Catherine the Great.

the throne; and it was especially the marks on their bodies that made others believe in them and support them.[40] Thus, for example, a beggar who turned up in 1732 in the Tambov province proclaimed:

> I am no peasant and no son of a peasant; I am an eagle, the son of eagles, and my destiny is to be an eagle. I am the Tsarevich Aleksei Petrovich . . . I have a cross on my back and a birthmark in the form of a sword on my thigh . . . [41]

Compare the evidence of the Pugachev investigation:

> He had been at Eremina Kuritsa's [the name of a Cossack] for two days, when the latter called Emel`ka [Pugachev] to the bathhouse and Emel`ka said to him: "I have no shirt." Eremina Kuritsa replied: "I'll give you mine." Then the two of them went alone to the baths. When they arrived and Emel`ka undressed, Eremina Kuritsa saw the scars of a disease on Emel`ka's chest, just under the nipples, and asked him: "What's that you have there, Pugachev, on your chest?" And Emel`ka replied to Eremina Kuritsa: "Those are the marks of a sovereign." Hearing this, Eremina said: "That is good, if it is so."

Further on in the same deposition we read:

> When we had sat down, Karavaev said to Emel`ka: "You call yourself a sovereign, yet sovereigns have the royal signs on their bodies," whereupon Emel`ka stood up and, ripping open the collar of his shirt, said: "There! If you do not believe that I am the sovereign, just look—here is the royal sign." First of all he showed the scars under his nipples left by an illness, and then the same kind of mark on his left temple. The Cossacks—Shigaev, Karavaev, Zarubin, Miasnikov—looked at the signs and said: "Well, now we believe you and recognize you as sovereign."[42]

In 1822 a certain townsman by the name of Startsev wrote to Alexander I about a man who maintained that he was Paul I:

> I know that he bears upon his body, on his back between the shoulder-blades, a cross the like of which none of your subjects can have except those of supreme power; for this reason it must be supposed that he has a similar sign also on his chest. Now since he is vouchsafed such a cross on his body he cannot be a man of simple birth, neither can he be a nobleman: he must almost certainly be the father of Your Imperial Majesty . . . [43]

In 1844 a peasant by the name of Kliukin stated that he had been in the baths with a man who called himself the Tsarevich Constantine Pavlovich, and "I saw the hair on his chest formed in the shape of a cross, which no man has, save one of royal blood."[44] Such examples are very common and it would be easy to adduce many more. There is no reason in such cases to suspect a conscious attempt at mystification: for there is no doubt that the pretenders themselves were convinced that the presence of such a mark on their bodies specifically attested to their having been singled out.

The notion of divine election, of the belief that the Tsar is mystically preordained, most likely explains not only the specific conception of royal power in early Russia, which we discussed above, but also the psychology of the pretender. In the absence of any clear-cut criteria on how to distinguish between a true and a false Tsar, the pretender could evidently to some degree believe in his predestination, in his election. It is significant that the most striking pretenders—the False Dmitrii and Pugachev—crop up precisely at those moments when the natural (i.e. hereditary) order of succession has been broken and when the actual occupier of the throne could in fact be regarded as a pretender. Boris Godunov who, in Ivan Timofeev's words, acceded to the throne "by an act of his own will" (see above) could be regarded in this way, as, of course, could Catherine the Great, who had no right to the Russian throne at all. The presence of one pretender (a pretender on the throne) provokes the appearance of others; and there is a kind of competition between pretenders, each of whom claims to be marked (elect). At the basis of this psychology, however paradoxical it may seem, there lurks the conviction that it is not man, but God who must judge who is the real Tsar.[45] It follows, therefore, that royal imposture is a quite predictable and logically justified consequence of the conception of royal power which we have been discussing.

However, the specific psychology of royal imposture is based to a considerable degree on a *mythological act of identification*.[46] It is indicative in this connection that Pugachev, who called himself Petr Fedorovich,* should have called his closest associate, I. N. Zarubin, Chika, "Count Chernyshev."[47]** In addition, the other self-styled Peter III—the *skopets* Kondratii Selivanov, discussed above—had his own "Count Chernyshev" (this was another leader of the *skoptsy*, A. I. Silov[48]). The case of the "mother of God" to the *skoptsy*, Akulina Ivanovna, who, as mentioned above, called herself "Empress Elizabeth" (at the end of the eighteenth century, i.e. after Elizabeth Petrovna's death) is exactly analogous. She had a close associate who called herself E. R. Dashkova;[49]

---

*   I.e. Peter III, husband of Catherine the Great.
**   Count Z. G. Chernyshev (d. 1784) and his brother Ivan held high positions under Catherine.

the fact that the real, not self-styled E. R. Dashkova* was an associate not of Elizabeth, but of Catherine, only serves to underline the purely functional role of such an appellation. In these cases the *name* has become, as it were, a function of the *position*. No less remarkable in this context is the portrait of Pugachev in the Moscow Historical Museum, where Pugachev is painted over the portrait of Catherine:[50] if a portrait is a pictorial parallel to a person's name, then the repainting of a portrait is equivalent to an act of renaming.[51]

5. Thus the very concept of royal power in early Russia presupposed an opposition between true, genuine Tsars and Tsars in outward appearance only, i.e. pretenders. In this sense the behavior of a pretender is viewed as carnival behavior: in other words, pretenders are seen as mummers (*riazhenye*).

Furthermore, royal imposture is obviously connected with the "game of Tsar" which was played in Muscovy in the seventeenth century; people would play at being the Tsar, i.e. would *dress up* as Tsars and act out the attendant ceremonies. Thus in the record book of the Muscovite court for February 2, 1634 we read:

> The same day, Prince Matvei, Prince Ofonasei and the Princes Ivan and Ondrei Shakhovskie were brought before the Tsar, where the following was said to them: In the year 7128 [i.e. 1620] Ondrei Golubovskoi laid a charge against you to the Sovereign Tsar and Grand Prince Mikhailo Fedorovich of all Russia** that one evening you went to Ileika Bochkin's house and that you, Prince Ofonasei, Prince Ondrei, Prince Ivan and Ileika Bochkin did in a rascally and cunning [i.e. playful] way call you, Prince Matvei, Tsar, and that you, Prince Matvei, did call the prince and his comrades your boyars; indeed, you yourselves confessed to such rascality. The boyars' verdict was that you should be condemned to death for that misdeed. And then his Majesty the Tsar and Grand Prince Mikhailo Fedorovich of all Russia, at the entreaty of His Majesty's father, the Great Sovereign and Most Holy Patriarch of Moscow and all Russia, Filaret Nikitich, was merciful to you and spared your lives. His Majesty commanded that you be sent for your great crimes to separate prisons in the towns downriver [from Moscow]. But now His Majesty the Tsar and Grand Prince Mikhailo Fedorovich of all Russia, in blessed memory of his father, the Great Sovereign and Most Holy Patriarch of Moscow and all Russia, Filaret Nikitich, has taken pity on you and ordered you to be reprieved from disfavor and brought back from Moscow to appear before the Sovereign. Henceforth you, Prince Matvei, and your comrades are to redeem your great crimes through service.[52]

---

*   Princess E. R. Dashkova was one of the outstanding women of her time.
** I.e. Mikhail Romanov.

Another such case has been preserved in the archive of the Ministry of Justice. On the Wednesday of the first week of Lent in 1666, a landowner from Tver` by the name of Nikita Borisovich Pushkin made a petition in Moscow, in which he called down on his peasants "the Sovereign's word and deed":

> It seems the peasants from my villages around Tver`, to wit from the villages of Vasil`evskoe and Mikhailovskoe, have got up to some kind of unholy mischief: they chose one of their number—I do not know whom—as their leader, and *having given him a high-ranking title,* went with him this Shrovetide Saturday and made an uproar with flags and drums and rifles.

The evidence for the case revealed that the peasants "called one of their number a man of high rank—the Tsar;" moreover, they paraded their elected Tsar, Mit`ka Demidov, "through the village on a litter with a funnel placed on his head,"

> and carried before him *varenets* [boiled soured milk, the ritual repast of Shrovetide]; they also tied a sheaf of straw to a pole [cf. the carrying and burning of sheaves of straw or a scarecrow stuffed with straw in ritual processions at Shrovetide], and the customary basket [sic], and tied a garment instead of a standard to another pole and carried with them instead of a rifle, roofing-timbers.

Next the peasants chose as their Tsar, instead of Mit`ka Demidov, Pershka Iakovlev, who unleashed a royal punishment upon his subjects:

> In the village of Mikhailovskoe, at Pershka's command, his brother peasants beat a certain peasant—I forget his name—with sticks, and the peasant pleaded with them, saying: "Sire, have mercy"; and Pershka was wearing a green caftan at the time with a shoulder-belt and a maiden's fox-fur hat upon his head. And for a flag they tied a woman's veil to a pole.[53]

Both of these peasant "Tsars" had two fingers of their right hands cut off. Both they and their accomplices were whipped "mercilessly" and exiled together with their families to Siberia.[54] It is highly significant that all these events should have taken place at Shrovetide and be characterized by the typical attributes of Shrovetide festivities (the sheaf of straw, the *varenets,* etc.). Dressing up as Tsar similarly emerges as one of the aspects of Shrovetide mummery.[55] Unfortunately we do not know at what season of the year the Shakhovskie princes "played at tsar," but we have every reason to suspect that it happened at Yuletide or at Shrovetide.

"Playing at Tsar" is reflected not only in historical but also in folklore and ethnographical documents. We find a characteristic description of the game in a fairy tale recorded in the Perm` province:

The boy grew not year by year, but hour by hour. He started playing with his friends. They began to *play at Tsar*. The blacksmith's son said to his friends: "Shout to the river to flow backwards! The one who succeeds will be Tsar!" They all shouted and shouted, but nothing happened; then he gave a shout, and the river began to flow backwards. They played the same game again: "Shout to the forest to bow down to the damp earth!" The others shouted and shouted, but nothing happened; he gave a shout, and the forest bowed down. "So, I am Tsar a second time!" They played a third time: "Shout to the animals in the forest to be silent!" [Omission in the text.] "So, lads, I'm Tsar for the third time! I can kill whoever I like since no court can try me," he said. So they agreed to this.[56]

Here we have a very clear reflection of the sacred properties of the Tsar: "playing at Tsar" in this context is seen as playing at being a sacred, omnipotent being.

The "game of Tsar" is essentially a variant of royal imposture, though one completely divested of any kind of political pretensions whatsoever: it is royal imposture in its purest form, so to say. It was no accident that the "game of Tsar" was ruthlessly punished in the seventeenth century, and the fact that despite persecution the game was still played and even left its mark in folklore is extremely significant.[57]

6. The extent to which the "game of Tsar" was found in early Russia is demonstrated by the fact that it could be played not only by pretenders, but also by real Tsars, who forced *another* man to be the false, inauthentic Tsar—a Tsar in outward appearance only. Thus Ivan the Terrible in 1567 forced his equerry, the boyar Ivan Petrovich Fedorov (Cheliadnin), who was suspected of conspiracy, to be dressed up in the Tsar's clothes, given the sceptre and other insignia of royalty and be seated on the throne; after which, having bowed down to the ground before him and paid him all the honors befitting a Tsar, Ivan killed the travesty Tsar with his own hand. This is how Slichting describes the incident:

When he [I. P. Fedorov] arrived at the palace, the tyrant caught sight of him and immediately commanded that he be given the raiment which he [Ivan] was wearing himself and that he should be arrayed therein, that he be given the sceptre which sovereigns are wont to hold, and then ordered him to mount the royal throne and take his seat in the place where the Grand Prince himself always sat. As soon as Ioann [I. P. Fedorov] had done this, albeit with vain protestation (there is after all no sense in trying to justify oneself before a tyrant), and had seated himself on the royal throne in the princely raiment, the tyrant himself rose, stood before him and, baring his head and bowing, knelt before him, saying: "Now you have what you sought, what you aspired to—to be Grand Prince of Muscovy and to occupy my place. So now you are the Grand Prince; rejoice now and enjoy the power after which you thirsted." Then after a short pause he began again, thus: "However, as it lies in my power to seat you upon this throne, so does it also lie in my power to unseat you." Thereupon, seizing a knife he thrust it into his chest several times and made all the soldiers there at the time stab him with their daggers.[58]

This scene is full of the most profound symbolism: Ivan accuses Fedorov of unlawfully claiming the Tsar's throne and yet makes him Tsar, but Tsar in outward appearance only—a *pretender-Tsar.* Such behavior is fairly typical of Ivan in general and—as we shall see below—is not by any means necessarily linked with the desire to rid himself of an unworthy man or quench his thirst for revenge; rather it is connected with the masquerading and dressing up so typical of Ivan and his entourage,[59] in fact, with the game which outwardly might remind one of playing the holy fool, but which is in reality radically different from it.[60]

Even more indicative is the incident when in 1575 Ivan crowned Simeon Bekbulatovich Tsar, handed over to him all his royal ceremonial and all the royal insignia, himself assuming the name of Ivan of Moscow and playing the role of a simple boyar; in the words of the chronicler:

> Ivan Vasil`evich was pleased to make Simeon Bekbulatovich Tsar of Mos-cow . . . and crowned him Tsar, and himself assumed the name of Ivan of Moscow, left town and went to live in Petrovka; he handed over all his royal ceremonial to Simeon, while he himself travelled simply, like a boyar, in a cart and when he came into Simeon's presence he would seat himself far away from the royal throne, together with the boyars.[61]

According to some sources, Simeon Bekbulatovich even underwent the sacred rite of coronation,[62] but even this could not make of him a genuine, authentic Tsar.[63] The enthronement of Simeon Bekbulatovich was directly bound up with the institution (or to be more precise, with the reinstatement) of the *oprichnina,* which also had many features of the masquerade to a marked degree; while Ivan entrusted the *zemshchina* to Simeon Bekbulatovich, he himself controlled the *oprichnina*:[64] the term *zemshchina* (from *zemlia* = land, earth) is correlated with the original land, while the word *oprichnina* signifies that which is separate, unconnected, on the outside.[65] We should point out that I. P. Fedorov too was the head of the *zemshchina* government,[66] so that in both cases the person at the head of the *zemshchina* plays the part of the travesty Tsar; and this, of course, is no mere coincidence.

It is highly significant, moreover, that Simeon Bekbulatovich should have been a direct descendant of the Khans of the Golden Horde, i.e. of those who in their time wielded the real power over the territory of Russia and who *called themselves Tsar* (we have already mentioned that the Tatar Khans were called precisely this);[67] the Tsarevich Bekbulat, father of Simeon Bekbulatovich, was the grandson of Akhmat, the last Khan of the Golden Horde—the very man of whom Vassian Rylo wrote in his *Epistle to the Ugra* in 1480 that he was a false Tsar, a pretender (see above)—and was, in addition, one of the strongest claimants to the Khanate of the fragmented Tatar Horde.[68] So it was that Ivan placed the Tatar Khan on the throne of Russia. *The role of travesty, pretender-Tsar is played by one who would formerly have possessed the right to call himself Tsar and to rule over the Russian state;* such a Tsar is now revealed to be a false Tsar, a Tsar in outward appearance only—and by the same token, the previous Tatar Khans are also seen as false Tsars, not true ones.[69] What we have before us is as it were the last stage in the struggle with Tatar rule, a semiotic stage. In his time, having overcome the Khan (Tsar), the Russian Grand Prince became Tsar, i.e. began to take the name used by the Khans; and now it was the Khan who became the *pretender*-Tsar. [70] It was quite in character that Ivan the Terrible should have behaved like this; for he was the first Russian Tsar officially crowned Tsar, i.e. the first monarch to enjoy the *formal* right to assume the title of Tsar of Russia.

It could be said that in each case, both in that of I. P. Fedorov and in that of Simeon Bekbulatovich, the "game of Tsar" had a symbolic character for Ivan the Terrible and served the function of a *political "unmasking"*: in the first case an actual person (I. P. Fedorov, accused of laying claim to royal power) was unmasked, and in the second, a state principle (the rule of the Tatar Khans). In both cases it was the *head of the zemshchina* who was subjected to being unmasked.

We know of another Tsar who indulged in this game: Peter the Great. In much the same way as Ivan designated Simeon Bekbulatovich Tsar while he himself became a subject, so Peter designated F. Iu. Romodanovskii "Prince-Caesar" [*kniaz`-kesar`*], calling him *korol`* (*konich* [sic], king) and "His Majesty," while he called himself the latter's "serf and lowliest slave," and was awarded various ranks and promotions by him.[71] Setting out in 1697 on his journey abroad, Peter entrusted the government of Moscow to Prince-Caesar Romodanovskii, and in his letters from abroad addressed him as monarch, emphasizing his own subject status.[72] All the highest ranks—those of Colonel (1706), Lieutenant-General and *shoutbenakht*, i.e. Rear-Admiral (1709)—were awarded to Peter by the Prince-Caesar.[73] Nobody dared drive into Romodanovskii's courtyard—the sovereign himself used to leave his carriage at the gates[74]— and in their mock ceremonies Peter would kiss Romodanovskii's hand.[75]

This "game" also had its point of symbolic unmasking. It is characteristic, for example, that at the wedding of the Tsar's jester, Shanskii, in 1702,

Romodanovskii should have been dressed in the robes of a seventeenth century Tsar of Russia, while Nikita Zotov was dressed as the patriarch:[76] this parody of the Russian Tsar as it were anticipates Peter's assumption of the title of Emperor.[77] After F. Iu. Romodanovskii's death (in September 1717), the title of "Prince-Caesar" was inherited by his son, I. F. Romodanovskii (from April 1718); at the wedding of the "Prince-Pope," P. I. Buturlin, in 1721—that is, just before Peter was proclaimed Emperor!—I. F. Romodanovskii again appeared in the costume of Tsar of Russia, his wife was dressed as Tsarina and the crowd of servants wore traditional Russian costume.[78] In this connection we should remember that both Romodanovskiis were known as adherents of traditional Russian customs and in their private lives kept up the traditional boyar ways.[79] Broadly speaking, the Prince-Caesar may be considered an equivalent of the Prince-Pope: the Prince-Caesar being a parody of the Tsar, and the Prince-Pope a parody of the Patriarch; just as the parody of the image of the Tsar preceded the assumption of the title of Emperor, so the parody of the image of the Patriarch preceded the abolition of the Patriarchate [1721]. At the same time we have here a parody of the very principle (ultimately derived from Byzantium) of the coexistence of the priesthood and monarchy, i.e. the division of power into ecclesiastical and secular, a division which was in opposition to the one-man power of Peter.[80] Finally, we should not forget that the Romodanovskii family, unlike the Romanovs, traced their descent from Riurik. Thus, in this case too—as in that of Simeon Bekbulatovich—the role of the monarch is played by one who could previously have laid claim to the title.

Moreover, for both Ivan the Terrible and Peter the Great, this masquerade is intimately bound up with the notion of royal imposture, and can be seen as simply another aspect of the same phenomenon. Its basis is the opposition between genuine and apparent Tsars (pretenders) mentioned above: in all these cases the true, real Tsar, by shedding the *external* signs of his status as Tsar and forcing another to play what is to all intents and purposes the role of pretender, is in fact emphasizing as it were his own *authentic* right to the royal throne, independent of any formal attributes of kingship. Ivan and Peter clearly shared the conception of royal power which we discussed above, and indeed their behavior derives from that conception. It is indicative that Ivan should have renounced the throne several times in the course of his reign (in 1564 in connection with the institution of the *oprichnina,* and in 1575 in connection with its reinstatement and the installation of Simeon Bekbulatovich as Tsar), as if in the full certainty that, come what might, he still remained the true and genuine Tsar: a Tsar by nature, "by the will of God, and not by the unruly whim of mankind," as he puts it himself in his letter to Stephen Batory.[81] In just the same way Ivan could, in a critical situation, ostentatiously abandon Moscow, leaving his throne behind him (in 1564 he left Moscow for Aleksandrovskaia Sloboda) and nonetheless still remain Tsar.[82]

It is also significant that both Ivan and Peter should have named another man not only *Tsar,* but *saint;* their contemporaries—not without justification— saw overt blasphemy in this.[83] Bearing in mind the sacred nature of the title of Tsar, we can say that we have essentially the same type of behavior in both cases.

7. It should be borne in mind that any kind of masquerade or dressing up was inevitably thought of in early Russia as *anti-behavior;* i.e. a sinister, black-magic significance was attributed to it in principle. This is quite plain from the example of the mummers of Yuletide, Shrovetide, St. John's Night and other festivals, who, it was assumed (by participants in the masquerade as well as spectators!), depicted devils or unclean spirits; correspondingly, the dressing up was accompanied by extremes of disorderly behavior, often of an overtly blasphemous character.[84]

This is how imposture too, and, evidently, "the game of Tsar," was perceived in early Russia. Dressing up in the Tsar's clothes should be seen in this context as a typical case of anti-behavior, to which, on the level of content, there corresponds the blasphemous attempt to procure sacred attributes through outer simulation. It is no accident that Ivan and Peter took part in this masquerade, for they were both Tsars of whom anti-behavior was on the whole typical, whether expressed by dressing up or by the blasphemous imitation of church rituals—cf. in this connection Ivan's *"oprichnyi* monastery"[85] and Peter's "All-Jesting Council."[86] In this sense the link between the installation of Simeon Bekbulatovich as Tsar and the institution of the *oprichnina* [or *oprichina*], mentioned above is highly typical: the word *oprichnina* means both "separate, unconnected," and at the same time "on the outside" [*kromeshnoe*]; it is, therefore, by the same token connected with the *other world,* the travesty element of demons. Thus the *oprichniki* were seen as *kromeshniki* [people on the outside] (cf. *t`ma kromeshnaia* [outer darkness] as a term for purgatory), i.e. as special kinds of mummers, who assumed diabolical appearance and diabolical behavior.[87] And indeed the manner in which the *oprichniki* acted recalls the behavior of mummers at Yuletide or other festivals; thus, Ivan's *oprichnyi* monastery in Aleksandrovskaia Sloboda—in which the *oprichniki* dressed up in monks' habits and the Tsar called himself the Abbot of this carnival monastery—would seem in all probability to have arisen under the influence of those Yuletide games of which the icon-painter of Viaz`ma, the *starets* Grigorii, wrote in 1651, in his petition to Tsar Aleksei Mikhailovich. In Viaz`ma, he wrote,

> there are various vile games from Christmas Day to the vigils of epiphany, during which the participants designate some of their number as saints, invent their own monasteries and name for them an archimandrite, a cellarer and startsy.[88]

In exactly the same way the blasphemous entertainments indulged in by Peter, exemplified above all by the ceremonies of the All-Jesting Council, were originally intended primarily for Yuletide and Shrovetide (they soon, however, extended to the whole period from Christmas to Lent), and correspondingly contained elements of Yuletide and Shrovetide ritualism.[89] It should be noted in addition that by forcing his people to wear "German," i.e. European, clothes, Peter had in the eyes of his contemporaries transformed his entourage into mummers (just as Ivan's *oprichniki* had appeared in their time as mummers too): it was said that Peter had "dressed people up as devils."[90] Indeed, European dress in pre-Petrine times was perceived as a "mockery," a masquerade, and in icons devils could be depicted in German or Polish dress.[91]

By the same token, royal imposture as a specific type of behavior falls wholly into the traditional Russian situation which presupposes, along with correct, normative behavior, some form or other of anti-behavior[92]; in other words royal imposture is part of the tradition of anti-behavior in Russia.

8. Royal imposture, then, is perceived in early Russia as anti-behavior. The fact that the False Dmitrii was regarded as a sorcerer ("a heretic"), i.e. that features characteristic of the behavior of sorcerers were ascribed to him in the popular consciousness, is indicative of this. Indeed, it is precisely this kind of view which is reflected in historical songs about the False Dmitrii, for example:

> *The unfrocked Grishka, son of Otrep`ev, stands*
> *Before his crystal mirror*
> *And in his hands he holds a book of magic*
> *And casts spells, this unfrocked Grishka, son of Otrep`ev;[93]*

And:

> *He distributes Lenten food to the people,*
> *While he himself eats non-Lenten food [on a Friday!];*

> *He makes his bed on the icons there are around him*
> *And tramples underfoot the miracle-working crosses.*[94]

Similar views were seemingly held even during the False Dmitrii's lifetime: an anonymous account of 1605 states that after the False Dmitrii's appearance in the political arena Boris Godunov sent emissaries to the Polish Sejm and "they spread the rumor that Dmitrii is the son of a priest and is a widely-known sorcerer." Later on, the same rumor was put about by Boris in Moscow, too; from the same account we learn that on his way to Moscow the False Dmitrii captured Grishka Otrep'ev, "the great and widely known magician, of whom the tyrant Boris spread the rumour that he was the real Dmitrii."[95] In any case the evidence provided by folklore sources is thoroughly corroborated by the tales about the Time of Troubles,* in which, for example, we find the "heretical book" (i.e. book of magic or sorcery) which the False Dmitrii was said to be constantly reading;[96] it is stated that he began "to eat veal and other unclean foods on Wednesdays and Fridays."[97] No less characteristic are the rumours that a *skomorokh's* mask hung instead of icons on the False Dmitrii's wall, and that icons lay about under his bed;[98] *skomorokhi* and sorcerers were identified with each other in early Russia, and it was believed that, during the act of sorcery icons were placed on the ground, icons or the cross were trodden on, and so on.[99]

Historical songs about the False Dmitrii tell of how he sets off to the bathhouse at the time when people are going to church; this is also a characteristic behavior of sorcerers, inasmuch as in early Russia the bathhouse was thought of as an "unclean place," a kind of antipode to the church—and hence sorcerers could be recognized by the fact that they went to the bathhouse instead of going to church.[100] See, for example:

> *The time had come for the Great Day,*
> *For the Great Day, for Christ's Day,*
> *And in Ivan-the-Great's bell-tower*
> *The biggest bell of all was rung.*
> *All the boyar-princes went to the liturgy,*
> *To Christ's midnight Easter service,*
> *But that thief Grishka the Unfrocked went to the bathhouse*
> *With his sweetheart Marinushka Iur'evna.*
> *All the boyar-princes are praying to God;*

---

* The period between the death of Fedor (eldest son of Ivan the Terrible) in 1598 and the accession of Mikhail Romanov in 1613.

That thief Grishka the Unfrocked is washing in the bathhouse
And fornicating with his sweetheart Marinushka.
The boyar-princes come back from the service;
That thief Grishka the Unfrocked comes from the bathhouse
With his sweetheart Marinushka Iur`evna.[101]

Cf.:

All the people went to Christian mass,
But Grishka the Unfrocked and his Tsarina Marishka,
Marina Ivanovna, daughter of the Prince of Lithuania—
They didn't go to Christian mass;
They went to the steam-baths,
To the clean wash-tub,
And steamed themselves in the steam-bath.
They washed themselves in the wash-tub
During Christ's midnight Easter service.
The people come away from Christian mass,
But Grishka the Unfrocked comes from the steam-bath
With his Tsarina Marina Ivanovna.[102]

The description of the model intended to represent hell, which the False Dmitrii is supposed to have erected for his amusement, is particularly interesting in this connection. In the *Tale of the Reign of Tsar Fedor Ioannovich:* we read:

And so that accursed heretic, ever thirsty for power in this brief life and in the one to come, built for himself the image of his eternal dwelling, the like of which has never been in the realm of Russia since the beginning of the world; what he desired, that did he inherit. He made a great pit right opposite his palace on the other side of the Moscow river and placed a great cauldron of pitch there, prefiguring his own future place, and placed above it three great and awesome bronze heads; their teeth were made of iron and inside there was noise and clanging, and by some cunning contrivance the jaws were made to yawn open like the jaws of hell, and the teeth were pointed and the claws were like sharp sickles ready to clutch at you. When they began to yawn it was as if a flame spurted out of the gullet; sparks were continually shooting out of the nostrils and smoke was ceaselessly issuing from the ears. From inside each head could be heard a great noise and clanging, and people looking at it were terrified. And out of the mouth hung down a great tongue, at the end of which was an asp's head, which looked as if it wanted to swallow you up. The accursed one, foretelling his eternal dwelling-place with his father the Devil and Satan, was very fond of that hellish place and was always looking at it out of his palace windows, so as to achieve his heart's desire, the outer darkness of hell; and what he coveted, that did he inherit. And that accursed heretic ordered those Orthodox Christians who denounced his accursed heresy to be thrown into it to their death.[103]

This description corresponds fairly closely to the iconographic representation of hell as a fire-breathing serpent (see such depictions on Russian icons of the Last Judgement, for example).

The False Dmitrii was accordingly given a sorcerer's burial: whereas his accomplice, Basmanov, who was killed together with him, was buried near a church, the False Dmitrii was buried in a "God's house" [*ubogii dom*] or *skudel'nitsa* (i.e. where suicides were buried).[104] Subsequently, however, the corpse was exhumed and burnt.[105] The reason for the exhumation was doubtless the idea that the earth would not accept the body of a sorcerer, i.e. the earth's anger was feared.[106] Compare also the statement that when the False Dmitrii's body was exhibited "for shame," before being interred,

> the earth itself did abhor it, and the beasts and the birds abhorred such a foul body and would not come to eat of it . . . the earth disdained to carry upon it the accursed and vile corpse, and the air was poisoned and would not send rain from the heavens; where the accursed corpse lay, the earth brought forth no fruit and the sun would not shine because of the foul stench, and the stench covered all the fruits and they dried up; and the Lord took away from the earth both wheat and grapes until the corpse had disappeared.[107]

Foreigners' accounts of the vilification of the False Dmitrii's body are also significant:

> for further ridicule they threw a hideous and shameless *mask* on the belly of the dead sovereign . . . , and stuffed a reed-pipe into his mouth . . . with which to bribe the door-keeper of Hell.[108]

The mask and the pipe were seen as the attributes of the inverted world of the sorcerer and were intended to demonstrate the False Dmitrii's adherence to that world; at the same time we see here an exchange between top and bottom, which is characteristic of mummers who aim to resemble unclean spirits.[109] Compare also the characteristic rumours of devils playing like *skomorokhi* over the False Dmitrii's body:

> And as his body lay in the field many people in the middle of the night, even until cockcrow, heard much dancing and playing of bells and pipes, and other devilish games being enacted over his accursed body; for Satan himself was rejoicing at his coming . . . [110]

It is characteristic that even the False Dmitrii, recognizing Boris Godunov as
a false Tsar, i.e. a pretender (he ordered his body to be transferred from the
Arkhangel`skii Cathedral and interred outside the Kremlin, in the Church of
St. Ambrose), should see a sorcerer in him and "fearing spells and magic, gave
orders to demolish . . . to its foundations" Boris's palace.[111]

Pretenders, then, are perceived as sorcerers, and elements of anti-behavior
are attributed to them. And conversely Peter the Great, whose conduct seemed
to his contemporaries nothing more nor less than anti-behavior,[112] is perceived
essentially as a pretender: popular rumour, even during Peter's lifetime,
proclaimed him to be not a genuine ("natural") Tsar, but rather *a substitute
Tsar* who had no right to the throne. Here, for example, is one of the many
testimonies which express just such a view: in 1722

> the *staritsa* Platonida said of his Imperial Majesty: *he is a Swede put in the place
> of the Tsar,* for just fancy—he does what is displeasing to God; christenings
> and weddings are celebrated 'against the sun';[113] and images are painted of
> Swedish people,[114] and he does not abstain during Lent,[115] and he has taken
> a liking to Swedish dress,[116] and he eats and drinks with Swedes and will not
> leave their kingdom . . . [117] and the Grand Prince Peter Alekseevich was born
> already with teeth of a Swedish woman, he is the Antichrist.[118]

Rumors to the effect that a substitute had been exchanged for the
real Tsar (either while he was abroad or else in infancy) and that another
man sat upon the throne in his stead—i.e. a pretender, a Tsar in outward
appearance only—were widespread in Peter's reign and were extraordinarily
persistent.[117] These rumors stimulated the appearance of a whole succession
of pretenders who played the role of the legitimate heir of the authentic, real
Peter; for the most part they were False Alekseis, giving themselves the name
of the Tsarevich Aleksei Petrovich.[120] It is remarkable that the first False
Aleksei appeared even during the lifetime of Aleksei Petrovich (in 1712, i.e.
six years before his execution).[121] This seemingly testifies to the fact that
viewing Peter as a "substituted" Tsar could be transferred to his son: in as
much as Peter is seen as a false Tsar, his son may be seen as the false heir;
it was presumed that the real Peter had a real heir who was called Aleksei
Petrovich.[122] The absence of pretenders playing the role of Peter himself is
entirely understandable if we bear in mind the widespread opinion that Peter
had been *killed* when he was "substituted"; this opinion is one component of
the legend of the "substitute" Tsar.[123]

Thus, along with the myth of the return of the Tsar-Deliverer (which
has been analysed in connection with the question of royal imposture by

K. V. Chistov), there existed the fairly persistent myth of the *pretender on the throne,* which was based on a specifically Russian concept of royal power, i.e. on the distinction between true and false Tsars. The coexistence of these myths considerably assisted the spread of royal imposture in early Russia.

Translated by David Budgen

NOTES

1 K. V. Chistov, *Russkie narodnye sotsial`no-utopicheskie legendy* (Moscow, 1967) 29.

2 V. O. Kliuchevskii, *Sochineniia* (Moscow, 1956-1959), vol. III, 27.

3 K. V. Chistov, *Russkie narodnye sotsial`no-utopicheskie* legendy, 32, 179-180.

4 Ibid.

5 On the history of the process of sacralization of monarchic power in Russia, see B. A. Uspenskij, V. M. Zhivov, "Tsar and God," in this volume, 1-112.

6 Feofan Prokopovich specifically justifies the legitimacy of such a title in his *Discourse on the Tsar's Power and Honour* and subsequently in his *Inquiry upon the Pontifex* and *Discourse on the Coronation Day of Catherine the First.* See Feofan Prokopovich, *Arkhiepiskopa Velikogo Novagrada i Velikikh Luk, Sviateishago Pravitel`stvuiushchego Sinoda Vitse prezidenta, a potom pervenstvuiushchego Chlena Slova i rechi pouchitel`nyia, pokhval`nyia i pozdravitel`nyia* (St. Petersburg, 1760-1768), part I, 252; part II, 178-179; Idem, *Rozysk istoricheskii, koikh radi vin, i v iazykovom razume byli i naritsalis` imperatory rimstii, kak iazychestii, tak i khristianstii, pontifeksami ili arkhiereiami mnogobozhnogo zakona* (St. Petersburg, 1721), 37. For the history of the naming of the Russian monarch as "Christ," see especially B. A. Uspenskij, V. M. Zhivov, "Tsar and God," in this volume, 25.

7 The religious connotation of the word "tsar" can be traced back also in sporadic instances of its use in the titles of the Russian princes before the title of Tsar was officially assumed. See Wladimir Vodoff, "Remarques sur la valeur du term 'tsar' applique aux princes Russes avant le milieu du XV siecle," *Oxford Slavonic Papers* 11 (1978).

8 Quoted in N. Ustrialov, *Skazaniia sovremennikov o Dmitrii Samozvantse* (St. Petersburg, 1859), part I, 254—translation from the French; Margeret's spelling of titles has been preserved.

9 Archpriest Avvakum wrote in his exegesis of Psalm XLIV: "Christ . . . by command of the Father on high is anointed by the Holy Ghost and is filled with grace and truth. It is for this reason that he is called Christ, or the Anointed One, or Tsar." See *Russkaia istoricheskaia biblioteka, izdavaemaia Arkheografícheskoiu komissieiu* (St. Petersburg, Petrograd, Leningrad, 1872-1927), vol. XXXIX, 459.

10 The opposition between the "corruptible Tsar" and the "incorruptible" one (God) dates from a work by the sixth century Byzantine writer Agapetos, which was widely quoted in early Russian writing. The twenty-first chapter of this work, in which it is said that the Tsar is like men in his corruptible nature, but like God in his power, found its way into the early Russian *The Bee* [*Pchela*] (V. Semenov, *Drevniaia russkaia Pchela po*

pergamennomu spisku (St. Petersburg, 1893), 111-112). We find reflections of this opposition in the chronicle story of the murder of Andrei Bogoliubskii (*Polnoe sobranie russkikh letopisei* (St. Petersburg, Petrograd, Leningrad, Moscow, 1841-1989), vol. I, 370; vol. II, 592); in an extract from Iosif Volotskii's *Letter to the Grand Prince* (*Poslaniia Iosifa Volotskogo* (Moscow, Leningrad, 1959), 184); and in the sixteenth discourse of the same author's *Enlightener [Prosvetitel`]* (Iosif Volotskii, *Prosvetitel`* (Kazan, 1855), 602). In the latter the monarch is directly named "corruptible [mortal] tsar" (Ibid., 420). Aleksei Mikhailovich often called himself this, for example in his epistle to the Troitse-Sergievo Monastery of 1661 (*Akty, sobrannye v bibliotekakh i arkhivakh Rossiiskoi imperii Arkheograficheskoi ekspeditsieiu imp. Akademii nauk* (St. Petersburg, 1836), vol. IV, no. 127, 172).

11   The practice of calling the Tsar "earthly God" is also Byzantine in origin (cf. the same appelation in the works of the eleventh century Byzantine writer Kekavmenos: *Sovety i rasskazy Kekavmena. Sochinenie vizantiiskogo polkovodtsa XI v.* (Moscow, 1972), 275). Foreigners were the first to report that the Russians considered their Tsar to be the "earthly God," e.g. Pastor Oderborn in his pamphlet on Ivan the Terrible in 1588 ("*Irrdliche Gott*": see P. Oderbornius, *Wunderbare, Erschreckliche, Unerhörte Geschichte, und warhaffte Historien: Nemlich, Des nechst gewesenen Großfürsten in der Moschkaw, Joan Basilidis, (auff jre Sprach Iwan Basilowitz genandt) Leben* (Hörlitz, 1588), d 3; in the Latin edition the word used for this quality is *divinitas*: see Paul Oderborn, *Ioannis Basilidis Magni Moscoviae Ducis Vita* (Wittenberg: heirs of Johann Crato, 1585), x 4); cf. Isaac Massa in his description of Siberia of 1612 (M. P. Alekseev, *Sibir` v izvestiiakh zapadnoevropeiskikh puteshestvennikov i pisatelei* (Irkutsk, 1932), 252); Iurii Krilsanich in his *Politika* of 1663-1666 (Iurii Krilsanich, *Politika* (Moscow, 1965), 206). In Russian sources the title of "earthly God" or "earthly divinity" as applied to the monarch is recorded later, from the mid-eighteenth century onwards (see B. A. Uspenskij, V. M. Zhivov, "Tsar and God," in this volume, 30-33).

12   "Righteous sun" is a name often given to Christ in liturgical texts (see, for example, the Christmas troparion, the troparion for the feast of the Purification of the Mother of God, the fourth and fifth verses of the Easter canon, etc.). In the new edition of the liturgical texlts established after Patriarch Nikon's reforms, the corresponding expression is "sun of righteousness" (cf. Malachi 4:2).

13   N. T. Voitovich, *Barkalabauska letapis* (Minsk, 1977),198.

14   Cf. Simeon Polotskii's address to Tsar Aleksei Mikhailovich of 1656: "We greet you, Orthodox Tsar, righteous sun" (I. Tatarskii, *Simeon Polotskii (ego zhizn` i deiatel`nost`). Opyt issledovaniia iz istorii prosveshcheniia i vnutrennei tserkovnoi zhizni vo vtoruiu polovinu XVII veka* (Moscow, 1886), 49).

15   V. Kel`siev, *Sbornik pravitel`stvennykh svedenii o raskol`nikakh* (London, 1860-186), vyp. III, 62-98.

16   Ibid., 75, 81.

17   Ibid., 63, 81, 106-107. "The *skoptsy* believe that their Redeemer [Kondratii Selivanov] was incarnate of the Empress Elizabeth Petrovna, of blessed memory, who, according to their mythology, was like the real Mother of God, a pure virgin at the birth, before the birth and after the birth, since she conceived and bore the Redeemer, according to the Gospel, not from the will of the flesh, but from the Holy Ghost. The most widely held opinion among them is that the Empress Elizabeth was delivered of her burden in Holstein, and then, on her return to Russia, being predestined for a saintly and ascetic life, in fact ruled for only two years (although others maintain she did not

rule at all) and gave up her throne to one of her favorites who bore a perfect likeness to her in both her facial features and her spiritual virtues—while she herself retired to the province of Orel, where she settled in the house of a peasant *skopets* and lived out the remainder of her days under the name of a simple peasant woman, Akulina Ivanovna, in fasting, prayer and good works, and on her death was buried in the garden there, where her relics remain to this day. Other *skoptsy* relate that Elizabeth Petrovna's delivery took place in Russia, and that her son, Peter III, the Redeemer, was despatched the moment he was born to Holstein, where on reaching adolescence, he underwent castration." (Ibid., 63).

[18] Ibid., 108.

[19] See N. N. Pokrovskii, "Sibirskii Il`ia-prorok pered voennym sudom prosveshchennogo absoliutizma," *Izvestiia Sibirskogo otdeleniia AN SSSR. Ser. obshchestvennykh nauk* 6, vyp. 2 (1972).

[20] When in the 1790's Kondratii Selivanov was in hiding from the authorities among the Fedoseev Old Believers of the Moscow province, he was treated with great respect, since he led an ascetic life and kept silent. Subsequently, at the investigation, the Old Believer Ivan Gavrilov testified as follows: "We called him, in our local speech, Elijah the Prophet, or Enoch, or John the Divine" (P. I. Mel`nikov, "Materialy dlia istorii khlystovskoi i skopcheskoi eresi," *Chteniia v Obshchestve istorii i drevnostei rossiiskikh* 3 (1872): 47). This could not possibly be simply a rhetorical trope, since such appellations would normally be totally inadmissible among the Old Believers (they consider it sinful, for example, to call people by the sobriquets of their patron saints: to address Nikita, say, as "Nikita Sokrovennyi [the Concealed]," if his nameday is the day of the Holy Nikita Sokrovennyi; see P. I. Mel`nikov (Andrei Pecherskii), *Polnoe sobranie sochinenii* (St. Petersburg, 1897-1898), vol. IV, 251). It is characteristic in this context that Kondratii Selivanov should have proclaimed himself not only God and Tsar, but prophet too, stating that: "I am God of Gods, Tsar of Tsars and prophet of prophets" (V. Kel`siev, *Sbornik pravitel`stvennykh svedenii o raskol`nikakh*, vyp. III, 81; appendices, 12).

[21] S. M. Solov`ev, *Istoriia Rossii* (Moscow, 1962-1966), vol. VII, 429.

[22] V. G. Druzhinin, *Raskol na Donu v kontse XVII veka* (St. Petersburg, 1889), 97, 148, 267, 277.

[23] That is, Prince Michael, mentioned in the Old Testament; according to the prophecy of Daniel, he was called upon to destroy the unfaithful (Daniel 12, 1). Concerning the legend of Tsar Mikhail, see A. N. Veselovskii, "Opyty po istorii khristianskoi legendy," *Zhurnal Mimisterstva narodnogo prosveshcheniia,* April-May (1875); V.Istrin, *Otkrovenie Mefodiia Patarskogo i apokrificheskie videniia Daniila v vizantiiskoi i slaviano-russkoi literaturakh. Issledovaniia i teksty* (Moscow, 1897), 180 ff.; cf. the evidence of Kuz`ma Kosoi at the investigation in 1687: "He claims to be Grand Duke Mikhail and, on the evidence of the Holy Scripture and the testimony of various holy books, the Lord God Our Saviour Himself" (V. G. Druzhinin, *Raskol na* Donu, 277). In defence of his plenary powers Kuz`ma Kosoi stated that he had a book which was written in God's own hand before the making of the world and the creation of the universe, and showed a transcript from this book (Ibid., 97; cf. Supplement to *Akty istoricheskie, sobrannye i izdannye Arkheograficheskoiu komissieiu* (St. Petersburg, 1841-1842), vol. XII, no. 17, 133).

[24] K. V. Chistov, *Russkie narodnye sotsial`no-utopicheskie legendy*, 90; cf. Supplement to *Akty istoricheskie*, vol. XII, no. 17, 139. In addition, the biblical Prince Michael, mentioned in the Book of the Prophet Daniel, could be associated with the Archangel Michael

and at the same time with the Tsar Mikhail Fedorovich, the founder of the Romanov dynasty. Thus a founder of the Old Believers, Father Lazar̀, compared Mikhail Fedorovich with the legendary Tsar (Prince) Michael (N. Subbotin, ed., *Materialy dlia istorii raskola za pervoe vremia ego sushchestvovaniia, izdavaemye bratstvom sv. Petra mitropolita* (Moscow, 1875-1890), vol. V, 225), while a certain Old Believer, Martyn son of Kuz̀ma, stated under torture in 1682: "when Tsar Michail Fedorovich reigned, it was not he, but the Archangel Michael" (S. M. Solov̀ev, *Istoriia Rossii*, vol. VII, 428). As N. N. Pokrovskii points out, the legend of the Tsar Mikhail "unleashed on the reigning tsar (and sometimes the entire dynasty after Aleksei Mikhailovich) an enormous accumulation of eschatological views which had grown up over the centuries in popular consciousness" (Ia.N. Pokrovskii, "Predstavleniia krest̀ian-staroobriadtsev Urala i Sibiri XVIII veka o svetskikh vlastiakh," in *Ezhegodnik po agrarnoi istorii Vostochnoi Evropy, 1971 g.* (Vilnius, 1974), 167).

25   *Russkaia istoricheskaia biblioteka*, vol. XIII, 300, 393.

26   Ibid., 351.

27   Ibid., 326, 336, 356.

28   V. Val̀denberg, *Drevnerusskie ucheniia o predelakh tsarskoi vlasti* (Petrograd, 1916), 362, 364, 365, 369, 372.

29   *Russkaia istoricheskaia biblioteka*, vol. XIII, 1237.

30   Ibid., 1247.

31   V. Val̀denberg, *Drevnerusskie ucheniia*, 366.

32   *Polnoe sobranie russkikh letopisei*, vol. VI, 228; vol. VIII, 211.

33   *Akty istoricheskie,*, vol. I, no. 40, 79, 82. The "spiritual blindness" of Dmitrii Shemiaka is evidently contrasted here with the physical blindness of Vasilii the Blind (whom Shemiaka blinded in 1446).

34   See especially the *Discourse Selected from the Holy Scriptures which is in Latin* [Slovo izbranno ot sviatykh pisanii ezhe na latyne] (1460-1461) in the edition of A. Popov, *Istoriko-literaturnyi obzor drevnerusskikh polemicheskikh sochinenii protiv latinian (XI-XV v.)* (Moscow, 1875), 384, 394. (Prince Vasilii is called "Tsar" in this work twelve times in all). The title of "Tsar" applied to Vasilii the Blind is used also by Metropolitan Iona in his epistle to Pskov (*Russkaia istoricheskaia biblioteka*, vol. VI, no. 90, 673; though in the other copy of this epistle the words "of the Russian Tsar" as applied to Vasilij the Blind do not occur: see *Akty istoricheskie*, vol. I, no. 60, 107), and he is also called this in the chronicle for 1472 (*Polnoe sobranie russkikh letopisei*, vol. XXV, 260; A. Popov, *Istoriko-literaturnyi obzor*, 379). The history of Russian princes' being honored with the title of "Tsar" has been researched by Vodoff (see Wladimir Vodoff, "Remarques sur la valeur du term 'tsar' applique aux princes Russes avant le milieu du XV siecle"); for the term *samoderzhets* [autocrat] see V.Skol̀skii, *Uchastie russkogo dukhovenstva i monashestva v razvitii edinoderzhaviia i samoderzhaviia v Moskovskom gosudarstve v kontse XV i pervoi polovine XVI v.* (Kiev, 1902), 68n3; Ostrogorsky, G. "Zum Stratordienst des Herrscher in der byzantinisch-slavischen Welt," *Seminarium Kondakovianum* 7 (1935): 168.

35   See Iona's epistle to the Pskovians (*Russkaia istoricheskaia biblioteka*, vol. VI, no. 90, 673), supposedly dated 1461, but possibly earlier (on the question of the date see E. Golubinskii, *Istoriia russkoi tserkvi* (Moscow, 1917), vol. II, 498n2).

36   See Val̀denberg, *Drevnerusskie ucheniia*, 223-4.

37   See Ivan Timofeev's *Chronicle* (*Vremennik*), *Russkaia istoricheskaia biblioteka*, vol. XIII, 373.

38   Maxim the Greek wrote in his epistle (about 1545) to the young Ivan the Terrible that "the earthly Tsar was none other than the living and visible form (that is, the spirit embodied) of the Tsar of Heaven Himself" (Maksim Grek, *Sochineniia* (Kazan, 1859-1862), vol. II, 350; A. F. Ivanova *Slovar` govorov Podmoskov`ia* (Moscow, 1969), no. 217); and Metropolitan Filipp Kolychev said to Ivan: "If, O Tsar, you are revered as the image of God, you were nevertheless created with the clay of the earth" (V.Skol`skii, *Uchastie russkogo dukhovenstva i monashestva v razvitii edinoderzhaviia i samoderzhaviia v Moskovskom gosudarstve v kontse XV i pervoi polovine XVI v.*, 198). No less significant is the fact that Patriarch Nikon protested specifically at the Tsar's being called "God's likeness" (Zyzykin, M. V. *Patriarkh Nikon: ego gosudarstvennye i kanonicheskie idei* (Warsaw, 1931-1939) vol. II, 14). The Patriarch of Jerusalem, Dosifei (Dositheus), also links the righteousness of the Tsar with his status as the image of God in his document [*gramota*] to Tsar Fedor Alekseevich dated 27 June 1679 (Kapterev, N. F. "Snosheniia Ierusalimskikh patriarkhov s russkim pravitel`stvom," *Pravoslavnyi Palestinskii sbornik* 43 (1895): 239). This idea, generally, has its roots in Byzantium (see B. A. Uspenskij, V. M. Zhivov, "Tsar and God," in this volume, 43-44).

39   *Russkaia istoricheskaia biblioteka*, vol. XIII, 367.

40   K. V. Chistov, *Russkie narodnye sotsial`no-utopicheskie legendy*, 44, 66, 67, 71, 86, 118, 126, 127, 148-9, 185, 210.

41   Ibid., 126; G. V. Esipov, *Liudi starogo veka. Rasskazy iz del Preobrazhenskogo prikaza i Tainoi kantseliarii* (St. Petersburg, 1880), 434.

42   *Vosstanie Emel`iana Pugacheva. Sbornik dokumentov* (Leningrad, 1935), 123, 125126; K. V. Chistov, *Russkie narodnye sotsial`no-utopicheskie legendy*, 148-149.

43   Ibid., 185; B. Kubalov, "Sibir` i samozvantsy. Iz istorii narodnykh volnenii v XIX v.," *Sibirskie ogni* 3 (1924): 167.

44   K. V. Chistov, *Russkie narodnye sotsial`no-utopicheskie legendy*, 210. This motif of the "royal marks" turns up unexpectedly after the French Revolution, when a runaway French convict appeared in Russia exhibiting a royal lily (the mark with which capital offenders were branded in pre-Revolutionary France) and went around assuring Russian landowners that this was how the princes of the blood were distinguished; this fabrication was remarkably successful (Léonce Pingaud, *Les Français en Russie et les Russes en France; l'ancien régime, l'émigration, les invasions* (Paris, 1886), 89; Iu.M. Lotman, *Roman A. S. Pushkina "Evgenii Onegin." Kommentarii* (Leningrad, 1980), 45). Ippolit Zavalishin (the brother of the Decembrist)—an adventurer who clearly believed in his own divine election—demanded upon his arrest that note be taken of special marks on his body: "that he had a birthmark in the form of a crown on his chest, and on his shoulders another in the form of a sceptre" (V. P. Kolesnikov, *Zapiski neschast-nogo, soderzhashchie puteshestvie v Sibir` po kanatu* (St. Petersburg, 1914), 22; see also Iu. M. Lotman, B. A. Uspenskii, *The Semiotics of Russian Culture*, Ann Shukman, editor (Ann Arbor, 1984), 202-204). Clearly belief in the royal marks was not only widespread among the common folk but was shared by very different classes of Russian society.

45   Ancient Rome provides us with a typologically similar picture: with the violation of the natural order of succession, the usurper or adopted son who gets the throne pretends to refuse power, i.e. does not consider himself Emperor, as it were, and in fact presents himself as a false monarch. He accepts power only when a sign from God (a victory over his rival, for example) or social opinion endorses his authority and his mystical power. It is precisely from the moment of this first manifestation of

supreme power that the days of his rule are calculated; and by the same token, the day of his predecessor's death does not always coincide with the successor's *dies imperii*; see J. Beranger, *Recherches sur l'aspect ideologique du principal* (Basel, 1953) (this book was kindly brought to my notice by M. L. Gasparov).

[46] On mythological identification in general, see Iu.M. Lotman, B. A. Uspenskii, "K semioticheskoi tipologii russkoi kul`tury XVIII veka," in *Khudozhestvennaia kul`tura XVIII veka (Materialy nauchnoi konferentsii 1973 g.)* (Moscow, 1974), 285, 296, 299, 300, passim.

[47] *Dokumenty stavki E. I. Pugacheva, povstancheskikh vlastei i uchrezhdenii. 1773-1774* (Moscow, 1975), 55, 57, 127-39, 152, passim; no. 50, 54, 156-76, 198, passim. Moreover, Zarubin-Chika was called Ivan Nikiforovich Chernyshev, in contrast with the real Count Zakhar Grigo`revich Chernyshev.

[48] See F. V. Livanov, *Raskol`niki i ostrozhniki. Ocherki i rasskazy* (St. Petersburg, 1868-1873), vol. I, 207-208; K. V. Chistov, *Russkie narodnye sotsial`no-utopicheskie legendy*, 182.

[49] Ibid.; F. V. Livanov, *Raskol`niki i ostrozhniki*, vol. I, 426.

[50] M. Babenchikov, "Portret Pugacheva v Istoricheskom muzee," *Literaturnoe nasledstvo* 9-10 (1933).

[51] The phenomenon of mythological identification is seen most graphically among the *skoptsy* and the *khlysty* who see in actual people the direct incarnation of the Lord of Sabaoth, of Christ or of the Mother of God, and give these people the corresponding names. In the same way the *Pavlikiane* ["Paulicians"] (who are in many ways similar to the *khlysty* and may well have a common origin) called themselves after the Apostle Paul and his disciples and fellow workers; they saw themselves as their incarnations (see Iu. Iavorskii, "Legenda o proiskhozhdenii pavlikian," in *Stat`i po slavianskoi filologii i russkoi slovesnosti (Sbornik statei v chest` akad. A. I. Sobolevskogo)* (Leningrad, 1928), 506).

[52] *Russkaia istoricheskaia biblioteka*, vol. IX, 550-551, 529.

[53] See I. I. Polosin, "'Igra v tsaria' (Otgoloski Smuty v moskovskom bytu XVII v.)," *Izvestiia Tverskogo pedagogicheskogo instituta* I (1926): 59-61.

[54] Ibid., 62.

[55] Compare, for example, the description of the Shrovetide processions in the reminiscences of A. K. Lelong: "At about two o'clock they would harness two or three sledges and on one of them would put a vat or barrel instead of a mattress, and on this would sit Vissarion Rodionovich: (a peasant) dressed up in a cloak made of matting and a hat, similarly adorned with bast feathers. He would ride on ahead, while other sleighs rode behind, full to bursting with our house servants, who would be singing and playing the accordion. This convoy would go round the whole village and be joined by other mummers from the village on their own sleighs; they would go round other villages, singing, and be joined by still more people on sleighs and in disguise. Under the leadership of our Vissarion. an enormous convoy would be formed" (A. K. Lelong, "Vospominaniia," *Russkii arkhiv* 6-7 (1913): 65). Just as characteristic was the custom of dressing up as a priest at the end of Shrovetide and imitating the church ritual of the burial service (see, for example, P. V. Shein, *Velikoruss v svoikh pesniakh, obriadakh, obychaiakh, verovaniiakh, skazkakh, legendakh i t.p.* (St. Petersburg, 1898-1900), 333; M. I. Smirnov, "Kul`t i krest`ianskoe khoziaistvo v Pereslavl`-Zalesskom uezde. Po etnograficheskim nabliudeniiam," in *Trudy Pereslavl`-Zalesskogo istoriko khudozhestvennogo i kraevednogo muzeia* (Pereslavl`-Zalesskii,1927), vyp. I, 22-23). The same kind of travesty can be observed in the Yuletide rituals as well (see V. E. Gusev,

"Ot obriada k narodnomu teatru (evoliutsiia sviatochnykh igr v pokoinika)," in *Fol`klor i etnografiia. Obriady i obriadovyi fol`klor* (Leningrad,1974); cf. the petition of the *starets* Grigorii, quoted below, which tells us that at Yuletide "they designate some of their number as saints, invent their own monasteries and name for them an archimandrite, a cellarer and *startsy*").

It is very significant that in the case of 1666 quoted above, there was a *maiden's* cap on the head of the peasant "Tsar" Pershka Iakovlev: dressing up in the clothes of the opposite sex—and especially men dressing up as women—is characteristic of mummers at Shrovetide, Yuletide and other times.

[56] D. K. Zelenin, *Velikorusskie skazki Permskoi gubernii. S prilozheniem dvenadtsati bashkirskikh skazok i odnoi meshcheriakskoi* (Petrograd, 1914), no. 40, 271.

[57] In connection with the "game of Tsar" Makarov's reminiscences of a certain landowner from Chukhloma are interesting: N. Makarov's story about a landowner from Chukhloma may be seen as an example of imitating the tsar's order, a peculiar type of "playing at tsar": "From a multitude of cynical and blasphemous pranks I will tell of one, known then in the Chukhloma district under the name of 'Entry into Jerusalem.' He once gathered his field and house serfs of both sexes, and even children, and lined them up in two rows between his estate and the nearest village, for a length of several hundred feet. He ordered each person to take a palm frond in their hand, and he himself, seated on an old nag, rode by slowly from the village to his estate between the rows of his subordinates, who waved their palm branches at him." See N. Makarov, *Moi semidesiatiletnie vospominaniia i s tem vmeste moia polnaia predsmertnaia ispoved`* (St. Petersburg, 1881-1882), part I, 28. Unfortunately, the memoirist makes no mention as to the season in which the performance took place. In as much as the Tsar is seen as a living image of God (see above), the "game of Tsar" is indirectly linked with the likeness to the Divinity; whereas what we have here is a *direct* imitation of God. It is not impossible that the behavior of this landowner reflects memories of the ritual "ride on a donkey" performed by the Patriarch on Palm Sunday (a ritual which had lapsed since 1696), or of the triumphal reception of Peter in Moscow after the victory of Poltava (December 21, 1709), when he was met by children dressed in servants' robes, waving palm branches and singing "Blessed is he that cometh in the name of the Lord"; in one instance Christ was represented by the Patriarch and in the other by the Tsar.

[58] A. I. Malein, trans. ed., *Novoe izvestie o Rossii vremeni Ivana Groznogo. "Skazanie" Al`berta Shlikhtinga* (Leningrad,1934), 22. A similar account of I. P. Fedorov's execution is given by Oderborn (P. Oderbornius, *Wunderbare, Erschreckliche, Unerhörte Geschichte, und warhaffte Historien*, f.v. M3, fo. R2-f.v. R2; Veronensis Alexander Gwagnmus, *Sarmatiae Europeae decriptio, quae Regnum Poloniam, Lituaniam, Samogitiam, Russiam, Masoviam, Prussiam, Pomeraniam, Livoniam et Moschoviae, Tartariaeque partem complectitur...* ([Cracovia], 1578), f.v. 28·f.v. 30). See also N. M. Karamzin *Istoriia gosudarstva Rossiiskogo* (St. Petersburg, 1892), vol. IX, 113; for typological analogies see O. M. Freidenberg, "Proiskhozhdenie parodii," *Trudy po znakovym sistemam* VI (1973): 492.

[59] In addition this disguise very often bears the character of a symbolic *unmasking*. Thus, for example, when in 1570 Ivan the Terrible flew into a rage with the Archbishop of Novgorod, Pimen the Black, he ordered him to be arrayed as a *skomorokh*. Cf. Shlikhting's account: ". . . he ordered that his tiara be snatched from his head; he also divested him of his episcopal vestments as well as stripping him of his rank as a bishop, saying: 'It is not fitting that you be a bishop, but rather a *skomorokh*. Therefore

I will give you a wife in marriage.' The tyrant ordered that a mare be brought forth, and turning to the bishop said: 'Receive from me this wife, mount her now, saddle her, set out for Muscovy and enter your name on the reigster of the *skomorokhi.*' Then, when the bishop had climbed on the mare Ivan ordered that his feet be tied to the animal's back; and having sent him out of town in this fashion, he commanded him to follow the Moscow road. When he had already gone some way, Ivan sent for him to appear before him again and gave him a musical instrument to hold, bagpipes and a stringed lyre. 'Practice in this art,' said the tyrant, 'for there is nothing more for you to do, especially now that you have taken a wife.' And so this bishop, who had no idea before this of how to play the lyre, rode off on the command of the tyrant in the direction of Moscow on the back of the mare, strumming on the lyre and blowing the pipes" (A. I. Malein, trans. ed., *Novoe izvestie o Rossii*, 29-30; cf. N. M. Karamzin *Istoriia gosudarstva Rossiiskogo*, vol. IX, 172). According to other sources the Tsar threatened the Archbishop that he would make him lead a bear about, as the *skomorokhi* do (Veronensis Alexander Gwagnmus, *Sarmatiae Europeae decriptio*, fol. 34-35; Adam Olearii, *Opisanie puteshestviia v Moskoviiu i cherez Moskoviiu v Persiiu i obratno* (St. Petersburg, 1906), 127-129). The priest-figure and the *skomorokh* are perceived as antipodes, and by dressing the archbishop up as a *skomorokh,* Ivan is, as it were, attaching him to the inverted world of anti-behavior: if the mummers during the Yuletide and Shrovetide rituals can dress up as priests (see above), then here we have a case of the opposite — of a priest becoming a mummer.

60   For a discussion of the similarities and differences between Ivan's behavior and that of the Holy fool (*iurodivyi*), see Iu. M. Lotman, B. A. Uspenskii, *The Semiotics of Russian Culture*, Part I, Chap. 2.

61   S. M. Solov`ev, *Istoriia Rossii*, vol. III, 565; Ia.V. Lileev, *Simeon Bekbulatovich khan Kasimovskii, velikii kniaz` vseia Rusi, vposledstvii velikii kniaz` Tverskoi. 1567-1616 g. (Istoricheskii ocherk)* (Tver, 1891), 25-26; A. Nikolaev, "Simeon Bekbulatovich" in *Russkii biograficheskii slovar`* (St. Petersburg, 1904), 466-467. Cf. the petition handed to Simeon Bekbulatovich by Ivan the Terrible and his sons on October 30, 1575, which observes all the rules of epistolary etiquette laid down for addressing the monarch: "Unworthy Ivan Vasil`ev and his children, little Ivan and little Fedor, do petition thee, great Lord and Prince Semion [sic] Bekbulatovich of all Russia, that thou, O Lord, shouldst show them mercy . . ." The petition concludes in the manner proper in such cases with the words: "How, O Lord, dost thou decree? We petition thee, O Lord, for everything. O Lord, have mercy, take pity!" (*Poslaniia Ivana Groznogo* (Moscow-Leningrad, 1951), 195-196).

62   Ia.V. Lileev, *Simeon Bekbulatovich*, 26, 36; cf. however A. Nikolaev, "Simeon Bekbula-tovich," 467-468.

63   The fact that Simeon Bekbulatovich was legitimately installed as Tsar is confirmed by the latest text of the oath of allegiance to Boris Godunov (in 1598) and to his son Fedor Borisovich (in 1605): those swearing allegiance undertook not to wish "the Tsar Simeon Bekbulatovich" to be ruler of Moscow (S. M. Solov`ev, *Istoriia Rossii*, vol. IV, 353,421). It is also significant that the False Dmitrii ordered Simeon Bekbulatovich to take the tonsure, seeing in him a claimant to the throne (A. Nikolaev, "Simeon Bekbulatovich," 470).

64   Cf. the evidence of the Chronicles: "And so Tsar Ivan Vasil`evich became an ally of those who do multiply the sins of Orthodox Christianity and was filled with anger and violence: he began maliciously and mercilessly to persecute the serfs in his power and to shed their blood; and the kingdom which was entrusted to him by God he divided

into two parts: one part he made over to himself, and the other he entrusted to Tsar Simeon of Kazan̄. Then he went away from several small towns and went to one called Staritso, where he took up residence. He called his half the *oprichniki* and Tsar Simeon's part the *zemshchina;* and he ordered his half to assault, slaughter and plunder the other half . . ." (S. M. Solov̄ev, *Istoriia Rossii*, vol. III, 733n85; cf. K. Popov, "Chin sviashchennogo koronovaniia (istoricheskii ocherk obrazovaniia china)." *Bogoslovskii vestnik* II (1896): 284; Ia.V. Lileev, *Simeon Bekbulatovich*, 22-23). See also the commentary by Ia. S. Lur̄e in *Poslaniia Ivana Groznogo*, 634n2. Simeon Bekbulatovich ruled from October 1575 to July 1576.

65 The term *oprichnina* was not invented by Ivan the Terrible: it is met earlier in business documents, signifying a separate territory (see Ia.I. Sreznevskii, *Materialy dlia slovaria drevnerusskogo iazyka po pis̄mennym pamiatnikam* (St. Petersburg, 1893-1912), vol. II, 694; A. Diuvernua, *Materialy dlia slovaria drevnerusskogo iazyka* (Moscow, 1894), 122; S. M. Solov̄ev, *Istoriia Rossii*, vol. II, 484). However, in Ivan's time—and possibly even earlier—the word had a second meaning associated with the "outer [darkness]" *[kromeshnyi]*, i.e. the inverted, demonic principle; this will be discussed in more detail below.

66 See S. B. Veselovskii, *Issledovaniia po istorii klassa sluzhilykh zemlevladel̄tsev* (Moscow, 1969), 93-94.

67 The naming of the Tatar Khan as "Tsar" was reflected in the title of the Russian monarch. Thus, Ivan the Terrible and the Russian monarchs following him were called "Tsar of Kazan̄" and "Tsar of Astrakhan̄" (after the capture of Kazan̄ in 1552 and of Astrakhan̄ in 1557): the Khanate (or kingdom) of Kazan̄ split away from the Golden Horde in 1445 and that of Astrakhan̄ came into being after the collapse of the Golden Horde in 1480, i.e. both Khanates were in one way or another connected with the Golden Horde.

68 Ia.V. Lileev, *Simeon Bekbulatovich*, 3; A. Nikolaev, "Simeon Bekbulatovich," 466.

69 In his capacity of Khan of Kasimov, Simeon Bekbulatovich was related by direct line of succession to the Khans of the Golden Horde and was called Tsar even before he was installed on the Russian throne (see V. V. Vel̄iaminov-Zernov, *Issledovanie o kasimovskikh tsariakh i tsarevichakh* (St. Petersburg, 1863-1866), vol. II, 1, 13-14, 15-16, 20-21, 25). Ivan the Terrible made him Tsar or Khan of Kasimov in 1567; prior to this he was called, like his father, Tsarevich: evidently in his capacity as descendant of the Khans (or Tsars) of the Golden Horde. The rulers of the kingdom of Kasimov in general held the title of Tsarevich, except for those who were already Khans before their installation as ruler of Kasimov; these retained the title of Tsar (Khan). Simeon Bekbulatovich (even before he was converted to Orthodoxy and while he still bore the name Sain-bulat) was the first ruler of Kasimov personally to receive the title of Tsar (Khan). See Ibid., 25-26.

The kingdom of Kasimov was created by Vasilii the Blind in 1452 as a reaction to the recently formed kingdom (or Khanate) of Kazan̄, and the rulers of Kasimov were appointed by the ruler of Moscow: power was not hereditary and was conferred on the person who was considered most useful to Moscow. Kasimov (the former town of Gorodets) was so named in the same year, 1452, after the prince of the Golden Horde, Kasim, the son of the Khan Udu-Mukhammed, who went over to Vasilii the Blind in 1446, for protection against his brother Mukhmutek, the Khan of Kazan̄ (immediately after the latter had formed the kingdom of Kazan̄ in the autumn of 1445:

see V. V. Vel`iaminov-Zernov, *Issledovanie o kasimovskikh tsariakh*, vol. I, 3-4). In 1449 Kasim defeated the troops of the Khan of the Golden Horde, Seid-Akhmat, and in 1467 led an unsuccessful campaign against Kazan`. Thus the kingdom of Kasimov may be seen as a kind of Muscovite model of the Golden Horde.

70 The assumption by the Russian Grand Prince of the title of Tsar is connected with the fall of the Byzantine Empire, an event which led to the idea of Moscow as the new Constantinople, or the Third Rome (see Iu. M. Lotman, B. A. Uspenskii, *The Semiotics of Russian Culture*, Part I, Chap. 1).

Moreover, in its time, the title of Tsar united the Emperor *(basileus)* of Byzantium, to whom Russia was culturally subject (the Russian church lay under the jurisdiction of Constantinople), and the Khan of the Golden Horde, to whom the Russian lands were politically subject; both of these rulers were called "Tsar" in early Russia. During Tatar rule the Russian church prayed for the Tatar "Tsar," i.e. he was named in the liturgy (see G. M. Prokhorov, *Povest` o Mitiae. Rus` i Vizantiia v epokhu Kulikovskoi bitvy* (Leningrad, 1978), 53, 84); we may assume that before the Tatar-Mongol conquest the prayer for the Tatar "Tsar" had been preceded by prayer for the Greek "Tsar," i.e. the Emperor of Byzantium. After the collapse of the Byzantine Empire and of the Golden Horde (with the subsequent conquest of the Tatar lands), the Grand Prince of Moscow emerges as the successor not only of the Tsar (Emperor) of Byzantium, but also of the Tsar (Khan) of the Golden Horde. On the one hand, with the fall of Byzantium the Grand Prince was the only Orthodox ruler left (with the exception of the ruler of Georgia, which was distant and peripheral), i.e. the only independent ruler of the Orthodox *oikoumene* [inhabited, i.e. civilized, world]; it was generally assumed that there was only one Tsar in the Orthodox world (see *Russkaia istoricheckaia biblioteka*, vol. VI, supplement, no. 40, 274 ff.; cf. M. A. D`iakonov, *Vlast` moskovskikh gosudarei. Ocherki iz istorii politicheskikh idei drevnei Rusi do kontsa XVI v.* (St. Petersburg, 1889), 25-26; V. Savva, *Moskovskie tsari i vizantiiskie vasilevsy. K voprosu o vliianii Vizantii na obrazovanie idei tsarskoi vlasti moskovskikh gosudarei* (Kharkov, 1901), 200 ff.), and this position, formerly occupied by the Emperor of Byzantium, was now occupied by the Prince of Russia. On the other hand, the territory which had formerly belonged to the Golden Horde now belonged to the Grand Prince. Thus the Russian Tsar now united in his own person both the Tsar (Khan) of the Golden Horde and the Tsar (Emperor) of Byzantium: if in a territorial sense he was successor to the Tatar Khan, then in a semiotic sense he was successor to the Greek Emperor.

71 M. I. Semevskii, *Slovo i delo. 1700-1725* (St. Petersburg, 1885), 283; A. Petrov "Romo-danovskii, kniaz` Fedor Iurevich," in *Russkii biograficheskii slovar`* (Petrograd, 1918), vol. "Romanova-Riasovskii," 132. Peter's first letter to Romadanovskii addressing him as "king" is dated May 19, 1695. It begins with the words *"Min Her Kenich* [My Lord King]. The letter written by Your Illustrious Majesty, my most merciful sovereign, in· the capital town of Preshpurkh [Presburg] on the 14th day of May, was handed to me on the 18th day, for which sovereign mercy of yours we are bounden to shed our blood, even to the last drop . . ." The letter is signed "The eternal slave of your most Illustrious Majesty bombadier *Piter"* (*Pis`ma i bumagi imperatora Petra Velikogo* (St. Petersburg-Moscow, 1887-1977), vol. I, no. 37, 29-30). Later on, similar letters frequently occur.

In his *History of Tsar Peter Alekseevich and of Those Persons Close to Him*, Kurakin recounts that already in 1689, at the time of the military exercises, Peter had proclaimed F.Iu. Romodanovskii to be Tsar of Presburg, with his residence in

Preobrazhenskoe, in the small town Presburg (Plezpurkh) on the river Iauza, and
I. I. Buturlin to be Tsar of Semenovskoe with his residence in Sokolinyi court on
Semenovskoe meadow (*Arkhiv kniazia F. A. Kurakina* (St. Petersburg-Saratov-Moscow-
Astrakhan`, 1890-1902), kn. I, 65). Subsequently. in the mock battles of Kozhukhovo
in 1694 Buturlin was referred to as "the Polish King" (*Zapiski Zheliabuzhskogo s 1682 po 2
Iiulia 1709* (St. Petersburg, 1840), 32-33; M. M. Bogoslovskii, *Petr I. Materialy dlia biografii*
(Moscow, 1940-1946), vol. I, 195); he suffered a defeat by Romodanovskii, who by this
act emerged, as it were, as the Russian potentate (they were both, however, referred
to as "generalissimus" as well). It is highly significant that in these mock battles (at
Semenovskoe in 1691 and Kozhukhovo in 1694) Peter took part on Romodanovskii's side,
acting as his subordinate, and so consequently Romodanovskii's victory over Buturlin
was in fact predetermined (see Ibid., 125-128, 196-206). In addition, in these contexts
Buturlin had under his command a concentration of the old Muscovite troops (*streltsy*),
whereas Romodanovskii had new-style soldiers (*soldaty*); the former played a passive,
and the latter an active, role, i.e. Buturlin's forces were doomed to defeat beforehand (see
Ibid., 195, 197, 199, 206). According to Zheliabuzhskii, it was precisely after his victory
in the Kozukhovo mock battle of October 1694 that Romodanovskii received his "new
appellation" and began to be called "*gosudarich*" ["son of the sovereign" or "little lord":
gosudar` could mean either "sovereign" or "lord"] (*Zapiski Zheliabuzhskogo*, 39). In his speech
to the troops after this victory, Romodanovskii is mentioned as "Our Most Elevated
Generalissimus, Prince Fedor Iur̀evich of Presburg and Paris and conqueror of All the
Iauza" (M. M. Bogoslovskii, *Petr I*, vol. I, 201). Wittram supposes that Romodanovskii
had the title of "*gosudar`*" in May 1692 (R Wittram, *Peter I, Czar und Kaiser. Zur Geschichte
Peters des Grossen in seiner Zeit* (Göttingen, 1964), vol. I, 110), basing his supposition on
the letter from the shipwrights of Pereaslavl` which states that Peter was building
a ship on the orders of "his Lord [*gosudar`*], Generalissimus Prince Fedor Iur̀evich" (see
M. M. Bogoslovskii, *Petr I*, vol. I, 143); this context is not, however, very significant, in
as much as the word "*gosudar`*" could in this case refer to the title of "generalissimus."
M. M. Shcherbatov writes of Romodanovskii: "Some time before his departure for
foreign parts, he (Peter) gave the title of 'Prince-Caesar' to this man [Romodanovskii],
while he himself pretended to be his subject, and in so doing set an example of
obedience. Having accepted from him various ranks and, supposedly, instructions, he
left him ruler of Russia when he himself went to foreign parts in 1697; and when he
returned he continued both the title and his ostensible respect to him: he would call
him 'Lord' [*gosudar`*] both verbally and in writing, and he used his [Romodanovskii's]
sternness and severity to repress the arrogance of the bojars and to track down and
punish crimes even unto his death" (M. M. Shcherbatov, *Tetrati zapisnyia vsiakim
pis`mam i delam, komu chto prikazano i v kotorom chisle ot E. I.V. Petra Velikago 1704, 1705
i 1706 godov s prilozheniem primechanii o sluzhbakh tekh liudei, k kotorym sei gosudar` pisyval*
(St. Petersburg, 1774), 15). Golikov tells us that, on going abroad in 1697, Peter "founded
a new government": "'The Great Lord entrusted the government of the state to his most
faithful bojars, Prince Romodanovskoi and Tikhon Nikitich Streshnev, and gave them
as assistants the most loyal of his boyars, namely Lev Kirilovich Naryshkin and the
Princes Golitsyn and Prozorovskii. And so that the Chief Ruler, Prince Romodanovskii,
should be the more respected, he gave him the title of Prince·Caesar and Majesty, and
himself pretended to be subject to him" (I. I. Golikov, *Deianiia Petra Velikogo* (Moscow,
1788), part I, 290).

After the victory of Poltava Peter considered it his duty to congratulate Romodanovskii, in as much as it meant that thenceforth Petersburg would become the residence of "His Majesty": "We congratulate Your Majesty on this victory which is unprecedented in the entire world. And now beyond any doubt the desire of Your Majesty to take up residence in Petersburg has been attained through this final downfall of the enemy" (*Pis`ma i bumagi imperatora Petra Velikogo*, vol. IX, no. 3281, 246).

[73] A. Petrov "Romodanovskii, kniaz` Fedor Iur̀evich," 135; P. V. Verkhovskoi, *Uchrezhdenie Dukhovnoi Kollegii i Dukhovnyi Reglament* (Rostov-na-Donu, 1916) , vol. I, 92.

[74] A. Petrov "Romodanovskii, kniaz` Fedor Iur̀evich," 138.

[75] *Zapiski Iusta Iulia, datskogo poslannika pri Petre Velikom* (Moscow, 1900), 297.

[76] I. I. Golikov, *Deianiia Petra Velikogo*, part I, 76; M. I. Semevskii, *Slovo i delo*, 286-287.

[77] It is essential to bear in mind that Peter could have been called Emperor long before he officially assumed the imperial title in 1721. Feofan Prokopovich specifically remarks on this in his encomium on Peter, dated 1725, when he recalls how "with our entreaties we persuaded him to assume the title of 'Great' and 'Emperor'"; Feofan adds: "which is what he was already, and was called by everyone" (Feofan Prokopovich, *Arkhiepiskopa Velikogo Novagrada i Velikikh Luk,* part II, 163). Indeed, Peter is addressed as "Emperor" and "Father of the Fatherland" as early as 1708 in a speech delivered to him on behalf of all the clergy (K. V. Kharlampovich, *Malorossiiskoe vliianie na velikorusskuiu tserkovnuiu zhizn`* (Kazaǹ, 1914), 462n 4, with a reference to the Archive of the Typographical Library, no. 100, fol. 20). From that time on this title is frequently used to refer to Peter. Some examples follow. In 1709, on the occasion of the victory of Poltava, a publication appeared under the title of *The Wonderful Public Apotheosis of the most Praiseworthy Valour of the Hercules of All the Russias . . . of our Great Sovereign, Tsar and Grand Prince Peter Alekseevich, Emperor and Autocrat of All the Russios, Great, Small and White* (P. P. Pekarskii, *Nauka i literatura v Rossii pri Petre Velikom* (St. Petersburg, 1862), vol. II, no. 160; T. A. Bykova, M. M. Gurevich, *Opisanie izdanii grazhdanskoi pechati 1708—ianvar` 1725 g.* (Moscow-Leningrad, 1955), no. 26). In 1713 in the title of the *Book of Mars [Kniga Marsovaia]* it is stated that it was printed "by order of the Emperor, Peter the First, Autocrat of All the Russias," and on the frontispiece of this volume there appears a portrait of Peter done by Aleksei Zubov in 1712 with this inscription: "Peter the First, Most August [*prisnopribavitel̀*] Emperor, Tsar and Autocrat of All the Russias" (P. P. Pekarskii, *Nauka i literatura v Rossii pri Petre Velikom*, vol. II, no 233, 291; T. A. Bykova, M. M. Gurevich, *Opisanie izdanii grazhdanskoi pechati*, no. 68; *Portret Petrovskogo vremeni. Katalog vystavki* (Gos. Tret`iakovskaia galereia; Gos. Russkii muzei) (Leningrad, 1973), 206. The word *prisnopribavitel̀* [literally: "Eternally increasing") means "most august," cf. *augustus* from Latin *augeo,* "I increase, add"). Peter is referred to as "Emperor" (but not as "Tsar") in Serban Kantemir's *Panegyrical Burnt Offering [Panegiricheskoe vsesozhzhenie]* of 1714 (P. P. Pekarskii, *Nauka i literatura v Rossii pri Petre Velikom*, vol. II, no. 249; T. A. Bykova, M. M. Gurevich, *Opisanie izdanii grazhdanskoi pechati,* no. 85); it is noteworthy that in the manuscript of this work, preserved in the Library of the Academy of Sciences, the word *"Autocrat" (samoderzhets)* is used instead of "Emperor" (T. A Bykova, M. M. Gurevich, R. I. Kozintseva, *Opisanie izdanii, napechatannykh pri Petre I. Svodnyi katalog. Dopolneniia i prilozheniia* (Leningrad, 1972), no. 20): apparently the word "Emperor" was inserted during the process of publication. The title of the book *The Laurea or Crown of Immortal Glory [Liavrea ili Venets bezsmertnyia slavy]* (1714) uses the words "His Imperial Majesty" (P. P. Pekarskii, *Nauka i literatura*

v Rossii pri Petre Velikom, vol. II, no. 266; T. A. Bykova, M. M. Gurevich, *Opisanie izdanii grazhdanskoi pechati*, no. 112); in just the same way Peter is called "Emperor" in both editions of the *Book of Command or of Maritime Rights in the Navy* [*Kniga ordera ili vo flote morskikh prav*], which came out in the same year, 1714 (P. P. Pekarskii, *Nauka i literatura v Rossii pri Petre Velikom*, vol. II, no. 247, 249; T. A. Bykova, M. M. Gurevich, *Opisanie izdanii grazhdanskoi pechati*, no. 75, 79). See also Ibid., no. 243, 310, 320 (P. P. Pekarskii, *Nauka i literatura v Rossii pri Petre Velikom*, vol. II, no. 394), 366, 606 (P. P. Pekarskii, *Nauka i literatura v Rossii pri Petre Velikom*, vol. II, no. 478); T. A. Bykova, M. M. Gurevich, *Opisanie izdanii, napechatannykh kirillitsei 1689—ianvar` 1725 g.* (Moscow-Leningrad, 1958), no. 126, 128, 130, 131, 136, 138 (P. P. Pekarskii, *Nauka i literatura v Rossii pri Petre Velikom*, vol. II, no. 453), 149 (P. P. Pekarskii, *Nauka i literatura v Rossii pri Petre Velikom*, vol. II, no. 478); Ibid., no. 380, 450, 483. 1718 saw the publication of the *True Document of His Caesarine Roman Majesty . . . on whom the aforementioned Caesar in this his Document conferred the title of Caesar [Tsezar`] of all the Russias;* this document was referred to on the occasion of Peter's being presented with the imperial title (Ibid., no. 388; T. A. Bykova, M. M. Gurevich, *Opisanie izdanii grazhdanskoi pechati*, no. 298). We should also mention the portrait of Peter in the collection of the State Russian Museum, presumably dated 1697, which bears the inscription: *Petrus Alexandrowitz Moscowitarum Imperator cum magna legatione huc regio montem venit media May. Anno M: DCXCVII;* i.e. "Peter Aleksandrovich, Emperor of Muscovy, came here to the region of mountains together with the Great Embassy in the middle of May 1697" (*Portret Petrovskogo vremeni*, 119). Even earlier, in 1696, on the occasion of the victory of Azov, a medal was struck with a portrait of Peter and bearing the inscription: *Petrus Alexi; fil, Russor. Mag. Caes.* (G. Baier, *Kratkoe opisanie vsekh sluchaev, kasaiushchikhsia do Azova* (St. Petersburg, 1738), 267), where the word *Caes[ar]* signifies "Emperor". In 1709 the Viennese court expressed its disapproval of the Tsar's assumption of the title of "Emperor"; in 1710 the Austrian ambassador to Russia, General Velchek (Weltschek) notified Vienna to acknowledge the title of *"Majestät Kayser"*, i.e. the imperial title (A. V. Florovskii, "Stranitsa istorii russko-avstriiskikh diplomaticheskikh otnoshenii XVIII v.," in *Feodal`naia Rossiia vo vsemirno-istoricheskom protsesse. Sbornik statei, posviashchennyi L. V. Cherepninu* (Moscow, 1972), 390).

78 *Dnevnik kamer-iunkera F. V. Berkhgol`tsa, 1721-1725* (Moscow, 1902-1903), part I, 115-117; A. Petrov "Romodanovskii, kniaz` Fedor Iur`evich," 121. The wedding of the Prince-Pope took place on September 10, 1721, and Peter became Emperor on October 20 of the same year.

79 Ibid., 138, 123-124.

80 It should be emphasized that *"kesar`"* stands in the same relation to "tsar" as "pope" [*papa*] to "patriarch". Indeed, if *pope* signifies the supreme pontiff of Rome, then *kesar`* in Church Slavonic signifies the Roman Emperor. Thus *Prince-kesar`*, like Prince-Pope, would on the face of it appear to be Rome-orientated; however, just as the Prince-Pope in fact represents the Russian patriarch, so the Prince-*kesar`* represents the Russian Tsar.

81 *Poslaniia Ivana Groznogo*, 213.

82 It is indicative that in 1682, at the time of the Revolt of the *strel`tsy* and the disputes with the Old Believers, the Tsarevna Sophia Alekseevna broke off the discussions and threatened to leave Moscow with the two young Tsars (Ivan and Peter) [i.e., Ivan V and his half-brother Peter I (the Great); Sophia, their elder sister, was Regent until 1689]

(S. M. Solov`ev, *Istoriia Rossii*, vol. VII, 288); this threat had the desired effect. Cf. in this connection Peter's own departure in 1689 for the Troitse-Sergievo Monastery.

When, however. Patriarch Nikon did the same thing (in 1658 Nikon, having quarrelled with Aleksei Mikhailovich, ostentatiously left the patriarchal throne and retreated to the Monastery of the Resurrection), he ceased to be considered Patriarch. The difference in attitude to secular and ecclesiastical power is thrown into particular relief here: in a certain sense the Tsar emerges as a more sacred figure than the Patriarch, in as much as he is Tsar by nature and not by virtue of his having been installed upon the throne.

[83] Similarly. Ivan the Terrible mockingly called Nikita Kazarinov Golokhvastov an "angel" (see the testimony of Kurbskii in his *History of the Grand Prince of Moscow, Russkaia istoricheskaia biblioteka*, vol. XXXI, 308; cf. N. M. Karamzin *Istoriia gosudarstva Rossiiskogo*, vol. IX, 186). In an exactly comparable way Peter the Great later named one of the participants in his fools' performances (Vasilii Sokovnin) "a prophet," and this directly corresponds to the blasphemous tendency of Peter's merrymaking (cf. Kurakin's testimony in his *History of Tsar Peter Alekseevich and of Those Persons Close to Him* in *Arkhiv kniazia F. A. Kurakina*, vol. I, 73). In conditions where the non-conventionality of the sign is prevalent this kind of linguistic behavior is highly significant.

[84] Cf., for example, the eloquent description of Yuletide mummers in the Petition of 1636 from the priests of Nizhnii Novgorod, apparently drawn up by Ioann Neronov: "On their faces they place shaggy and beast-like masks and the like in clothing too, and on their behinds they fix tails, like demons made visible, and they wear shameful members on their faces, and goat-like bleat all manner of devilish things and display their shameful members, and others beat tabors and clap and dance and perform other improper deeds" (N. V. Rozhdestvenskii, "K istorii boŕby s tserkovnymi besporiadkami, otgoloskami iazychestva i porokami v russkom bytu XVII v. (Chelobitnaia nizhegorod-skikh sviashchennikov 1636 goda v sviazi s pervonachal`noi deiatel`nost`iu Ivana Neronova)," *Chteniia v Obshchestve istorii i drevnostei rossiiskikh* 2 (1902): 24-26); the features described here correspond exactly to the iconographic image of the demon, which is also characterized by the tail, the shagginess and the interchange between top and bottom (the face and the sexual organs). In just the same way the behavior of the mummers in the picture represented here corresponds to the idea of devilish behavior. The description of Yuletide games which appears in the Life of Ioann Neronov is no less characteristic: "In those days the ignorant used to assemble for games of devilry . . . putting on their faces various frightening masks in the guise of demons' faces" (N. Subbotin, ed., *Materialy dlia istorii raskola za pervoe vremia ego sushchestvovaniia, izdavaemye bratstvom sv. Petra mitropolita* (Moscow, 1875-1890), vol. I, 247). Numerous ethnographic descriptions testify that the mummers themselves called their masks "the mask of the Devil," "the devil's mug," "the devil's grimace" and so on, and by the same token considered that donning them constituted a terrible sin which would require future atonement. Very often, therefore, any kind of Yuletide mask at all, whatever it represented, was seen as a devil's mask (see. for example, P. S. Efimenko, "Materialy po etnografii russkogo naseleniia Arkhangel`skoi gubernii. Chasti I-II," *Izvestiia imp. Obshchestva liubitelei estestvoznaniia, antropologii i etnografii pri Moskovskom universitete* XXX (1877-1878): 138; S.Maksimov, *Sobranie sochinenii* (St. Petersburg, 1908-1913), vol. XVII, 39-40). In early Russia a particular form of penance was laid on those who donned a mask.

It is no accident, therefore, that the *oprichniki* of Ivan the Terrible, whose form of behavior was to a significant degree based on the principles of anti-behavior (see below), should have danced in masks: it is well-known that Prince Mikhailo Repnin preferred death to the donning of the sinful *"mashkara"* (*Russkaia istoricheskaia biblioteka*, vol. XXXI, 279; S. M. Solov̀ev, *Istoriia Rossii*, vol. III, 541). Kurbskii testifies that the Tsar ordered that Repnin be killed in church, near the altar, during the reading of the Gospel; this is, of course, highly significant: the wearing of a mask was shown in this case to be the antipode to the church ritual.

[85] See A. I. Malein, trans. ed., *Novoe izvestie o Rossii*, 27; I. I. Polosin, *Sotsial̀no-politicheskaia istoriia Rossii XVI—nachala XVII v. Sbornik statei* (Moscow, 1963), 154; N. M. Karamzin *Istoriia gosudarstva Rossiiskogo*,vol. IX, pp. 98-99; R. G. Skrynnikov, *Ivan Groznyi* (Moscow, 1975), 123. Metropolitan Filipp (Kolychev) viewed the wearing of monastic cowls by the *oprichniki* as sacrilege. See N. M. Karamzin, *Istoriia gosudarstva Rossiiskogo*, vol. IX, 98, 118-119.

[86] See M. I. Semevskii, *Slovo i delo*, 282-336; R. Wittram, *Peter I, Czar und Kaiser*, vol. I, 106-110.

[87] Kurbskii, for example, often calls the *oprichniki* *"kromeshniki"* (see especially *Russkaia istoricheskaia biblioteka*, vol. XXXI, 155, 273, 306, 307, 323) and puts into the mouth of Metropolitan Filipp Kolychev the following words addressed to the Tsar: "If thou wilt promise to repent of thy sins and dismiss from thy presence that Satanic regiment which thou hast assembled to the great detriment of Christianity, that is to say, those *kromeshniki*, though they are called *aprishnitsy* [*oprichniki*], I will bless thee and forgive thee, and will return . . . to my throne" (Ibid., 316). On this subject S. B. Veselovskii wrote: "The words *oprich̀* and *krome* are synonymous. In those days the idea of the after-life, of 'the kingdom of God,' was a realm of eternal light beyond the confines of which (outside [*oprich̀*] which, without [*krome*] which) was the kingdom of eternal gloom, 'the kingdom of Satan' . . . The expressions *kromeshnyi* and *kromeshnik*, formed by analogy with the words *oprich̀*, *oprichnyi* and *oprichnik*, were not merely a play on words, but at the same time branded the *oprichniki* as the progeny of hell, as servants of Satan. Kurbskii, too, on many occasions in his writings, calls the adherents and servants of Tsar Ivan, and in particular his *oprichniki*, 'the Satanic regiment,' from which it followed, or was implied, that Tsar Ivan was like Satan" (S. B. Veselovskii, *Issledovaniia po istorii oprichniny* (Moscow, 1963), 14; cf. also N. M. Karamzin *Istoriia gosudarstva Rossiiskogo*, vol. IX, 95). In exactly the same way Ivan Timofeev also recounts in his *Chronicle* (*Vremennik*) that the Tsar laid "dark," i.e. infernal, signs on his *oprichniki*: "He separated his favorites, who were as wolves, from those he hated, who were as sheep, and laid on the chosen warriors dark signs: he clothed them all in black from head to foot, and ordered that they also have their own horses, identical in color to their clothing; he made all his men in every way like demonic servants" (*Russkaia istoricheskaia biblioteka*, vol. XIII, 272). That it is possible to put such an interpretation on the word *oprichnik* seems to be inherent in the word itself: *oprichnik* seems to be etymologically connected with the Ukrainian *oprishok* ("robber"), and this corresponds to the connection between robbers and the world of outer darkness [*kromeshnyi*] and of sorcery (cf. the widespread association of robbers with sorcerers). In this context the name introduced by Ivan is highly significant: it is surely this that also explains the prohibition in 1575 of the name *oprichnina* (see S. M. Solov̀ev, *Istoriia Rossii*, vol. III, 565; I. I. Polosin, *Sotsial̀no-politicheskaia istoriia Rossii*, 183; G. Shtaden, *O Moskve Ivana*

Groznogo. Zapiski nemtsa oprichnika (Moscow, 1925), 110; R. G. Skrynnikov, *Ivan Groznyi*, 190).

N. F. Kapterev, *Patriarkh Nikon i ego protivniki v dele spravleniia tserkovnykh obriadov* (Sergiev Posad, 1913), 181. The custom of dressing up as a monk at Yuletide was partially kept up even into the twentieth century (see G. K. Zavoiko, "Verovaniia i obychai velikorossov Vladimirskoi gubernii," *Etnograficheskoe obozrenie* 3-4 (1914): 138; V. I. Chicherov, *Zimnii period russkogo zemledel`cheskogo kalendaria XVI-XIX vekov (Ocherki po istorii narodnykh verovanii)* (Moscow, 1957), 210, and also the description of the "monk game" in, for example, M. I. Smirnov, *Etnograficheskie materialy po Pereslavl`-Zalesskomu uezdu Vladimirskoi gubernii. Svadebnye obriady i pesni, pesni krugovye i prokhodnye, igry. Legendy i skazki* (Moscow, 1922), 58). The information given by the chronicler of Piskarev (in the beginning of the seventeenth century) about the entertainments indulged in by the young Ivan the Terrible in 1545-1546 is very interesting in this connection: "And he also amused himself in this way: he would do the spring ploughing and sow buckwheat with his boyars, and his other amusements were walking on stilts and *dressing up in a shroud"* (see *Materialy po istorii SSSR*, II (Moscow, 1955-9, 73-4). This should be compared with those ethnographical accounts which testify that Yuletide mummers sometimes dressed up in "the clothes of the deceased" and pretended to be corpses (see, e.g. F. Zobnin, S. Patkanov, "Spisok Tobol`skikh slov i vyrazhenii," *Zhivaia starina* 4 (1899): 517); cf. also the Yuletide game of "dead-man", in which one of the participants also imitated a dead person (see V. E. Gusev, "Ot obriada k narodnomu teatru (evoliutsiia sviatochnykh igr v pokoinika)," in *Fol`klor i etnografiia. Obriady i obriadovyi fol`klor* (Leningrad, 1974), 50 ff; S. Maksimov, *Sobranie sochinenii* (St. Petersburg, 1908-1913), vol. XVII, 14ff.; K. Zavoiko, "V kostromskikh lesakh po Vetluge reke (Etnograficheskie materialy, zapisannye v Kostromskoi gubernii v 1914-1916 gg.," in *Etnograficheskii sbornik* (Kostroma, 1917), 24). Both corpses and representatives of the Devil belong to the "other world" and can be directly associated with each other; thus in a broad sense mummers depict all dwellers of the "other world."

Thus the *oprichniki* should evidently be associated with mummers and in this sense identify with the "other world" of outer darkness [*kromeshnyi*]. It is, moreover, characteristic that the *oprichniki* should, in their turn, perceive the representatives of the *zemshchina* as belonging to another, alien world: for which very reason it was as if in their eyes they did not even exist. Cf. Shtaden's testimony: "The *oprichniki* did indescribably terrible things to the *zemskie* [members of the *zemshchina]* so as to extort from them money and goods. Even the field of battle [i.e. God's judgement—whichever side won in a battle to settle a dispute was taken to have been granted success by God's judgement] had no force in this case: all those who fought on the side of the *zemskie* acknowledged themselves to be defeated; though they were alive they were thought of as if they were dead . . ." (G. Shtaden, *O Moskve Ivana Groznogo*, 86). Thus the *oprichniki* consider the *zemskie* to be no better than *corpses*: the *oprichnina* and the *zemshchina* belong to different worlds, which are opposed to each other in the same way as the "other world" and this world are.

The *oprichniki* were supposed to avoid associating with the *zemskie* (see Ibid., 93), and this forcibly reminds one of those restrictions on association which were common in the case of denominational disagreements (cf. the Old Believers' later refusal to have contact with the Nikonites for eating, drinking and praying); it was most likely this that Ivan Timofeev had in mind when he wrote in his *Chronicle* that Ivan the Terrible, in founding the *oprichnina*, "in his anger, by division and splitting into two, divided a united people and as it were created two faiths" (*Russkaia istoricheskaia biblioteka*, vol. XIII, 271). The *oprichniki* moreover cut themselves off from their parents and in so doing automatically became outcasts, standing in opposition to the rest of the world. The punishment for contact between an *oprichnik* and a member of the *zemshchina* was death for both, so association with a representative of the opposite party was just as dangerous as contact with a representative of the "other world".

[89] Kurakin, in his *History of Tsar Peter Alekseevich*, describes Peter's jesting entertainments as "Yuletide pranks," remarking, however, that the Patriarch of All the Fools "prolonged his celebration from Christmas throughout the entire winter until Shrovetide, visiting all the noble households of Moscow and the suburb and the houses of the best-known merchants, and chanting the way they usually do in church" (*Arkhiv kniazia F. A. Kurakina*, kn. I, 72 ff.); the behavior of the travesty "Patriarch" is, moreover, extremely reminiscent of the behavior of Yuletide carol-singers. Information on this jesting celebration at Yuletide can also be found in *Zapiski Zheliabuzskogo*, 59, 225, 279; *Zapiski o Rossii pri Petre Velikom, izvlechennye iz bumag grafa Bassevicha* (Moscow, 1866), 119-120; *Zapiski Iusta Iulia*, 128-129; Johann Georg Korb, *Dnevnik puteshestviia v Moskoviiu (1698 i 1699 g.)* (St. Petersburg, 1906), 109 ff.; and *Dnevnik kamer-iunkera F. V.Berkhgol'tsa*, vol. II, 10-11; vol. III, 186. Golikov, following Strahlenberg, enumerates all that Peter was accused of and mentions in particular "His Majesty's celebration at Yuletide" (I. I. Golikov, *Deianiia Petra Velikogo*, part I, 3; cf. Ph.J. von Strahlenberg, *Das Nord- und Ostliche Theil von Europa und Asia, In so weit solches Das gantze Rußische Reich mit Sibirien und der grossen Tatarey in sich begreiffet, In einer Historisch-Geographischen Beschreibung der alten und neuern Zeiten, und vielen andern unbekannten Nachrichten vorgestellet* (Stockholm, 1730), 231-232); it is quite clear that the "All-Jesting Council" could indeed be seen as a Yuletide performance. According to Berkhgol'ts, Yuletide celebrations in 1724 were signalized by all the senators and members of the Imperial Colleges being dressed up in disguise and being obliged to wear masks and the appropriate costumes even in their audience chambers (*Dnevnik kamer-iunkera F. V. Berkhgol'tsa*, vol. IV, 16-17).

Even later in the eighteenth century jesting performances were often associated with either Yuletide or Shrovetide and included features of the corresponding rituals. So, for example, the public masquerade "Minerva Triumphant" which took place in Moscow in 1763 after Catherine the Great's accession was arranged to coincide with Shrovetide. Poroshin describes the Yuletide games which Catherine organized in Petersburg, in which men dressed up in women's clothing (S. A. Poroshin, *Zapiski, sluzhashchie k istorii ego imperatorskogo vysochestva Pavla Petrovicha* (St. Petersburg, 1881), 560), in a similar way to that of Yuletide mummers. Dressing up in the clothes of the opposite sex was in general characteristic of court masquerades in the eighteenth century (see for example *Zapiski imperatritsy Ekateriny II* (St. Petersburg, 1906), 100-1; S. A. Poroshin, *Zapiski*, 555, A. V. Khrapovitskii, *Dnevnik s 18 ianvaria 1782 po 17 sentiabria 1793 goda* (Moscow, 1901), 205).

[90] Ia.V. Lileev, *Simeon Bekbulatovich*, 208; T. S. Rozhdestvenskii, "Pamiatniki staroobriad-cheskoi poezii," *Zapiski Moskovskogo arkheologicheskogo instituta* VI (1910), xxxiv.

[91] See B. A. Uspenskii, "Historia sub specie semioticae" in *Kul'turnoe nasledie Drevnei Rusi. Istoki, stanovlenie, traditsiia* (Moscow, 1976), 290. In exactly the same way the prominent Old Believer Ivan Smirnov testified in the 1720's that Peter was making "the male sex female, to the extent that he orders the male sex to let their hair grow

long and to shave their beards" (P. S. Smirnov, *Iz istorii raskola pervoi poloviny XVIII veka po neizdannym pamiatnikam* (St. Petersburg, 1908), 160); as already pointed out, assuming the attributes of the opposite sex is typical in general of mummers: men disguising themselves in women's clothing, imitating women and so on. Such an opinion as the one quoted above must have been reinforced by the behavior of Peter himself, who was prone to all kinds of disguises and to the assumption of other names or titles which corresponded to them ("Sergeant Peter Mikhailov", "bombardier" or "captain Piter", and so on).

[92] See Iu. M. Lotman, B. A. Uspenskii, *The Semiotics of Russian Culture*, part I, chapters 1 and 2.

[93] V. F. Miller, *Istoricheskie pesni russkogo naroda XVI-XVII vv.* (Petrograd, 1915), 590.

[94] Ibid., p. 621.

[95] *Istoricheskoe i pravdivoe povestvovanie o tom, kak moskovskii kniaz` Dimitrii Ioannovich dostig ottsovskogo prestola*. With introduction and trans. from Czech by V. A. Franzev (Prague, 1908), reprinted in *Starina i novizna* 15 (St. Petersburg, 1911).

[96] *Russkaia istoricheskaia biblioteka*, vol. XIII, 827.

[97] Ibid., 56. Apart from the prescriptions laid down for fasting on Wednesdays and Fridays, the Russians and the other Eastern Slavs placed a special prohibition on veal (see D. Zeienin, *Russische (Ostslavische) volkskunde* (Berlin-Leipzig, 1927), 116). According to Shlikhting, who records that Muscovites ate no veal at all, Ivan the Terrible ordered that people who sampled veal out of hunger should be burnt at the stake (A. I. Malein, trans. ed., *Novoe izvestie o Rossii*, 39): thus it is quite clear that a doctrinal signIficance was seen in this prohibition.

[98] SeeN. Ustrialov, *Skazaniia sovremennikov o Dmitrii Samozvantse* (St. Petersburg, 1859), vol. II, 196, 238.

[99] See, e.g., S. Maksimov, *Sobranie sochinenii*, vol. XVIII, 128, 146; vol. X, 184; Ia.A. Nikitina, "K voprosu o russkikh koldunakh," *Sbornik muzeia antropologii i etnografii AN SSSR* VII (1928): 309-310; D. Zeienin, *Russische (Ostslavische) volkskunde*, 45; P. S. Efimenko, "Materialy po etnografii," 221.

[100] Ia.A. Nikitina, "K voprosu o russkikh koldunakh," 311-312.

[101] V. F. Miller, *Istoricheskie pesni*, 585.

[102] Ibid., 591; cf. also 587, 588, 589, 593, 595, 597, 601, 602, 620, 62.

[103] *Russkaia istoricheskaia biblioteka*, vol. XIII, 818-820. Cf. also in *Another Story* [Inoe skazanie]: "And he created for himself in this transient life an entertainment which was also a token of his eternal dwelling-place in future ages, the like of which no-one in the state of Russia or in any other state, save in the infernal kingdom, has ever before seen on earth: an exceedingly vast hell, having three heads. And he made both its jaws of bronze which jangled greatly; and when it opened wide its jaws, the onlookers saw what seemed like a flame spurt from inside them and a great jangling noise issued from its gullet; its teeth were jagged and its claws seemed ready to grab, and out of its ears flames seemed to be bursting forth; and the accursed one placed it right on his Moskva river as a reminder of his sins, so that from the highest vantage points in his residence he could gaze upon it always and be ready to settle in it for endless ages with other like-minded associates" (Ibid., 55-56).

[104] Samuil Kollinz, *Nyneshnee sostoianie Rossii, izlozhennoe v pis`me k drugu, zhivushchemu v Londone* (Moscow, 1846), 22, describes these burial places as follows: "[the corpses] are sent to the *Bosky* or *Boghzi Dome* (i.e. God's House) which is a great pit in the fields

arched over, wherein they put an hundred or two hundred and let them rest till Midsummer, and then the popes go and bury them, and cover them with earth."

[105] S. M. Solov'ev, *Istotiia Rossii*, vol. IV, 455; Adam Olearii, *Opisanie puteshestviia v Moskoviiu i cherez Moskoviiu v Persiiu i obratno* (St. Petersburg, 1906), 238.

[106] For customs associated with the burial of "unclean" bodies in general, see D. K. Zelenin, *Ocherki russkoi mifologii* (Petrograd, 1916).

[107] *Russkaia istoricheskaia biblioteka*, vol. XIII, 831, 59.

[108] N. Ustrialov, *Skazaniia sovremennikov o Dmitrii Samozvantse*, vol. I, 347; cf. S. M. Solov'ev, *Istoriia Rossii*, vol. IV, 455.

[109] Cf. the description of the Yuletide mummers in the Petition of 1636 from the priests of Nizhnii Novgorod quoted above, note 84.

The reed-pipe stuck into the False Dmitrii's mouth "for payment to the gatekeeper at the entrance to hell" seems to be a travesty substitute for the money which was ordinarily placed with the deceased so that he would be received into the next world; moreover, the money was sometimes placed in the deceased's *mouth* (see Samuil Kollinz, *Nyneshnee sostoianie Rossii*, 21; *Polnoe sobranie russkikh letopisei*, vol. I, 178; cf. also A. Fischer, *Zwyczaje pogrzebowe ludu polskiego* (Lwow, 1921), 173 ff.; L. Niederle, *Slovanske starozitnosti. Oddil kulturni. Zivot starych Slovanu* (Prague, 1911-1921), vol. I, 266-268). In addition, the whistle could also have corresponded functionally to the ·so-called "permit," which, it was supposed, was destined for the gate-keeper of Paradise, who was usually thought to be either St. Nicholas or St. Peter.

[110] *Russkaia istoricheskaia biblioteka*, vol. XIII, 831, 59.

[111] *Istoricheskoe i pravdivoe povestvovanie,* 25, 31. For our purposes here it is sufficient to note that pretenders were *perceived* as sorcerers, in as much as they were seen as self-appointed, travesty Tsars. The question arises as to how far anti-behavior was inherent in these pretenders and how far it was attributed to them by public opinion. It must be supposed that this was a question of the degree of self-awareness of the pretender, which varied in each actual case. As we have already said, many pretenders undoubtedly believed that they were genuine Tsars, yet among them there were also some adventurers who were perfectly well aware of the unlawfulness of their claims. *A priori* it must be assumed that anti-behavior was in the main characteristic of the pretenders in the second category, i.e. those who perceived themselves as mummers.

[112] See especially on this B. A. Uspenskii, "Historia sub specie semioticae."

[113] What is meant here is walking around the lectern against the sun (in other words, counter-clockwise) in the course of the celebration of a christening or a wedding; this practice was introduced by Patriarch Nikon, whereas previously the accepted form of this ritual movement was in the opposite direction, 'sun-wise.' The opponents of Nikon's reforms considered this change a blasphemous violation of the ritual, imparting to it the nature of a demonic action.

[114] This refers more particularly to the spread of the art of secular portraiture. Formerly only icon-painting was allowed in Muscovite Russia, i.e. it was permitted to depict only the saints, not ordinary people.

[115] What is presumably meant here is the violation of fasts, a common feature of life in Petrine Russia, and the exemption of soldiers from fasting, which was introduced into Russia on Peter's insistence.

[116] That is, the enforced introduction of foreign dress under Peter.

[117] Formerly it was forbidden to eat, drink or pray with persons of another faith (foreigners); this prohibition survived among the Old Believers. .

[118] G. V. Esipov, *Raskol`nich`i dela XVIII veka* (St. Petersburg, 1861-1863), vol. II, 41.

[119] See K. V. Chistov, *Russkie narodnye sotsial`no-utopicheskie legendy*, 91-112; N. B. Golikova, *Politicheskie protsessy pri Petre I po materialam Preobrazhenskogo prikaza* (Moscow, 1957), 122-161,168-176, 172-219, 266-275.

[120] See K. V. Chistov, *Russkie narodnye sotsial`no-utopicheskie legendy*, 114-130.

[121] Ibid., 118-119.

[122] Such a duality, as we have seen, is quite characteristic for the ideology of imposture: just as the pretender Peter III (Pugachev) had his own "Count Chernyshev" (see above), so the "pretender" Peter the Great was assumed to have a pretender heir, Aleksei Petrovich.

[123] Chistov (Ibid., 113-114), who thinks that the historical image of Peter did not correspond to the utopian image of the Tsar-Deliverer, explains this phenomenon differently—and in our opinion unconvinclngly. Inasmuch as Peter was perceived as a Tsar by "indirect" line of succession, and as a "substitute" Tsar, his historical image bears no relation at all to the problem: the real Peter who existed in the consciousness of his contemporaries has nothing whatsoever to do with the person who *should have been* occupying his place.

ENTHRONEMENT IN THE RUSSIAN
AND BYZANTINE TRADITIONS

B. A. Uspenskij

After the fall of Byzantium, the Muscovite state attempted to enact a restoration of the Byzantine Empire. Thus originated the kingdom of Muscovy, which subsequently became the Russian Empire. This kingdom was modeled as a theocratic one, with Moscow conceived as the New Constantinople and the Third Rome. In conformity with this conception, there appeared in Moscow, as in a New Constantinople, a tsar, that is, a βασιλεύς (basileus), or emperor. Notably, the Byzantine emperor had been called "tsar" in Russia, so that Peter I's assumption of the title of emperor in 1721 designated a change of cultural orientation and not an elevation in rank. As a result of its new orientation towards Byzantium, Russia acquired both a tsar and a patriarch. However, by this time Byzantium had been long gone; and, what is more, long after Byzantium fell, contacts between Moscow and Constantinople had remained severed. Thus the Russians modeled themselves not on a tradition that actually existed, but on a certain notion of a theocratic state, in which ideology played a far greater role than real facts.

I

The tradition of enthronement (*postavlenie na tsarstvo*) began in Rus` on January 16, 1547, when Ivan IV was crowned tsar. Ivan IV's ceremony of enthronement, composed by Metropolitan Makarii, had nothing in common with the Byzantine emperors' (tsars') rite of enthronement, but rather derived from Dmitrii Ivanovich's rite of enthronement as Grand Prince that had taken place on February 4, 1498 (Dmitrii Ivanovich was the grandson of, and co-ruler with, Grand Prince Ivan III).[1]

There exist two basic textual versions of Ivan IV's order of enthronement as tsar, the Formulary Edition[2] and the Chronicle Edition; sometimes distinguished in the latter is the Nikonian version, as presented in the Nikonian and L`vov Chronicles; in the Chronicle of the beginning of the reign; in the Piskarevsk Chronicle[3]; and in the Illuminated (*Litsevaia*) version, presented in the "Royal Book" (*Tsarstvennaia kniga*);[4] a special variant of the Formulary Edition is contained in the order of services published by N. I. Novikov.[5] The oldest copies of the Chronicle Edition (within the Nikonian and L`vov Chronicles) are dated to the second half of the 1550s, the oldest copies of the Formulary Edition—to the beginning of the 1560s.

The Formulary Edition has a more general character, and was undoubtedly compiled after Ivan IV's enthronement. Thus allowance is made here for the presence of the tsar's father, who was no longer alive ("if there is a father . . . ," "if there is no father . . . "), and Tsaritsa Anastasia and the tsar's children are mentioned (although Ivan had only married one month after his enthronement and couldn't yet have had children), as is the patriarch ("the holy patriarch or right reverend metropolitan, your father, summons you . . . ").[6] As we see, various possibilities are allowed for here—participation in the ceremony of enthronement by the Grand Prince alone or together with his father; and the involvement of either a metropolitan or a patriarch—and this is clearly connected to the formulary character of the given document, which was to serve as the norm for the future enthronement of tsars. Thus we may discern two levels in the text of the Formulary edition: the narrative connected with the real ceremony of enthronement that took place in 1547, and the formulary proper, that provides for other potential situations.

We can date the composition of the Formulary Edition more or less precisely. There is every reason to believe that it was composed no earlier than 1547 and no later than 1560. The *terminus post quem* is the date of Ivan IV's enthronement as tsar (1547); the *terminus ante quem* is the death of Tsaritsa Anastasia (1560), who is mentioned in the metropolitan's greeting. At the same time it is possible to define the date more exactly on the basis of some general considerations. The Formulary Edition came into existence at the moment when the demand arose that the international community recognize the tsar's title, that is, no earlier than the mid-1550s.[7] We may assume that this version was composed before the trip by Archimandrite Feodorit (missionary to the Lapps, known by the name of Feodorit Kol`skii) to Constantinople in 1557 to have Ivan IV's enthronement as tsar blessed.[8] Thus the composition of the Formulary Edition of Ivan IV's elevation to the kingdom may with a large degree of certainty be dated to the mid-1550s.

In 1561 Ioasaph, metropolitan of Evripos, brought to Moscow the decree of the Patriarch of Constantinople, Ioasaph, of December 1560, that confirmed Ivan IV's title as tsar. [9] Acknowledging Ivan IV's rank, the patriarch nevertheless pointed out that only the patriarchs of Rome and Constantinople were entitled to enthrone somebody, and proposed that Ivan have the metropolitan of Evripos repeat the ceremony as the patriarch's exarch.[10] The metropolitan also brought to Moscow *The Order and Charter of Coronation and Enthronement as Emperor,* a book which described the Byzantine emperors' ceremony of enthronement, which significantly differed from the way Ivan IV had been crowned.[11] However, Ivan IV did not accept this proposal; subsequent ceremonies of enthronement for Russian tsars were based on the Formulary Edition of Ivan IV's enthronement.[12]

We are thus forced to admit that familiarity with Byzantine imperial practice had no substantive influence on Russian tsars' own rite of enthronement. It was only for Boris Godunov's enthronement as tsar on July 21, 1605, that the description of the Byzantine enthronement ceremony received from Patriarch Ioasaph was used to some degree, but only in particular aspects.[13] We may add to this that in Metropolitan Makarii's Great Reading Menalogion (compiled c. 1529-1554) under August 31 there is a description of the enthronement of Manuel II Paleologus as emperor in 1392.[14] The author of this description is Ignatii Smolianin, who was present at the event.[15] Thus the Byzantine order of enthronement as emperor was to some extent known in Russia; nonetheless it was not reflected in Ivan IV's order of enthronement as tsar[16] or on later Russian tsars' ceremonies of enthronement.

II

The basic difference between the Formulary Edition of Ivan IV's elevation to the tsardom and the Chronicle Edition concerns the anointing of the tsar. Only the Formulary version contains a description of the anointing, which is presented as a separate article ("Order and rule how a tsar or grand prince should be anointed with chrism"), but mention of anointment is also made in the general order of service. It is significant that it is precisely in this context that the patriarch is also mentioned: "You are summoned by the holy patriarch or right reverend metropolitan, your father, together with the entire holy community, to the anointment with holy and great chrism and for communion in the holy and life-giving divine sacraments of Christ"; before this only the metropolitan had been mentioned. Apparently, the introduction of this rite into the elevation to the tsardom's order of service presumed the participation of the patriarch in principle, and therefore also presumed the establishment of a patriarchate.

One may thus suppose that Ivan IV's elevation to the tsardom in 1547 occurred in conformity with the order of service described in the Chronicle Edition, which very closely corresponds to the service order for Dmitrii Ivanovich's elevation to Grand Prince in 1498; in the Chronicle Edition anointing of the tsar is not mentioned.[17] However, subsequent elevations to the kingdom took place in accord with the order of service presented in the Formulary Edition. The first Russian tsar consecrated with sacred unction was Fedor Ivanovich, enthroned on May 31, 1589,[18] in conformity with the Formulary version of the order of enthronement of his father, Ivan IV. All subsequent Russian tsars were likewise anointed with chrism during the ceremony of enthronement.

III

Anointment with chrism during accession to the throne was practiced in Byzantium as well as in the West.[19] It is not important for us that this custom appeared in Byzantium under Western influence;[20] those who composed the Russian order of elevation to the kingdom (Metropolitan Makarii and his collaborators) undoubtedly took the already existing Byzantine tradition as their point of departure.[21]

Neither in Byzantium nor the West was anointing with chrism during enthronement identified with the sacrament of Chrismation, which in the Orthodox Church is, as a rule, is performed directly after Baptism.[22] However, in Russia, the two were identified.[23] Here it is necessary to emphasize that mere anointment with chrism by no means signifies the sacrament of Chrismation. Thus, for example, we may piously wash our faces with water from the baptismal font, but this will not mean a second baptism; similarly, traditional bathing in the "Jordan" (that is, a baptismal ice hole), arranged for Epiphany, is not the same as Baptism, even though it was an accepted practice to baptize adults who were converting to Orthodoxy in it.[24] In precisely the same way, during Baptism in the Catholic Church the priest daubs the one being baptized with chrism, although this is not considered a special sacrament; subsequently, however, during confirmation, when a bishop anoints a person with it, this is perceived as a sacrament.[25]

Accordingly, in Constantinople as well as in the West, anointment during the ceremony of enthronement was clearly distinguished from the rite of

Chrismation, while in Moscow both rites turned out to be absolutely identical: we can speak here about one and the same ritual, that is, the performance of the same sacrament. Most likely, the Russian hierarchs knew that in Byzantium anointment took place during the enthronement of emperors, but at the same time they did not possess a description of exactly how the given ritual was performed in Constantinople; therefore, they introduced the rite they were familiar with into the order of service for elevation to the tsardom.[26]

Thus, in particular, if the Constantinopolitan patriarch proclaimed "Holy, Holy, Holy"[27] when anointing the emperor, the Muscovite metropolitan or later the patriarch pronounced "The seal and the gift of the Holy Spirit" when anointing the tsar (in a later version: "The seal of the gift of the Holy Spirit"),[28] that is, precisely the words that were said in performing Chrismation. In Constantinople they anointed (crosswise) only the head of the monarch being crowned,[29] while in Moscow they anointed the brow, ears, breast, shoulders, and both sides of each hand, each time repeating the words "The seal and the gift of the Holy Spirit," as is done during Chrismation.[30] In a similar way as after Baptism and Chrismation, it was accepted practice not to remove one's white baptismal clothes and not to wash for seven days, so as not to remove any of the chrism;[31] after anointment the tsar could only wash and change clothes on the eighth day.[32]

Notably, the proclamation "Holy, Holy, Holy" referred to Old Testament tradition,[33] and in particular, to the Old Testament tradition of anointing a king,[34] while the words "The seal and the gift of the Holy Spirit" obviously refer to the New Testament. The proclamation "Holy, Holy, Holy" indicates that the one becoming tsar has been divinely chosen (as is the case with Old Testament kings), while the declaration of the sacramental words during Chrismation likens the tsar to Christ, whom "God anointed . . . with the Holy Spirit."[35] Thus both in Byzantium and the West when a monarch was anointed he was likened to the kings of Israel, while in Russia the tsar was equated to Christ Himself. Hence in the West unjust rulers were compared to impious Biblical kings, whereas in Russia they were juxtaposed to the Antichrist.[36]

IV

And so, consecrating a tsar in Russia—in distinction from consecrations in Byzantium—did not in principle differ from Chrismation, which was performed over every Orthodox Christian after his or her Baptism. Accordingly, if in both the West and in Byzantium the anointing of the monarch preceded the crowning, in Russia it occurred after.[37] At the same time, the crowning itself was likened in an obvious way to Baptism; Chrismation in this case was performed after crowning because in usual practice it was performed after Baptism.

Together with this, anointing the tsar was directly part of the liturgical action. Indeed, anointment took place during the liturgy after the chanting of "Holy to the holies" (*Sviataia sviatym*), and directly after the anointing the metropolitan (or later the patriarch) addressed the tsar with the words: "Come, tsar, as you are worthy, anointed, to take communion"—after which communion would take place.[38] Thus the tsar communes with the Holy Sacraments precisely in his capacity as the anointed and is likened to Christ by the very act of anointment. It is worth noting here that the ritual of crowning, which precedes anointment, is structured like an abbreviated morning service (*utrenia*).[39] Thus the crowning is correlated with Matins and anointment with the liturgy. Accordingly, anointing as tsar is the culminating point of the entire ceremony of enthronement.[40]

At the same time, the "tsar's place" in the middle of the church, where the crowning takes place, correlates with the "tsar's doors" that lead to the altar and before which the anointment is performed; it is worth noting that during this period the label "tsar's doors" (as opposed to the earlier period) relates to Christ as Tsar of Glory.[41] The two tsars—heavenly and earthly—are thus juxtaposed within the space of the temple, in other words, they are located in a spatially defined order. It is not accidental that since the time of Ivan IV the "tsar's place" in the Moscow Cathedral of the Dormition was called "the throne"[42]—the throne of the earthly tsar, situated amid the cathedral, was again clearly juxtaposed to the throne of the heavenly Tsar, located at the altar.[43]

Characteristically, when the tsar was invited for anointment, he was called "holy."[44] Generally speaking, the epithet "holy" was part of the Byzantine emperor's title,[45] although in this context it turns out to be directly connected to the exclamation (*vozglas*, Gr. ecphonesis) "Holy to the holies" that usually precedes communion, but in this case preceded anointing and communion.[46] Thus the connection between anointment and communion was emphasized in the liturgical action.

Anointment to the kingdom defines the special liturgical status of the tsar as manifested in the nature of his taking the Holy Sacraments. After the introduction of anointing with chrism to the rite of elevation to the tsardom the manner in which tsars took communion began to be distinguished from that of laymen, to some degree likening it to the communion of clergymen. Later, from the mid-seventeenth century, the tsar began to take communion exactly the same way as clergy did.[47]

Having been placed in the liturgical context, anointing the tsar gave him a specific sacral status, a special charisma.[48] Hereafter the tsar's special charisma—the charisma of power, conferred precisely through anointment with chrism—was particularly emphasized by the Russian Church. According to Russian specialists in modern canonical law, anointment with chrism "summons a special grace of the Holy Spirit onto the anointed sovereign. Our church teaches that those who do not recognize this grace are subject to anathema and exclusion. On the feast of the Triumph of Orthodoxy that takes place on the first Sunday of Lent, in the Order of Service that is established for this occasion, among other things it is proclaimed: 'To those who think that Orthodox sovereigns are not raised to the throne by God's special will, and that at anointment the gifts of the Holy Spirit are not poured into them for carrying out their great calling; and also to those who dare to raise revolt against them or commit treason—anathema!'"[49]

V

As we know, the sacrament of Chrismation is in principle unrepeatable, just like the sacrament of Baptism that is connected with it. The sacrament of Baptism is only repeated in cases when the earlier baptism is declared invalid or if the very fact of its having taken place is in doubt. Similarly, the repetition of Chrismation, generally speaking, suggests that the previous ritual is being recognized as invalid. However, in the given case the ritual that had been performed over the future tsar after his baptism would not have been put in doubt; the repetition of Chrismation indicated that after crowning the tsar took on a qualitatively new status, different from that of all other people. Chrismation is performed on the same person, but he has taken on a new quality, defined by the ritual of crowning.

In this sense later clarifications by Russian theologians are characteristic:

> The anointing of tsars with holy chrism upon their ascension to the throne was established by God Himself. God, having blessed the regal power for the people of Israel, ordered those selected for kingship to be anointed at the moment they were chosen. Saul, David and other kings of the Jewish people were thus anointed (1 Kings 10:1, 16:2, etc.). On this divinely established basis, and with this same understanding, the Christian Orthodox Church performs the sacrament of Chrismation over Orthodox sovereigns when they are crowned to the tsardom. This is not a special sacrament just because it has

the same basis as Chrismation and the same form; in any case, the Orthodox Church unchangingly recognizes only seven sacraments. This is not the repetition of the same sacrament, because it has an exclusive significance and use; the church recognizes the general sacrament [that is, Chrismation] as unrepeatable. It is only a special variant of the sacrament of Chrismation, or, so to speak, its highest degree, since through it the particular, highest gifts of grace are communicated, corresponding to its supreme mission in the world and in Christ's Church . . . [50]

And also:

Finally, one must not forget to mention in particular, brethren, the strength and grandeur of the sacrament of Chrismation in its use for the crowned head of the Christian people. Who does not know that our devout sovereigns, in ascending the throne, accept holy Chrismation for their great service on the same day as they accept the crown and other marks of greatness? This is not a repetition [of the sacrament] of Chrismation, no, the sacrament is not repeated, just as Baptism, or spiritual birth [cannot be performed twice]; this is another, supreme degree of communicating the gifts of the Holy Spirit that is required for another exalted state and service! Neither is the sacrament of Ordination repeated, but has degrees of elevation; the laying on of hands crowns servitors of the faith for the highest service again and again. Thus we say that holy anointment of tsars is another, supreme degree of a sacrament, when a special Spirit descends onto the head of peoples. "You are my Son, I today gave birth to you" (Psalms 2:7), says the Lord to the tsar on that day when He Himself creates him anew as an exalted person, adorned with all of the gifts of His grace. To this new-born person is added another gift of the Holy Spirit through holy anointment for the Lord's select. [51]

As for the holy action when the Orthodox Church anoints devout Sovereigns with holy chrism upon their elevation to the tsardom . . . this is not a repetition of the sacrament of Chrismation, through which all believers commune with the powers of grace, which are essential for spiritual life itself. No, this is another, supreme level of communion of the gifts of the Holy Spirit that is required for the special, extraordinarily important service of the tsar, specified by God Himself (Daniel 4:22, 29) . . . As is known, the sacrament of Ordination is also not repeated; however, it has its gradations, and the repeated laying on of hands crowns servitors of the faith for the highest service. Thus we say that holy anointment of tsars is but a special, supreme degree of the sacrament, an extraordinary Spirit that descends onto the head of God's anointed ones. [52]

This holy action is indispensable for Orthodox sovereigns, as tsars over a people that has received grace (see 1 Peter 2:9), and for whose governance a ruler is needed who has also received grace in the highest degree. In the tsar's anointment by the Holy Church a special grace of the Holy Spirit is passed on which gives wisdom and strength to divinely-crowned sovereigns for the holy task of tsar's service that faces them. In this way this anointment is not a separate sacrament or a repetition of the sacrament that is performed over every Orthodox Christian after Baptism . . . but merely a special type or supreme degree of the sacrament of Chrismation in which—in view of the special mission of the Orthodox Sovereign in the world—special supreme gifts of grace, of royal wisdom and strength, are communicated to him.[53]

Repetition of Chrismation of one and the same person cannot occur, for reason of the nature of this sacramental action. . . . The Church has never allowed repetition of this sacrament for the same person: "This mystery is not revealed twice"—it says of Chrismation in the Orthodox confession of faith. Only in two cases has the Church permitted its repetition: when crowning a tsar and when someone converts to Orthodoxy from a serious heresy. . . . In the first case the Church has clear Divine command as basis for its behavior. God, in establishing the royal power over his chosen people, ordered the anointing of those chosen for this high merit. . . . For this reason the Christian Church also, in anointing tsars, has as its aim to communicate to them more than the gift of the Holy Spirit that is common to all Christians but a special power of the Holy Spirit which will strengthen them in carrying out their royal responsibilities that are beyond the capability of ordinary people.[54]

Arguing against this kind of assertion, the well-known historian of church law Professor N. S. Suvorov asserted that, on the contrary, the anointment of tsars is a special—eighth!—sacrament, noting that Russian theologians were hesitant to call it so exclusively "from fear of destroying the symmetry of seven sacraments, established at the start by scholastics in the West."[55] This sacrament, in his opinion, was destined to communicate the special gift of ruling the state as well as the Church to tsars:

Russian sovereigns are not dedicated by the church hierarchy but instead receive Holy Chrismation that is performed at coronation. . . . We in Russia have no doubt about its sacramental character, that holy action by which the tsar, by means of Church prayer together with the anointment with chrism, receives power and holy wisdom from above to rule and to judge. Theologians who interpret this act merely as a sacramental descent of the gifts of the Holy Spirit onto the sovereign forget that there is no other person over whom the sacrament may be performed, and that the grace of the Holy Spirit that is necessary for ruling the whole Russian Church is invoked. In contrast, bishops are ordained [by church authority] to rule only an individual diocese . . . but in order to rule the Russian state as a whole and not in parts the beneficent gifts of the Holy Spirit are communicated. Otherwise a theologian would find it difficult to explain why the grace-giving gifts of the Holy Spirit are granted [during the consecration as tsar] for governing the Russian state, while no grace-giving gifts of the Holy Spirit are required for governing the whole Russian Church, not its parts, and consequently for exercising the central Church power.[56]

And further:

In the sacrament of Chrismation the Russian Orthodox tsar receives beneficent gifts for ruling not only the Russian state but also the Church which constitutes the Russian people from itself . . . The tsar is not consecrated into the religious hierarchy, as was the case with the Byzantine emperor, and does not claim the power to perform and teach in church, but receives strength and high wisdom in order to carry out the highest administrative power in both state and Church.[57]

It is curious to juxtapose these statements by Russian scholars of the liturgy with the following evaluation of a Western church historian:

The rite of anointing the tsar [in Russia] has the clear character of a special sacrament, like Chrismation, which is applied to the already anointed tsar in order to emphasize the sacred character of his person and power and to suggest the special grace of his being. At the same time, the crowning and anointment communicate to the tsar the quality of a Christian leader, although they do not give him the authority to carry out this or that liturgical action; accordingly, the tsar takes communion from the hands of a metropolitan like a layman. In this sacred character the [Russian] tsar is completely different from the Byzantine emperor. The tsar, crowned and anointed, occupies a totally unique position among the members of the Church, always remaining only a layman.[58]

In this way, Russian theologians describing the Synodal period unanimously recognize anointing the tsar as a sacrament; at the same time, some have considered this a unique sacrament, different from ordinary Chrismation, and others as a special type of Chrismation sacrament, its supreme degree. In essence, the understanding of the tsar's anointment as a sacrament was defined by the rules of anathematization, cited above. The notion of various (higher and lower) degrees of the same sacrament seems uncanonical. If one understands anointment of the tsar as a special sacrament, different from Chrismation, then one must evidently speak of a special ritual that communicates special charismatic qualities to the anointed tsar. In this case we would have a unique situation in which two rituals that are absolutely identical in every detail would be recognized as different. It would be hard to accept this as anything but canonical nonsense.

It only remains to note that the non-canonical repetition of Chrismation could come into conflict with a person's confessional conscience. Thus, Bishop Andrei (Prince Ukhtomskii) wrote in 1926:

> Everyone knows that during their coronation Russian tsars were anointed with chrism. From a canonical and dogmatic point of view this was [merely] anointment with chrism and in no way the sacrament of Chrismation. I myself personally considered this a sacrament even as a fifth-year gymnasium student, but when I began to make sense of ecclesiastical directives, I began to become critical of puerile textbooks.[59]

But, had Bishop Andrei thought this way, for this he would have been subject to anathema . . .

Translated by Marcus C. Levitt

NOTES

[1]   See Dmitrii Ivanovich's ritual of elevation in: A. I. Pliguzov, G. V. Semenchenko et al., eds., *Russkii feodal'nyi arkhiv XIV-pervoi treti XVI veka* (Moscow, 1986-1992), vyp. 3, prilozhenie, 604-625, no. 16-18; E. V. Barsov, *Drevnerusskie pamiatniki sviashchennogo venchaniia tsarei na tsarstvo v sviazi s grecheskimi ikh originalami. S istoricheskim ocherkom chinov tsarskogo venchaniia v sviazi s razvitiem idei tsaria na Rusi* (Moscow, 1883), kn. 1, xxvii-xxviii, 32-38; P. Catalano, V. T. Pašuto, eds., *L'idea di Roma a Mosca (secoli XV-XVI). Fonti per la storia del pensiero sociale russo* (Rome, 1993), 67-77; Sigizmund Gerbershtein, *Zapiski o Moskovii* (Moscow, 1988), 79-82.

[2]   E. V. Barsov, *Drevnerusskie pamiatniki,* 42-90; P. Catalano, V. T. Pašuto, *L'idea di Roma,* 78-95; *Dopolnenie k Aktam istoricheskim, sobrannym i izdannym Arkheograficheskoiu kommissieiu* (St. Petersburg, 1846-1875), vol. 1, no. 39, 41-53.

[3]   *Polnoe sobranie russkikh letopisei* (St. Petersburg, Petrograd, Leningrad, Moscow, 1841-1989), vol. XIII/1, 150-151; vol. XX/2, 468-469; vol. XXIX, 49-50; vol. XXXIV, 180-181; *Sobranie gosudarstvennykh gramot i dogovorov, khraniashchikhsia v gosudarstvennoi kollegii inostrannykh del* (Moscow, 1813-1894), part. II, no. 33, 41-53.

[4]   *Polnoe sobranie russkikh letopisei,* vol. XIII/2, 452-453; Ia.N. Shchapov, "K izucheniiu 'China venchaniia na tsarstvo' Ivana IV" in *Rimsko-konstantinopol'skoe nasledie na Rusi. Ideia vlasti i politicheskaia praktika. IX Mezhdunarodnyi Seminar istoricheskikh issledovanii "Ot Rima k Tret'emu Rimu." Moskva, 29-31 maia 1989 g.* (Moscow, 1995), 214f.

[5]   *Drevniaia rossiiskaia vivliofika* (Moscow, 1788-1791; The Hague, Paris, 1970), part 7, 4-35; see M. V. Shakhmatov, "Gosudarstvenno-natsional'nye idei 'chinovnykh knig' venchaniia na tsarstvo moskovskikh gosudarei," *Zapiski Russkogo nauchnogo instituta v Belgrade* 1 (1930): 249-252.

[6]   In the order of service published by N. I. Novikov (*Drevniaia rossiiskaia vivliofika,* ch. 7, 4f) the name of Tsaritsa Anastasia is not mentioned (and neither is Ivan's; in general, the exposition here is consistently impersonal). Mention of the patriarch is also absent.

[7]   I. A. Tikhoniuk, "O vizantiiskom obraztse tsarskoi koronatsii Ivana Groznogo," at press.

8 See *Russkaia istoricheskaia biblioteka, izdavaemaia Arkheograficheskoiu komissieiu* (St Petersburg, Petrograd, Leningrad, 1872-1927), vol. XXXI, 340; V. Savva, *Moskovskie tsari i vizantiiskie vasilevsy. K voprosu o vliianii Vizantii na obrazovanie idei tsarskoi vlasti moskovskikh gosudarei* (Kharkov, 1901), 150; W. Regel, ed., *Analecta byzantine-russica* (St. Petersburg, 1891), lif.

9 For the text of the document, see Ibid., 75-85; P. Catalano, V. T. Pašuto, eds., *L'idea di Roma*, 96-104; B. L. Fonkich, "Grecheskie gramoty sovetskikh khranilishch" in *Problemy paleografii i kodikologii v SSSR* (Moscow, 1974), 247-252; B. L. Fonkich, comp., *Grechesko-russkie sviazi serediny XVI—nachala XVIII veka. Grecheskie dokumenty moskovskikh khranilishch, Katalog vystavki* (Moscow, 1991), 8-9, no. 1-3.

10 See V. Savva, *Moskovskie tsari i vizantiiskie vasilevsy*, 150-151.

11 This book has come down to us in a collection from the 1640s: *Chin i ustav o venchanii i o postavlenii tsarskom. Perevodil na Moskve mitropolit Egrivskoi Iasaf s patriarsha Potrebnika tsaregradskago leta 7070 mesiatsa dekabria 13 den`*, RGADA, f. 177, d. 30, ll.26-42. See also I. A. Tikhoniuk, "O vizantiiskom obraztse." In the description (*opis`*) of the tsar's archive it mentions the "book of the tsar's elevation" that was received together with Patriarch Ioasaph's blessing. See *Akty, sobrannye v bibliotekakh i arkhivakh Rossiiskoi imperii Arkheograficheskoi ekspeditsieiu imp. Akademii nauk* (St. Petersburg, 1836), vol. I, 349, no. 289. Another copy of the same text was preserved at the Kirillov Monastery; see P. M. Stroev, "Bibliologicheskii slovar` i chernovye k nemu materialy," *Sbornik Otdeleniia russkogo iazyka i slovesnosti Akademii nauk* 19/4 (1882): 141; Andrei Kurbskii mentions it in his *History of the Grand Prince of Moscow* (*Russkaia istoricheskaia biblioteka*, vol. XXXI, 340), as does the Moscow Chronicle of 1552-1562 ("Letopisets russkii [Moskovskaia letopis` 1552-1562] po rukopisi, prinadlezhashchei A. N. Lebedevu, soobshchil Andrei Lebedev," *Chteniia v Obshchestve istorii i drevnòstei rossiiskikh pri imp. Moskovskom universitete,* kn. 3, otd. 1 (1895): 149).

12 Something similar occurred in 1589 when the first Russian patriarch Job was ordained. Before the elevation of Job the Russians thought it necessary to question the Patriarch of Constantinople, Jeremiah II, about how the patriarch of Constantinople was put into office. However, they were dissatisfied with the Greek ceremonial order and ultimately turned to the Russian tradition for elevating a metropolitan (which involved a second consecration [*chirotony*]). See B. A. Uspenskii, *Tsar` i patriarkh. Kharizma vlasti v Rossii* (*Vizantiiskaia model` i ee russkoe pereosmyslenie*) (Moscow, 1998), 85-87.

13 Ibid., 136-139.

14 See Arkhimandrit Iosif, *Podrobnoe oglavlenie Velikikh Chetkikh Minei vserossiiskago mitropolita Makariia, khraniashchikhsia v Moskovskoi patriarshei (nyne sinodal`noi) biblioteke* (Moscow, 1892), 499.

15 See A. I. Pliguzov, G. V. Semenchenko et al., eds., *Russkii feodal`nyi arkiv,* vyp. 2, 273-275, no. 86; G. P. Majeska, "Russian Travelers to Constantinople in the Fourteenth and Fifteenth Centuries," *Dumbarton Oaks Studies* 19 (1984): 104-113.

16 On several of the Greek sources used in compiling the Formulary Edition, see Kh. Loparev, "O chine venchanii russkikh tsarei," *Zhurnal Ministerstva narodnogo prosveshcheniia* 252 (1887): 312-319.

17 In one of the chronicles ("The Royal Book") there is an editor's note that mention of anointment was required; the note was made after Ivan IV's elevation to the tsardom in 1547 and has no historical significance; see B. A. Uspenskii, *Tsar` i patriarkh*, 21-22, 21-22n17. The same goes for the description of Ivan IV's elevation to the tsardom in

a manuscript from the Pogodin collection (RNB, Pogod. 1567), in which it says that Ivan "was most gloriously elevated to the tsardom of all Rus`... according to the law of a tsar's flawless elevation and most holy Anointment [sic] to the throne of the ancient paternal heritage ... with the blessing and consecration of the primate, Metropolitan of all Rus` Makarii ... which was in the year 7055, January 20 [sic]." This description also mentions the "Tsar's place," that is, the tsar's throne in the Cathedral of the Dormition, set up in 1551, and so indicates that this was composed after the fact. See I. Zabelin, "Arkhaeologicheskaia nakhodka: Reshenie voprosa o Tsarskom meste, ili tak nazyvaemom Monomakhovom trone (po rukopisi Pogodinskogo drevlekhranilishcha)," *Moskvitianin* no. 11, kn. 1, otd. 3 (1850): 55. See also a description of Ivan IV's enthronement in the "Kazan History": "and he ascended the throne and was elevated to the tsardom with a great royal elevation. ... And he was consecrated with sacred unction and decorated with the neck-yoke and the crown of Monomakh, according to the ancient royal law, just as Roman, and Greek, and other Orthodox tsars had been elevated" (T. F. Volkova, "Kazanskaia istoriia," in *Pamiatniki literatury Drevnei Rusi: Seredina XVI veka* (Moscow, 1985), 360). The protograph of the "Kazan History" is dated to 1564-1565, that is, when the Formulary Edition of Ivan IV's elevation to the tsardom already existed; at the same time, the surviving manuscript copies contain traces of editing from the late sixteenth century, during the rule of Fedor Ivanovich, who as we know was not consecrated as tsar with sacred chrism. Thus the document reflects later notions about the procedure of enthronement.

Equally unreliable historically is the report in the Vologda Chronicle concerning the fact that in 1547 Ivan IV "got anointed as tsar for the sake of tsardom" in *Polnoe sobranie russkikh letopisei*, vol. XXXVII, 173. The Vologda Chronicle was compiled in the late seventeenth to early eighteenth century, and correspondingly reflects the ideas of that time about enthronement. Mention of Ivan IV's anointment in the "Chronicle of Novgorod's Divine Churches" (*Novgorodskie letopisi (tak nazyvaemye Novorodskaia vtoraia i Novgorodskaia tret`ia letopisi)* (St. Petersburg: Izd. Arkheograficheskaia komissiia, 1879), 329), as well as in one of the copies of the "Book of Degrees" (see N. M. Karamzin, *Istoriia gosudarstva rosiiskogo* (St. Petersburg, 1842-1843), vol. 8, 24n161) can be explained exactly the same way. In the *History of the Grand Prince of Moscow*, Andrei Kurbskii calls Ivan "the divinely appointed" and speaks of the "the dignity of the tsar's anointing" (*Russkaia istoricheskaia biblioteka*, vol. XXXI, 261, 239); similarly, in an epistle to the elder Vas`ian Kurbskii says that "tsars and princes in the Orthodox faith from ancient generations until today are anointed by God to do justice and to protect [us] from the enemy" (Ibid., 394). These words should not be taken literally: anointing appears here as a necessary attribute of the tsar's rank, deriving from the biblical archetype.

[18] See the order of service in: P. Catalano, V. T. Pašuto, eds., *L'idea di Roma*, 117-118; *Sobranie gosudarstvennykh gramot i dogovorov*, ch. II, 83, no. 51; A. Ia. Shpakov, *Gosudarstvo i tserkov` v ikh vzaimnykh otnosheniiakh v Moskovskom gosudarstve. Tsarstvovanie Fedora Ioanovicha. Uchrezhdenie patriarshestva v Rossii* (Odessa, 1912), prilozhenie 2, 120-122; *Polnoe sobranie russkikh letopisei*, vol. XXXIV, 232.

[19] See B. A. Uspenskii, *Tsar` i imperator: Pomazanie na tsarstvo i semantika monarshikh titulov* (Moscow, 2000), 5-26.

[20] It was adopted between the mid-ninth and mid-tenth century. See Ibid., 26.

[21] Metropolitan Makarii's words addressed to Ivan IV describing elevation to the tsardom are characteristic. In accord with the Formulary Edition of the order of service,

the metropolitan said: "Your father Grand Prince Vasilii Ivanovich, autocrat of all Russia . . . ordered you, his son Ivan, to become Grand Prince and to be anointed and to be crowned with the divinely-crowned tsar's crown, according to the ancient tsar's rite" (E. V. Barsov, *Drevnerusskie pamiatniki*, 49, 74; P. Catalano, V. T. Pašuto, eds., *L'idea di Roma*, 82). The statement about anointment "according to the ancient tsar's rite" cannot, of course, refer to the Russian tradition of enthronement, but most likely to the Byzantine tradition (and, indirectly, to the Biblical tradition). See also note 17 above.

[22]   In his description of the Byzantine coronation rite Simeon of Thessalonica nowhere gives the emperor's anointment the significance of a sacrament and in no way relates it to Chrismation. See: J. P. Migne, ed., *Patrologiae cursus completis. Series graeca* (Paris, 1857-1864), vol. CLV, 351-358; M. Arranz, "L'aspect ritual de l'onction des empereurs de Constantinople et de Moscou," in *Roma, Constantinopoli, Mosca* (Naples, 1983), 413; Idem, "Les Sacrements de l'ancien Euchologue constantinopolitain, X: La consecration de saint Myron," *Orientalia Christiana Periodica* 2 (1989): 319n3; A. Kniazeff, "Les rites d'intronisation royale et imperial," in A. M. Triacca, A. Pistoia eds., *Les benedictions et les sacramentaux dans Liturgie: Conférences Saint-Serge, XXXIVe semaine d'études liturgique. Paris, 23-26 Juin 1987* (Rome, 1988), 155. Likewise, anointing the monarch during his enthronement was not perceived as a sacrament in the West. See E. H. Kantorowicz, "Deus per naturam, Deus per gratiam: A Note on Medieval Political Theology," *The Harvard Theological Review* 45 (1952): 253-277.

[23]   See: M. Arranz, "Évolution des rites d'incorporation et de readmission dans l'Eglise selon l'"Euchologe byzantine," in *Gestes et paroles dans les diverses familles liturgiques. Conférences Saint-Serge, XXIVe semaine d'études liturgique. Paris, 28 Juin-1er Juillet 1977* (Rome, 1978), 66; Idem, "L'aspect ritual de l'onction," 413, 415; Idem, "Les Sacrements," 319n3; Idem, "Couronnement royal et autres promotions de cour: Les Sacrements de l'institution de l'ancien Euchologe constantinopolitain, III/1," *Orientalia Christiana Periodica*, 1 (1990): 86n5.

[24]   In this context, Olearius' mistake is characteristic; he assumed that it was accepted practice to baptize "Chaldeans" (that is, mummers) who took part in the "Fiery Furnace Play" (*Peshchnoe deistvo*) a second time in an ice hole (A. Olearii, *Opisanie puteshestviia v Moskoviiu i cherez Moskoviiu v Persiiu i obratno* (St. Petersburg, 1906), 301-303); actually they only bathed in the ice hole, which was called "the Jordan [River]." We may also mention in this connection the ancient practice in the Orthodox Church of sprinkling with water blessed on Epiphany; see A. Neselovskii, *Chiny khitrotesii i khirotonii. Opyt istoriko-arkheologicheskogo issledovaniia* (Kamenets-Podol´sk, 1906), 87.

[25]   See B. A. Uspenskii, *Tsar´ i imperator*, 7-11. Bishop Andrei (Prince Ukhtomskii) wrote in this connection: "Many priests, the most pious ones, after anointment with chrism of newly-baptized children, instead of wiping off the brush with some rag, anointed their own forehead or head with what was left over . . . Well then, may this behavior by devout priests be seen as the sacrament of Chrismation?" See A. Znatov. ed., "Ep. Andrei (Ukhtomskii), 'Istoriia moego staroobriadchestva (1926)'," *Nash sovremennik*, 1 (2007): 212.

[26]   It is not impossible that the Russians based their practice on the epistle of the Constantinopolitan Patriarch Antony IV to Grand Prince Vasilii (Basil) I of 1393, in which it was emphasized that the Byzantine emperor was the head of all Christians and that he had been anointed with chrism: "He is anointed with the great chrism and elevated to tsar and autocrat of all Romans, that is, all Christians." See *Russkaia istoricheskaia biblioteka*, vol. VI, prilozhenie no. 40, 271-272; Fr. Miklosich, I. Müller,

eds., *Acta Patriarchatus Constantinopolitani, 1315-1402* (Darmstadt, 1860-1868), vol. 2, 190, no. 447. This epistle might have been a source of misunderstanding, as anointment with chrism (*pomazanie mirom*) could have been taken to mean Chrismation (*miropomazanie*). True, this epistle was only known in the Greek original; at least, manuscripts with a Russian translation have not been preserved. On the history of the epistle, see D. Obolensky, "A Late Fourteenth-Century Byzantine Diplomat. Michael, Archbishop of Bethlehem," in *Byzance et les Slaves: Études de civilisation: Mélanges Ivan Dujcev* (Paris, 1979), 305-306.

[27] For example, in: Jean Verpeaux, ed., *Pseudo-Kodinos: Traité des offices* (Paris, 1966), 258; L. Schopen, ed., *Ioannes Cantacuzenos (Ioannis Cantacuzeni historiae libri IV)* (Bonn, 1828-1832), vol. 1, 197; or in Simeon of Thessalonica in J. P. Migne, ed., *Patrologiae cursus completis. Series graeca*, vol. CLV, 353-354. See also the anonymous description of the anointment of Emperor Manuel II in 1392 in Jean Verpeaux, ed., *Pseudo-Kodinos*, supplement VI, 354-355.
According to the Byzantine order of enthronement of the emperor from the Medici library the words "Holy, Holy, Holy" were pronounced by the patriarch (and then repeated by the archdeacon and other clergy) directly before the anointment rather that at the moment of anointment. See Kh. Loparev, "K chinu tsarskogo koronavaniia v Vizantii" in *Sbornik statei v chest` Dmitriia Fomicha Kobeko: ot sosluzhivtsev po Impe-ratorskoi publichnoi biblioteke* (St. Petersburg, 1913), 3, 8. This differs from what other authors report.

[28] This formula was prescribed by the seventh rule of the I Constantinopolitan (II Ecu-menical) Council (of 381). For the history of the text of the formula in the Russian liturgical rite, see: *Russkaia istoricheskaia biboioteka*, vol. VI, 93, no. 6; V. N. Beshenevich, *Drevne-slavianskaia kormchaia. XIV titulov bez tolkovanii* (St. Petersburg, Sofia,1906-1987), vol. 2, 182, no. 32; A. Almazov, *Istoriia chinoposledovanii kreshcheniia i miropomazaniia* (Kazan, 1884), 417-418, 422; prilozhenie, 48, 51, 62, 65; E. Golubinskii, *Istoriia russkoi tserkvi* (Moscow, 1917), vol. 2/2, 518; M. Arrants, "Chin oglasheniia i kreshcheniia v Drevnei Rusi," *Simvol* 19 (1988): 89-90; I. Rumiantsev, *Nikita Konstantinov Dobrynin* (*"Pustosviat"). Istoriko-kriticheskii ocherk* (Sergiev Posad, 1916), prilozhenie, 257.
As far as we know, in only one case was anointing as tsar accompanied by other words, and thus formally differing from Chrismation, and that was at the coronation of Catherine I (May 7, 1724), when instead of "The seal and the gift of the Holy Spirit" were pronounced the words: "In the name of the Father and the Son and the Holy Spirit." See *Opisanie koronatsii Ee velichestva imperatritsy, Ekateriny Aleksievny, torzhestvenno otpravlennoi v tsarstvuiushchem grade Moskve 7 maiia 1724 godu* (St. Petersburg, 1724), 14. This may be explained by the fact that Catherine was crowned as the emperor's spouse rather than as ruling empress (which was an unprecedented phenomenon in Russia, and which may be explained by Peter I's western cultural orientation). At the same time, after Peter's death Catherine's coronation was the formal basis for her ascension to the throne on January 28, 1725, which took place without any special rituals. Thus Catherine I's coronation represents an exception, when during a monarch's anointing the rite of Chrismation was not repeated. See B. A. Uspenskii, *Tsar` i patriarkh*, 162-164; Idem, "Liturgicheskii status tsaria v russkoi tserkvi. Priobshchenie k tainam" in B. A. Uspenskii, *Etiudy o russkoi istorii* (St. Petersburg, 2002), 229-278, esp. 238-241.

[29] St. Simeon of Thessalonica explains that the head alone is anointed because the emperor of Byzantium is the head of all Christians. See J. P. Migne, ed., *Patrologiae*

cursus completis. Series graeca, vol. CLV, 353-354; D. M. Nicol, "Kaisersalbung: The Unction of Emperors in Late Byzantine Coronation Ritual," *Byzantine and Modern Greek Studies* 2 (1976): 48-49. Thus here there is a play on the two meanings of "head" (κεφαλή)—the concrete and the abstract. This interpretation is the result of a later reconsideration: historically the anointing of the head during elevation to the kingdom apparently derives from the western Baptismal rite. See B. A. Uspenskii, *Tsar` i imperator*, 12.

30 E. V. Barsov, *Drevnerusskie pamiatniki*, xxviii, 8, 63, 87; M. Arranz, "L'aspect ritual de l'onction," 413. In modern times it is also usual to anoint the feet during the sacrament of Chrismation (see K. Nikol`skii, *Posobie k izucheniiu ustava bogosluzheniia pravoslavnoi tserkvi* (St. Petersburg, 1874), 67), although they did not do this earlier in Russia. See A. Almazov, *Istoriia chinoposledovanii*, 412-413, 415-416, 418, 420, 423; prilozhenie, 48, 51, 62, 65; E. Golubinskii, *Istoriia russkoi tserkvi*, vol. 1/2, 432; vol. 2/1, 73; vol. 2/2, 518; N. Odintsov, *Poriadok obshchestvennogo i chastnogo bogosluzheniia v drevnei Rossii do XVI veka: Tserkovno-istoricheskoe issledovanie* (St. Petersburg, 1881), 76-77, 260-261; "Posledovanie tainstv v tserkvi russkoi v XVI stoletii, po rukopisiam Novgorodskoi-Sofiiskoi i Moskovskoi-Sinodal`noi biblioteki," *Strannik* (1880): 565; Ieromon. Filaret, *Opyt slicheniia tserkovnykh chinoposledovanii po izlozheniiu tserkovno-bogoslyzhebnykh knig moskovskoi pechati, izdannykh pervymi piat`iu rossiiskimi patriarkhami, s ukazaniem predstavliaemykh simi knigami vazhneishikh razlichii i nesoglasii v izlozhenii tserkovnykh chinov* (Moscow, 1875), 29-30; *Russkaia istoricheskaia biblioteka*, vol. VI, 33, 55, no. 2; 93-94 no. 6; V. N. Beshenevich, *Drevne-slavianskaia kormchaia*, vol. 2, 182, no. 32; M. Arranz, "Les Sacrements de l'ancien Euchologe constantinopolitain, VI-IX: L'Illumination de la nuit de pâques," *Orientalia Christiana Periodica* 1 (1987): 88-89; M. Arrants, "Chin oglasheniia," 89-90. Cf. however: "Chast` 1: Sluzhby kruga sedmichnogo i godichnogo i chinoposledovaniia tainstv. Istoriko-arkheologicheskoe issledovanie," in A. Dmitrievskii, *Bogosluzhenie v russkoi tserkvi v XVI veke* (Kazan, 1884), 294. See also the Old Believers' protest against the anointing of feet in N. Subbotin, ed., *Materialy dlia istorii raskola za pervoe vremia ego sushchestvovaniia, izdavaemye bratstvom sv. Petra mitropolita* (Moscow, 1875-1890), vol. 6, 286, 323; vol. 7, 349; P. S. Smirnov, *Iz istorii raskola pervoi poloviny XVIII veka po neizdannym pamiatnikam* (St. Petersburg, 1908), 201. Still, generally speaking anointing feet is a very ancient tradition. See, in particular, F. C. Conybeare, ed., *Rituale Armenorum* (Oxford, 1905), 98. In general, the ritual of anointing was not stable (see M. Arrants, *Kreshchenie i miropomazanie: Tainstva Vizantiiskogo Evkhologiia* (Rome, 1998), 153-154), and this could affect the ritual of anointing as tsar.

In this connection, we note that when Aleksei was enthroned as tsar (on September 28, 1645), the patriarch also anointed his beard and under his beard with holy chrism. See: *Drevniaia Rossiiskaia Vivliofika*, part 7, 290; Arhimandrit Leonid (Kavelin), ed., "Chin postavleniia na tsarstvo tsaria i velikogo kniazia Alekseia Mikhailovicha," *Obshchestvo liubitelei drevnei pis`mennosti, Pamiatniki drevnei pis`mennosti* 7 (1882): 32; E. V. Barsov, *Drevnerusskie pamiatniki*, xxxi-xxxii; N. Pokrovskii, "Chin koronovaniia gosudarei v ego istorii," *Tserkovnyi vestnik* 19 (1896): 607; E. Karnovich, "Koronovanie gosudarei," *Russkii arkhiv: Russkii istoricheskii zhurnal* 1 (1990): 50. This was conditioned by the special attitude toward beards, which were generally accorded sacred status. See B. A. Uspenskii, *Filologicheskie razyskaniia v oblasti slavianskikh drevnostei (Relikty iazychestva v vostochnoslavianskom ku`te Nikolaia Mirlikiiskogo)* (Moscow, 1982), 173-175. A case is known of daubing boys' chins with chrism when performing Chrismation.

See Kh. Ia. Nikiforovskii, *Prostonarodnye primety i pover'ia, suevernye obriady i obychai, legendarnye skazaniia o litsah i mestakh v Vitebskoi Belorussii* (Vitebsk, 1897), 21, no. 136; this practice might possibly have influenced the rite of the tsar's enthronement. The special attitude toward the beard might have been supported in this case by the words of the Psalter about the myrrh that streamed from Aaron's head onto his beard (Psalm 132: 2 [133:2]). See also St. Augustine's commentary on this passage: "In capite ipsius unguentum, quia totus Christus cum Ecclesia: sed a capite venit unguentum. Caput nostrum Christus est: crucifixum et sepultum resuscitatum ascendit in coelum; et venit Spiritus Sanctus a capite. Quo? Ad barbam. Barba significat fortes; barba significat iuvenes strenuos, imprigros, alacres" (J. P. Migne, ed., *Patrologiae cursus completis. Series latina*, vol. XXXVII, 1733), and also a thirteenth century lyric: "Unguentum in capite quod descendit in barbam, barbam Aaron, quod descendit in oram vestimenti eius, mandavit dominus benedictionem in seculum" (E. Lodi, "Enchiridion euchologicum fontium liturgicorum," *Bilbiotheca "Ephemerides liturgicae"* 15 (1979): 1678, no. 3349b).

[31] See A. Almazov, *Istoriia chinoposledovanii*, 470f; K. Nikol'skii, *Posobie k izucheniiu ustava*, 676; N. Odintsov, "Posledovanie tainstv," 571; Idem, *Poriadok obshchestvennogo i chastnogo bogosluzheniia*, 83, 152; A. Dmitrievskii, *Bogosluzhenie v russkoi tserkvi*, 307. On an analogous custom among the Greeks, see, in particular, Simeon of Thessalonica in J. P. Migne, ed., *Patrologiae cursus completis. Series graeca*, vol. CLV, 235-236. As Amalarius of Metz testifies, the same thing took place in the Western church at one time. See: I. M. Hanssens, ed., "Amalarii episcopi opera liturgica omnia," *Studi e testi* 2 (1949): 186; J. P. Migne, ed., *Patrologiae cursus completis. Series latina*, vol. CV, 1070; N. Odintsov, *Poriadok obshchestvennogo i chastnogo bogosluzheniia*, 79-80.

[32] See: E. V. Barsov, *Drevnerusskie pamiatniki*, 63, 87-88, 96; P. Catalano, V. T. Pašuto, eds., *L'idea di Roma*, 92, 118; *Drevniaia rossiiskaia vivliofika*, part VII, 31, 291-292, 360, 465; *Polnoe sobranie zakonov Rossiiskoi imperii. Sobranie pervoe* (St. Petersburg, 1830), vol. 2, 64, no. 648; 435, no. 931; *Sobranie gosudarstvennykh gramot i dogovorov*, part II, 83-84, no. 51; part 3, 85, no. 16; Arhimandrit Leonid (Kavelin), ed., "Chin postavleniia na tsarstvo," 32-33; A. Ia. Shpakov, *Gosudarstvo i tserkov'*, prilozhenie 2, 122; RNB, Dukh. akad., d. 27, l. 64.

M. Arranz suggests that these special features of the Russian ritual of anointing as tsar were determined by the fact that Metropolitan Makarii did not consider himself comparable to the patriarch of Constantinople, who alone was invested with the appropriate divine authority. See M. Arranz, "L'aspect rituel de l'onction," 415; Idem, *Istoricheskie zametki o chinoposledovaniiakh tainstv po rukopisiam Grecheskogo Evkhologiia. Leningradskaia dukhovnaia Akademiia, 3-i kurs* (Rome, 1979), 67. We find a different explanation in A. Kniazeff, who is inclined to think that here the tendency was felt to repeat especially important rituals, something which the author feels was characteristic of Russians. (See A. Kniazeff, "Les rites d'intronisation," 157.) It is impossible to agree with either explanation; see our discussion of the question of a special cheirotonia (*khirotoniia*, placing of hands) by Russian metropolitans and patriarchs which Kniazeff mentions in B. A. Uspenskii, *Tsar' i patriarkh*, 30-107.

[33] Isaiah 6:3.

[34] In the prayer which the patriarch of Constantinople pronounced during the emperor's enthronement (which begins with the words "Lord, Our God! To the Tsar ruling and

the Lord reigning" [*Tsariu tsarstvuiushchim i Gospod` gospodstvuiushchim*] in the Slavonic translation), King David's anointment is mentioned ("Lord, our God . . . for Samuel the prophet chose his slave David and anointed him king [*tsar`*] over his people Israel . . . "), and so David thus turns out to be prototype of the crowned emperor. See M. Arranz, "Couronnement royal," 127. As Simeon of Thessalonica and several other sources attest, it was precisely after this prayer that anointment took place in Byzantium. See: J. P. Migne, ed., *Patrologiae cursus completis. Series graeca*, vol. CLV, 353-354; Kh. Loparev, "K chinu tsarskogo koronavaniia," 3, 8; M. Arranz, "L'aspect rituel de l'onction," 413; A. Kniazeff, "Les rites d'intronisation," 155. For the Greek text of this prayer, see E. V. Barsov, *Drevnerusskie pamiatniki*, 27-28. Cf. in this context the perception of the monarch as "new David" which was typical for both Byzantium and for the Medieval West. See B. A. Uspenskii, *Tsar` i imperator*, 4, 60n41. This prayer also became part of the Muscovite order of service for elevation to the throne, although there it preceded the actual ceremony of enthronement and was not directly connected to the anointment. See B. A. Uspenskii, *Tsar` i patriarkh,* 137; in particular, we find it in the offices of enthronement of Dmitrii Ivanovich in 1498 (see *Russkii feodal`nyi arhiv,* vyp. 3, 610, 616, 622, no. 6-18; *Polnoe sobranie russkikh letopisei,* vol. XII, 247), and then of Ivan IV in 1547 (see Ibid., vol. XIII/1, 150; vol. XIII/2, 451-452), although neither was anointed as tsar or Grand Prince.

35 Acts 10:38. According to St. Simeon of Thessalonica's interpretation, in Byzantium anointment was administered on behalf of Christ: a cross was made on the emperor's head using chrism because "Christ himself anoints the basileus, protecting him with his cross from failures, giving him power and making him the head." See J. P. Migne, ed., *Patrologiae cursus completis. Series graeca,* vol. CLV, 353-354; and the Slavonic translation by Evfimii of Chudov in RNB, Dukh. akad., d. 27, l. 28 verso; BAN, f. 32.5.12, l. 20; f. 32.4.19, l. 69 verso; also see in this connection M. Arranz, "Couronnement royal," 125. Hence the idea of anointment turns out to be significantly different in Byzantium and Russia; if in Byzantium Christ anoints the tsar (basileius), in Russia the tsar resembles Christ as a result of his anointment.

In this connection, the polemic between Patriarch Nikon and the Metropolitan of Gaza Paisios Ligarides in 1664 is curious. Ligarides taught that the tsar is anointed by God, according to the Greek tradition, but Nikon countered: "If you say that the tsar went to the altar because he is anointed by God, you are lying. He is anointed through the hierarch [i.e. patriarch] as tsar." See V. A. Tumins, G. Vernadsky, eds., *Patriarch Nikon on Church and State: Nikon's "Refutation"* [Vozrazhenie ili razorenie smirennago Nikona, Bozhieiu milostiiu patriarkha, protivo voprosov boiarina Simeona Streshneva, ezhe napisa Gazskomu mitropolitu Paisiiu Likaridiusu i na otvety Paisiovy, 1664 g.] (Berlin; New York: Mouton, 1982), 621-622; V. K-v, "Vzgliad Nikona na znachenie patriarshei vlasti," *Zhurnal Ministerstva narodnogo prosveshcheniia* 212 (1880): 243n2. On this polemic, see B. A. Uspenskii, *Tsar` i patriarkh*, 158-159; B. A. Uspenskii, "Liturgicheskii status tsaria v russkoi tserkvi. Priobshchenie sv. tainam," *Uchenye zapiski. Rossiiskii pravoslavnyi universitet ap. Ioanna Bogoslova* 2 (1996): 235-236.

36 This observation belongs to S. Averintsev (oral communication). On the perception of unjust tsars in Russia, see: B. A. Uspenskii, "Historia sub specie semioticae" in *Kul`turnoe nasledie Drevnei Rusi: Istoki, stanovlenie, traditsii* (Moscow, 1976), 286-292 (on Peter I); Idem, "Tsar and Pretender: *Samozvanchestvo* or Royal Imposture in Russia as a Cultural-Hisotrical Phenomenon" in this volume, 115 (on the False Dmitrii);

A. M. Panchenko, B. A. Uspenskii, "Ivan Groznyi i Petr Velikii: kontseptsii pervogo monarkha," *Trudy Otdela drenerusskoi literatury* XXXVII (1983): 54-78 (on Ivan IV).

[37] See in this connection B. A. Uspenskii, *Tsar` i patriarkh*, 136-143. In Russia the so-called cap of Monomakh served as the tsar's crown; see B. A. Uspenskii, "Vospriiatie istorii v Drevnei Rusi i doktrina 'Moskva—tretii Rim'" in *Russkoe podvizhnichestvo. Sbornik statei k 90-letiiu D. S. Likhacheva* (Moscow, 1996), 468-469, 480-483, notes 11-24.

[38] E. V. Barsov, *Drevnerusskie pamiatniki*, 63, 87; P. Catalano, V. T. Pašuto, eds., *L'idea di Roma*, 92, 118; *Sobranie gosudarstvennykh gramot i dogovorov*, part II, 83, no. 51; part III, 85, no. 16; Arhimandrit Leonid (Kavelin), ed., "Chin postavleniia na tsarstvo," 32-33; A. Ia. Shpakov, *Gosudarstvo i tserkov`*, prilozhenie, 122.

[39] See A. Kniazeff, "Les rites d'intronisation," 159.

[40] In the "Royal Book," which contains the Chronicle Edition of the order of service for Ivan IV's elevation to the kingdom, there is an editor's note written in *skoropis`* script that indicates the necessity of making reference to anointment. Here we read: "In the liturgy after the Cherubims' song anointment with oil, after 'She is worthy,' anointment with chrism, and just then write Eucharist" (*Polnoe sobranie russkih letopisei*, vol. XIII/2, i452n1). Hence anointing with chrism, according to this source, is performed not immediately before communion (as it is prescribed in the Formulary Edition and as it was subsequently practiced) but right after the presentation of the Gifts. This note obviously reflects the process of working out the future order of enthronement as tsar; it is posited that the editorial corrections to the chronicle belong to the 1570's. See Ia.N. Shchapov, "K izucheniiu 'China venchaniia na tsarstvo'," 215. It is curious that according to this source anointment is performed at the time when it was customary to ordain deacons (see K. Nikol`skii, *Posobie k izucheniiu ustava* bogosluzheniia, 433-436, 706), which generally speaking correlates to the understanding of the liturgical status of the Byzantine emperor. See in this connection B. A. Uspenskii, *Tsar` i patriarkh*, 156; B. A. Uspenskii, "Liturgicheskii status tsaria," 233. Nonetheless, this order of service was not adopted, which is also quite indicative.

[41] See B. A. Uspenskii, *Tsar` i patriarkh*, 144-150.

[42] In the description of Ivan IV's enthronement as tsar, composed after the fact (i.e., after he had already become tsar), we read: "This very Tsar's place, which is the throne, was built in the year 7060 [1552], on the first day of September, in the fifth year of his power, kingdom, and governance." See I. Zabelin, "Arkheologicheskaia nakhodka," 55. The fact that the tsar's throne in the Cathedral of the Dormition was established on the first day of the new year may be significant.

[43] The equation of these two thrones was manifested very eloquently in Emel`ian Pugachev's behavior. After seizing a city he went to the cathedral, went into the altar through the tsar's gates, and sat on the throne. See B. A. Uspenskii, "Liturgicheskii status tsaria," 274n44. At the same time this kind of association may also be traced in more well-educated circles, for example, that of Bishop Innokentii Borisov: "Why do our most devout sovereigns ascend the throne? . . . For the peoples too there must be a continuous Tabor on which the will of the heavenly lawgiver can be discerned, where the light of God's glory is reflected on the face of the crowned representatives of the people. This Sinai, this Tabor—is the tsar's throne." See B. A. Uspenskij, V. M. Zhivov, "Tsar` and God. Semiotic Aspects of the Sacralization of the Monarch in Russia" in this volume, 77. The word "throne" (*prestol*) goes back to the Slavonic Bible; see on King Solomon: "And the king created a throne [*prestol*] . . . " (1 Kings 10:18).

44   See the address to the tsar in the Formulary Edition of the order of service for the enthronement of Ivan IV (which, as already noted, had been composed after Ivan had already become tsar, and which defined the order for all later enthronements): "Lord Holy Divinely-Crowned Tsar, the holy patriarch summons you, or the most holy metropolitan, your father, with the entire holy council, to anointing with holy and great chrism, and to communing with the holy and life-giving, divine sacraments of Christ." See E. V. Barsov, *Drevnerusskie pamiatniki*, 62, 86; P. Catalano, V. T. Pašuto, eds., *L'idea di Roma*, 91. The same salutation of the tsar as "holy" is also met in the order of service for the enthronement of Fedor Ivanovich (Ibid., 118; *Sobranie gosudarstvennykh gramot i dogovorov*, part 2, 83, no. 51; A. Ia. Shpakov, *Gosudarstvo i tserkov`*, prilozhenie 2, 121), as well as in that of Mikhail Fedorovich (*Sobranie gosudarstvennykh gramot i dogovorov*, part 3, 84, no.16) and of Aleksei Mikhailovich (*Drevniaia rossiiskaia vivliofika*, part VII, 288, 291, 31). However, this address is absent in the order of service for Boris Godunov's elevation to the kingdom (*Dopolneniia k Aktam istoricheskim*, vol. 1, 247, no.145), as well in that of Fedor Alekseevich (*Drevniaia rossiiskaia vivliofika*, part VII, 357; *Polnoe sobranie zakonov*, vol. II, 63, no. 648) and that of Ivan Alekseevich and Peter Alekseevich (*Drevniaia rossiiskaia vivliofika*, part VII 7, 462; *Polnoe sobranie zakonov*, vol. II, 434, no. 931). See also: V. Savva, *Moskovskie tsari i vizantiiskie vasilevsy*, 151n3, 153; B. A. Uspenskij, V. M. Zhivov, "Tsar and God," in this volume, 14.
The form of address "lord" (*gospodi*) is also noteworthy in relation to the tsar, as apparently juxtaposed in the given context to the form "*gospodine*," which was usual in addressing simple mortals. While "*gospdine*" represented the vocative form of "*gospodin*," "*gospodi*" was the vocative of "*gospod`*." In the order of service for Boris Godunov's enthronement we find the form "*gosudar`*." See *Dopolneniia k Aktam istoricheskim*, vol. 1, 247, no. 145. The same form of address is used in Patriarch Nikon's epistle to the Constantinopolitan Patriarch Dionisios in 1665. See E. Matthes-Hohlfeld, "Der Brief des Moskauer Patriarchen Nikon an Dionysios, Patriarch von Konstantinopel (1665). Textausgabe und sprachliche Beschreibung von zwei bisher nicht veröffentlichten Handschriften," *Bibliotheca Slavonica* 3 (1970): 285.

45   Theophanes Continuatus (III, 10) relates how Emperor Michael II (820-829) ordered that he not be called "holy," insofar as "he took it into his head that this word could only apply to God"; the writer found this incorrect. See I. Bekker, ed., *Theophanes Continuatus, Ioannes Cameniata, Symeon Magister, Georgius Monachus* (Bonn, 1838), 99; Ia. N. Liubarskii, ed., *Prodolzhatel` Feofana. Zhizneopisaniia vizantiiskih tsarei*, (St. Petersburg, 1992), 46.

46   See: B. A. Uspenskij, V. M. Zhivov, "Tsar and God," in this volume, 23-24. A. Ia. Shpakov, *Gosudarstvo i tserkov`*, prilozhenie 2, 120-121. After the introduction of anointment into the Byzantine enthronement rite the epithet "holy" as applied to the emperor was associated with the exclamation "Holy, holy, holy," that was pronounced during the royal anointment in Byzantium; in any case, the epithet was connected with the special status of the emperor as the anointed one. In the words of Simeon of Thessalonica, "the pious emperor is holy through anointment, and the high priest is holy through the laying on of hands" (J. P. Migne, ed., *Patrologiae cursus completis. Series graeca*, vol. CLV, 431-432); in another place Simeon says that the exclamation "agios" while anointing as emperor signifies that the emperor "is made holy by the Holy Spirit and dedicated by Christ as the emperor of the sanctified" (Ibid., 353-354). At the same time, Makarios of Ancyra, an author of the fourteenth-fifteenth century, asserts that "the emperor, the Lord's anointed, is holy through anointment and belongs to the

clergy ... [He] is a hierarch, priest and teacher of the faith" (*Leonis Allatii de ecclesiae occidentalis atque orientalis perpetua consensione, libri tres* (Cologne, 1648), 219, s.l., 1970; V. Savva, *Moskovskie tsari i vizantiiskie vasilevsy*, 65). In Balsamon's opinion it was precisely the anointment of emperors that made them equal to clergymen, giving them the right to approach the altar, use the thurible, burn incense like priests, bless with the triple-branched candlestick like hierarchs, and, finally, to teach the faith (See Ibid., 73-74; J. P. Migne, ed., *Patrologiae cursus completis. Series graeca*, vol. CXXXVII, 751-754; vol. CXIX, 1165-1166). Pachymeres cites a characteristic episode when Patriarch Joseph I (1267-1275) composed his testament; he didn't call Emperor Michael Paleologue ἅγιος, as it was accepted for emperors who had been anointed with chrism. It turned out that this word had actually been in the original text of the testament but was later left out by monastic copyists who considered it blasphemous in reference to the emperor, whom they considered a heretic. See: I. Bekker, ed., *Georgii Pachymeris de Michaele et Andronico Paleologis libri tredecim* (Bonn, 1835), vol. 1, 507; A. Failler, ed., "Georges Pachymérès. Relation historique," *Corpus fontium historiae byzantinae* 24/2 (1984): 639-639; Georgii Pakhimer, *Istoriia o Mihaile i Andronike Paleologakh* (St. Petersburg, 1862), vol. 1, 468; D. M. Nicol, "Kaisersalbung," 46-47; I. E. Troitskii, *Arsenii, patriarkh Nikeiskii i Konstantinopol'skii, i arsenity. K istorii vostochnoi tserkvi v XIII veke* (St. Petersburg, 1873), 190.

Thus both in Byzantium and in Russia the epithet "holy" in relation to the tsar (emperor) was associated with anointing, although in Byzantium it was associated with the exclamation "Holy, holy, holy," while in Russia it was understood through its connection to the exclamation "Holy to the holies."

[47]   See: B. A. Uspenskii, *Tsar' i patriarkh*, 151f; Idem., *Tsar' i imperator*, 232f.

[48]   B. A. Uspenskij, V. M. Zhivov, "Tsar and God," in this volume, 10-11.

[49]   P. Vozdvizhenskii, *Sviashchennoe koronovanie i venchanie na tsarstvo russkikh gosudarei s drevneishikh vremen i do nashikh dnei* (St. Petersburg, Moscow, 1896), 3; K. Nikol'skii, *Anafematstvovanie (otluchenie ot tserkvi), sovershaemoe v pervuiu nedeliu Velikogo posta: Istoricheskoe issledovanie o chine Pravoslavii* (St. Petersburg, 1879), 263. This order of service was compiled in 1766 (Ibid., 49-50); the corresponding exclamation was repealed by decision of the All-Russian Orthodox Council (*Pomestnyi Sobor*) of 1917-1918 (A. G. Kravetskii, "Diskussii o tserkovnoslavianskom iazyke (1917-1943)," *Slavianovedenie*, 5 (1993): 124). On the eighteenth-century sacralization of the monarch in general, see B. A. Uspenskii, V. M. Zhivov, "Tsar and God," in this volume, 1-112.

[50]   "Obzor tserkovnykh postanovlenii o Kreshchenii i Miropomazanii," *Pravoslavnyi sobesednik*, February (1859): 179-180.

[51]   Archbishop Ignatii (Semenov), *O tainstvakh edinoi, sviatoi, sobornoi i apostol'skoi Tserkvi: Opyt arkheologicheskii* (St. Petersburg, 1849), 143.

[52]   Mitr. Makarii (Bulgakov), *Pravoslavno-dogmaticheskoe bogoslovie* (St. Petersburg, 1895-1905), vol. 2, 360-361; see also K. Nikol'skii, *Posobie k izucheniiu ustava bogosluzheniia*, 686; *Sviashchennoe miropomazanie russkikh Gosudarei i ego znachenie* (Moscow, 1896), 2-3.

[53]   S. V. Bulgakov, *Nastol'naia kniga dlia sviashchenno-tserkovno-sluzhitelei: Sbornik svedenii, kasaiushchikhsia preimushchestvenno prakticheskoi deiatel'nosti otechestvennogo dukhovenstva* (Moscow, 1913; 1993), 995n1; P. Lebedev, *Nauka o bogosluzhenii Pravoslavnoi Tserkvi* (Moscow, 1890), part 2, 138.

[54]   S. Pospelov, *Rassuzhdenie o tainstve Miropomazaniia* (Moscow, 1840), 58-59.

[55]   N. Suvorov, *Kurs tserkovnogo prava* (Iaroslavl', 1890), vol. 2, 27.

56 Ibid., 26. The author accompanies this argument with the following remarkable comment: "Meanwhile, every bishop, at the very moment of his consecration, is clear about the existence of the supreme power that determines his juridical limits and communicates legal authority. The consecrated hears the royal decree announcing that the sovereign *orders* and the Holy Synod blesses him to be a bishop, that is, to exercise those spiritual gifts that are created by his dedication as bishop, within particular juridical bounds, while the consecrated person 'thanks, accepts, and does not demur.' And the members of the Holy Synod (which title is also granted to them at the will of the sovereign) upon their entry into this supreme central ruling establishment *swear an oath* to recognize 'the monarch of all Russia, our all-gracious sovereign, as the ultimate judge of the spiritual college'" (Ibid.). From Suvorov's point of view, the Synodal administration embodies the essence of the Orthodox tradition. See in this connection, B. A. Uspenskij, V. M. Zhivov, "Tsar and God," in this volume, 22.

57 N. Suvorov, *Kurs tserkovnogo prava*, vol. 2, 28. A. M. Loviagin literally says the same thing: "According to the teaching of Orthodox theologians, anointment, which accompanies coronation, is a special sacrament: the tsar is not consecrated into the religious hierarchy as it was with the Byzantine emperor, and does not take on the power to perform and teach in church, but receives strength and high wisdom in order to carry out the highest administrative power in both state and Church" (A. M. Loviagin, "Koronatsiia ili koronovanie" in F. A. Brokgauz, I. A. Efron, eds., *Entsiklopedicheskii slovar`* (St. Petersburg, 1895), vol. 16, 320-321). Compare with this the accusation against the Russian Church by representatives of the Ukrainian Autocephalous Church: "The Muscovite hierarchy established a number of imperial (tsarist) holidays and 'services' and punished those priests who didn't carry out the emperor's cult by defrocking them. It [the Muscovite hierarchy] even introduced a completely new sacrament of 'Chrismation' to the tsardom that went against the Christian faith" (V. Chekhovskii, *Za tserkvu, Khristovu gromadu, proti tsarstva t`mi* (Frankfurt on Main, 1947), 8). The author says approximately the same thing as N. S. Suvorov and A. M. Loviagin: that the anointment of the monarch has the character of a special sacrament in the Russian Church, even though they give the given idea completely opposite evaluations.

58 G. Olšr, "La Chiesa e lo Stato nel cerimoniale d'incoronazione degli ultimi sovrani Rurikidi," *Orientalia christiana periodica*, 3-4 (1950): 296. The author is not fully accurate in the description of the tsar's communion. On this see: B. A. Uspenskii, *Tsar` i patriarkh*, 151-186; Idem., "Liturgicheskii status tsaria," 229-278.

59 A. Znatov. ed., "Ep. Andrei (Ukhtomskii)," 213.

EUROPE AS METAPHOR AND METONYMY
(IN RELATION TO THE HISTORY
OF RUSSIA)

B. A. Uspenskij

1. It seems obvious that Europe is not so much a geographical notion as a cultural-historical and ideological one. Not many people are aware that from the geographical point of view the center of Europe is Vilnius, the capital of Lithuania: from the cultural-historical viewpoint Vilnius belongs rather to the European periphery. When one speaks about Europe one hardly has in mind Turkey or Kazakhstan; however, strictly speaking, these may be regarded as European countries, since a certain part of their territory belongs to Europe.

2. *What about Russia? Does it belong to Europe?*

From the geographical point of view this question certainly presumes a positive answer. It is true that the major part of Russia is in Asia; however its central and most representative part is in Europe, and historically Russia is a European country which expanded into Asia. (This constitutes the difference between Russia and Turkey, not to mention Kazakhstan.) The Asiatic part of Russia belongs to its periphery and actually, very often, is not called Russia. Inhabitants of Siberia distinguish between Russia and Siberia: in particular, when travelling to the European part of the Russian Federation they use the expression "to go to Russia", just as inhabitants of the outskirts of Moscow say "to go to the city".

Also from the cultural-historical point of view the appurtenance of Russia to Europe raises no doubts: Russian culture is undoubtedly European. Russian literature, music and figurative art are generally acknowledged as outstanding achievements of the European cultural tradition. It is hardly possible to imagine European culture without Russian novels, Russian poetry, Russian ballet, Russian symphonic music, Russian avant-garde painting, or Russian cinema.

Nevertheless the question whether Russia really belongs to Europe is always present to our minds and is an object of constant discussion. The question was explicitly formulated by Petr Chaadaev at a time when Russia was one of the leading European countries and when, consequently, it seemed pleonastic.

Why then? What is the cause of these doubts, if the answer seems so evident?

3. The diffusion of a name related to a certain cultural-historical center and representing a particular cultural-historical tradition, generally speaking, may be based either on the principle of metonymy or on the principle of metaphor. Correspondingly the name of Europe, as we shall see, may function both as metonymy and as metaphor.

In the one case we have a *cultural expansion*, i.e. when a name related to a center becomes applied to the periphery of a given region. This is a natural process.

In the other we have a *cultural orientation*. This is an artificial process.

Let us cite two examples to illustrate the two cases.

The first example. Île de France, a feudal domain of Hugh Capet, in the 10th century became the center of a country which today is called France. Thus the name "France" as the definition of a country came into being.

The second example. In the process of the colonization of the New World (America) and subsequently of the Newest World (Australia, New Zealand), very often European names were given to new towns and regions: this evidences a clear tendency to transfer European cultural space to a newly assimilated territory. Thus we have New York (originally called New Amsterdam), New England, New Zealand, etc. Later on in America we also have such names as Ithaca, Syracuse, etc. Tom Sawyer, the celebrated hero of the eponymous novel of Mark Twain, lived in a small town which had the name of the capital of the Russian Empire, St. Petersburg. There actually is a St. Petersburg in the state of Florida, but, characteristically, Tom Sawyer's St. Petersburg is on the banks of the Mississippi River; apparently the writer considered it a typical name for an American town. Once when I was in the United States I met a charming old lady who asked me where I was from. When she learned that I was from Moscow, she asked what state Moscow belonged to. She was sure that Moscow was an American town.

The difference between these two cases is obvious. In the first we have a natural process of cultural expansion, while in the other we face an artificial process of cultural orientation. In the former case we have a metonymy, in the latter a metaphor, since metaphor is based on comparison[1] and metonymy on the *pars pro toto* principle. In the one case centrifugal forces are manifested (the principle of metonymy), in the other centripetal forces prevail (the principle of metaphor).

It is notable that in the case of metaphor (metaphorical toponymy revealing a cultural orientation) we usually meet the attribute "new": New York, New Amsterdam, New Orleans, New London (there are several towns of this name in the United States), New England, Nova Scotia (a province in Canada) with a town named New Glasgow, New South Wales, New France (the name of the French territories in Canada until 1763), New Holland (the first name of Australia), New Zealand, New Caledonia, New Georgia (one of the Solomon Islands), New Guinea, New Ireland and New Britain (islands in the Bismarck Archipelago; previously they were called New Mecklenburg and New Pomerania), New Spain (a Spanish colony in Central America near Mexico City, founded in 1522), New Galicia (the area to the west and north of Mexico City), New Granada (a Spanish colony in South America, founded in 1538), New Siberia (one of the New Siberian Islands), New Brunswick, New Jersey, New Mexico, New Hampshire, New Hebrides, etc.; the list may be continued without difficulty. Such names may be repeated: if nowadays the name of New England is applied to a north-east region of the United States, in the 11th century it was the name of a territory on the north coast of the Black Sea, which was consigned by the emperor Alexis to his British body-guards: the towns of this territory, "Nova Anglia", were called correspondingly London, York, etc.

However, in the case of metonymy (metonymical toponymy revealing a cultural expansion) we usually find the attribute "great" attached to the locality. Thus, for example, the name of Boston, primarily referring to the city of Boston, may extend to its suburbs, i.e. the territory lying outside the city borders, including Cambridge, Lexington, Watertown, etc.; in this case the expression "Great(er) Boston" is used. Here the word "great" properly means "in the broad sense of the word". Examples of this kind are very usual in toponymy. Thus the name of Bretagne as the result of colonization was extended to England and Scotland and, consequently, we call the whole country "Great Britain" (later, in 1707, it was reinterpreted as the union of England and Scotland). Similarly Southern Italy with its original Greek population bears the name of "Magna Grecia" (i.e. Great Greece). In 1819-1830 when the Spanish colonies in South America were struggling for their independence, the republic of "Great Colombia" was founded, the country of Colombia being the center of this republic.

The same phenomenon may be observed in the history of Russia. Thus the name of Rus` (the ancient name of Russia) originally referred to Kiev and the surrounding territory which corresponds to the present Ukraine. The northern lands of contemporary Russia (such as Novgorod, Vladimir, Suzdal`, etc.) were outside Rus` and, consequently, were not called Russian. Later on, however, they began to be considered parts of the "Great Rus`" (i.e. Great Russia), just as the suburbs around Moscow included more or less recently within the territory of Moscow may be called nowadays "Great Moscow". In a Byzantine list of dioceses compiled in the 12th century, those dioceses are indicated which are governed by the Metropolitan of "Great Rus`" (τῇ μεγάλῃ Ῥωίσᾳ) whose residence was Kiev. Among them we find the bishoprics of Novgorod, Smolensk and Suzdal`: these towns did not belong to Rus` (Russia) in the proper sense of the word, but they were considered parts of Great Rus` (Great Russia) (see *Appendix, Table I*).

Then the name "Great Rus`" (μεγάλη Ῥωίσᾳ) became semantically identical with the name "All Rus`" or "Whole Russia" (πᾶσα Ῥωίσᾳ) which was a component of the official title of the Kievan metropolitan: at least from the second half of the 12th century he was called "metropolitan of Kiev and All Rus`". The opposition "Rus`" and "Great Rus`" was not mutually exclusive, but the name "Rus`" turned out to be the marked member of the opposition. Indeed, at this stage the name "Rus`" had a double meaning: on the one hand this name was related to the Kievan lands, on the other hand it could refer to a larger territory under the rule of the Kievan metropolitan. In relation to Kiev and the adjacent territory the names "Rus`" and "Great Rus`" were interchangeable, but in relation to Novgorod or Rostov they were contrasted (*Appendix, Table II*). Successively the name of "Rus`" was extended to the northern territories so that "Rus`" and "Great Rus`" became more or less synonymous (*Appendix, Table III*).

Later on, however—after the transportation of the metropolitan's residence from Kiev to Vladimir in 1299, caused by the Tartar invasion and devastation of Kiev—the name "Great Rus̀" began to be associated primarily with the northern lands: from this time on it signified not so much "All Rus`" ("Whole Russia") as those territories of "All Rus`" which were not included in the original (Kievan) "Rus`" (*Appendix, Table IV*).

Since the notion of "Great Rus`" began to be associated with the northern lands, which were becoming more and more important, at the next stage the territory originally called "Rus`" began to be called "Little Rus`" ("Little Russia"). The name "Little Rus`" for contemporary Ukraine was obviously formed by contrast with "Great Rus`", which means that the perspective of Great Rus` was adopted. As a result, the former opposition of "Rus`" and "Great Rus`" was transformed into the opposition of "Little Rus`" and "Great Rus`", the exclusive one. Ukrainians nowadays consider the name "Little Russia" as pejorative and offensive. They prefer the name "Ukraine" but both names have substantially the same significance (etymologically "Ukraine" means outskirts, borderline). Indeed, both the name "Little Rus`" and the name "Ukraine" manifest the same idea: the idea of periphery. Both names are due to the exchange of the center and periphery: the center (the territory which used to be called "Rus`") becomes the periphery ("Little Rus`" or "Ukraine", i.e. outskirts), while the periphery, vice versa, becomes the center.

Thus in the course of time "Rus`" becomes a general notion associated with the territory of both Great Rus` (the northern lands of the country) and "Little Rus` (the southern lands). Then it became possible to define Moscow or Novgorod as towns belonging to "Rus`" or, more particularly, to "Great Rus`", but it was not possible to define these towns as belonging to "Little Rus`". In the same way Kiev or Chernigov could be referred to as towns belonging to "Rus`" or, more particularly, to "Little Rus`"; however it was not possible to define them as towns of "Great Rus`". At this stage the opposition of "Rus`" and "Great Rus`", as well as the opposition of "Rus`" and "Little Rus`", was not mutually exclusive: both "Rus`" and "Great Rus`", on the one hand, and "Rus`" and "Little Rus`", on the other hand, were contrasted as a general and a particular concept. However the opposition of "Great Rus`" and "Little Rus`" appeared as a mutually exclusive one. Indeed, any locality which belonged to "Great Rus`" also belonged to "Rus`" but not vice versa (the converse affirmation is not true: it would be wrong to affirm that any locality which belonged to "Rus`" also belonged to "Great Rus`"). Analogously, any locality that belongs to "Little Rus`" belongs also to "Rus`", but not vice versa.

Finally, when the name "Little Russia" was substituted by the name "Ukraine" the mutually exclusive opposition of "Great Rus`", and "Little Rus`" was transformed into the opposition of "Rus`" and "Ukraine". Thus a territory which originally was called "Rus`" became opposed to a territory which in the course of time acquired this very name (*Appendix, Table V*).

It is worth noting that at the time when in the Kievan perspective the northern part of the country was called "Great Rus`", in the Scandinavian perspective the whole country (both "Rus`" as such, i.e. Kievan Rus`, and "Great Rus`") could be called "Great Sweden". In both cases the word "great", or its equivalent in the Scandinavian languages, has the same meaning: it refers to a periphery which is opposed to a center.

Something similar seems to have happened in Poland. We have here an opposition of "Little Poland" (Mala Polska) and "Great Poland" (Wielka Polska) but "Little Poland" similar to "Little Rus`" presents the historical center of the Polish territory: just as we have Kiev in "Little Rus`" we have Kraków in "Little Poland".

Generally a toponymic model of nomination with the attribute "great" is associated with a zone of colonization, not with a metropolis (mother country). Thus the name "Great Britain" refers to the perspective of continental "Britain", i.e. Bretagne, "Great Greece" (Magna Grecia) refers to the perspective of historical Greece, "Great Colombia" to the perspective of historical Colombia, etc. Analogously the name "Great Rus`" refers to the perspective of what was originally called "Rus`" and what later on—from the perspective of "Great Rus`"—came to be defined as "Little Rus`" or "Ukraine".

4. It is evident that the extension of a toponymic name—the application of a traditional name to a different territory—may appear either as metonymy or metaphor. When England was called "Great Britain", it was the result of a metonymic association. When a town in America received the name New Amsterdam or New Orleans, it was the result of a metaphoric association.

The use of the attribute "great" (e.g., when we say "Great Britain" or "Great Rus`") implies an *identification* of a peripheral territory with the historical center.

The use of the attribute "new", however, is based on a different presumption: it implies a *comparison*, and comparison, according to Aristotle, is the basis of metaphor. Indeed, metaphor is based on comparison, which presupposes common *characteristics*. Metonymy is based on the association of objects or events, which have common *coordinates*. In this sense metaphor is based on similarity, metonymy on the contiguity of the associated phenomena.

A comparison presumes an initial distinction in the compared phenomena: we can compare only that which is recognized as different.

In the one case, when we use the attribute "great" in a toponymic nomination, we deal with a gradual relationship of a more or less general territory, otherwise, when we use the attribute "new", relations of mutual exclusion are present. In the first case the opposed phenomena are not necessarily in a complementary distribution, in the second case they usually are.

This is why when we define something (in particular, a locality) as "new", it is natural to define the opposite notion as "old". Thus after the discovery of the "New World", i.e. America, Europe acquired the name of the "Old World". Analogously, after the appearance of the "New Testament" the Hebrew Bible was understood as the "Old Testament"; after the French revolution the previous order received the name of "ancien régime"; after the introduction of the Gregorian calendar which was defined as the "new style" the Julian calendar began to be called "old style", etc.

When we define something as "great", however, we do not usually define the opposite notion as "little" (even if, on occasion, we do, as in the case of the opposition "Great Rus`" and "Little Rus`" or "Great Poland" and "Little Poland"; however, these are rather exceptional cases, which are due to the change of a center and a periphery in the corresponding territory; see above).

In the case of a toponymic nomination based on metonymy the problem of *center* and *periphery* is actual; in the case of a toponymic nomination based on metaphor, the problem of *old* and *new* prevails. Generally speaking, metonymy is connected with relations in *space*, while metaphor is connected with relations in *time*. While a periphery is not necessarily contrasted to the center, the relations of old and new as a matter of principle appear as a contrasting opposition: the new is created as the antithesis of the old. When Constantine the Great in 330 founded the new capital of the Roman Empire, which received the name "New Rome", along with the name "Constantinople", the New Rome turned out to be opposed to the Old Rome as a Christian capital to a pagan one (later on this opposition turned into the opposition of an Orthodox center and a Catholic one). More or less the same happened after the Florentine union of 1439 (the union of the Catholic and Orthodox Churches) and the subsequent Fall of Constantinople in 1453. The Fall of Constantinople and the victory of the Turks over Byzantium were seen in Russia as divine punishments for the betrayal of Orthodoxy, after which Russia remained the only independent Orthodox country representing true Orthodoxy. As a result Moscow was declared the Third Rome and the New Constantinople, Constantinople being the second Rome. Moscow as Third Rome was opposed both to the first (Old) Rome and the first Constantinople. Moscow was understood as a center which had preserved the Orthodox tradition, while both Rome and Constantinople had lost it. In both cases a toponymic name (e.g. "New Rome", "New Constantinople", "Third Rome", etc.) is based on metaphor, and this is revealed in the use of the attribute "new". In both cases we have a distinct contrast of new and old, typical of the metaphoric principle of naming.

5. It remains to note that the name of Europe itself is based on metonymy. Indeed "Europe" originally was the name of Greece, more precisely of continental Greece, while the islands of the Aegean Sea as well as the Ionian Coast of Asia Minor belonged to "Asia". Gradually the name of Europe was extended to other territories—first to the territories close to Greece and then, step by step, to more distant ones. The extension of the name revealed the metonymic principle of identification. The Ionian geographers, such as

Anaximander applied the name of Europe to the territory to the north of the Mediterranean sea, while the territory to the south was called "Asia". Thus the opposition of Europe and Asia was originally associated not with the opposition of West and East, as it is nowadays, but with the opposition of North and South.

6. Returning to Russia one may say that Russia belongs to Europe not in a metonymic but in a metaphoric sense. In other words, the appurtenance of Russia to Europe appears as a result not of the expansion of Europe as the center of civilization to adjacent lands, but rather as a conscious and conspicuous orientation towards Europe: this was not a centrifugal but a centripetal process.

In the opposite case Russia would have become, so to say, a part of *Great* Europe, i.e. a zone on the periphery of Europe to which the European cultural model had been extended. It would have been a process of gradual and consequent evolution, and historically such an evolution was quite possible. Indeed, the europeanization (westernization) of Russia began at the end of the 15th and beginning of the 16th century: it started with Boris Godunov and continued with the False Dmitrii. The process was resumed after the Time of Troubles, especially in the second half of the 17th century.

This evolution, however, was impeded by the reforms of Peter I, which had not an evolutionary, but a revolutionary character—not a natural but an artificial one. As a result Europe became for Russia not a metonymy, but a metaphor: instead of becoming an organic part of Europe (i.e. a *Great* Europe), Russia became a *New* Europe.

But conscious orientation of this type presumes a contradistinction of Europe and Russia as two contrasted entities: indeed, the orientation towards Europe suggests that previously Russia did not belong to Europe.

This idea was a starting point of the reforms of Peter I.

What I am saying may seem a paradox. As a matter of fact Peter I is known as a *Kulturträger*. It is generally accepted that as a result of his reforms Russia adopted European cultural values and became a European country. But at the same time, I believe, Peter created a cultural contrast between Russia and Europe, which did not exist (at least in this form) previously. In the words of Pushkin (which go back to Algarotti), Peter cut a window from Russia to Europe. Adopting this metaphor I would say that in order to cut his window Peter had to build a wall separating Russia from Europe. And it is not by chance that Peter and his associates proclaimed Russia after the reforms to be a *new* country.

7. The artificial character of the reforms of Peter I is recognizable from their initial stage. It is notable that Peter begins with the adoption of the *signs*, i.e. the forms of European culture, obviously presuming that the content should follow the form (this is typical in cases in which the processes of civilization bear the characteristics of a *metaphoric* assimilation). This artificiality later on determines the subsequent development of Russia: signs (forms) precede content. Thus Lenin developed the impossible idea of realizing Karl Marx's program by making an anti-capitalist revolution in an agricultural country. Both the initiative of Peter and the initiative of Lenin had a conspicuously utopian character: they were based not on what *was*, but on what *should be*, not on an actual state of affairs but on a state of affairs which had to be achieved.

In 1698 Peter returned from the first of his foreign travels: he had been touring across Europe—Prussia, Sweden, Curland, Holland, England, Austria—under the name of Sergeant Peter Mikhailov, and it was the first case in the history of Russia that a tsar had left his country. On the day following his arrival in Moscow Peter began cutting—with his own hand—the beards of the boyars, or old-Russian noblemen, forcing them also to dress in foreign clothes. This act was intended to symbolize the beginning of a new and European stage of Russian history. Later on beards as well as Russian national clothes involved expulsion from society: a nobleman who refused to shave his beard or preferred to wear traditional clothes automatically lost his nobility.

It is difficult to find anything European in these acts: they remind us rather of an aborigine who wants to dress like a white man.

Such performances obviously demonstrate a proclivity towards Europe, a desire to be European; at the same time they create a contrast between Russia and Europe. Dressing in German clothes does not transform a Russian into a German; on the contrary, it increases the contrast between them. Indeed, there is an obvious difference between a German who wears German clothes and a Russian who is *obliged* to wear such clothes. This is analogous to the difference between a German who speaks German and a foreigner who speaks German as a foreign language. A man who speaks a foreign language is not free in his linguistic behavior, he has to be oriented towards a native speaker who defines the norms of speech, for the native speaker has natural habits of speech, having mastered his language in a natural, not an artificial way. In a sense the difference between a German speaking German and a Russian speaking German is greater than the difference between a German speaking German and a Russian speaking Russian, because in the latter case each uses his own language.

8. Dressing in foreign clothes produces the effect of a masquerade. It should be noted that in pre-Petrine Russia West European clothing was considered comical and was used in contemporary masquerades (in particular, demons in icon-painting could be painted in West European clothing, which corresponded to their carnival costumes). A Russian nobleman, shaved and dressed in foreign clothes, would at first have felt like a mummer, like a carnival merry-maker. At the same time traditional Russian clothes in official carnivals arranged by Peter and his collaborators were used as motley, as the costume of buffoons.

As a result two contrasting cultures were found in Russia: the traditional culture which was declared to be obsolete and obscure, and the new culture which was proclaimed as enlightened and progressive: from the point of view of one culture, the other may appear unnatural, comic, and carnivalesque. On the one hand, in Petrine buffoonery fools were dressed in Russian national costume. On the other, in Russian folk rituals it was possible to represent demons dressed in European clothes (characteristically in an ethnographic novel by Gogol` a demon wears German clothes).

Russian official life turned out to be extremely carnivalesque. Carnival became an element of Russian court life; participation in carnivals was obligatory. The tsar himself felt obliged to take part in carnival ceremonies since they belonged to the cultural program which was compulsory for his milieu. Masks could be used even in official institutions, which appeared very strange to foreign visitors. We learn of an occasion when Peter ordered all the senators and administrators of the highest level to be masked. We can only imagine what an assembly of the Senate looked like: it must have been something similar to a nightmare . . . At first carnival ceremonies were coordinated with Russian traditional festival periods, such as Yuletide or Shrovetide -traditional occasions for carnival amusements,—but gradually they were extended to the entire year.

9. Characteristically the reforms of Peter I intended to turn Russia into a European country in many cases began with carnival sport. In particular, "toy soldier regiments" created in the beginning of the 1680s became the basis of the Russian regular army; one might say that the military reform started by playing soldiers. In a similar way Peter's church reform of 1721, when relations between Church and State were adopted from the European model accepted in Protestant countries, was preceded by the buffoonery of the "All-Jesting Council", also called the "Most Holy Council of Drunkards and Fools"; it could be said that ecclesiastical reform began with an obscene and blasphemous parody of the Church. Analogously, the parody of a traditional image of the tsar in buffoon weddings (a burlesque "tsar" took part in these ceremonies) preceded the assumption by Peter of the imperial title: in 1721 he officially began to be styled "emperor" and "Otets otechestva" (i.e. *pater patriae*), just as Roman emperors were called (one should bear in mind that the word *tsar* previously meant "emperor", not "king")[2]. At the same time Peter began to be called "the Great", similar to Constantine the Great and Charlemagne and also "the First": he was named "the Great" and "the First" because western monarchs—never Russian rulers!—were styled in this way.[3] (Subsequently the Russian emperors Paul, Alexander and Nicholas were called "the First", although there was no Paul II in Russian history, while both Alexander II and Nicholas II appeared much later).

All this strikingly recalls a child who imitates the behavior of an adult.

Carnivalization, re-naming—all this manifested a general cultural program which reveals the artificial character of the europeanization (westernization) of Russia. In the time of Peter towns with foreign names appeared, such as "Sankt Peterburg" (Saint Petersburg), "Shlissel`burg" (Schlüsselburg), and others. Previously, such names were understood as burlesque (e.g. the young Peter had built a town "Presburg" for his "play" troops); subsequently, however, the capital of the Russian empire itself was named in the same way.

Together with new clothing and new names a new Russian alphabet was created. The new forms of letters (projected by Peter himself) were assimilated to Latin letters, at the same time being conspicuously different from the traditional forms. The letters remained the same, only their form was changed. From the practical point of view there was no need to change the forms of the letters: the letters, so to say, acquired a European appearance similar to the people who were dressed in European clothes.

10. Peter began the construction of the new, European Russia with the building of Saint Petersburg. The new capital of the new state was built as a European city with a European name, specifically as a city of Saint Peter, which obviously recalled Rome. Characteristically the coat-of-arms of Saint Petersburg was very similar to that of the papal capital ("Claves Ecclesiae Romanae") and may be seen as a transformation of the latter: the crossed keys in the papal arms correspond to the crossed anchors in that of Saint Petersburg; the fact that the anchor flukes are turned up is especially telling, since they correspond to the position of the key-bits in the papal coat-of-arms. In this way the arms of Saint Petersburg corresponded semantically to the name of the city: name and blazon were the verbal and visual expressions of the same idea.

It is remarkable that the new capital of the future empire was erected not in the center of the country but in its periphery. In this sense Saint Petersburg was contrasted with Moscow, which occupies a central position. This constitutes a rare case (in fact, Istanbul, formerly Constantinople, is also in the periphery of its country, but this is not typical: the new capital of Brazil was built in the center of the country, while the former capital had been in the periphery; also in Kazakhstan the capital was transferred from the periphery to the center of the country). However, the intentions of Peter are clear: on the Western border of his country he built a small European enclave, which was intended to expand subsequently to cover the entire Russian territory. The opposition of West and East, of Europe and Asia, was transferred in this way within the borders of Russia.

Together with the building in stone of Petersburg—a city intended to represent the whole of Russia—Peter prohibited stone buildings elsewhere in the country. In this way, along with the image of Saint Petersburg, the image of a backward, wooden Russia was created as the antithesis of the new city. Saint Petersburg was associated with the Russia of the future; what was actually created, however, was not only an image of the future country but also an image of its past. And this latter image did not completely correspond to reality: traditionally Moscow was described as "built of white stone", now it had to be perceived as wooden. The creation of a new culture involved a conspicuous discrediting of the old: the new was created at the expense of the old, as its antithesis.

In an analogous way Peter prohibited monks to write; they were not allowed even to have paper or ink in their cells. In pre-Petrine Russia monasteries had been notable cultural centers; monks were busy with literary activities, which might even be mentioned in their monastic vows. Now monasteries could be considered as centers of the obsolete traditional culture, and consequently monks could be prohibited to write.

All this is very far from europeanization: what we perceive is merely the desire to imitate Europe . . .

Thus together with the building of a new Russia the image of old Russia was formulated to symbolize the old, traditional culture. From the point of view of new Russia old Russia appears as its opposite, as "anti-Russia",—and vice versa. In this way two cultures were set up which were antagonistically opposed.

There is a scene in Tolstoy's *War and Peace* in which Natasha, a noble girl, is portrayed in a village; the peasants treat her as if she were a doll: they touch her body and her clothing and they discuss her in her presence. From the point of view of the new Russia, peasants could be understood as mummers, but from the point of view of traditional Russia it was the nobles who appeared as mummers. This was the result of conscious cultural policy, a result of the cultural contrast which was created by the reforms of Peter I and which was conditioned by the artificial character of these reforms.

Nothing of the kind is to be found in the history of France or Germany; it appears to be a specific characteristic of Russia—the new Russia created by Peter I.

Later, under the influence of the ideas of Herder and Hegel concerning "the spirit of the people" (*Volksgeist*), the concept of the people as a moving force of historical development became popular. This concept received in Russia specific connotations: the notion of the people turned out to be opposed to the notion of civilization. This determined a special role for the Russian *intelligentsia* which was intended to become a link connecting the people and civilized society.

11. It is evident that the desire to europeanize Russia does not always make Russia similar to Europe: in many cases the differences between Russia and the Western countries may be determined precisely by the importation of Western culture. Russian culture after Peter I was highly semiotic: it was directed to the assimilation of signs, when new forms of expression were adopted in order to achieve a corresponding content. Usually content generates expression; here, on the contrary, expression was intended to generate content.

Such an orientation towards Europe could lead to paradoxical results. In the 18th century, along with the ideas of the Enlightenment, serfdom was established in Russia. Russian serfdom was based on the personal attachment of a peasant to his landowner, and not to the land owned by the latter. As a result it became possible to sell peasants without land, to separate the members of a family, etc. The enslaving of peasants in Russia in the 18th century was realized in most inhuman forms. The practice of selling peasants without land began in the second half of the 17th century but in the 18th century it became a widespread phenomenon. This was determined by the bureaucratic reforms of Peter I, viz. the population census and the introduction of a poll-tax, when free peasants and serfs were registered under the same heading: as a result free peasants became serfs. The mentioned reforms were part of the general process of bureaucratic centralization and modernization—the process directly connected with the tendency to europeanize the Russian bureaucratic system (the census was an element of bureaucratization, the reduction of catalogues was an element of modernization). It should be recalled that in the *western* countries neighboring Russia, such as Poland or Prussia, serfdom still existed, and this might justify the enslaving of peasants in Russia; it was natural for Peter to imitate his western neighbours.

Characteristically, literacy was drastically reduced following the reforms of Peter. In pre-Petrine Russia people were basically literate, i.e. they could read and write (learning to read was a part of religious education). As the result of the reforms of Peter and his followers—the reforms characteristic of europeanized Russia—the overwhelming majority of the peasants became illiterate.

Thus Peter I created European Russia, but at the same time he created its opposite: the image of Asiatic Russia as backward, obscure and ignorant. Consequently, he is responsible for the basic cultural tension which determined the subsequent evolution of Russian culture and, more generally, the course of Russian history.

Translated by Boris Uspenskij

APPENDIX:

THE SUCCESSIVE EVOLUTION OF THE RELATION BETWEEN "RUS`" AND "GREAT RUS`"

I.

	Southern territories	Northern territories
Rus`	+	-
Great Rus`	-	+

II.

	Southern territories	Northern territories
Rus`	+	-
Great Rus`	+	+

III.

	Southern territories	Northern territories
Rus`	+	+
Great Rus`	+	+

IV.

	Southern territories	Northern territories
Rus`	+	+
Great Rus`	-	+

V.

	Southern territories	Northern territories
Rus`	-	+
Great Rus`	-	+

NOTES

1   According to Aristotle, a metaphor is essentially nothing other than a hidden or implied comparison. Thus, "When the poet [Homer] says of Achilles that he 'leapt on the foe as a lion,' this is a simile; when he says of him 'the lion leapt,' it is a metaphor— here, since both are courageous, he has transferred to Achilles the name of 'lion'" (Ars rhetorica, III, 4). Aristotle evidently refers to the description of Achilles in Iliad, XX, 164.

Quintilian (Inst. Orat. VIII, 6, 9) is in essential agreement with Aristotle: "On the whole, *metaphor* is a shorter form of *simile*, while there is this further difference, that in the latter we compare some object to the thing which we wish to describe, whereas in the former this object is actually substituted for the thing. It is a comparison when I say that a man did something 'like a lion'; it is a metaphor when I say of him, 'He is a lion'."

2   The expression "Otets otechestva" literally means "father of the fatherland", at the same time "father of fatherhood". This expression is nothing other than a literal translation of the Latin *pater patriae*, an honorary title of the Roman emperors: it clearly reveals the conspicuous orientation of Peter towards the Roman empire as a cultural model. In the Russian cultural context, however, the expression had a very different effect. Since paternity (fatherhood) in general can refer either to blood or to spiritual kinship, and Peter obviously was not the people's father in the sense of blood kinship, the title was understood as a pretension to spiritual kinship. But it is only a priest who can be a spiritual father; in its turn, the title "Otets otechestva" could be applied only to a bishop as the spiritual father of priests, and—first and foremost—to a patriarch. Actually the ecumenical patriarch of Constantinople as well as the patriarch of Alexandria were both addressed in this way. Moreover, in so far as the official adoption of this title coincided with the abolition of the patriarchate in Russia (it occured in the same year), when the Russian church began to be entirely dependent on the state, and the monarch was subsequently declared to be "Supreme Judge" of the Ecclesiastical College, this title could be interpreted in the sense that Peter had become the head of the Church and had declared himself patriarch. As a matter of fact this is precisely how it was interpreted. But according to canon law only a bishop is able to head the Church. Peter, therefore, was accused of willfully "assuming ecclesiastical power by naming himself *otets otechestva*".

The notion that the tsar had proclaimed himself to be a spiritual or even holy person must have been furthered by Peter's command to be called without his patronymic, for that was precisely how clerical persons and saints were addressed. He called himself Peter *tout court* (without patronymic), whereas his father was called Aleksei Mikhailovich (i.e. Alexis, son of Michael), his grandfather Mikhail Fedorovich (Michael, son of Theodor), and so on. If Peter had been a monk or a priest, he would have been called without patronymic—simply Peter—but he was not. If he had been a saint he would have been called St. Peter, also without patronymic; thus this kind of naming could be understood as a claim to sainthood.

As a result Peter was perceived by his contemporaries and by the Old Believers of subsequent generations as the Antichrist, a view which in turn called forth a whole series of allegations derogatory to the emperor.

Certainly Peter knew the cultural language of his epoch and could therefore foretell the effect of his actions. It looks as if Peter deliberately disregarded his native "cultural language" as erroneous and accepted as the only correct language that of the imported West-European cultural ideas.

3   Generally, pre-Petrine Russian culture was characterized by the identification of persons and objects with the corresponding persons and objects found on a hierarchically general plane which in this sense appeared as ontologically initial or "the first". Thus Constantinople was identified with Rome and Jerusalem and accordingly was called the "second" Rome and the "new" Jerusalem, just as the Russian monarch could be called the "second" Constantine or the "new" David. What is at stake is the identification that reveals the underlying ontological essence of what or who is named in this way. Naturally in such a system of views the title "Peter the First" must have been interpreted as the unlawful pretension of being a point of departure, or origin, a status only applicable in general to the sacred sphere. The fact that Peter began calling himself "the Great" was far less immodest in the eyes of his contemporaries than his naming himself "the First".

If Peter had been a Roman emperor he could have been called "Petrus primus, pater patriae", but he was not—he was a Russian tsar . . .

CULTURAL REFORMS IN PETER I'S SYSTEM OF TRANSFORMATIONS

V. M. Zhivov

1. CULTURAL REFORMS AND SEMIOTIC PROPAGANDA

The Petrine reforms brought about a break in Russian cultural and political consciousness that was no less acute than those in the state structure and in economics. The goal of the Petrine reforms was not only the creation of a new army and navy, a new state administrative apparatus and new industries, but also the creation of a new culture; cultural reforms took up no less a place in Peter's activities than reforms of a more obviously pragmatic character. The change in clothing, shaving of beards, renaming of state offices, instituting of "assemblies" (*assamblei*), and the constant production of various kinds of public spectacles were not accidental byproducts of the era of transformations, but a most essential part of state policy aimed at reeducating society and establishing a new conception of state power. It was not by chance that Feofan Prokopovich wrote in the "Truth of the Monarch's Will," an apologia for Petrine autocracy and the reforms, that "A sovereign monarch can lawfully demand of the people not only whatever is necessary for the obvious good of his country, but indeed whatever he pleases, provided that it is not harmful to the people and not contrary to the will of God. The foundation of this power, as stated above, is the fact that the people has renounced its right to decide the common weal in his favor, and has conferred on him all power over itself: this includes civil and ecclesiastical ordinances of every kind, changes in customs and dress, house-building, procedures and ceremonies at feasts, weddings, funerals, etc., etc., etc."[1] Setting forth the theory of the social contract after Hobbes and Pufendorf,[2] Prokopovich specially underscores the monarch's right to make cultural (semiotic) innovations. But European theoreticians of absolutism had no need to make such declarations, and comparing their arguments to those of

Prokopovich indicates that cultural transformation was assigned a unique role in the Petrine transformation that had no direct analogies in Europe.

Peter saw a guarantee of the new order's staying power precisely in cultural transformation. The new culture was negatively juxtaposed to the old. From Peter's perspective, traditional culture was considered ignorant, barbarous, and even as "idolatry."[3] From the perspective of traditional culture, the new culture appeared to be demonic, the kingdom of the Antichrist, and the creators of the new culture were unquestionably aware of this.[4] In the context of this opposition, propaganda took on prime importance as a basic way to establish the new culture. This propaganda was called upon to fulfill two purposes: to inculcate new cultural values, and to discredit the old ones. This propaganda had to reach the masses, and this is what motivated the predilection for grand ritual and spectacle; in the framework of traditional culture, only this kind of propaganda could be effective and influence mass psychology. Other forms of propaganda, say, distributing political pamphlets, that were so significant for the England of Peter's day, could only be of peripheral importance in Russia. As far as we can judge from the surviving evidence, neither Stefan Iavorskii's "Speech on the Antichrist" nor Feofan Prokopovich's "Truth of the Monarch's Will" and "Investigation of the Pontifex" had a comparably broad resonance either in the capitals or the provinces. Public ceremonies were a different matter. Insofar as traditional culture had a most intimate connection with rituals,[5] innovations in this area were a crucial component of cultural transformation, transmitting all of the basic ideas of the cultural reform. It was precisely for this reason that Prokopovich emphasized the emperor's right to introduce changes in this sphere.

At the same time, in the framework of traditional culture ritual had always been tied to religious values. Ritual and faith were completely allied. In pre-Petrine Rus' Orthodoxy was unthinkable without the liturgy, and popular magic—without corresponding magical rites. Moreover, when taking part in rituals, a Russian not only manifested his or her faith, but also revealed its content, so that participation in an altered ritual necessarily meant a change in faith itself (the clearest and most famous example of this process was the schism). The new rituals therefore gave birth to a new faith, and the new order propagandized by the new rituals became fixed not so much via new convictions as by practice ("conversion" in the etymological sense), even if through coercion. Choice between the new and old culture became something of a religious decision that obligated a person for his or her whole life. Becoming part of the new culture served as a magical rite of denying traditional spiritual values and accepting totally opposite new ones. This is precisely how Prince

I. I. Khovanskii looked upon his induction into Peter's All-Jesting Council, for example:

> They took me to Preobrazhenskoe and in the central court Nikita Zotov consecrated me as metropolitan, and they gave me a panchart (*stolbets*) for renunciation, and I repudiated [my faith] in accordance with this writing, and during this renunciation they asked me 'Do you drink?' instead of 'Do you have faith?' And by this renunciation I ruined myself more than by shaving my beard, because I did not protest, and it would have been better for me to have accepted a crown of martyrdom than to have made this renunciation.[6]

Thus, accepting Petrine cultural innovations had the character of entering a new faith, and obliged a person to have a positive attitude toward an entire complex of changes, from the cult of Peter himself to the reorganization of the state administration. Acceptance of Petrine culture thus turned out to be a pledge of loyalty to all of the changes being implemented, something like that "spilt blood" which Peter Verkhovenskii (of Dostoevskii's *Demons*) used to cement his cell of five "into one knot." It is indicative that F. I. Strahlenberg, who listed all of the accusations that Peter's opponents brought against him, began with his creation of the All-Jesting Council and its blasphemous ceremonies; according to Strahlenberg, it was precisely these ceremonies that served as Peter's original means of threatening Russian society, forcing the young tsar's more reasonable advisors to be silent and paving the way for the violent changes that were destroying the country: "People in the city of Moscow were so terrified that no one dared to say anything openly critical of the tsar or his favorites."[7]

This religious and semiotic aspect is extremely important for understanding the nature of the "Europeanization" which is associated with Peter's transformative program. Of course, the European customs and institutions that were being transferred to Russia had no organic pre-history there, and this alone fundamentally distinguished them from their European counterparts. Yet the means by which Peter inculcated European civilization involved something more. When, for example, the Great Embassy arrived in Leiden in April, 1698,[8] one of the places that the tsar and his cohort chose to visit was an anatomical theater; when the tsar's companions were unable to hide their disgust at the spectacle of a dissected human body, the tsar forced them to rip the corpse's muscles with their teeth.[9] This was in punishment for their "unenlightened" feelings and to make them appreciate that they had to assimilate European practices whether they liked it or not. And when he returned to Moscow Peter created an anatomical theater there as well. As

Korb reports, on February 7, 1699, "Dr. Zoppot began to practice anatomy in the presence of the Czar and a great number of Boyars, who, to their disgust, were coerced by the Czar's commands."[10]

This particular example clearly shows that Europeanization bore a primarily semiotic function; the anatomical theater was clearly of symbolic rather than pragmatic value. Peter demanded that his subjects overcome themselves, that they demonstratively reject the ways of their fathers and grandfathers and accept European practices as rituals of a new faith; understandably, overcoming fear and disgust were natural components of a ritual of initiation, and the anatomical theater was perfect for this role. To a greater or lesser extent, elements of this kind were also present in the tsar's other European innovations, and comprise exactly that which differentiated Peter's measures from other European models. They also constitute the specific nature of Petrine Europeanization when compared to the European influences under previous tsars.

The semiotic (ritual) propaganda of the new Petrine culture was implemented in various forms. Church rituals underwent certain changes, various civil ceremonies that came together as a special "civil cult" took on a systematic mass character, and rituals and spectacles of a parodic, blasphemous type became widespread. Each of these innovations was motivated by particular political and cultural ideas. Obviously, each of these forms of semiotic activity was adapted to express different particular ideas, but in view of the fact that all of these ideas were part of a single larger complex, all of these spheres of semiotic activity were interwoven; the church cult overlapped with the civil and civil ceremonies carried over into the parodic and blasphemous. A survey of all of these forms of semiotic innovation, however superficial, will allow us to clarify this larger complex, and therefore the content of Peter's cultural reform.

2. INNOVATIONS IN CHURCH RITUAL

Church ritual offered the least room for innovation. At the same time it could not remain unaffected, insofar as it was in this area that traditional cultural values were most strongly preserved, and in which basic notions of ethical norms and social order were asserted. In pre-Petrine Rus̓ the liturgy remained the center of belief and any substantive changes in it would have been perceived as sacrilege, so that Peter's reforming activity in this sphere was extremely restricted. For this reason, Peter did not attempt liturgical reform but only sought to limit the liturgy to the periphery of cultural space, forcefully trying to disassociate faith and ritual as phenomena that were connected only by convention. This was embodied, for example, in abolishing fast days and fasting in the army during campaigns,[11] as well as in a series of articles in the "Spiritual Regulation" that directly or indirectly condemned excessive attention to ritual (*obriadoverie*),[12] and so on.

At the same time several changes were nevertheless made in church ritual.[13] Among the most significant was the elimination of the procession on a donkey (*shestvie na osliati*) on Palm Sunday, which was cancelled in 1697, that is, while Patriarch Adrian was still alive; its termination reveals a very clear ideological agenda. In the second half of the seventeenth century, this ritual was perceived as a direct expression of the normative relations between church and state. The patriarch was seated on a donkey (actually, a horse with long ears that were tied back), appearing as the image of Christ entering Jerusalem, and the tsar would lead him by the bridle (during the joint rule of Peter and Ioann, both took part), which symbolized the humility of secular before divine power that the patriarch represented.[14]

Furthermore, the subtext of this ritual was not only the gospel event celebrated on this day, but also the Tale of the White Cowl, and specifically the section that deals with the Donation of Constantine.[15] According to the legend, after Pope Sylvester cured Constantine the Great he gave the pope a white cowl as a sign of the highest merit and assigned himself (and all of his successors) the role of the pope's equerry, thus recognizing the superiority of spiritual over secular authority. In the tale, Constantine says:

> We enact as law that it is an honor due our father Sylvester, the highest bishop, and all of his successor bishops, to clothe themselves in the cincture and to wear the crown that we gave him from our own head, which is made of the choicest gold and precious stones and exquisite pearls; they must wear it to the glory of God and for the honor of blessed Peter ... [But Sylvester] did not like to wear the golden crown and instead of it we put upon his most holy head with our own hands the whitest [white cowl], designating the bright resurrection of the Lord, and we held the reins of the steed in our own hands, giving ourselves up to him as an equerry in honor of blessed Peter. We order all bishops after him to enact the same custom and rite in all their processions, in imitation of our kingship ... [16]

With the establishment of the patriarchate the idea of the religious authority's superiority received new stimulus. And it is completely understandable that during the bitter debates between Aleksei Mikhailovich and Patriarch Nikon over the relative power of church and state Nikon would refer to the procession on a donkey as the prototype of relations between the head of the church and the emperor that according to legend had been established by Constantine the Great. In his "Objection or Ruination" (*Vozrazhenie ili razorenie*) he wrote: "The same was done by Constantine the Great for Saint Sylvester and by Justinian for Agapetos who consecrated Mina as patriarch of Constantinople. And Justinian held the reins of the horse on which Agapetos was sitting, in the same manner as most pious tsar Aleksei Mikhailovich does on Palm Sunday."[17]

It was this conception of the ritual that made it odious to Peter, who considered it a Russian form of papism, or, as Feofan Prokopovich later formulated it, "similar pipe dreams [*zamakhi*] that used to exist here as well."[18] There are various testimonies to the tsar's hatred for the procession on a donkey (by Petr Alekseev and Ivan Golikov)[19] and the All-Jesting Council performed an irreverent parody of it (see below). In 1697 and 1698 the ceremony was called off since the tsar was on the Great Embassy abroad, and in 1699 he consciously refused to take part in the "Palm [Sunday] ritual," which was part of his radicalized campaign against traditional practices that followed the Great Embassy and Streltsy Revolt. Revoking this practice anticipated (and predetermined) the abrogation of the patriarchate.

Peter's battle against the limitations on secular (that is, tsarist) power, and against the idea of the symphonic cooperation between secular and religious authority, was not limited to this innovation, and changes introduced into ritual practice were no less significant than concrete reforms of church administration. At the same time, as we have seen, Peter connected the idea that the autocrat's power was limited and not extending to the church sphere with the tale of the Donation of Constantine. Therefore all elements of ritual that were in one way or another associated with the tale were subject to elimination. The procession on a donkey represents a particular illustration of this. Peter also denied metropolitans the right to wear a white cowl.[20] In general, Peter strove to destroy those ritual differences that existed among church officials of various ranks that were perceived as testimony to the special power of the patriarch and metropolitans and which collectively limited the monarch's power.[21] Thus in 1702 the tsar began to bestow the saccus on particular bishops[22] and in 1705 gave the order that all bishops could wear the saccus.[23] In the same year, Peter allowed archimandrites to wear the miter.[24] The tsar's interference in these ritual details was not caused by a sudden interest in ecclesiastical grandeur but by his hatred for the symbolism they represented. And just as the abolition of the procession on a donkey presaged the abolition of the patriarchate, the rejection of distinctions in clothing anticipated doing away with the rank of metropolitan after the establishment of the Synod.

In asserting and promoting his single rule, Peter consistently rooted out those ritual elements that indicated symphonic relations between secular and religious power and as far as possible replaced them with indications of the absolute character of his own authority. It is indicative that in the vow that members of the Synod took they professed "with an oath that the ultimate judge of this Spiritual Collegia is the very all-Russian monarch, Our Most Gracious Sovereign."[25] The designation "ultimate judge," which could be taken to be sacrilegious (for example, by Arsenii Matseevich)[26] was apparently associated with calling the patriarch "the ultimate saintly cleric (*krainii sviatitel`*)," familiar from the very same tale of the Donation of Constantine and from many other documents that specified the patriarch's prerogatives.[27] Finally, it is worth recalling that one of Peter's first decrees after establishing the Synod was a directive forbidding obeisance to places in the Cathedral of the Ascension and in the Church of the Twelve Apostles that were dedicated to the patriarch, and commanding that the patriarchal staffs—which could also serve as objects of veneration—be stored away in the sacristy.[28] A short time later Peter ordered that they "prepare a place in Moscow, in the Synod's *Krestovaia palata* [main ceremonial hall], for His Imperial Majesty, and above it [place] a canopy of good velvet with golden braid."[29] Here too Peter sought to eliminate signs of patriarchal authority and to replace them with those of his own.

Naturally, the development of elements in the church service that fostered such ideas as the divine basis for tsarist power; the tsar's special charisma; and the country's power as illustration of God's particular care and concern for the ruling monarch, were now encouraged. Under Peter an eortological system of so-called "high triumphal" days (*vysokotorzhestvennye* or *tabel`nye dni*) began to take shape, celebrations that included saints' days and birthdays of members of the ruling family as well as the sovereign's coronation and ascension days. "The register of festival and victory days that were celebrated in St. Petersburg in 1723, with or without prayer services," included 44 such celebrations;[30] failure to conduct the special services that were arranged for these holidays was considered a serious offense.[31] Together with various other unscheduled services for things like military victories, these celebrations created a specific cycle of worship that was connected with the cult of the monarch and that inculcated the notion of the new state culture as divinely-protected successor to Holy Russia.

This religious sanction for the new order was underscored by the fact that its enemies were condemned as heretics. Later, such condemnation, in general terms, was included in the anathema delivered during the Triumph of Orthodoxy (the first Sunday of the Lent), together with anathematizing Arians,

Nestorians, etc. Here we read: "To those who think that Orthodox sovereigns are not raised to the throne by God's special will, and that at anointment the gifts of the Holy Spirit are not poured into them for carrying out their great calling; and also to those who dare to raise revolt against them or commit treason—anathema!"[32] This idea was also spelled out in Feofan Prokopovich's "First Lesson to Youth" (*Pervoe uchenie otrokom*) where obedience to the tsar and the struggle against his enemies are presented as the basic duty of a Christian according to the fifth commandment, insofar as: "The first order of fathers is constituted by the higher powers that were established by God to govern people, and the first among them is the highest power of the tsar," because "Tsars have to supervise all subordinate authorities, spiritual, military, and civil, [to see] whether they manage their business as they should."[33]

During Peter's reign Mazepa and Stepan Glebov were subjected to anathematization.[34] In the first case, the anathematization was especially significant insofar as it corresponded to references to Mazepa as the second Judas in the yearly "Service of Thanksgiving for the Victory near Poltava". In the sedalen (sessional hymn) from the morning service it says: "A second Judas appeared, who imitated the previous one in a vile manner, a slave and flatterer who behaved like an irredeemable son, a devil in his nature and not a man, thrice an apostate, Mazepa, who abandoned the Lord Christ, his lord and benefactor, and attached himself to the evil one, scheming to render evil for good, malfeasance for beneficence, hatred for mercy. But God meted out justice to the second Judas in the same way as to the first, in accordance with their deeds;"[35] and further, in the stikhira after the Psalm 50: "let the terrestrial angels, those who did not follow the rebellious devil, be praised with you; let those who did not consort with Mazepa, the second Judas, but gave their souls for their lord, be revered in the same way as the Apostles."[36] Right after the hetman's betrayal, Peter had called Mazepa "a second Judas" and ordered his anathematization.[37] Holiness was thus very explicitly associated with loyalty to the monarch, and disobedience with apostasy, and what is more, this idea was asserted by the tsar himself.

As we have seen, Peter's cultural and political position was expressed very clearly in those few changes he made in the ritual sphere of Russian church life. They testified unmistakably, in a way that was very clear to contemporaries, to a fundamental revision of the traditional conception of power. The idea that underwrote the innovations we have described was basically negative: getting rid of the spiritual and moral limitations on the omnipotence of the tsar. At the same time, the ideology of secular rule was not promoted. This task had to be undertaken by other forms of propaganda that were not constrained by tradition. These new forms of propaganda were developed and carried out over the entire course of Peter's reign, and belong perhaps to the tsar-reformer's most radical innovations.

3. THE CIVIL CULT

In the first place, such an innovation was the creation of a special civil cult which featured multiple rituals and diverse celebratory ceremonies such as triumphal entries, launching of ships, etc. The elements of these rituals are easily recognized in themselves and have direct parallels in Western European and classical culture. In Russia, however, they were implemented in a cultural space that had little in common with Western Europe and hence assumed new and different significance. The very idea of a triumph as a reward for personal valor and as testimony to service was unusual and alien for traditional Russian consciousness.[38] The services of thanksgiving performed for victories did not express this idea, and focused attention not on the achievements of the monarch and his warriors but on God's blessing, given to the whole people.[39] Understandably, in this case Peter did not try to destroy traditional notions, but in the new context they no longer emphasized that victories and well-being depended on the people's faith rather than on human efforts. Within the framework of the church, traditional ritual was supplemented with a sermon in which, as a rule, the bravery and power of the tsar and his warriors were praised, and within the framework of the celebration as a whole, prayers were supplemented by a civil ceremony that also emphasized this idea.

At the same time, on Russian soil these civil ceremonies themselves took on special religious significance. Indeed, in terms of religion, a new type of state culture emerged that centered more than anything else on a special civil cult of the monarch, which was parallel to his church cult but connected to a different complex of ideas. The religious connotations of the corresponding ceremonies were obvious for contemporary cultural consciousness. In 1704 Peter returned to Moscow after a rather successful campaign against the Swedes. His triumphal entry into the city was modeled on those of imperial Rome, although Muscovites, unused to such spectacles, were apt to interpret its symbolism and significance via a thoroughly different cultural code. For this reason a brochure written by the prefect of the Moscow Academy, Iosif Turoboiskii, was immediately published, in which the images on the triumphal arches were not only explained but the general significance of this kind of celebration was also spelled out. Turoboiskii writes:

I assume that you will be surprised, my Orthodox reader, that this triumphal arch (as also in past years) is purposefully decorated not on the basis
of the Holy Scriptures but [with material] taken from secular stories, not by
saints, but either from tales by secular historians or from those by poets about
fictional persons and likenesses of beasts, reptiles, birds, trees, and other
things. You should know this. First, this is not a temple or a church built in
the name of one of the saints, but a political, that is, civilian, commendation
of those who labored for the integrity of their fatherland and who defended it
against its enemies with the help of God and through their labors; this custom
was established among political (not barbarian) peoples from ancient times,
as in the case of the Roman tsar Constantine who vanquished Maxentius . . .
For this reason in all Christian countries that are free from the barbarian
yoke grateful citizens have the custom of making triumphal wreaths [i.e.,
arches] for glorious champions when they return from war in triumph and
[to decorate] them from both types of writings. [They are taken both] from
Scripture in churches . . . and from secular stories, so that each of them can
receive befitting and proper honor, in celebrations, in the streets and other
places appropriate for the general public's observation [*vsenarodnomu zreniiu
prilichnykh*] . . . And in this publicly announced and designated place, with
the help of secular and civilian stories, by means of triumphal arches, like
victorious wreaths, these most precious verbal wells, which with God's help
shower our fatherland with joy, health, freedom and glory from the living
water of the sweat [of their brow], we honor . . . his most radiant tsarist
majesty and all of his victorious heroic companions, in the manner and
tradition of the ancient Romans.[40]

Turoboiskii especially emphasizes that triumphal gates are not a "temple."
Clearly he has in mind the traditional perception that a ritual structure
could only fulfill a religious function. Insofar as this structure was clearly
not a Christian church, it could only represent a pagan temple, antagonistic
to Christianity and heralding the appearance of the Antichrist.[41] Turoboiskii
expressly warns against such a view: "Because you, pious reader, will not be
surprised by what we have written, nor be jealous of the uninformed person
who knows nothing and has seen nothing, but who like a turtle in its shell
never ventures out, and as soon as he sees something new is shocked and
belches out various unholy claptrap."[42] "Unholy claptrap" (*bliadoslovie*) clearly
refers to the anti-Christ and the notion of such celebrations' demonic character.
At the same time it is significant that Turoboiskii does not completely reject
all associations of triumphal ceremonies with church ritual, but refers to
their parallelism, something which can't help but confer a certain religious
significance on the "civil cult." Turoboiskii specifies that this cult has its
own sources and its own tradition, but argues that it has the same goal as

church ritual—to glorify a monarch who has done battle for the faith and the fatherland; hence the civil cult, while autonomous, does not contradict Orthodoxy or threaten traditional values. Turoboiskii thus suggests to readers that the new ideas do not contradict the old. It's hard to say to what extent this ruse was conscious for this graduate of the Kiev Mohyla Academy; in any case, for those raised in traditional culture the two contrasting value systems could in no way be reconciled.

What were these new notions that the civil cult wanted to impress on "pious readers"? Peter's triumphs were consciously modeled on those of imperial Rome. The Roman connection is clearly visible in the triumphal celebrations of 1703. Both the overall conception and various details testify to this. For example, "on the capitals [of the columns] on both sides four angels are throwing flowers in the manner of ancient conquerors for whom the Appian Way was paved with various flowers when they were coming to the Capitoline Hill."[43] Peter is compared to Julius Caesar:

> At the bottom of the same picture there are naval instruments with a naval sphere placed on a sail, and at the top there is a boat led by a tsar with the inscription: *non timet caesaris fortunam vehit*, that is, 'it is not afraid, it carries Caesar's well-being.' This signifies the courageous audacity of his tsarist most illustrious majesty and his courageous warriors who were not afraid to attack big ships with small boats in the seaside estuary, counting on God's help and his most illustrious tsarist majesty's fortune. We have taken this inscription from the sayings of Julius Caesar of Rome; when he sailed across the sea in a small boat and saw great waves he said to his frightened pilot: "do not be afraid, you carry Caesar's well-being."[44]

The symbolism of imperial Rome was repeated in many other celebrations. For example, at the very top of the triumphal gates of 1704 a "persona" (portrait) of Peter was depicted with "Glory, a winged figure with a trumpet, laying a date palm crown upon the head of his most illustrious tsarist majesty dressed in Roman clothes."[45] One could multiply similar examples.[46] They have much more than decorative interest. In connecting Russia with imperial Rome, the adepts of the new state culture were asserting a new type of legitimacy: the monarch drew his rights and his charisma not from his role as defender of the faith (as the "single Orthodox tsar anywhere under the sun" within the framework of the conception of Moscow as Third Rome), but as the leader of peoples, the father of the fatherland, whose power was an inalienable component of the cosmic establishment, and which did not depend directly on faith.[47] Indeed, the sources of information that were accessible to Russian readers from chronicles and chronographs portrayed the Roman Empire as part of the universal process of history, together with the Babylonian and Persian Empires, as well as that of the Ptolemies, all of which anticipated the "Christian kingdom" that began with the reign of Constantine the Great.[48] This view of cultural succession pictured the Russian monarchy as a category of cosmic being, independent of religious sanction.

A significant element that suggested this succession was references to "Caesar Augustus" that are often encountered in sermons from the Petrine period in connection with civil celebrations, and which were reflected even in the ritual of elevation to the kingdom.[49] An old dynastic legend thus became an element of the new political conception.[50] However, the key figure here turned out not to be Augustus but Constantine the Great.[51] Interest in this emperor and the glorification of Peter as "the new Constantine" created a long-standing tradition in the Petrine and post-Petrine period that was especially reflected in Ivan Golikov's voluminous book, expressively entitled "A Comparison of the Characteristics and Deeds of Constantine the Great, First Christian Emperor of the Romans, With the Characteristics and Deeds of Peter the Great, the First All-Russian Emperor, and of the Events that Took Place During the Reigns of Both These Monarchs."[52] The figure of Constantine the Great as predecessor and prototype for Peter also appears in panegyric literature, in triumphal ceremonies, and even in church services, and in frequency and significance far exceed any other imperial references.

What is important here, however, is not simply the fact of references to Constantine but the function that they played. For the pre-Petrine reader, Constantine was known primarily as the first ruler of the "Christian kingdom," under which the First Ecumenical Council was held: "[When] Constantine, son of Saint Helen, [was] 31 years of age, the First Council of Nicaea [consisting] of three hundred and eighteen holy fathers took place in the twelfth year of his reign and was against Arius, an Alexandrian priest who divided the divinity."[53] To this image accrued information derived from the tale of the Donation of Constantine and connected the creation of the Christian empire with the miraculous cure brought about by Pope Sylvester. In Petrine propaganda Constantine took on a completely different role. Here the main event was Constantine's victory over Maxentius, which of course had been known in Russia earlier but which now under Peter came to serve the interests of a particular ideological position.[54]

Thus, after the second Azov campaign in 1696, triumphal gates were erected for the return to Moscow. "On the pediment was the inscription: 'God is with us, and nobody can be against us...The inconceivable has happened . . . ' In the middle of the gates hung a green wreath. From it fell gold braided espaliers; on one were the words 'Tsar Constantine's return from victory' and on another 'Tsar Constantine's victory over the impious Tsar Maxentius of Rome'."[55] On the triumphal gates of 1704 there was depicted "a banner on which the name of Christ the Savior was written in the same way as seen on the banner of Tsar Constantine,"[56] i.e., a labarum (Constantine's military standard), and in Turoboiskii's commentary the appropriateness of "civil praise" was justified by reference to Constantine and his victory over Maxentius (see above). In the victory service for Poltava in the song of the third canon it was proclaimed: "Equal to the Apostles, Tsar Constantine, having seen the image of the cross in the sky, bright with stellar light, became strong against the impious Maxentius; by the same vision our cross-bearing tsar, the second Constantine, vanquished the power of the Swedish Maxentius and praises God with gratitude."[57] This same motif repeatedly occurs in panegyric sermons. It is no less indicative that "practically all of the examples of Russian banners from the Petrine period bore Constantine's cross on their panels."[58] In this case as well a polemic against the preceding tradition is clear: the creation of the "Christian kingdom" appears not as the result of miracles performed by the pope but due to the emperor's wise decisions and victorious actions; at the same time, the emperor is directly connected to God, who gives him signs and reveals that "in this you will conquer" (Constantine's legendary motto). Thus it is the emperor who establishes the religion; the church authorities have no role in it, so that it is precisely the emperor who assumes supremacy and no longer has to take on the role of the pope's equerry.

Consequently, here again the conception of the tsar's single rule—his power that embraces both the secular and religious spheres—is propagated. It turns out that it is precisely the monarch (the emperor) who is the true leader of Christian peoples, while the pope (or patriarch) only usurps his authority. For this very reason, Feofan Prokopovich in "Investigation of the Pontifex" demonstrates that it is the emperor's right to appoint bishops, based on references to none other than Constantine the Great. He writes: "Constantine declared external episcopal activities, not civil but ecclesiastical administration, to be his business. He declared his own complete supervision over these external [i.e., church] activities, over matters of religion, its rules, regulations, the convocation of councils, [rendering] justice and the punishment of those who fought against true piety, for both laity and clergy, including bishops"; therefore, "the tsar is, as Constantine used to be, *the common bishop over everyone*."[59] The Petrine empire is thus portrayed as the true realization of the model Christian state as established by Constantine, which was thereafter distorted both in the West due to papist intrigues and in the East "since the times of Justinian."[60] It was precisely this idea of replacing a false model by a correct one that was meant by relating St. Petersburg's coat of arms to that of the Vatican;[61] Petersburg emerges as the true Rome, rejecting both Western precedents as well as the native (pre-Petrine) tradition.[62]

The change of the ruler's title was also connected to the establishment and propagation of this correct model; presented as the "second Constantine," Peter becomes emperor and father of the fatherland. This symbolic renaming was popularized long before the official shift in titulature in the 1720s. Thus in explaining the decorations of the 1703 triumph we read:

> We have written on the cornice: *pio fel. sereniss, potent, inuictissimo que monar Petro Alexiewicz rosso imp. monocrat, patri patriae, triumph, suec, rest, plus quam qo annis inique detentae haered, fulmini liuon* . . . That is, to the Most Pious, Most Felicitous, Most Illustrious, Most Imperial, Most Invincible Monarch, Great Lord Tsar and Grand Prince Petr Alekseevich, the Autocrat of Great, Small and White Russia, father of the fatherland, conqueror, and recoverer of the possessions that were unjustly kept by Sweden for more than ninety years, who strikes Livonia with thunderbolts.[63]

True, here Peter is only called emperor in a Latin inscription, but "father of the fatherland" has already moved into the section in Slavonic.

The change in title symbolized the change in conception of power, and this was precisely the way it was perceived by representatives of traditional culture.[64] For them the assumption of the title of emperor meant that Peter was not an Orthodox tsar, and therefore derived his power from the devil. Thus the change in political conception was raised to a metaphysical level. Peter himself was undoubtedly conscious of this, and it evidently figured into his plans.[65] The "father of the fatherland" was spiritual head of the people, and "emperor"—master of the cosmos.[66] These titles thus put the Russian monarch's status into eschatological perspective, and turned the issue of the tsar's power to administer the church into one of transforming history itself. Claiming the role of apocalyptic leader of peoples (which traditional consciousness perceived to be a mark of the antichrist), Peter also ascribed to himself the power of a demiurge, the creator of a new order (e.g., on the model of the millennial kingdom). It was no accident that in the speech in church when Peter was given the title of "father of the fatherland" in 1721 it said that "Through your Tsarist Majesty's glorious and courageous political and military deeds alone, we, due to your incessant labors and leadership, have been led from the darkness of ignorance to the universal theater of glory and, so to speak, from non-existence to existence, and become part of the society of political nations, as is known not only by us but by the whole world."[67] The formula "from non-existence to existence," constantly repeated from then on in eighteenth-century panegyric literature, refers to the most important prayer of the liturgy (Praefatio, Ἅγιος ὁ Θεός) "Oh, Righteous God, Who has led everything from non-existence to existence . . . " The new order that Peter created represents not only a new political construct but also a new religious reality that humanity is entering. It was precisely thanks to the Petrine transformation that, in Antiokh Kantemir's words, "we suddenly became a new people."[68] This new reality gave Peter complete freedom and removed all responsibility for the break with thousand-year-old moral values and traditions. Russia became a *tabula rasa* on which Peter could freely sketch out plans for the state that he wanted to build. The only obstacle was people's devotion to old ideas and ways of doing things, and doing battle with this became a continual objective that embraced virtually the whole of Peter's reign.

4. PARODY AND BLASPHEMY AS RITUALS OF THE PUBLIC SPHERE

Traditional ideas and customs were discredited using all means of propaganda including the secular and religious rituals examined above. Beyond these, parodic and blasphemous ceremonies served as a special type of weapon. In carrying out this most important function in Peter's cultural politics, these rituals were characterized by traits that are inherent in all state institutions, e.g., consistency, regularity, compulsoriness, and public visibility. The interpretation of this activity as a kind of "entertainment" for the monarch, which was common in nineteenth-century historical writings, clearly contradicts these characteristics, and the failure to consider this crucial aspect of their function indicates a weakness in their overall conception of the Petrine reforms.[69]

Peter began to play at his All-Jesting and All-Drunken Council as early as 1692[70] and he continued this activity until his very death. The All-Jesting Council thus endured for more than thirty years, outliving all of the other "serious" institutions Peter established. Mock weddings were carried out again and again with ever greater scope, and with all of their repetitiousness could hardly have been entertaining to anyone.[71] Masquerades that contained elements of blasphemy and intentional official propaganda were held yearly. Funerals of dwarfs, public practical jokes on April First, Yuletide and Carnival games, and so on, played an analogous role. This type of phenomenon became an institution and a long-standing part of Russian social life.

Peter took a direct part in organizing these ceremonies and performed in them himself. In particular, the determination and seriousness with which he worked on the All-Jesting Council are evident in the extensive file that contains the rules—written in Peter's own hand—for the selection and elevation of the pope-prince for the ceremony that was to take place after the death of Nikita Zotov in 1717. Peter diligently toiled over this work, and several copyists' versions are covered with the tsar's corrections.[72]

In many cases games and merry-making were compulsory for the participants. It was also impossible to refuse to take part in feasts or masquerades, just as it was impossible to refuse appointment to this or that state service. Participation was a necessary sign of loyalty and readiness to be reeducated, recreating oneself according to the model Peter had established. Among the points posed to Tsarevich Aleksei during his interrogation of May 12, 1718, was the following: "When he was summoned to eat and for the launching [of a new ship; a required banquet followed], he said, 'Better hard labor or to be on my back with fever than that.' The Tsarevich answered, 'perhaps I said that'."[73] This coercion functioned on a mass scale. Thus for example on October 24, 1721, there was a masquerade and banquet to celebrate the peace with Sweden. Those who did not appear at this celebration were brought together in the Senate building a week later and forced to get drunk, and among those subjected to this punishment were approximately thirty women of the court.[74]

To be released from a masquerade one needed a special order from the tsar, and a request for one of these excuses has come down to us in which the petitioner explains in detail his inability to attend due to the demands of service and the threat of "losing payments."[75] For the main participants of the merry-making there was generally no choice. Thus, for example, the wife of the pope-prince Burturlin (widow of the former pope-prince Nikita Zotov) was married to him against her will after a year of refusals. We don't know what her feelings were, but Zotov's son, Konon Zotov, a faithful follower of Peter, asked the emperor to call off this enterprise that he found very demeaning; but he met with a refusal. Among the archival materials about Zotov's marriage in 1715 a register of participants has been preserved with their signatures attesting that they had "heard the order" and pledged to attend;[76] people were thus formally obliged to appear at the fools' ceremonies.

The coercive character of these ludic activities was apparently especially so in the case of the All-Jesting and All-Drunken Council, participation in which turned out to be a life-long obligation (and sometimes even passed on to heirs). Determining the Council's full contingent would require special research, which would reveal its principles of formation and changes in the selection of participants. However, the existing data is sufficient to clarify several crucial issues. Thus among the members of the Council two groups are clearly distinguishable: the professional jesters, for whom the Council was their main if not their only occupation (for example, P. I. Buturlin and the "abbess" Rzhevskaia), and high state officials, for whom drunken orgies combined with carrying out the most important state responsibilities (for example, T. N. Streshnev, F. M. Apraksin, I. A. Musin-Pushkin, F. Iu. Romodanovskii).[77] These officials belonged to the old aristocracy and to the elder generation of Peter's followers, so it is hard to imagine that they shared the tsar's revulsion against native traditions and customs.

As early as 1699 the Austrian ambassador I. G. Korb noted that "distingui-shed Muscovites" masqueraded as various religious figures *according to the tsar's choosing*."[78] However, as demonstrated by the Streltsy Revolts, during which representatives of many old families were subjected to harsh repressions (for example, the Romodanovskiis), these nobles did not have their own solid social base and were forced to seek support and defense from the tsar. At the same time, Peter did not reject the old aristocracy.[79] Rather, he tried to make use of its experience in ruling,[80] while obtaining its unconditional loyalty to his cultural politics and shattering "boyar pride and arrogance."[81] Repayment for Peter's support was these people's willing or unwilling acceptance of the tsar's ritual and culturological innovations. Such acceptance, as mentioned earlier, was the clearest guarantee of their loyalty. At the same time it demonstrated public support for the Petrine reforms on the part of the old state apparatus.

It is hardly likely that first-hand testimony concerning Peter forcing involvement in the All-Jesting Council and other blasphemous undertakings will be uncovered, at least from its main participants; in conditions of harsh control over the behavior of the social elite, historical figures do not usually record their dissatisfaction and disagreement on paper. In such situations, studying the reactions of various social groups to state policies requires work with indirect sources, some that might seem quite insignificant at first glance. For example, prince-pope Nikita Zotov consistently signed his name in documents to Peter (including business documents, written as the head of a chancellery) by parodying religious titulature: "Humble Anikit with his power-wielding hand."[82] In contrast, F. Iu. Romodanovskii, to whom Peter constantly refers (even in purely business correspondence) as "Min Her Kenich [i.e. *Mein Herr König*, My Lord King]" and "Your Majesty,"[83] never signs himself with a playful title, and this may reflect the fact that he never accepted the duties of tsar-in-jest of his own free will. It is suggestive that Tsarevich Aleksei, listing the people on whose support he hoped to count in the case of Peter's death, testified that "I also put my hope on the late prince-ceasar and prince-pope, as on friends,"[84] that is, he named Romodanovskii and Zotov as among his sympathizers. This is not easy to explain, but it does cast some doubt on Romodanovskii's devotion to his responsibilities as jester.[85]

It is significant that the various parodic rituals that Peter created, and in which members of the social elite played leading roles, were public events, so that blasphemous apostasy was acted out deliberately and before the eyes of the entire people. The marriage of the prince-pope Zotov was just such a public event, as numerous courtiers rode in the marriage procession dressed up in masquerade costumes, and the people "whose confluence was innumerable" cried out "with great laughter," "the patriarch has gotten married, the patriarch has gotten married!"[86] There was a similar scene at P. I. Buturlin's marriage in 1721, when the newlyweds accompanied by all-jesting cardinals (metropolitans) were carried across the Neva River in a specially contrived vehicle[87] in the presence of a great many people; and then the marriage ceremony was performed on Senate Square.[88] No less extravagant was the masquerade in 1723 that lasted from August 30 until September 6. More than fifty groups of performers took part, and each one rode in its own separate carriage. The emperor was in the group of "restless brethren" and beat on drums together with General Buturlin and Major Mamonov.[89] Members of the All-Jesting Council made up a separate group, riding dressed up as high church leaders.[90]

Parodic rituals, as public and socially significant, interacted with public events of different kinds and could be included as part of diverse civil ceremonies and celebrations. Thus, for example, during the triumphal entry into Moscow of 1710 after the Poltava victory, the jester Vymeni, "King of the Samoyeds," rode in the procession, coming after the prisoners of war and part of the Semevovskii guards and before the Preobrazhenskii regiment; he was accompanied by nineteen sleighs in which actual Samoyeds were riding.[91] The jester king's participation in the triumph was evidently meant to symbolize the imperial dimensions of the triumphal power into whose orbit "wild" peoples were included,[92] and at the same time it was an insult to the Swedes whose defeat ostensibly put them on the same level as other vassals of the Russian monarch. Together with this, the inclusion of parodic elements into the triumphal procession underscored the new system of values that the victorious monarch was establishing and controlling, asserting his right to act in an arbitrary manner on the basis of his victory. In an analogous way during the celebration of the peace treaty with Sweden in 1721, after the service of thanksgiving in Trinity Church, the tsar "immediately went off to Prince Romodanovskii as the prince-caesar and informed him of the peace treaty."[93] Understandably, the very combination of church ritual and blasphemous parody indicated the fact that the tsar's will was beyond the pale of traditional values and traditional ecclesiastical notions about the source of victory and well-being.

5. BLASPHEMY IN THE PARADIGM OF THE NEW POWER

Thus even a very superficial examination of the parodic and blasphemous rituals that Peter introduced and developed shows that they were characterized by consistency, compulsoriness, and public visibility, and this testifies to their importance for the tsar's program; these were not merry entertainments for the leader's relaxation but determined labor designed to transform public consciousness.[94] The challenge, then, is to define the ideas that were being promulgated through this kind of activity.

The functions of the All-Jesting and All-Drunken Council emerge most clearly. As R. Wittram suggests, at first this parodic institution arose "out of profound dissatisfaction . . . as the young tsar's reaction to his failure during the selection of the patriarch in 1690." Subsequently, however, the Council was used as a fully conscious part of the tsar's ecclesiastical policy, and its goal was "the discrediting of the patriarch's status and of all clerical claims."[95] This is just how I. I. Golikov, who remained one of Peter's apologists, viewed the All-Jesting Council; he fully appreciated Peter's anti-clerical ideas and—unlike later historians—did not try to portray him as the model of a pious Russian monarch or as an enlightened European sovereign. Speaking of the All-Jesting Council, Golikov tells how "little by little Peter created disrespect for the patriarch of Russia,"[96] and he directly connected the staging of the marriage of the prince-pope Zotov in 1715 that excited the entire capital to Peter's recent decision to do away with the patriarchate completely and to establish the Synod: "To prepare people for this . . . the monarch's invention of such a silly ceremony of marrying this sham patriarch served this end."[97] Citing the tales of eyewitnesses, Golikov reports that "when the one portraying the patriarch mounted the horse, [the tsar] held the steed's stirrup in the same way as several Russian tsars had when the patriarch had mounted a horse on the specified days."[98] Thus the theme of the procession on a donkey, which as we have seen was so clearly connected in Peter's mind with the clergy's hateful pretensions to power, once again appeared, here in connection with the All-Jesting Council and subjected to mockery.

The combining in the All-Jesting Council of parodies of Western (Catholic) ecclesiastical establishments and those of the Russian Orthodox Church symbolized the equation of these two kinds of "clericalism" which were juxtaposed to single tsarist rule. Hence at the head of the All-Jesting Council stood a prince-pope, who was also called the all-jesting patriarch, and its members could be called cardinals as well as metropolitans. They wore miters of a Western type, although their clothing evidently also included elements of Orthodox bishops' vestments.[99] The prince-pope could be called "most holy" or patriarch,[100] which parodied Orthodox tradition, and at the same time the parodic Novgorod metropolitan T. N. Streshnev received letters from Peter addressed to "Min Her heilige Vader,"[101] indicating the Catholic subtext. Elements of both Catholic and Orthodox derivation were also combined in the mock ritual of selection and elevation of the prince-pope. Thus during the prince-pope's selection mock cardinals took part in a "specially prepared conclave"[102] in which one of three candidates was elected by vote; the parody of the selection process was emphasized by playing on the story of the Papess Joanne,* which was often used in anti-Roman Protestant pamphlets, and was here assimilated by Peter as another argument discrediting the papacy.[103] Together with this the ceremony of elevation (both of the all-jesting patriarch and of the bishops) precisely followed the Orthodox ritual of bishops' khirotonia (the laying on of hands), both the order of its formulas and its language.[104] The idea behind this juxtaposition left no room for doubt: the institution of the patriarchy was depicted as a form of papism and in light of this was subject to destruction.

The connection between these parodic and Orthodox rituals was obvious for contemporaries who saw them precisely as a desecration of piety and the overthrow of church authority. Thus in a denunciation of the All-Jesting Council written around 1705 it said:

> [Peter] chose for himself just such an enemy of God, a peasant, a rogue, a whore's son, and calls him his teacher, Nikita Zotov; and he made him a false patriarch with a [ceremony of] elevation that was supposed to represent how patriarchs are elevated. In the same way, all of the hierarchs' clothing, that of the Kiev and Novgorod metropolitans, and others, was faked. I have heard

---

* *Translator's note:* Papess Joanne (or Pope Joan) was allegedly a female pope who reigned sometime in the Middle Ages.

from a worthy person of the highest rank (*sinkliticheskii san*), how his elevation was performed. They imitated the service book and in desecration of God and repudiation [of Him], promised all their faith to believe in someone called Gad. And going around the nobles' courtyards they abuse all of the church sacraments, they consecrate oil and insult the other sacraments, and make many affronts to the holy church.[105]

In this context the function of the prince-pope becomes clear, a role which R. Wittram considered "hard to comprehend."[106] The prince-caesar and prince-pope emerge as a "holy pair" whose model was Emperor Constantine the Great and Pope Sylvester from the legend of the Donation of Constantine. The existence of these parodic rulers discredited the very idea of a "symphonic" relationship between secular and religious power which Peter associated with the Tale of the White Cowl, which he considered an illicit clerical attack on the indivisibility of tsarist authority. The concrete precedent which he might have had in mind here was calling the tsar and patriarch "the divinely wise holy pair (*dvoitsa*), chosen by God" and "doubly chosen by God," etc., in Nikon's Service Book,[107] as well as Nikon's use of the title "Great Sovereign," which was held against him after his exit from the Moscow pulpit.[108] Notably, "both Romodanovskii and Buturlin appeared in clothing like that of seventeenth-century Russian monarchs"[109]—an unmistakable parodic reference to the earlier state structure and to previous political notions.

One may also read the jester-prince-caesar's procedure of inheritance as meant to parody traditional political ideas. When in 1717 the prince-caesar F. Iu. Romodanovskii died his son became the new one. This "correct" line of succession by the eldest son took place while Peter was preparing vengeance against Tsarevich Aleksei and had certainly already thought about establishing a new order of inheritance for the Russian throne; the new edict, according to which the ruling monarch chose his successor, went into effect in 1722.[110]

Peter's own parodic service, which the prince-caesar Romodanovskii rewarded with successive military ranks on the occasion of various victorious battles, carried obvious ideological weight. From bombardier Peter became captain, from captain lieutenant, and so on.[111] Together with Peter's usual, deliberate appearance in the role of "sailor and carpenter," his parodic career also embodied the idea of a ruler who received power as a reward for merit and not as a divine gift for which the monarch was beholden to God. By the way, it was in just this vein of meritocracy that A. Nartov, who had fully assimilated Petrine ideology, understood these promotions in rank. He wrote: "The rank of vice-admiral was announced by the prince-caesar for Tsar Petr Alekseevich, previously rear-admiral, in the Senate, where the prince-caesar sat on the throne amid all of the senators and gave an audience to the tsar, reading a written relation of his victories, as a model to others that military advancement is awarded exclusively for merit and not according to lineage or fortune."[112] This idea that was propagated at triumphs and other civil ceremonies (as discussed above) here received mythological embodiment, as it referred to the fairytale story of the simple worker (or solider) who thanks to his cleverness and skill becomes tsar or governor of a city. This mythologized scheme was also apparently meant to discredit the old order and advertise the new, as well as the fairytale possibility of earning power and glory. At the same time it focused attention on Peter as the singlehanded creator of the new Russia, as a demiurge who fashioned a new order of being.[113]

The entire complex of the emperor's ludic enterprises that confronted Russian society year after year also supported this idea. To this group, for example, belong the public masquerades that were continually staged. By itself wearing costumes and appearing in masks was no new thing in Russia, as Shrovetide games were part of traditional customs. However, they were not a religiously neutral occupation but served as an element of anti-behavior that was included in the yearly cycle and connected to an "unclean" (demonic) period; Christmas games demanded repentance at Epiphany. In extending carnival behavior outside its usual frame Peter destroyed traditional practice in a fully intentional way, and made anti-behavior the standard modus vivendi. In this way he reversed the accepted world view. By introducing the masquerade into the structure of state life (and in particular, into civil holidays) he gave the semiotic "bottom" the function of the "top." In the perception of traditional society this meant changing the God-given established order, a demiurgic activity. The emperor demonstrated that he commanded divine power, and society had the choice of either accepting this inhuman superiority or rejecting it as a satanic enterprise. In any case these ludic enterprises posed a religious dilemma for society. The encroachment on the traditional order is even more apparent in such of the tsar's entertainments as the burial of a dwarf, when a human death as well as the Christian ritual consecration of a soul's release were treated playfully; someone who asserts his will in this sphere assigns himself power over human souls, that is, he claims divine rather than human authority.[114]

Mixing blasphemous and parodic elements with those of official (state) activity was a fairly characteristic, if not constant, trait of the Petrine period. Several examples—the participation of the jester-king of the Samoyeds in the triumph of 1710, the prince-caesar's arrival with news of the peace with Sweden—have already been mentioned. Others are easily cited. Thus for example prince-caesar Romodanovskii could occupy the first, tsar's, place at a celebratory feast, "having alongside himself both bishops, of Pskov and Novgorod, and also some of the members of the Synod."[115] Romodanovskii's imperial worthiness may have been a joke, but at the same time Feofan Prokopovich and Feodosii Ianovskii's rank was fully real. Understandably, this kind of juxtaposition not only gave a special status to play, but also communicated an air of carnival to real life: the prince-caesar's semiotic ambivalence created an analogous ambivalence for the genuine bishops. And when in 1699 during the execution of the Streltsy a Streltsy priest was to be put to death, the function of executioner fell to Nikita Zotov, on the strength of his belonging to the clerical station.[116] In this case as well a macabre dualism arose that brought sacral elements into the context of a blasphemous game. Similarly, a real priest from the existing church performed the marriage of the prince-pope and his bride according to the actual Orthodox ceremony, and this introduction of the sacred into the blasphemous erased the boundary between real and unreal.

The same erasure of boundaries also took place when, according to Berkhgol'ts' report, during the masquerade in February 1723 "all members of the imperial collegiums (kollegii) were obliged to come to work in masks, which seems improper to me, the more so since many of them were not dressed as befits old men, judges and councilors."[117] Understandably, a petitioner appearing at a collegium at such a moment would have received a rather complicated notion of state activity in the country that Peter revolutionized. In all of these cases, in making reality ambivalent Peter stood above it all, as if empowered to turn reality into parody and vice versa according to his whim. In this sense blasphemous and parodic activities no less emphasized the demiurgical omnipotence of the tsar than proclaiming him "father of the fatherland" who brought his subjects "out of non-existence into being."[118]

Interweaving real state activity with parodic play could give the latter a prognosticative character when real transformations were played out beforehand in the tsar's mocking capers. Thus for example the establishment of the All-Jesting Council with a prince-pope at its head took place while the last patriarch was still alive and presaged the abrogation of the patriarchate. In the very same way the formation of its mock-hierarchy consisting of only metropolitans was a harbinger of ending this rank in the Russian church itself (on the reasons for Peter's hatred of this position, see above). Peter's "toy soldiers" (poteshnyi polk) and the Kozhukhov campaign are often seen as a rehearsal of his subsequent military activity, although a researcher needs to keep in mind that he or she is dealing with a ludic mechanism, directly tied to the All-Jesting

Council.[119] Indeed, the "toy soldier regiments" took part in the Kozhukhov campaign under the command of the prince-caesar F. Iu. Romodanovskii, while the Streltsy formations were under the command of "the Polish King" I. I. Buturlin.[120] Understandably, the fate of these play military maneuvers was predetermined; the Polish king as well as the Streltsy regiments had to meet defeat.[121] The Streltsy's defeat modeled Peter's later military reform and served as an omen of the sad fate that awaited the Streltsy themselves. Various details also predicted the future. Thus the clothing of the "toy soldiers" (of European cut) later became required for state servitors, while the feast of Romodanovskii and Buturlin, the conqueror and conquered, emerged after the Kuzhukhov campaign as the prototype of the banquet, celebrated in literature, that Peter held with the defeated Swedish commanders after the Poltava victory.[122]

These materials allow us to interpret Peter's ceremonial innovations as all part of a single larger complex that is united by the ideas being propagated and the interconnections among the concrete acts themselves. These innovations were aimed at creating an image of the new Russia to which Peter gave birth as demiurge. The new Russia took on the status of a universal empire like that of Rome, its supreme leader endowed with divine power that combined sacral elements of classical paganism and Byzantine theocratic concepts. The emperor rose above reality and, wielding the power of life and death, transformed that reality according to his desire, turning age-old customs into blasphemous entertainments and playful inventions into state institutions. Together with this, Petrine propaganda not only created an image of the new Russia but also one of the old Russia that was directly opposed to it. In a sermon of 1716 Feofan Prokopovich asked: "What was foreign peoples' previous opinion of us, in what respect were we held? By those who were refined we were considered barbarians, by the proud and majestic we were disdained, by the learned deemed ignoramuses, by the predatory—a desirable target, by all—ignored, by all—insulted . . . While today . . . the ones who disdained us as coarse zealously seek our friendship, those who dishonored us, praise us, those who threatened us, fear us and tremble, those who scorned us are not ashamed to serve us."[123] This historiographical scheme was worked out with Peter's own direct influence[124] and was assimilated by many subsequent generations. The juxtaposition of old and new Russia was built on a set of mutually contradictory features that did not allow any room for continuity. Therefore, in ascribing enlightenment to the new Russia, the old was declared ignorant, in describing wealth and grandeur to the new Russia, to the old fell the lot of being squalid and poverty-stricken. It was as if the new Russia had drawn a caricature of the old, and through this depiction that was so far from reality there clearly emerged the self-image of the new culture turned inside out. This is why discrediting the traditional system of values took on such great significance and the affirmation of the new ideas became a kind of choice of religion. The various rituals that Peter created in every sphere of social life that gave every kind of behavior semiotic significance were all subordinated to this goal.[125]

6. CONCLUDING REMARKS

Peter's propaganda, which depended on mechanisms of religious perception that had developed over centuries, had decisive importance for the subsequent development of Russian cultural consciousness. It led to a profound cultural schism in Russian society that was the basis for later social cataclysms. That section of society that remained faithful, at least in part, to traditional notions of power and its religious basis were cut off from the cultural and political development of the new state, and were rendered socially disadvantaged and unreceptive to later governmental changes. The other part of society that assimilated Petrine ideas ceased to understand their less enlightened fellow citizens and experienced a painful, unresolvable contradiction between religious fidelity to Petrine ideas (in their various embodiments—monarchist, progressive, etc.) and consciousness of their isolation from the majority of the population, from "the people"; this sense of alienation also took on various forms. For all their diversity they all reveal a genetic connection to Petrine propaganda, and in becoming a dominant trend in cultural consciousness they were extrapolated into political activity, social construction, as well as scholarship. The present study cannot offer detailed analysis of this filiation of Petrine mythology, which is a subject that deserves separate consideration. Some fragmentary remarks, however, may help clarify some lines of analysis.

The fundamental proposition that Peter inculcated into cultural conscious-ness and that became established over many decades was faith in the root juxtaposition between old and new Russia, and the lack of practically any cultural continuity between them. Peter's reign is perceived as a genuine historical and cultural watershed, and the life of pre-Petrine Ruś as an ethnically alien way of life, juxtaposed to the later "European" way of life, and provoking the same sense of alienation as that felt toward unenlightened native peoples. In the last analysis this perception conditioned an almost religious devotion to the Petrine legacy as the indispensable basis for one's own life and worldview. The "choice of religion" that Peter demanded retained its power for many, many years. The sentiments of M. P. Pogodin, expressed a hundred and fifty years after Peter's death, eloquently testify to this. Having acquainted himself with the materials that N. G. Ustrialov published illuminating the murder of Tsarevich Aleksei and the suggestion that not only the entire trial but that the attempted escape of the tsarevich itself were set up by the tsar, Pogodin nevertheless could not bring himself to condemn Peter: "What verdict, then, will we pronounce upon Peter in the matter of his son . . . We are speaking in the academy founded by Peter the Great! . . . The city in which this academy has been laboring for a hundred and fifty years received its name from him, and at every step, every stone here, it seems, proclaims his memory, and in every wave of the Neva we hear his name. No, ladies and gentlemen, our tongue cannot bear to form words that would pronounce judgment on Peter the Great[126] . . . " Pogodin expressed similar thoughts about Peter in another work:

> We awake. What day is it today? January 1, 1841—Peter the Great ordered us to count the years from Christ's birth; Peter the Great ordered that we number the months starting from January. It is time to get dressed—our clothes are sewn according to the style designated by Peter the Great, and our uniform is of his design . . . Our eye falls on a book—Peter the Great introduced that alphabet, and himself carved the letters. You begin to read—it was under Peter that this language became written, literary, having forced out the former church language. They bring in newspapers—it was Peter the Great who began them . . . After dinner you go visiting—this is [the legacy of] Peter the Great's "assemblies." You meet ladies there—they were permitted into male company on Peter the Great's command . . . You are given a rank—from Peter the Great's table of ranks; the rank makes me a noble—that's what Peter the Great established. I need to file a complaint—Peter the Great defined its form. It is accepted—in front of Peter the Great's "zertsalo." A judgment is made—according to [Peter's] General Regulations . . . Whatever we may think, or say, or do, everything, harder or easier, nearer or farther, I repeat, leads us back to Peter the Great. He holds the key, or the lock itself.[127]

The organic connection of modern Russian society with Peter's semiotic transformation is responsible for the conviction shared by Westernizers and Slavophiles alike that the Petrine period is the crucial watershed in Russian history and Russian historical consciousness. It has also made its way into scholarship, defining the periodization in all historical disciplines—in history itself, in the history of culture, literature, the literary language, art, and so on. A revolution indeed took place and historical consciousness certainly underwent transformation, but to be objective about this process demands a precise clarification of its sphere of action. First of all the conception of power changed. Petrine propaganda completely rejected old Russian notions about the just and unjust ruler, replacing them with the idea of the omnipotent monarch who represents the source of law. This conception, deriving from Justinian's law code, underwent a special transformation under Peter insofar as the emperor emerged not only as the highest court of appeal in regulating properly juridical procedures but also as the one who could establish any norm or practice in general, including religious, moral, cultural and behavioral ones. Of central importance in this innovation was Peter's church reform, under which the church which had served as an independent setter of norms was now forced to become part of the state structure. The charismatic omnipotence of the tsar, asserted by Ivan the Terrible (and evidently undermined as a fundamental value by the events of the Times of Trouble and the rule of Mikhail Fedorovich), was institutionalized under Peter and took on the character of a legal standard, without particular relationship to past practice. In his capacity as creator of this new order Peter was perceived as the "father" of new Russia, and historical development began to be described within the framework of those institutions which formed as a result of his policies. By virtue of this the Petrine era became the starting point for modern Russian history, whatever particular area of the historical process (cultural, literary, etc.) that was involved.

Consequently, those elements of continuity which exist between pheno-mena of the pre-Petrine and post-Petrine periods—in social structures, mechanisms of cultural and religious perception, the literary process, and so on—have been forced to the periphery of scholars' interest or simply ignored. This lack of attention has two aspects. On the one hand, for many years the living traditional culture that to a significant degree rejected Petrine innovations was excluded from Russian cultural consciousness. I have in mind here the development of the pre-Petrine cultural, literary traditions and worldview of the Old Believers as well as that of the lowest level of society. Notions about power, about the religious organization of society, social structure, about the development of urban culture, and so on, which the greater part of the Russian population professed and which had defining influence on mass social movements, all have remained practically unstudied. In particular, the evolution of the lowest level of social consciousness remains unexamined, although it was by no means static (as references to the most recent ethnographic material by researchers of old Russian culture suggest), but reflected a specific, unique response to the reigning culture.

On the other hand, the "old" within the "new" culture has also been ignored. Only those developments which openly manifested a debt to the Petrine reforms have attracted attention; the connection of these new traditions with the old culture that was declaratively rejected by representatives of the new culture, has, as a rule, unsurprisingly, remained hidden. The connection of eighteenth-century panegyric literature that spread Petrine state propaganda with seventeenth-century Baroque literature is a particular though characteristic example of this. All too often the seventeenth century as a whole is relegated to "ancient Rus`," so that the innovations of Peter's predecessors are written off as exceptional, without scope or importance. This widespread view also affects national cultural psychology, and, to a certain extent, historical scholarship. The idea of the demiurgical reorganization of the country which Peter incessantly promoted in his propaganda has preserved its influence right down to the present day. Therefore, in order to reconstruct the social and cultural history of the post-Petrine period it is necessary to reveal the genesis of modern Russian cultural consciousness and its fundamental connection to the historiosophical assertions of the tsar-transformer. This analysis of Peter's propagandistic undertakings as a special sphere of his activity may serve as an introduction to such future study.

Translated by Marcus C. Levitt

NOTES

[1] *Polnoe sobranie zakonov Rossiiskoi imperii. Sobranie pervoe* (St. Petersburg, 1830), vol. VII, 68, no. 4870. Translation is from A. Lentin, trans. and ed., *Peter the Great: His Law on Imperial Succession. The Official Commentary* (Oxford, 1996), 223). In an analogous way, Feofan wrote in his expansive speech "in praise of Peter the Great" in 1725:

> If he could not share his personal and individual virtues with his fatherland he did not regard them as virtues . . . And how much did he produce by his personal efforts? What we see blooming now but unknown to us before, is this not all his initiative? If we look at the smallest things that are yet estimable and useful, for instance, at our more dignified dress, friendly amenities, banquets and feasts, and other gallant manners, do we not recognize that Peter has taught us these skills? And what we boasted about before we are ashamed of now. (Feofan Prokopovich, *Arkhiepiskopa Velikogo Novagrada i Velikikh Luk, Sviateishago Pravitel`stvuiushchego Sinoda Vitse prezidenta, a potom pervenstvuiushchego Chlena Slova i rechi pouchitel`nyia, pokhval`nyia i pozdravitel`nyia* (St. Petersburg, 1760-1768), part II, 148-149.)

The French Ambassador Campredon also wrote specifically about this aspect of Peter's transformations in a dispatch of March 14, 1721: "This prince has taken it into his head to change the spirit, ways and customs of his people entirely, from black to white." See *Sbornik Russkogo istoricheskogo obshchestva* (St. Petersburg, Petrograd, 1867-1916), vol. XL, 180.

[2] See G. D. Gurvich, *'Pravda voli monarshei' Feofana Prokopovicha i ee zapadnoevropeiskie istochniki* (Iur`ev, 1915).

[3] See Peter's preface to the Naval Regulation in N. G. Ustrialov, *Istoriia tsarstvovaniia Petra Velikogo* (St. Petersburg, 1858-1859), vol. II, 397. See also Prokopovich's preface

to Apollodorus' "Library"—*Appolodora grammatika afineiskago biblioteki ili o bogakh* (Moscow, 1725), predislovie, 13-15.

[4] See B. A. Uspenskii, "Historia sub specie semioticae" in *Kul`turnoe nasledie Drevnei Rusi. Istoki, stanovlenie, traditsiia* (Moscow, 1976); V. M. Zhivov, B. A. Uspenskii, "Metamorfozy antichnogo iazychestva v istorii russkoi kul`tury XVII-XVIII vv." in *Antichnost` v kul`ture i iskusstve posleduiushchikh vekov* (Moscow, 1984), 216-221.

[5] See N. S. Trubetzkoy, *Vorlesungen über die altrussische Literatur* (Firenze, 1973).

[6] S. M. Solov`ev, *Istoriia Rossii* (Moscow, 1962-1966), vol. VIII, 101.

[7] Ph. J. von Strahlenberg, *Das Nord- und Ostliche Theil von Europa und Asia, In so weit solches Das gantze Rußische Reich mit Sibirien und der grossen Tatarey in sich begreiffet, In einer Historisch-Geographischen Beschreibung der alten und neuern Zeiten, und vielen andern unbekannten Nachrichten vorgestellet* (Stockholm, 1730), 232; see also Golikov's refutation of Strahlenberg in I. I. Golikov, *Deianiia Petra Velikogo* (Moscow, 1788), part I, 14-15; see also A. M. Panchenko, *Russkaia kul`tura v kanun petrovskikh reform* (Leningrad, 1984), 116f.

[8] M. M. Bogoslovskii, *Petr I. Materialy dlia biografii* (Moscow, 1940-1946), vol. II, 390.

[9] S. M. Solov`ev, *Istoriia Rossii*, vol. VII, 554.

[10] Johann Georg Korb, *Dnevnik puteshestviia v Moskoviiu (1698 i 1699 g.)* (St. Petersburg, 1906), 121. Translation is from Count Mac Donnel, trans. and ed., *Diary of an Austrian Secretary of Legation at the Court of Czar Peter the Great by Johann-Georg Korb* (London, 1863), 244-245.

[11] According to an ukase of 1718; see *Polnoe sobranie zakonov*, vol. V, no. 3178.

[12] See *Dukhovnyi Reglament Vsepresvetleishego derzhavneishego gosudaria Petra Pervogo, imperatora i samoderzhtsa vserossiiskogo* (Moscow, 1904), 20-24; J. Cracraft, *The Church Reform of Peter the Great* (London, 1971), 290-293.

[13] A change in the oaths that were recited and signed during the service for installing a bishop came in 1691. For a complete collection of these pledges for 1672—1700, see GIM, Sin., ms. 1044; see also A. V. Gorskii, K. I. Nevostruev, *Opisanie slavianskikh rukopisei Moskovskoi Sinodal`noi biblioteki* (Moscow, 1855-1917), otd. III, 2, 441-444. A comparison of the bishop's oaths taken by Evfimii of Sarsk and Podonsk, installed on August 22, 1688, and Ilarion of Pskov and Izborsk, seated on February 1, 1691, reveals that after the death of Patriarch Ioakim an item forbidding consorting with heretics and prohibiting marriages between Orthodox and non-Orthodox was removed from the oath. Before Ioakim's death the text read:

> Moreover, I vow that I shall not hold intercourse with Catholics and with Lutherans or with Calvinists and with other heretics should it happen that any of these come to the capital city of Moscow; nor will I allow anyone of the Orthodox faith in my entire see to enter into marriage with them, or be in a fraternal or godparent relationship with them, and the same goes for people of all heretical faiths, if they previously have not converted to the Orthodox Christianity of this Eastern Church. And should any cleric under me do such a thing without my knowledge then it is for me to punish such a priest according to the holy rules of the fathers. (GIM, Sin. ms. 1044, l. 2 verso.)

It was just this pledge that was removed after Patriarch Adrian took office. See the standard text of the pledge composed under the last patriarch in GIM, Sin. ms. 344, l. 27 verso-28 verso. It seems clear that this change was not introduced by the religious but by the secular authority that posed certain demands on the new patriarch as a condition of his selection. One can hardly doubt that this stipulation came from Peter himself (at that time eighteen years old) as a response to Patriarch Ioakim's testament, in which he had warned tsars against letting Orthodox and non-Orthodox consort. He had written: "and let them, sovereigns, never allow Orthodox Christians in their kingdom to have dealings with heretics of other faiths, with Latins, Lutherans, Calvinists, or godless Tatars . . . but should keep them away as enemies of God and denigrators of the church." See M. M. Bogoslovskii, *Petr I*, vol. I, 107; N. G. Ustrialov, *Istoriia tsarstvovaniia*, vol. II, 472. Peter's association with foreigners was beginning precisely at this time. Thus here we have one of Peter's first substantial actions in the area of cultural politics, and it is symptomatic that it relates specifically to the church and concerns church rituals. Notably, changes in the text of the bishop's oath are a very important historical source that to this day have practically never been used by scholars. On their significance for a series of other issues, see V. M. Zhivov, "Neizvestnoe sochinenie mitropolita Stefana Iavorskogo kak pamiatnik tserkovnoi mysli epokhi petrovskikh preobrazovanii" in *Vtoraia Mezhdunarodnaia nauchnaia tserkovnaia Konferentsiia, posviashchennaia 1000-letiiu Kreshcheniia Rusi 'Bogoslovie i dukhovnost` Russkoi Pravoslavnoi tserkvi,' Moskva, 11-19 maia 1987 goda* (preprint).

14 For a description of the ritual, see K. Nikol`skii, *O sluzhbakh russkoi tserkvi, byvshikh v prezhnikh bogosluzhebnykh knigakh* (St. Petersburg, 1885), 45-97; on its history, see B. A. Uspenskij, V. M. Zhivov, "Tsar and God," in this volume, 50; M. S. Flier, "Breaking the Code. The Image of the Tsar in the Muscovite Palm Sunday Ritual" in M. S. Flier, D. Rowland, eds., *Medieval Russian Culture* (Berkeley and Los Angeles, 1994), 213-242; Idem., "Court Ceremony in an Age of Reform. Patriarch Nikon and the Palm Sunday Ritual" in S. H. Baron, N. Sh. Kollmann, eds., *Religion and Culture in Early Modern Russia and Ukraine* (De Kalb: Northern Illinois University Press, 1997), 73-95. This was precisely the interpretation presented in the decisions of the Council of 1678. They stated that:

> Our most pious autocrats condescend [in the ceremony of the procession on a donkey] to demonstrate to the Orthodox people a model of their humility and virtuous submission to the Lord Christ, because they adopt a most humble custom in which they chasten their royal loftiness when the Patriarch mounts a steed in memory of the Lord's entry in Jerusalem and they take into their noble scepter-bearing hands the reins of this donkey and lead it to the cathedral church in service of the Lord Christ. This is a praiseworthy deed because seeing such humility of the terrestrial Tsar before the heavenly Tsar many people relent [of their hard-heartedness]; having acquired the spirit of contrition they descend into profound salvific humility and from the treasuries of their hearts they give forth a warm sigh to the Lord Christ and sing with devout lips: 'Hosanna in the highest, blessed is he who comes in the name of the Lord, the King of Israel'. (*Akty, sobrannye v bibliotekakh i arkhivakh Rossiiskoi imperii Arkheograficheskoi ekspeditsieiu imp. Akademii nauk* (St. Petersburg, 1836), vol. IV, 308-309.)

One may probably agree with M. Flier (M. S. Flier, "Breaking the Code") that the given ritual, that arose in Novgorod in the fifteenth century and relocated to Moscow in the 1540s under Metropolitan Makarii, at first symbolized not only the tsar's humility toward religious power but also had eschatological significance as archetype of the Second Coming in which the patriarch represented Christ in glory, and the tsar an earthly shepherd who was leading his people to the Heavenly Kingdom. However, in the second half of the seventeenth century, at a time of intense struggle between the secular and spiritual authority, this interpretation evidently ceased to be relevant.

[15]   See G. Ostrogorsky, "Zum Stratordienst des Herrscher in der byzantinisch-slavischen Welt," *Seminarium Kondakovianum* 7 (1935); R. O. Crummey, "Court Spectacles in Seventeenth-Century Russia: Illusion and Reality" in *Essays in Honor of A. A. Zimin* (Columbus, 1985).

[16]   Cited from *Kormchaia* (Moscow, 1653), 8 verso-9 (third foliation).

[17]   RGB, f. 178, d. 9427, l. 259.

[18]   P. V. Verkhovskoi, *Uchrezhdenie Dukhovnoi Kollegii i Dukhovnyi Reglament* (Rostov-na-Donu, 1916), vol. II, 32 (first pagination); *Dukhovnyi Reglament*, 17.

[19]   B. A. Uspenskij, V. M. Zhivov, "Tsar and God," in this volume, 52-53.

[20]   I. Smolitsch, *Geschichte der russischen Kirche, 1700-1917* (Leiden, 1964), 401.

[21]   Hierarchical regulation as a manifestation of church power was the main idea behind the decisions of the Council of 1675 that governed investiture. Concerning the patriarch's relationship to other church leaders they declared that "After the first head of the most Holy Church, Our Lord Jesus Christ, that has no beginning, exists forever, and is powerful beyond measure, its [next] head and its spiritual bridegroom is the most holy Patriarch in his entire domain; the other bishops serve either as eye, or hands, or other members of his body." See Amvrosii, *Istoriia rossiiskoi ierarkhii* (Moscow, 1807), 325. This view also determined the decision according to which "it has been defined and established in respect of privileges of patriarchs, metropolitans, archbishops, bishops and other clergy that the honorific privileges of patriarchal majesty in holy Churches should not be diluted and, as has been deemed by the Fathers, that their limits should not be transgressed." See Ibid., 326. Here, in particular, it was established that the patriarch and metropolitans, as opposed to other church leaders, could wear a saccus and miter; moreover, the patriarch's saccus, as opposed to that of metropolitans, was embroidered with epitrachelion (using pearls), and on top of the patriarch's miter—again as opposed to that of a metropolitan—there was a cross. See "Opredeleniia Moskovskogo Sobora 1675 g.," *Pravoslavnyi sobesednik* 1 (1864): 438-439. Here too may be seen a connection to the narrative about the Donation of Constantine insofar as the royal clothing that Constantine bequeathed to Pope Sylvester could be perceived as a saccus with woven epitrachelion. As concerns the structure of the patriarch's miter, the Council's decisions of 1675 directly stated that it was designed "according to the directive that Holy Tsar Constantine the Great, equal to the apostles, made to Holy Sylvester." See Amvrosii, *Istoriia*, 328. In this way, the clergy's superiority over the state and the special status of the patriarch as image of the Heavenly Sovereign—ideas Peter detested—were clearly expressed in the regulation of sacral clothing.

[22]   Ibid., 352.

[23]   P. Lebedev, *Nauka o bogosluzhenii Pravoslavnoi Tserkvi* (Moscow, 1890), vol. I, 134.

[24]   "O sviashchennykh odezhdakh," *Khristianskoe chtenie* 1 (1848): 344.

[25]   P. V. Verkhovskoi, *Uchrezhdenie Dukhovnoi Kollegii*, vol. II, 11.

[26]   See M. S. Popov, *Arsenii Matseevich i ego delo* (St. Petersburg, 1912), 97, 140, 390, 430.

[27]   See the quotation above from *Kormchaia* (note 16).

[28]   *Polnoe sobranie postanovlenii i rasporiazhenii po vedomstvu pravoslavnogo ispovedaniia* (St. Petersburg, Petrograd, 1869-1916), vol. I, 165, no. 148.

[29]   Ibid., 17, no. 348.

30 *Opisanie dokumentov i del, kraniashchikhsia v arkhive Sviateishego Pravitel`stvuiushchego Sinoda* (St. Petersburg, 1869-1914), vol. III, no. 393; prilozhenie XLI, cxcix-cci.

31 See N. D. Zol`nikova, *Soslovnye problemy vo vzaimootnosheniiakh tserkvi i gosudarstva v Sibiri (XVIII v.)* (Novosibirsk, 1981), 152f; B. A. Uspenskij, V. M. Zhivov, "Tsar and God," in this volume, 57.

32 Ibid., 120-121.

33 Feofan Prokopovich, *Pervoe uchenie otrokom* (St. Petersburg, 1723), 11.

34 *Polnoe sobranie zakonov*, vol. IV, no. 2213 and *Polnoe sobranie postanovlenii i rasporiazhenii*, vol. I, no 179, respectively.

35 Feofilakt Lopatinskii, *Sluzhba blagodarstvennaia, Bogu v Troitse sviatoi slavimomu o velikoi Bogom darovannoi pobede, nad svoiskim korolem Karolom 12, i voinstvom ego. Sodeiannoi pod Poltavoiu, v leto 1709* (Moscow, 1709), 16 verso-17.

36 Ibid., 19 verso.

37 See his letter to Stefan Iavorskii of October 31, 1708 in *Pis`ma i bumagi imperatora Petra Velikogo* (St. Petersburg-Moscow, 1887-1977), vol. VIII, 261.

38 E.g., the inscription on the triumphal gates of 1696: "a [public] figure is worthy of his recompense." See N. G. Ustrialov, *Istoriia tsarstvovaniia*, vol. II, 300.

39 See E. Anisimov, *Vremia petrovskikh reform* (Leningrad, 1989), 55-60.

40 V. P. Grebeniuk, ed., *Panegiricheskaia literatura petrovskogo vremeni* (Moscow, 1979), 154-155.

41 In general, this was the perception of mythological images, insofar as mythological characters were identified with the unclean force. An incident is known concerning Peter I's clash with Mitrofan, bishop of Voronezh, who protested against the statues of ancient gods that decorated Peter's residence there. See I. I. Golikov, *Deianiia Petra Velikogo* (Moscow, 1837-1843), vol. XV, 41-44; V. M. Zhivov, B. A. Uspenskii, "Metamorfozy antichnogo iazychestva." Venerating the unclean force was naturally seen as a mark of the antichrist and dovetailed with the view of Peter as antichrist (or herald of the antichrist) that was widely current among various levels of society and which was provoked in part by Peter himself. See B. A. Uspenskii, "Historia sub specie semioticae."

42 V. P. Grebeniuk, ed., *Panegiricheskaia literatura*, 156.

43 Ibid., 142.

44 Ibid., 147-148. And what is more, Peter, like Roman emperors, acted like an epiphany of Jupiter:

>On approach, the first painting on the left depicted the taking of the city of Kantsy, which is also named Schlotburg [i.e, Nyenschantz], this year on May 2, 1703. Above it was drawn Jove, the head of all heavenly and earthly powers (for the Greeks), throwing fiery arrows at the city, signifying the leader of all Russian cavaliers, His Most Imperial Highness, who by his presence and guidance forced the above-described city to surrender. (We will add: *quid stabit a facis ejus*, that is, 'What can withstand his sight?')." (Ibid., 139.)

Significantly, Christian material is combined with pagan, which was typical for Western Baroque but unseen in Russia; above Peter in the guise of Jupiter a Biblical quote is inscribed (Psalm 75:8). In this context the appearance of a single syncretic Christian-pagan divinity, a thundering God, becomes understandable. For examples of the European tradition see A. Ebert, *Allgemeine Geschichte der Literatur des Mittelalters im Abendlande bis zum Beginne des XI. Jahrhunderts* (Leipzig, 1889), vol. I, 144f. This synthesizes Jupiter-the-Thunderer, mentioned many times in the given description (see V. P. Grebeniuk, ed., *Panegiricheskaia literatura*, 143, 145), and "the God of glory, who thunders upon many waters, who showed his most illustrious tsarist majesty the way to this naval victory over Swedish ships and the way to the Finnish Gulf" (Ibid., 145—quoting Psalm 28 [29]:3). On mixing Christian and pagan terminology, see V. M. Zhivov, B. A. Uspenskii, "Metamorfozy antichnogo iazychestva."

45   V. P. Grebeniuk, ed., *Panegiricheskaia literatura*, 175-176.

46   See if only E. V. Barsov, *Drevnerusskie pamiatniki sviashchennogo venchaniia tsarei na tsarstvo v sviazi s grecheskimi ikh originalami. S istoricheskim ocherkom chinov tsarskogo venchaniia v sviazi s razvitiem idei tsaria na Rusi* (Moscow, 1883), 115.

47   Iu. M. Lotman, B. A. Uspenskii, "Otzvuki kontseptsii 'Moskva—Tretii Rim' v ideologii Petra Pervogo (K probleme srednevekovoi traditsii kul`ture barokko)" in *Khudozhestvennyi iazyk srednevekov`ia* (Moscow, 1982), 236-249.

48   See the "Short Chronicler" by Patriarch Nicephoros in V. N. Beneshevich, *Drevne-slavianskaia kormchaia XIV titulov bez tolkovanii* (St. Petersburg, Sofia,1906-1987), vol. II, 219-224.

49   E. V. Barsov, *Drevnerusskie pamiatniki sviashchennogo venchaniia*, 111.

50   The dynastic legend concerning Riurik's descent from Prus, brother of Emperor Augustus, comes from the epistle of Spiridon-Savva and the "Tale of the Vladimir Princes." See R. P. Dmitrieva, *Skazanie o kniaz`iakh Vladimirskikh* (Moscow-Leningrad, 1955). It appears in the context of secular power's struggle for ascendancy and for the limitation of ecclesiastical authority (Ibid., 85-86). This ideological mission also served as one of the stimuli for the later spread and affirmation of this legend. The reasoning behind this is understandable: having descended from "Augustus, Roman tsar of the whole universe" (Ibid., 161, passim), it is as if the Russian monarch has inherited his prerogatives—to divide up the universe at his will, giving or denying the church part of his power and might. In this respect one could compare the Russian dynastic legend to that of the Tudors, who traced their family back to Brutus the Trojan, who was in turn related to Aeneas, founder of Rome; this Brutus founded New Troy, which later turned into London. See F. A. Yates, *Astraea. The Imperial Theme in the Sixteenth Century* (Harmondsworth: Peregrine Books, 1977), 50. This legend was spread under Henry VIII and Elizabeth in a similar ideological context, as part of an imperial mythology that supported the monarch's claims for authority in the religious sphere, and it is not impossible that during Ivan the Terrible's reign this English model may have had some significance for Russian political thought. In any case, the development of imperial ideology (and in particular the imperial aspect of the conception of Moscow as Third Rome) should not be isolated from the notion of a universal kingdom and its national transformations that were actualized in Europe after Charlemagne. See F. A. Yates, *Astraea*, 2f.

51   For a different view, see Iu. M. Lotman, B. A. Uspenskii, "Otzvuki kontseptsii," 237.

52   I. I. Golikov, *Sravnenie svoistv i del Konstantina Velikogo pervogo iz rimskikh khristianskogo imperatora so svoistvami i delami Petra Velikogo, pervogo vserossiiskogo imperatora i proisshestvii v tsarstvovanie oboikh sikh monarkhov* (Moscow, 1810).

53   *Polnoe sobranie russkikh letopisei* (St. Petersburg, Petrograd, Leningrad, Moscow, 1841-1989), vol. IX, xix.

54   G. V. Vilinbakhov notes that "the cult of Constantine's cross was very strong" at the court of Aleksei Mikhailovich. See G. V. Vilinbakhov, "Osnovanie Peterburga i imperskaia emblematika," *Uchenye zapiski Tartuskogo universiteta* 664 (1984), 51. In

particular, Aleksei Mikhailovich wanted to obtain that cross itself from Mt. Athos, and his desire was fulfilled. See Ibid.; *Pis`ma russkikh gosudarei i drugikh osob tsarskogo semeistva* (Moscow, 1861-1896), vol. V, 33. These facts should be put into the context of Aleksei Mikhailovich's various acts whose goal was to appropriate the symbolic attributes of a Byzantine basileus for himself, such as: sending for an orb and diadem from Constantinople, made "according to the model of the pious Greek Tsar Constantine" (E. V. Barsov, *Drevnerusskie pamiatniki sviashchennogo venchaniia*, 138); changes in the coronation ceremony, giving his eldest son the status of "Great Sovereign"; and so on (see B. A. Uspenskij, V. M. Zhivov, "Tsar and God," in this volume, 25; V. M. Zhivov, "Istoriia russkogo prava kak lingvosemioticheskaia problema" in *Semiotics and the History of Culture. In Honor of J. Lotman* (Columbus, OH, 1988), 104). In all these cases Aleksei Mikhailovich was trying to equate his empire with Byzantium, so the issue here concerns a different political and ideological situation from that in Peter's era.

55 N. G. Ustrialov, *Istoriia tsarstvovaniia*, vol. II, 300.

56 V. P. Grebeniuk, ed., *Panegiricheskaia literatura*, 164.

57 Feofilakt Lopatinskii, *Sluzhba blagodarstvennaia*, 22-22 verso.

58 G. V. Vilinbakhov, "Osnovanie Peterburga," 52.

59 Feofan Prokopovich, *Rozysk istoricheskii, koikh radi vin, i v iazykovom razume byli i naritsalis` imperatory rimstii, kak iazychestii, tak i khristianstii, pontifeksami ili arkhiereiami mnogobozhnogo zakona* (St. Petersburg, 1721), 27-28; see also references to Augustus in Ibid., 12; P. V. Verkhovskoi, *Uchrezhdenie Dukhovnoi Kollegii*, vol. II, 9, 15 (second pagination).

60 We find the same idea about the tsar's authority in the spiritual realm with reference to Constantine the Great in Feofan Prokopovich's funeral sermon for Peter:

> Behold, oh Russian Church, your David and Constantine. Synodic government was his creation, his concern for our written and oral edification. Oh, how his heart groaned seeing our ignorance of the ways to salvation! With what ardor did he fight against superstition, false pretension, and against insane schism, hostile and pernicious! How much did he desire and promote the art of persuasion among priests, to spread divine wisdom among the people and to establish the best order in everything. (Feofan Prokopovich, *Slovo na pogrebenie Vsepresvetleishego Derzhavneishego Petra Velikago, Imperatora i Samoderzhtsa Vserossiiskago* (St. Petersburg, 1725), 3.)

The "Spiritual Regulation" also comments on the collapse of single imperial rule after Constantine: "These are not fancied imaginings, so that it is only possible to conjecture about this; but in very deed has this appeared more than once in many states. Do only delve into the history of Constantinople after the period of Justinian, and much of that will appear. And even the pope was able, by means not different from those, not only to cut the Roman Empire in half and to appropriate for himself a great part of it, but more than once even to shake other states almost to final destruction. Let us not recall similar convulsions among ourselves in the past!" Translation is from A. V. Muller, trans., *The Spiritual Regulation of Peter the Great* (Seattle: University of Washington Press, 1972), 11. See also P. V. Verkhovskoi, *Uchrezhdenie Dukhovnoi Kollegii*, vol. II, 32 (first pagination); *Dukhovnyi Reglament*, 17.

The reference to Constantine the Great in the context of asserting single imperial rule, the subordination of the religious sphere to the monarch, and the corresponding church reform is natural and has typological analogies. Thus Elizabeth I of England could also be juxtaposed to Constantine the Great. We find such a reference, for example, in Foxe's preface to the first English edition of his "Book of Martyrs" where it speaks in part of the usurping power of the Roman pope. The book concludes with a depiction of Elizabeth contained in the initial "C" that symbolizes Emperor Constantine. As F. Yates notes, "the picture of Queen Elizabeth trampling on the Pope in the initial C is . . . the climax of the whole book. She represents the return to the Constantinian, imperial Christianity, free from papal shackles, the kind of religion which Foxe regards as alone pure" (F. A. Yates, *Astraea*, 44). It is hard to imagine that this precedent could have been known to Peter or his cohort, but it is obvious that a similar purpose led to the use of identical historiographical schemes.

[61] See Iu. M. Lotman, B. A. Uspenskii, "Otzvuki kontseptsii," 239-240.

[62] (*Translators note*: this and other notes marked as supplementary were added to the original ones for the 2002 republication of this article and respond to various discussions, criticism, and publications that came out after its first appearance in *Iz istorii russkoi kul`tury* (Moscow: Iazyki russkoi kul`tury, 1996), vol. 3, 528-583.) Richard Wortman, in his book *Scenarios of Power*, that is extremely important for the issues treated in the third section of the present article (the civil cult), comments apropos of my interpretation of Constantine the Great as a model for Peter: "I tend to agree with Lotman and Uspenskij that the Roman images, embodied in Julius and Augustus Caesar, are dominant . . . The figure of Constantine in Peter's reign rather seems to be an effort to turn Byzantium into a mirror image of Rome." See R. S. Wortman, *Scenarios of Power. Myth and Ceremony in Russian Monarchy* (Princeton, 1995), vol. 1, 43n2. To prove that one of these models was significantly more important than another is quite difficult, and hardly necessary. Both had their strong points which Peter himself and his apologists eagerly exploited. The figures of Julius and Augustus Caesar as pagan Roman emperors helped Petrine Russia assume the image of the Roman Empire, with Peter in the role of a conquering emperor, a monarch triumphant. Together with this the imperial Roman model united Russia with Europe insofar as, in appropriating this model, Russia stood in the same relationship as successor to ancient Rome as did other European powers; the cultural and political fiction of Roman legitimacy extended to Peter's power as tsar-transformer.

The model of Constantine the Great also referred to imperial Rome and in this sense could fulfill the same function as that of Julius and Augustus Caesar. Of course, in this function Constantine was not the dominating figure, as the Roman emperors had priority, with Constantine as only their Byzantine reflection. However, unlike Julius and Augustus, the model of Constantine was polyfunctional and ambivalent, and in this lay its unique value. For Peter's church policies references to pagan emperors were of no help, while Constantine embodied a Christian monarch's broad mandate to act in the ecclesiastical sphere. Peter's religious policies were intimately tied to his cultural ones, so that Constantine's model was in no way less significant than that of classical Rome for the Petrine cultural transformation. What is more, while the Petrine image of Constantine as emperor was not clearly juxtaposed to Constantine the saint, this reconceptualization was well suited (as a paradigmatic strategy) for Peter's clash with traditional cultural consciousness. Nevertheless, the reconceptualization of the traditional view of history that was taking place may in no way be reduced to "an attempt to turn Byzantium into a mirror reflection of Rome."

V. M. ZHIVOV

[63] V. P. Grebeniuk, ed., *Panegiricheskaia literatura*, 148-149.

[64] See for example the reaction of the Old Believers in V. Kel'siev, *Sbornik pravitel'stvennykh svedenii o raskol'nikakh* (London, 1860-1862), vypusk IV, 253.

[65] See B. A. Uspenskii, "Historia sub specie semioticae."

[66] See references to Augustus Caesar in Russian monuments as "possessing the entire universe," e.g., in E. V. Barsov, *Drevnerusskie pamiatniki sviashchennogo venchaniia*, 111.

[67] *Opisanie dokumentov i del, kraniashchikhsia v arkhive Sviateishego Pravitel'stvuiushchego Sinoda*, vol. I, prilozhenie, cccclviii-cccclix.

[68] A. Kantemir, *Sobranie stikhotvorenii* (Leningrad, 1956), 75.

[69] Indeed, in this picture of eighteenth-century Russian social development as drawn by nineteenth-century historians (which to a significant extent has lived on) there is no room for phenomena of the type we are discussing. Thus for example in speaking of the All-Jesting Council S. M. Solov'ev suggested that it is impossible to interpret it as "mockery of the patriarchate, a desire to belittle a holy order which [Peter] wanted to destroy." In his opinion this was simply "playing at kings, popes, and patriarchs— a game comprehensible given the condition of the young society of the time." See S. M. Solov'ev, *Istoriia Rossii*, vol. VIII, 523. Naturally, analogous phenomena from other "young societies" are not cited. And V. O. Kliuchevskii, in analyzing the origin of the All-Jesting Council, asks "what was the reason for this, the need for coarse diversion after manual labor or the lack of the habit of thinking through one's actions"? See V. O. Kliuchevskii, *Sochineniia* (Moscow, 1956-1959), vol. IV, 39. How profound historians' lack of understanding of this phenomenon could be is demonstrated by Ivan Nosovich's short article "The All-Jesting Council Established by Peter the Great," in which he suggests that the drunken gatherings were set up to camouflage secret military conferences. See I. Nosovich, "Vsep'ianeishii sobor, uchrezhdennyi Petrom Velikim," *Russkaia starina* II (December 1874): 734-739. No less characteristic is M. I. Semevskii's view which placed materials on the history of the All-Jesting Council under the rubric "Peter the Great as a Humorist"! See M. I. Semevskii, *Slovo i delo, 1700-1725* (St. Petersburg, 1885), 281-338.

[70] See the report by Gordon in P. Gordon, *Dnevnik* (Moscow, 1892), part II, 360; see also M. M. Bogoslovskii, *Petr I*, vol. I, 131, 136-137; R. Wittram, *Peter I, Czar und Kaiser: Zur Geschichte Peters des Grossen in seiner Zeit* (Göttingen, 1964), vol. I, 106f.

[71] The first jesters' wedding we know about took place in 1695. Zheliabuzhskii reports:

> On the ... of January the jester Iakov, son of Fedor Turgenev, was married to a chancellery clerk's wife, and following him in the procession there were boyars and *okol'nichie*, and officials of the Duma, and courtiers of various ranks, and they rode on bulls, on goats, on swine, on dogs; they wore mock garments, bast sacks, bast hats, caftans of coarse fabric, decorated with squirrels' tales, straw boots, mouse gloves, bast caps. Turgenev rode in the sovereign's own best velvet-lined carriage and was followed by the Trubetskiis, the Sheremetevs, the Golitsyns, the Gagins, in velvet caftans ... And the wedding of Iakov was celebrated in tents in the field across from Preobrazhenskoe and Semenovskoe, and the great banquet lasted for three days. (*Zapiski Zheliabuzhskogo s 1682 po 2 Iiulia 1709* (St. Petersburg, 1840), 39-40.)

[72] RGADA, f. 9, o. I, d. 67. Also see the incomplete and imprecise publication of these texts by M. I. Semevskii in M. I. Semevskii, *Slovo i delo*. One may judge the nature of

Peter's editing from the following section of the rules for selecting a prince-pope (the material in corner brackets was crossed out and italics indicates the changes made in Peter's own hand):

> *After that* the prince-caesar orders that <eggs> *nuts* [i.e., testicles] be brought for the election and the servitors distribute two to each of the fathers, one natural and the other jacketed, and [that] they sit in their cloaks and secretly hold the <eggs> *balls. Then* the prince-caesar inspects the covered chalice and gives it his seal, and orders that his first name be announced, bringing the chalice to each <father> *of the fathers,* who has to place [one of] the <eggs> *balls* [into it], the natural one if he votes for the candidate and the jacketed one if he is against the candidate . . . " (RGADA, f. 9, o. I, d. 67, ll. 32-32 verso.)

73   N. G. Ustrialov, *Istoriia tsarstvovaniia Petra Velikogo,* vol. VI, 504, 245.
74   Berkhgol`ts reports:

> The emperor's command was so strict that not one of the ladies dared to stay at home. Several wanted to excuse themselves on account of illness, and in fact were sick, both today and last Sunday, but this was of no use, they had to show up. Moreover the worst thing was that they were told beforehand that they were being brought only to make them drink because of their absence the previous Sunday. They knew very well that the wines would be bad and what was still worse, if you please, [that it would be served] with an admixture of vodka, that is the local custom, not to mention the large portions of pure simple vodka that they would unconditionally be forced to drink. The good marshal's wife Olsuf`eva, a German by birth, a very sweet and humble woman, took this so to heart that this morning she gave premature birth. When on the eve she had been told of the emperor's order she immediately went to court and very humbly asked the empress to free her from the duty of going to the Senate; but her highness answered that it did not depend on her, that it was the sovereign's will, from which he would never back down . . . The poor marshal's wife suffered such torments all night that she gave birth to a dead child the next morning, which, they say, she sent to court [preserved] in spirits. (*Dnevnik kamer-iunkera F. V. Berkhgol`tsa. 1721-1725* (Moscow, 1902-1903), part I, 147-148.)

Clearly, the forcible participation in court debauches was an unusual form of terror that was specially directed at the highest level of society. Given this situation it was not surprising that the Danish envoy Just Juel refused to go to Russia a second time "because he knew from long experience what unpleasantness awaited him from drunkenness." See *Zapiski Iusta Iulia, datskogo poslannika pri Petre Velikom* (Moscow, 1900), 11.

75   See the chancellery official A. Protas`ev's petition of 1722 in M. I. Semevskii, *Slovo i delo,* 335-336.
76   See RGADA, f. 156, d. 129.
77   Of course, this division is not completely unambiguous, and at least one person occupies an intermediate position in this classification. I have in mind the all-jesting patriarch (or prince-pope) Nikita Zotov. Zotov was Peter's first teacher, who taught him grammar, the Breviary and Psalter, and then served as his clerk (*dumnyi d`iak*), and later as head of the tsar's personal (i.e., campaign) chancellery. His teaching as

a mock patriarch echoed his former duties as the tsar's instructor and apparently was a kind of payback for his former position. Zotov's ambivalent status is clearly evident in the episode of awarding him the title of count. This was given him on July 8, 1710, "upon receiving news of the taking of the city of Riga." See *Pis`ma i bumagi imperatora Petra Velikogo*, vol. X, 221. In the patent signed in Peter's hand it said: "At the request of, and for service [rendered], the prefix count is given to sir Mikita Moiseevich Zotov, also the rank of personal councilor and the general-president of the personal chancellery." See Ibid. This "prefix" (*nadanie*) of count evidently was parodic and did not transfer to Zotov's sons. However, Zotov's descendants managed to have the title returned to the family by order of Alexander I in 1802. See Count Mac Donnel, trans. and ed., *Diary of an Austrian Secretary*, vol. I, 199. The ambivalence of the title corresponds to the ambivalence of Zotov's activities as both a kind of jester as well as a kind of high-placed administrator.

The determination of membership in the All-Jesting Council, its social composition and changes that occurred in it, should be the goal of an especially detailed study. In the documents that have come down to us from this establishment, its participants mostly have made-up names, although other sources may allow them to be identified. Thus for example at the end of a letter from Peter to Menshikov on February 3, 1703, from Oranienburg, are the signatures: "Ianikii, metropolitan of Kiev and Gaditska Gadich, Gedeon archdeacon, Pitirim protodeacon," and others. See *Pis`ma i bumagi imperatora Petra Velikogo*, vol. II, 126-128. The first title is a parody of the official title of the Kievan metropolitan, "*mitropolit kievskii, i galitskii i vseia Malyia Rossii*" (1686-1722); "*gaditskii*" (instead of "*galitskii*," of Galicia) is a play on words, based on the root *gad* (disgusting). The latter two signatures belong to Prince Iu. F. Shakhovskoi and Peter himself, and the first, judging from Peter's cohort, masks the boyar I. A. Musin-Pushkin. See N. G. Ustrialov, *Istoriia tsarstvovaniia Petra Velikogo*, vol. IV, 223. In the "Notes Concerning the Mock Wedding of the Prince Pope" (RGADA, f. 156, № 129) there is a "Register of Lines" (Ibid., l. 22), that is, the order of sleighs in which the wedding procession was to proceed. In this list we read (corner brackets indicate crossing out, italics—additions): "metropolitan <Buturlin> *from here* // <Tikhon Nikitich> *metropolitan of Novgorod*." From this we learn that the "metropolitan of Novgorod" was T. N. Speshnev, and the one from Petersburg was the boyar Petr Ivanovich Buturlin. A large portion of the sources on the history of the All-Jesting Council remains unstudied.

78 Johann Georg Korb, *Dnevnik puteshestviia v Moskoviiu*, 11—my italics. Under January 13, 1699, Korb reports:

A sumptuous comedy celebrates the time of Our Lord's Nativity. The chief Muscovites, at the Czar's choice, shine in various sham ecclesiastical dignities. One represents the Patriarch, others Metropolites, Archimandrites, Popes, Deacons, Sub-Deacons, etc. Each, according to whichever denomination of these the Czar has given him, has to put on the vestments that belong to it. The scenic Patriarch, with his sham metropolites and the rest in eighty sledges, and to the number of two hundred, makes the round of the city of Moscow and the German Slowoda, ensigned with crolier, miter, and the other insignia of his assumed dignity. (Ibid., 111; translation is from Count Mac Donnel, trans. and ed., *Diary of an Austrian Secretary*, 222-223).

The most precise (although possibly biased) testimony concerning the gradual and forcible recruitment of the social elite into the All-Jesting Council is that of Strahlenberg. Recounting the beginning of the parodic "glorification," he writes:

> Soon after this activity received further development, as the tsar forced some senators and other high-placed servitors to ride with him. Insofar as they imagined that this was an innocent venture, they willingly invited the tsar and his suite into their houses to entertain them ... This entertainment, if it consisted as it did at the start only of drunkenness and other bawdiness, was still tolerable; however, insofar as all kinds of invective and gossip spread about these processions and the tsar's unusual behavior, the tsar intentionally set out to involve important and well-known people, and with this aim invited all of the courtiers and military ranks to take part, so that they formed a gathering of more than three hundred people. From this moment it became too important and aristocratic to have a simple clergyman or priest at its head (the which function Zotov fulfilled); it had to take on a more lofty character, and the entire suite be given a more imposing name. (Ph. J. von Strahlenberg, *Das Nord- und Ostliche Theil von Europa und Asia*, 231-232).

Insofar as participation in parodic ceremonies turned out to be a necessary mark of loyalty, foreigners living in Russia were also forced to create for themselves a kind of analogue of the All-Jesting Council. This was what became the so-called Bengo-collegium or the Great Britain Monastery. About this, S. F. Platonov wrote:

> The Bengo-collegium creates the impression of something base and obtuse, incompatible with the honorable names of the Keldermans, Farquarson, Gwynn, Pause. They would only have occupied themselves with such stupidity as was described in the five points of its "code" and in the three points of its "publication," and go to Yuletide celebrations with scallions and flags with English emblems in their hats, only ex officio, because they were forced to do so. They were forced by the sum of conditions that Peter had created, in his manner mixing business with nonsense; it was impossible to work with the government without taking part in official masquerades, drinking parties, compulsory assemblies [*assamblei*], and in collective sailing trips on the Neva. It was evidently thus also necessary for foreigners to have their "all-jesting" organization, just as Russian government circles did, in the image of the prince-pope and his suite that Peter dragged around with him all over the state. (S. F. Platonov, "Iz bytovoi istorii Petrovskoi epokhi. 1. Bengo-kollegiia ili Velikobritanskii monastyr` v S. Peterburge pri Petre Velikom," *Izvestiia AN SSSR* 7-8 (1926): 544).

[79] This is one of the myths of Peter's rule, connected with the idea of personal merit as the basis for power, that is, the propaganda of meritocracy—"he rewarded not breeding but merit, in whomever he found it." See I. I. Golikov, *Deianiia Petra Velikogo*, part I, 12.

[80] See R. O. Crummey, "Peter and the Boiar Aristocracy, 1689-1700," *Canadian-American Slavic Studies* 2 (Summer 1974): 274-287; Idem., "The Origins of the Noble Official. The Boyar Elite, 1613-1689" in W. M. Pintner, D. K. Rowney, eds., *Russian Officialdom. The Bureaucratization of Russian Society from the Seventeenth to the Twentieth Century* (Chapel Hill, 1980), 75.

[81] I. I. Golikov, *Deianiia Petra Velikogo*, part I, 13.

82   Here is a typical example of this kind of writing:

> To Mr. Colonel his grace P[etr]. A[lekseevich]. We make it known to your grace that we are helping Mr. Siniavin to ship supplies in accordance with your letters; I do so with hearty diligence; how much stuff and in how many carts were delivered during his stay and with him he will report himself. The bodies of their graces Shchepotev and Dubasov, invincible warriors of blessed memory, who are worthy of all honors (and who were indeed saintly) were buried with proper honors on October 21, and Mr. Vice-Admiral was also present. I write briefly so as to set your conscience at rest, and will report all the details as an eyewitness [when we meet]. I request your appropriate obedience. Leaving aside the sorrowful, please order that the town of Vyborg be sufficiently censed with military censers [i.e., cannons] so that its citizens will keep your presence there continually in mind. Simultaneously with this letter I am sending letters with Ulian Siniavin that have been sent to Fedor Matveevich Apraksin from Moscow from the Admiralty chancellery; among them there are letters to you and to others. Awaiting your return in good health and with victory, with divine help, we give you our peace and blessing. Humble Anikit [writing] with power-wielding hand. From Saint-Petersburg, October 22, year [1]706. (RGADA, f. 9, o. II, d. 5, l. 127. Also see a letter with similar practical content on ll. 136-137.)

83   *Pis`ma i bumagi imperatora Petra Velikogo*, vol. I, 29-30, 31-32, 34, 43, 46, 52, 227, 264; vol. II, 62; vol. IV, 305; vol. VIII, 108, 123, passim.

84   N. G. Ustrialov, *Istoriia tsarstvovaniia Petra Velikogo*, vol. VI, 511, 253.

85   All of the information derived from the affair of Tsarevich Aleksei and the other people who were investigated in the case raises certain doubts, because the testimony of the accused and of the witnesses was obtained through torture or as the result of threats. Yet this data is too important and unique for historians to ignore. In any case, it indicates that various social classes widely expected Peter's death to liberate them from the burdens of his rule. The social and cultural parameters of this expectation deserve special investigation, which, it seems, would be extremely valuable for understanding the reception of the Petrine reforms. It is obvious in any case that not only the clergy and lower levels of society awaited Peter's death with impatience, but also the elite, including many people close to the tsar. This is suggested by the stories Tsarevich Aleksei told to Count Schoenborn, by his testimony during the investigation, and from a series of other statements that were made. See Ibid., vol. VI, 68f, 371-372, 453, 509-511. Among the innovations expected to end with Peter's death were his "destruction of the old, good ways" and his "introduction of everything bad" (Ibid., 73), including, of course, blasphemous rituals.

86   I. I. Golikov, *Deianiia Petra Velikogo*, vol. VI, 289-290.

87   See its description in *Dnevnik kamer-iunkera F. V. Berkhgol`tsa*, part I, 120-121.

88   See the description of these ceremonies in Berkhgol`ts' diary:

> Having walked around the square for about two hours, amid thousands of people who had come, and having had a good look at one another, all of the masks, in the same order, headed for the buildings of the Senate and the Collegiums where the prince-pope was to treat them to a wedding dinner on numerous tables that had been prepared. The newlywed and his young bride of about 60 years sat at

a table under beautiful baldachins, he with the tsar and mssrs. Cardinals, and she with the ladies. Above the prince-pope's head hung a silver Bacchus, seated astride a barrel of vodka, which he directed into his glass and drank . . . After dinner they danced at first; then the tsar and tsaritsa, accompanied by numerous masks, led the young ones off to their nuptial bed. The groom in particular was unimaginably drunk. The nuptial rook was located in . . . a large and wide wooden pyramid that stood in front of the Senate house. The inside was intentionally lit with candles, and the bridal bed was strewn with hops and surrounded by barrels filled with wine, beer, and vodka. The newlyweds, in the tsar's presence, had to drink vodka once again, in bed, out of vessels in the shape of *partium genitalium* [gentalia] . . . that were, by the way, quite large. Then they were left alone; but there were holes in the pyramid through which one could see what the young people were doing in their intoxication. In the evening all the houses in the city were lit up, and the tsar ordered that this continue throughout the entire masquerade. (Ibid., 120).

[89] See Ibid., part III, 142-147; S. F. Platonov, "Iz bytovoi istorii Petrovskoi epokhi"; M. P. Alekseev, "Russko-angliiskie literaturnye sviazi (XVIII veka—pervaia polovina XIX veka)," *Literaturnoe nasledstvo* 91 (1982): 74-77.

[90] A contemporary description of this masquerade survives that in its external aspect (its writing, language, etc.) parodies church books. See RGADA, f. 156, o. 1, d. 186; published in *Dnevnik kamer-iunkera F. V. Berkhgol`tsa*, part III, 188f; many details of the text are not reproduced. See also the members of the All-Jesting Council listed here under no. 52:

> Bishops: Ianikandr dick, Metropolitan of Saint-Petersburg, Morai-dick, Metropolitan of Kronshlot and Kotlin, Tarai-dick, Metropolitan of Great New Dick and of Great Testicles [instead of Great Novgorod and Velikie Luki], Iakov, nimble dick, Metropolitan of Derbent and Midia, Gnil` [rotten] dick, Metropolitan of Siberia and Tobolsk; Bibabr, Metropolitan of the Okhta River and Seven Mills [River]; Mother-fucker, Metropolitan of Pskov and Izborsk; Feofan, red dick, Metropolitan of Smolensk and Dorgobuzh; Archdeacon Go-To-Dick Stroev; Sacristan Formosov-dick, Protas`ev.

[91] See Just Juel's description of the celebration in *Zapiski Iusta Iulia*, 118-119.

[92] On the symbolism of "wild" peoples in Russian panegyric texts, see V. M. Zhivov, "The State Myth in the Era of Enlightenment and its Destruction in Late Eighteenth-Century Russia," in this volume, 249-258.

[93] *Dnevnik kamer-iunkera F. V. Berkhgol`tsa*, part I, 110.

[94] *Supplementary note*: In the most recent monograph on Peter the Great by Lindsay Hughes, we again find the interpretation of the All-Jesting Council as an entertainment for the tsar, and at the same time Hughes asserts that this kind of entertainment was typical for European culture of the time. She writes:

> The Drunken Assembly was not an isolated phenomenon, either in the Russian or in an international context. There were elements reminiscent of the common culture of Saturnalia, the Feast of Fools, Lords of Misrule, and mystery plays (Russia had its own version, the Furnace play [*peshchnoe deistvie*]). There were

also links with Yuletide mummer customs. As Kurakin wrote, 'There is an old custom among the Russian people before Christmas and after to play at *sviatki,* that is friends gather together at someone's house in the evening and dress up in masquerade costume and the servants of distinguished people act out all sorts of funny stories. According to this custom His Majesty the tsar in his court also played at *sviatki* with his courtiers.' All over Europe at carnival time laymen and women donned the habits of priests, monks, and nuns, even impersonating the pope in *parodia sacra.* There were cross-dressing and erotic undertones. Within Russia, too, far from existing in isolation, the Drunken Assembly coexisted and overlapped with other cases of elaborate parody. To describe it as an 'influential social institution' is to misunderstand its essence, which was rooted in personal relationships and private jokes, and seemed more often than not to satisfy a need for letting off steam in male cameraderie rather than teaching the Russian people a lesson about the evils of overpowerful organized religion. Weber favoured a similar explanation: 'the Czar among all the heavy Cares of Government knows how to set apart some Days for the Relaxation of his Mind, and how ingenious he is in the Contrivance of those Diversions.' (L. Hughes, *Russia in the Age of Peter the Great* (New Haven and London: Yale University Press, 1998), 256-257.)

In my opinion this interpretation shows a profound lack of understanding of the role of cultural politics in the workings of the Petrine reforms. This lack of understanding is fully explainable on the part of foreigners contemporary to Peter, for example, of Weber, whom Hughes cites (Weber was an admirer of the tsar-reformer and was thus eager to explain the "peculiarities" of the tsar's court in categories that were comprehensible to a Western European reader). But it seems strange on the part of a researcher today who is trying to reconstruct a picture of Petrine Russia. Elements of carnival were clearly present in Peter's doings, and by the way not only Western European ones, but also properly Russian equivalents from Yule and Shrovetide games (although the furnace play that Hughes mentions is not relevant here). Furthermore, in the beginning the activity of the All-Jesting Council was timed to coincide with traditional carnival time, so that this is not a case of typological similarity but of a direct genetic link. This alone is not surprising. Although Peter took material for his blasphemous performances from diverse sources, it would have been strange if had not used what was close at hand. However, neither origin nor typological likeness says anything about the function of the corresponding elements (what use was made of them), and it is precisely this lack of differentiation between origin and function that indicates the author's lack of methodological perspective that leads to incorrect conclusions.

Indeed, as Hughes writes in another place, "Peter's masquerades were not true carnival at all, in the sense that 'people are liberated from authority, behavior is unfettered and hierarchy is suspended'" (Ibid., 266). For some reason Hughes takes the definition of carnival's functions from Stephen Baehr's book (S. L. Baehr, *The Paradise Myth in Eighteenth-Century Russia. Utopian Patterns in Early Secular Russian Literature and Culture* [Stanford: Stanford University Press, 1991], 59), which though very useful is not directly relevant to the matter at hand, and relies on M. M. Bakhtin's well-known (and pertinent) understanding of carnival. If, however, elements of carnival do not fulfill carnival functions, the question arises what function they *do* fulfill. The answer that Hughes provides is strikingly naïve, insofar as it appeals to psychology ("male camaraderie") as a timeless constant; we have no evidence of the first Russian emperor's inclination to familiar relations with his companions in arms, and we have no reason to think that monarchial "friendship" in the eighteenth century was of this type. The answer Hughes provides is also unconvincing in that it does not explain the known facts. "Private jokes" and letting off of male steam, of course, may have taken place in the private sphere, but this has no relation to the public ceremonies that attracted crowds of people (for example, to the mock weddings of the prince-popes or to masquerade processions). Like all of Peters' other innovations in the public sphere, his blasphemous actions had direct didactic significance and in this sense were "influential social institutions."

In the case of the blasphemous ceremonies the traditional attitude toward the church and religious authority was an obvious target. There is nothing fundamentally new in this conclusion. Both V. Kliuchevskii and R. Wittram (see R. Wittram, *Peter I, Czar und Kaiser*, vol. I, 106-11) as well as other historians held this view. Stephen Baehr also writes about this, speaking of the special functions of carnival in Petrine culture: "Peter throughout his reign combined festival, carnival, and theater to propagandize his projects and programs. Even his carnivalistic crowning of an 'All Fools' Pope' and creation of the 'Most Drunken Synod of Fools and Jesters' were revelry with a cause, condemning the excesses and immorality of the church and thus implying the need to place it under the control of the secular state" (S. L. Baehr, *The Paradise Myth*, 218). There is no reason to reject this view (apart from the desire to primitivize history, to make it more comprehensible for an inexperienced reader and make all explanations seem "natural" for contemporaries), although it is necessary to define more precisely what Peter's "projects and programs" were that inspired his blasphemy. I suggest that the issue does not concern the "excesses and immorality" of the church but the place of the church hierarchy in the reformed system of the Petrine state. This is precisely the project that is examined in this article.

95 R. Wittram, *Peter I, Czar und Kaiser*, vol. I, 109.
96 I. I. Golikov, *Deianiia Petra Velikogo*, vol. VI, 278.
97 Ibid., 279.
98 Ibid.
99 See Ibid., 278-279.
100 *Pis'ma i bumagi imperatora Petra Velikogo*, vol. I, 34, 52, 56, 58, 237, 521; vol. IV, 172, 286 passim.
101 Ibid., vol. I, 46, 54 passim.
102 RGADA, f. 9, o. 1, d. 67, l. 14.
103 A passage connected to this subject was inserted into one of the variants of the rules for election; I cite it from the draft written in Peter's hand:

> After that the prince-caesar orders the servitors of the p. p. [prince-pope] to inspect the chosen ones, and they, according to his order, examine whether they have everything in working order ["perfect nature"]. This is done in the following manner: the chosen one (or ones) sits on a chair with a notch cut into it and covered by a vestment. Then one who is entrusted by the prince-caesar stretches his hand under the cover and feels around; and if he finds it worthy he

cries out loudly: *habet, habet*; and if not, then *non habet*. (RGADA, f. 9, o. 1, d. 67, l. 30 verso.)

The Latin exclamation indicates the parodying of a western model in particular. In his book Strahlenberg reports that the Catholic model replaced the Orthodox one after the Astrakhan uprising of 1704:

> This glorifying continued right until the death of the emperor. However, since in Astrakhan the insurgents named among the other reasons for their rebellion that the emperor, deriding the church, had created a mock patriarch and mock bishops, these titles were changed, so that as a result Zotov received the title prince-pope, and his twelve bishops—the name of cardinals; this, to the detriment of the Russian state, created great dissatisfaction at Roman Catholic courts, and from electors at the Viennese and other German courts, [who disapproved of] the unauthorized use of the title prince-caesar. (Ph. J. von Strahlenberg, *Das Nord- und Ostliche Theil von Europa und Asia*, 234.)

As far as I know, there are no direct sources that indicate the use of the title "prince-pope" before 1704 (here further research is necessary), although this change hardly occurred as a response to the demands of the Astrakhan rebels, insofar as their uprising was cruelly suppressed and their demands rejected. In any case there is definite evidence that the Orthodox model (in particular, the titles of patriarch and metropolitan) was used over the entire existence of the All-Jesting Council, including the period after 1704.

In contrast, I. I. Golikov notes that in 1714 or 1715, Peter, having decided to deal with the patriarchate once and for all, "to this end transformed the Prince-Pope into the patriarch." See I. I. Golikov, *Deianiia Petra Velikogo*, vol. VI, 279. But in this case as well the writer does not perceive the significance of combining a parodic patriarchate and parodic papacy, and tries to separate them chronologically. Here again there is no factual basis for such a separation. On the juxtaposition of Orthodox and Catholic models, see also L. Hughes, *Russia in the Age of Peter the Great*, 255-256.

104 Here is the list of formulas of elevation, written in Peter's hand (corner brackets indicate things that Peter crossed out):

> 0 dear to Bacchus, elected candidates so-and-so are presented for installation as fathers of such-and-such cities
> 2 the strength of Bacchus be with you
> 1 what have you come for and what do you ask of us
> +1 drink myself to death in the taverns dear to Bacchus of such-and-such cities
> 3 and how do you drink
> 4 and present it in more detail <how>
> 5 the strength of Bacchus be with you, darkening [your mind] and making you tremble and making you mad all the days of your life (RGADA, f. 9, o. I, d. 67, l. 42).

Other of Peter's drafts offer significant variations. Thus in one we read:

> 1 for what reason have you come and what do you wish from our lack of moderation;
> answer: to be a son and collaborator in your lack of moderation

2 the gluttony of the most drunken Bacchus be with you

3 tell us in more detail how you drink

4 <the grace of> Bacchus' gluttony be with you darkening [your mind] and making you tremble and making you mad all the days of your life (Ibid., l. 35).

In another draft the answer to the question "for what reason have you come?" is given as:

+ (if a pope is installed then he says) to be the ultimate priest <of father> and first son of our father Bacchus (Ibid.).

For comparison, here are the corresponding places from the order of elevation of a bishop from the time of Patriarch Adrian:

The elected and confirmed candidate, dear to God, is presented to be installed as the bishop or archbishop or metropolitan of such-and-such cities, preserved by God . . . And the patriarch or another bishop who is to install him says:

For what reason have you come and what do you request from our moderation?

And the elected replies saying:

The consecration (khirotoniia) of the episcopal grace for the most holy metropolitanate or bishopric of so-and-so.

And the patriarch asks saying:

And how do you believe . . .

After delivering this speech the patriarch says while blessing him in the manner of the cross, the grace of God the Father and of Our Lord Jesus Christ and of the Holy Spirit be with you . . .

And the patriarch says to him:

Declare to us in more detail how you believe (GIM, Sin. 344, ll. 18 verso-20).

Labeling the elevated prince-pope "the ultimate priest" (krainii zhrets) deserves special attention; it has no direct parallel in the order of chirotony but is apparently connected to designating the patriarch as "ultimate saintly cleric" (krainii sviatitel`), a notion which Peter abhorred. It also relates to the proclamation of the tsar as "the ultimate judge" in the oath taken by members of the Synod (see above), whose text was formulated with Peter's input several years after these parodic documents.

[105] S. A. Belokurov, *Materialy dlia russkoi istorii* (Moscow, 1888), 539.

[106] R. Wittram, *Peter I, Czar und Kaiser*, vol. I, 110.

[107] *Sluzhebnik* (Moscow, 1656), 21, 22, 34, 40.

[108] See B. A. Uspenskij, V. M. Zhivov, "Tsar and God," in this volume, 94 n.204.

[109] N. Moleva, E. Beliutin, *Zhivopisnykh del mastera. Kantseliariia ot stroenii i russkaia zhivopis` pervoi poloviny XVIII veka* (Moscow, 1965), 12.

[110] *Polnoe sobranie zakonov*, vol. VI, no. 3893. 22. In this context Weber's report on the death of F. Iu. Romodanovskii, prefaced by the news of Tsarevich Aleksei's return to Russia, is curious:

Information has come from Novgorod that the tsarevich and Privy Councilor Tolstoi arrived there from Naples in order to continue on immediately to Moscow, and from the latter city it is reported that after the death there of the vice-tsar Romodanovskii His Tsarist Majesty preserved this high office for his single remaining son; he did not want the name of the ancient noble lineage to disappear, so that both sisters of the current vice-tsar, who has no heir and is the last offspring of his clan, have had to marry two grandees on condition that both of these men abandon the names they were born with and accept the Romodanovskii name. (F. C. Weber, *Das Veranderte Rußland, In welchem die ietzige Verfassung des Geist- und Weltlichen Regiments; Der Kriegs-Staat zu Lande und zu Wasser; Wahre Zustand der Rußischen Finantzen* (Frankfurt, 1721), 235-236.)

This concern with preserving the name and lineage of the prince-caesar (a title which Weber, who cannot imagine this sort of parodic game, takes for that of a high office) stands in sinister contrast to the reprisal that was just beginning to play out against Peter's own son and heir.

[111] See the ascent up the service ladder as reflected in Peter's correspondence in *Pis'ma i bumagi imperatora Petra Velikogo*, vol. I, 521, 533, 555, 559, 582; vol. II, 465; vol. IV, 1124 passim.

[112] *Rasskazy Nartova o Petre Velikom* (St. Petersburg, 1891), 58-59.

[113] The episode with the Order of Judas also emphasized Peter's sacral omnipotence with the help of models of anti-behavior. See S. F. Platonov, "Orden Iudy 1709 goda," *Letopis' zaniatii postoiannoi istoriko-arkheograficheskoi komissii za 1926 g.* I (1927): 193-198. Right after the Battle of Poltava a medal on a long silver chain was ordered that would have an image of the hanged Judas with thirty pieces of silver scattered below him. Prince Iu. F. Shakhovskoi, one of the active members of the All-Jesting Council who figured in it as the "Archdeacon Gedeon," wore this medal. He had asserted earlier that he understood Judas' behavior, but that in his place he would have asked Christ for a larger payment. See *Pis'ma i bumagi imperatora Petra Velikogo*, vol. VIII, 2, 472. S. F. Platonov suggests

> that the Order of Judas had another purpose, more serious than adorning a jester . . . We think that another more tangible betrayal was intended, most likely that of Mazepa. Peter hoped to catch Mazepa during his flight to Turkey . . . Mazepa's death on August 22, 1709, put a final end to this hope. If the Order of Judas had been prepared as a mockery of Mazepa's treason, with the hetman's death it no longer made sense, and Shakhovskoi the moocher could have been given it as a supplement to the goblet he had been rewarded with, as a person who did not disdain any pittance. (S. F. Platonov, "Orden Iudy," 197.)

Platonov seems to rationalize the behavior of those involved in this escapade a bit too much, and it remains completely unclear what use this order might have been even as retaliation against Mazepa if he were caught, and why it was appropriate for Shakhovskoi, about whom there is no factual basis at all to accuse of pathological greed. It is obvious, however, that the simultaneous preparation of the medal and Mazepa's betrayal were not simply a coincidence. As noted earlier, Mazepa was declared anathema for his treason to the state, as a second Judas, which thus gave it a religious dimension, likening Peter to Christ. While we can't reject Platonov's explanation out of hand, it seems more probable that here an ecclesiastical and governmental act, as in so many other cases, acquired a blasphemous parodic twin. Shakhovskoi with his Order of Judas was a constant reminder of Mazepa's betrayal as an immeasurable crime against God and that drew attention to Peter as "Sovereign Christ," a sacred ruler whose betrayal would inevitably end in shameful death.

Supplementary note: Recently E. Zitser has offered a new—and in our opinion fully convincing—interpretation of the Order of Judas and its presentation to Iu. Shakhovskoi. It suggests that the order was first prepared for the public execution of Mazepa, but later, insofar as Mazepa died and it wasn't needed, it was given to Shakhovskoi with quite different symbolic functions. See E. Zitser, "The Cavalier of the Order of Judas: Chivalry and Parody at the Court of Peter the Great" (Paper presented at the Early Slavists Seminar, Harvard University, February 8, 2002). This new interpretation does not fundamentally change anything in my argument.

Translator's note: Material from this work was subsequently included in chapter 3 (pp. 79-107) of E. Zitser, *The Transfigured Kingdom. Sacred Parody and Charismatic Authority at the Court of Peter the Great* (Ithaca and London: Cornell University Press, 2004).

[114] Berkhgol'ts describes the funeral of a dwarf in his diary under February 1, 1724. The funeral procession went along the streets of Petersburg:

> In front of everyone went thirty choristers, in pairs, all little boys. Behind them followed a tiny priest, in all of his vestments, who had been purposefully chosen out of all the local priests for his small stature. Then came a small sleigh of a completely special kind on which the body was laid out . . . Immediately behind them came a small dwarf, the emperor's favorite, in the office of marshal, with a big marshal's staff . . . He wore (as did all of his comrades) a long black mantle; he stood at the head of other dwarfs who followed in pairs, with the shorter ones at the front and the taller ones behind, and among them were no few ugly faces and big heads. Then came another, similarly small marshal at the head of the female dwarfs . . . On both sides of the procession moved huge guards soldiers with torches, at least fifty of them, and aside both of the women in mourning went four huge court legionnaires (*gaidiuki*) in black uniforms, and also carrying torches. One would hardly expect to see such a strange procession in Russia or anywhere else . . . The emperor together with Prince Menshikov came behind the procession on foot (but not in mourning clothes), from his own home to the avenue. When they put the dwarf there into the sleigh, they say that he [Peter] threw many of them [dwarfs] with his own hands. The dead dwarf was the same one for whom a great and famous wedding had been organized in 1710 for forty pairs of dwarfs who had been gathered from all over the state at the emperor's command. (*Dnevnik kamer-iunkera F. V. Berkhgol'tsa*, part IV, 13-14.)

For other descriptions of the wedding, see: F. C. Weber, *Das Veranderte Rußland*, 385-388; *Zapiski Iusta Iulia*, 261-264; and Peter's letter to Romodanovskii in *Pis'ma i bumagi imperatora Petra Velikogo*, vol. X, 271-272. Weber also describes another funeral for a dwarf which was also quite elaborate—F. C. Weber, *Das Veranderte Rußland*, 59.

Note that Peter acted not as a participant but as an observer of the procession, which definitely gave the entire spectacle a parodic and ludic cast.

It is worth mentioning that the tsar's interest in monstrosities also had a playful and blasphemous element. On February 13, 1718, he issued an ukase according to which his subjects had to send to Petersburg all kinds of natural curiosities; moreover, for a living human monstrosity was paid 100 rubles, for cattle or animal ones, 15 rubles, and for birds 7 rubles. See *Polnoe sobranbie zakonov*, vol. V, no. 3159. These were put in the Kunstkamera, which, like an anatomical theater, clearly not only served the progress of natural science but also the education of society. The Kunstkamera could also feature living monstrosities. See Berkhgol`ts's report: "There among other things was a living person without sexual organs, who had instead a kind of mushroom-shaped growth . . . This person, they say, is from Siberia, and his parents are well-to do simple folk. He would happily have given a hundred rubles and more to get his freedom and return home, from where his relatives had had to send him because of the tsar's order . . . The governors had been ordered to carry it out under threat of harsh punishment." See *Dnevnik kamer-iunkera F. V. Berkhgol`tsa*, part I, 106-107. Peter also had human monstrosities who died stuffed and mounted, thus denying them Christian burial. Clearly, in this case the tsar acted as the lord of nature, extending his activities into a sphere that has traditionally been considered beyond the pale of arbitrary human intrusion.

[115] Ibid., part III, 125.

[116] See Johann Georg Korb, *Dnevnik puteshestviia v Moskoviiu*, 187; the tsar himself took direct part in the executions and, at his insistence, so did many members of his court, including Zotov.

[117] *Dnevnik kamer-iunkera F. V. Berkhgol`tsa*, part IV, 17.

[118] *Opisanie dokumentov i del, kraniashchikhsia v arkhive Sviateishego Pravitel`stvuiushchego Sinoda*, vol. I, prilozhenie, cccclviii-cccclix; see above.

[119] See N. Moleva, E. Beliutin, *Zhivopisnykh del mastera*, 11.

[120] Buturlin's place in the All-Jesting Council is unclear, although in subsequent years Peter sent him the same kind of "play" dispatches as he did to Romodanovskii, so the fact that he was included in Peter's games is indisputable.

[121] See M. M. Bogoslovskii, *Petr I*, vol. I, 205-206; A. M. Panchenko, B. A. Uspenskii, "Ivan Groznyi i Petr Velikii: kontseptsii pervogo monarkha," *Trudy Otdela drenerusskoi literatury* XXXVII (1983): 56.

[122] See N. G. Ustrialov, *Istoriia tsarstvovaniia Petra Velikogo*, vol. II, 137.

[123] Feofan Prokopovich, *Arkhiepiskopa Velikogo Novagrada i Velikikh Luk*, part I, 114-115.

[124] See for example the notes of his statements in Berkhgol`ts' diary— *Dnevnik kamer-iunkera F. V. Berkhgol`tsa*, part II, 57.

[125] See Iu. M. Lotman, "Bytovoe povedenie i tipologiia kul`tury v Rossii XVIII v." in *Kul`turnoe nasledie Drevnei Rusi* (Moscow, 1976), 294-295.

[126] M. P. Pogodin, *Sud nad tsarevichem Alekseem Petrovichem. Epizod iz zhizni Petra Velikogo* (Moscow, 1860), 85-86; Idem., *Istoriko-kriticheskie otryvki* (Moscow, 1846-1867), vol. II, 375-376.

[127] Ibid., vol. I, 341-343; see also N. L. Rubinshtein, *Russkaia istoriografiia* (Moscow, 1941), 270-271.

THE MYTH OF THE STATE IN THE AGE OF ENLIGHTENMENT AND ITS DESTRUCTION IN LATE EIGHTEENTH-CENTURY RUSSIA*

V. M. Zhivov

I

The genesis of the Age of Enlightenment as a whole and of the mythology of the state as part of the foundation of that period's worldview is fairly complex. As Frances Yates has demonstrated, the Enlightenment, as generally understood, followed a "Rosicrucian Enlightenment," which in turn derived from two sources: Renaissance ideology (primarily scientific Hermeticism) and religious dissent.[1] Ever since the Reformation, religious discord had not only been an ecclesiastical issue (e.g., heresy and its eradication) but had also become a political problem. Religious wars and heterodoxy rendered prior views of state and polity moot, invalidating concepts of feudal fealty or notions of the monarch as God's anointed steward of his state.

Fratricidal chaos reigned in Europe and could be combated only by a new conception of the state. The depth of the attempts to find a solution that engulfed Europe in the late sixteenth and the early seventeenth centuries has evidently been undervalued until recently. But the intellectual achievements of that period had such a profound impact on the historical experience of subsequent centuries that without an appreciation of the relevant sources it is impossible to construct a spiritual history (*Geistgeschichte*) of the modern age.

The movement of interest to us strove scientifically (in the then-current understanding of "science," a holdover from the Renaissance) to

* English translation © 2010 M. E. Sharpe, Inc., from the Russian text, "Gosudarstvennyi mif v epokhu Prosveshcheniia i ego razrushenie v Rossii kontsa XVIII veka," in *Iz istorii russkoi kul'tury*, vol. 6: *XVIII–nachalo XIX veka* (Moscow: Iazyki russkoi kul'tury, 2000), pp. 657–83. Translated by Liv Bliss. Reprinted with permission of the author. Notes renumbered for this edition.—Ed.

uncover religious truths that rose above individual sectarian disputes and created an opportunity for religious reconciliation based on a far-reaching comprehension of the world system [*miroustroistvo*]. This theory had both anthropological and social aspects and assumed the transformation of a person as a microcosm who by assimilating the harmony of the macrocosm was filled with wisdom and love. It also assumed the transformation of society, in which learned initiates would gradually disseminate Hermetic knowledge and the principles of government founded thereon. That movement spread both internationally and interdenominationally: among others, Giordano Bruno, Tommaso Campanella, and Paolo Sarpi in Italy; Sir Philip Sidney, George Dye, and Robert Fludd in England; Johann Valentin Andreae and Michael Maier in Germany; and Jan Amos Komensky [Comenius] in what is now the Czech Republic were all associated with it in one way or another.

One expression of the movement's social program was the utopia, which never underwent more intensive development (Sir Frances Bacon's *New Atlantis,* Andreae's *Description of the Republic of Christianopolis,* Campanella's *City of the Sun,* Komensky's *The Way of Light,* Samuel Hartlib's *Macarius,* etc.). The aesthetic equivalent of the utopia was Arcadia or the Golden Age—both exemplars of undisturbed harmony; a perfect world from which enmity and discord, created by civilization gone astray, had been banished and in which the human (the social) had been brought into accord with nature, with the cosmos. Here Arcadia is the *locus magicus,* in which, due to the action of Hermetic science (practiced, for example, by Prospero in Shakespeare's *Tempest*), the microcosm is brought into equilibrium with the macrocosm. Prospero lays open the way to the perfect society of which Gonzalo dreams early in the play:[2]

> All things in common nature should produce
> Without sweat or endeavour: treason, felony,
> Sword, pike, knife, gun, or need of any engine,
> Would I not have; but nature should bring forth,
> Of its own kind, all foison, all abundance,
> To feed my innocent people. . .
>
> I would with such perfection govern, sir,
> To excel the golden age. (The Tempest, Act II, Scene I)

The Golden Age as a paradigm of the social organism renewed is also constantly present in the literature of this period, from Sidney's *Arcadia* to the Forest of Arden in Shakespeare's *As You Like It,* in which the old duke and his court "fleet the time carelessly, as they did in the golden world" (Act I, Scene I). In essence—although this is not readily perceived these days—we are dealing here with a tradition involving a scholarly art of a sort that, in partnership with Hermetic science, was expected to transform wayward humanity.

The intellectual/aesthetic movement here described had great political ambitions. The program for society's spiritual transformation was directly coupled with a political program, with a struggle against the old political structure of Europe that was supported by the Habsburgs. That intellectual/ political synthesis may be discerned in both the activity of Henry IV and in the schemes of the Union of German Protestant Princes. Hope for the establishment of a new order reached its apogee in the actions of Frederick V, Elector Palatine, who in 1619 accepted the crown of Bohemia offered to him in the course of a local rebellion against the Hapsburgs—the event that was to usher in the last struggle against the old order.[3] The future was portrayed as the gradual embodiment of the utopia or the attainment of Arcadia, involving an end to religious enmity, the establishment of a universal harmony of interests, and the rebirth of the inner person under the impact of the new science, scholarship, and art.

Frederick's accession to the throne of Bohemia marked the beginning, as we know, of the Thirty Years' War, which began with the devastation of the Palatinate. This was the last religious war in Europe, but its spiritual fruits were a far cry from the new harmony that had been so hoped for in the first decades of the seventeenth century. It led to a profound disenchantment in the transformation of human activity, in the transfiguring power of Hermetic science and art. The crisis of European consciousness in that period, so vividly reflected in, for example, Komensky's *Labyrinth of the World and Paradise of the Heart,* may be compared with the disillusionment as to civilization's achievements that seized Europe after World War I, since the latter instance, too, exhibits a reaction to the expectations of the preceding period, which tied in to the scientific and technical transformation of the world and even its religious and cosmic transfiguration (from Fourier and Compte to Nikolai Fedorovich Fedorov and Vladimir Ivanovich Vernadskii).

The spiritual crisis of the Thirty Years' War had various repercussions. In political thought, it led to the development of the theory of natural law and of the police state. An escape from the intransigence of religious discord was found in the idea of subordinating religion to the state, in the idea of a contract between the monarch and his or her subjects wherein those subjects renounce their individual will (including the manifestation of religious will) while the monarch takes responsibility for the public weal. (The revocation of the Edict of Nantes and the persecution of Catholics in England may be regarded as the practical product of this new political thought.) Just as rationalist philosophy was in a significant degree a reaction to the Hermetic thought of the preceding age, which originated in symbolic Neoplatonism, so the theory of the police state was a reaction to the idea of Rosicrucian thought: in both cases, reason and natural mechanics came to replace arcane knowledge and the policy of religious reconciliation founded on it.

But, however strong that reaction may have been, the rejection of the preceding era's thinking was far from complete and consistent. In the political ideology of Hermeticism, the monarch took part in arcane knowledge and employed it to establish peace, love, and a social harmony that embodied the cosmic harmony. Like Prospero in *The Tempest,* the monarch was, in essence, the mediator of the cosmic order in the social sphere. That role—lacking only the invocation of arcane knowledge—was now transferred to the absolute monarch, who ruled in accordance with the theory of the police state. But the monarch was still responsible for the establishment of global harmony, and on this was founded the Enlightenment ideology of the state. It was a relic of a long-gone confidence in a worldview system that afforded no logical basis for such confidence. A particular pointer to this genesis of the mythology is the symbolism of the Golden Age, which had been accepted by seventeenth-century literature and art and especially characterized the panegyric genres. That symbolism coalesced organically with the prior worldview system but was alien to the new. The idea of a reversion to primordial harmony, to the primeval order of the cosmos, was indeed a motive juncture of Hermetic and alchemical science but corresponded in no way to rationalist ideas of progress, which assumed not reversion but continuous forward motion.

As Lev Vasil'evich Pumpianskii at one time pointed out, the state and its outcomes were a motif organic to European classicism, which had made "classical politics" "a distinct theme for all neo-European literature."[4] The state was the subject of poetic rapture and philosophical meditation precisely because it was presented as the steward of cosmic harmony on earth. Therefore, the monarch's victories, welfare, alliances, and peace treaties were not only material for visual rendition but also a topic for philosophical and artistic introspection. The progress of the state was perceived as the progress of reason and enlightenment—not the individual progress of a given society but the universal development of a principle, a component part of an all-inclusive achievement. Such was French literature under Louis XIV, German literature in the first half of the eighteenth century, and Russian literature from Feofan Prokopovich to Derzhavin. The constant employment by this politico-philosophical literature, in its efforts to resolve the basic problems of the world system, of the pastoral and of pastoral symbolism points to its deep link with the mythology of the Golden Age and with vestigial notions of the monarch as the mediator between good order in the cosmos and good order in the social organism.

These manifestations are associated with the prehistory of the European Enlightenment in the narrow sense of the term. But the Age of Enlightenment—or at least the aspect of interest to us here—should obviously be measured from the moment when the state stopped managing culture, which in France happened in the early eighteenth century. In so doing, the state did not, of course, cease to be a subject of culture—a topic for philosophy, literature, and art. Instead, whereas the state had previously led the way to enlightenment, now enlightenment was, as it were, outpacing the state and presuming to show it the right path. The observer and bard of the state's successes yielded to the appraiser, wishful thinker, and mentor. Boileau expressed his philosophy of state as a panegyric; the encyclopedists saw it as a critical essay. We might call this the *emancipation* of culture: after having outstripped the state, culture was no longer restricted; it acquired autonomy and spontaneous self-direction.[5] But the task of this article is not to analyze the French Enlightenment: from this point, I will focus on Russia's makeover of these processes.

II

Russia gradually adopted the idea of a suprareligious state in which the monarch is steward of the public good from the reign of Aleksei Mikhailovich [1645-1676] on, as is particularly evident in Tsar Aleksei's church policy.[6] Peter [I, 1682/89-1725], though, used that idea as the starting point for his transformation of the state. This was not, however, the simple appropriation of a European model but a complex process of transplantation.[7]

In reality, European ideas did not fall on virgin soil in Russia but were imposed on an existing cultural tradition. The transplanted ideas, therefore, underwent changes here, taking on a life of their own. The idea of the monarch as the inaugurator of social harmony and the guardian of the public good combined here with the traditional messianic notions that were formulated in the concept of Moscow as the Third Rome.* The monarch, formerly the

---

* The idea that Moscow, as the last independent Eastern Orthodox kingdom, was the natural heir of the Roman and Byzantine empires and would lead the world to salvation.—Ed.

mediator of the cosmic order, accordingly became a demiurge, the creator of the new kingdom that would transform the world. That which the tsar created anew both formed the groundwork of the new world and, in terms of the European myth of the state, restored the primordial state of goodness. In that context, it is understandable that Peter and his entourage styled St. Petersburg "Paradise" and "Holy Land."[8] In the same context, Kantemir was able to write about the "new people" that Peter had created, while Lomonosov addressed the Swedes thus:[9]

> *Does this land draw you to itself,*
> *In which milk and honey flows?*
> *Press ahead, then; pass on! There is no wonderment!*
> *For you are already almost in Paradise*
> *Since our capital is so close to you![10]*

The new country that Peter had created was therefore a land of primeval bliss, once lost, while Peter was the savior of the world and the restorer of Paradise to earth. It is indicative that Arcadia here manifestly takes on the traits of the Promised Land, which is a direct reflection of a messianic makeover of the European myth of the state.[11]

In Russia, the European view of the monarch as the steward of the public good led to an unprecedented sacralization of the tsar, which expanded from Aleksei Mikhailovich's reign on and characterized Russia's entire imperial period. The Russian variant of this mythology of the state presented the monarch as an earthly god and an earthly savior linked by a mysterious, charismatic bond to God in heaven and Christ the Savior and as an apostle leading his realm along the path of salvation.[12] As Feofan Prokopovich preached ("in our Peter, in whom we first saw a great stalwart and after that an apostle"), it was Peter who had created in Russia "all the good things, beneficial and necessary for our temporal and eternal lives."[13]

The development of the imperial cult was of decisive significance to the construction of Russian culture in the eighteenth century. It was the keystone that ensured the synthesis—short-lived and illusory as it may have been—of two completely diverse traditions that shaped eighteenth-century Russian culture. These elements were, on the one hand, traditional Russian spirituality and, on the other, the rationalist culture of European absolutism. Since Petrine statehood included the reeducation [*perevospitanie*] of the populace among its crucial political tasks, the transformed empire assigned that synthesis to culture as its chief ideological mission.[14] Earlier we discussed how that mission modified the European contribution, introducing messianism into the state myth of absolute monarchy. But it exerted an equally substantial impact on the traditions of Russian spirituality.

Indeed, the growing cult of the monarch was bound, as a matter of principle, to conflict with the traditional Christian worldview. That conflict did take place, as is abundantly attested, but it did not determine the relationship between the state and the official Church.[15] Since the cult of the monarch and the mythology of the state were structured not outside the Christian tradition but within it, the Church had no choice but to disseminate and support both the mythology and the cult, accommodating the traditional categories of the Orthodox mindset to the state's new direction. The Church had no choice here because, in the above-mentioned politico-philosophical system that took shape after the Thirty Years' War, the Church was part of the state, one of its instruments in dispensing the public weal. Since the new ideology of state was combined in Russia with an existing and far more traditional messianism, that ideology became closely affiliated with the sphere of faith, which highlighted the importance of the Orthodox Church's involvement in affirming the new worldview. First and foremost, the Orthodox Church was charged with unifying traditional spirituality with a culture based on the idea of a progressive state and the monarch's absolute power. The Church did not accept that role without resistance, but by the beginning of Elizabeth's reign [1740-1762] it had given way and adopted the imperial cult as part of its mission. One expression of this trend was the development of the panegyrical homily, which is highly reminiscent in content and in form of the secular panegyrical ode (and served as one of its main sources).[16] As a result, both the spiritual and the secular literature of that period constitute a synthetic unity centered on the theme of the state.[17]

The basic elements of the new ideology of the state, mythology of the state, and the imperial cult became embedded in the fabric of autocracy in Russia, retaining their full significance until the beginning of Catherine's reign [Catherine II (1762-1796)], and supplied the mythological backdrop for Catherine's ventures. This is also the context in which Catherine's assimilation of the ideas of the French Enlightenment should be examined. As architects of a new world and Messiahs, Russian monarchs had a lively interest in the most radical ideas of their times. The newer the new world that was to arise on the Petersburg marshes and transform the universe, and the more Russian monarchs were revealed as arrangers of universal harmony, the more closely they would correspond to the myth of tsar-savior and tsar-demiurge. This was significant to the radicalism of both Peter and Catherine.

In my view, it also explains *why* the ideas of the French Enlightenment became the semiofficial ideology of Catherine's monarchy. But there is also another aspect: *how* that officially sanctioned ideology could coexist with despotic absolutism. The evident explanation is that eighteenth-century Russia lacked any direct link between the ideology of the state and the actual mechanism of state government. One stock example will suffice to illustrate how things stood in this regard.

In 1767 Catherine published her famous *Nakaz* [Instruction to the Legislative Commission], which mostly reiterated the findings of Montesquieu, Beccaria, and the encyclopedists. In one paragraph, the *Nakaz* states, "In Russia, the Senate is the repository of the laws,"[18] and elsewhere the Senate was granted the right "to represent that such or such an injunction is contrary to the Statute, that it is harmful, obscure, and is not capable of execution."[19] Here, the term "Statute" [*Ulozhenie*] implies the fundamental laws (a kind of constitution) and in the "right to represent" we immediately recognize the French parliament's *droit de remonstrance.* Seemingly the Russian autocracy was thus, in the most enlightened manner, restricting itself by the Fundamental Law.[20] Such, though, was only a superficial similarity that, as we well know, had nothing to do with reality. There was no Statute in eighteenth-century Russia and no Fundamental Law was ever compiled under Catherine.[21] At the same time, the Senate (which was, moreover, in no respect a representative body) never proffered any "representations" at all. The same is true of many other provisions in the *Nakaz,* which, although the eighteenth century's most progressive legal document, was quite obviously a legal fiction with no practical significance—a fact that is common knowledge and has been the subject of scholarly analysis on any number of occasions. I, however, am interested in another aspect, which is that, like the entire ideology of the state, the *Nakaz* belonged to the mythological sphere and fulfilled a mythological function. It was an attribute of a monarch engaged in establishing universal justice and creating harmony in the world.

The empress may have been the chief participant in this mythological pageant, but she was far from the only one. Its dramatis personae comprised all who were close to the court, regardless of their personal inclinations and convictions. That mandatory participation was what made the Enlightenment an officially sanctioned ideology, a state of affairs that is well demonstrated in the following episode (one of many).

In 1767, the year in which the *Nakaz* was published, Catherine and her entourage made a trip to the Volga, an Arcadian journey during which the assembled company occupied itself with the kind of project that courtiers rarely undertook—the translation of Marmontel's *Belisarius*. The book, widely known in Europe, was an admonition to enlightened monarchs that denounced despotism and extolled a rational concern for the subjects of the realm and at the same time a manifesto of enlightened deism that contrasted rational religion to clerical obscurantism. In France, the Sorbonne had censured it for its freethinking, but in Russia another fate awaited it. Catherine herself translated the chapter that condemned absolutism, had the book published, and arranged for its dedication to Archbishop Gavriil (Petrov). The dedication, written by Count Andrei Petrovich Shuvalov, an admirer and friend of Voltaire, read in part:

> The ancients were ever wont to offer their works to those whom they sincerely revered. We are following their example in offering our translation to Your Eminence. Your virtues are known; and especially the meekness, humility, moderation, and enlightened piety that reside in you and ought to adorn the soul of every Christian and even more so of a pastor of your rank. Moral edification is needful to all peoples and in all stations of life. The beatitude of society depends on the good conduct of its members, and so it is useful to them often to remind them of the duty owed by a man and a citizen; and . . . to ignite their hearts with a zeal to emulate the worthy men who lived before them. *Belisarius* is just such a work. . . . We candidly admit that *Belisarius* has taken possession of our hearts, and we are convinced that this work will please Your Eminence, because you are, in both thought and virtue, like unto Belisarius.[22]

This flattering dedication reads like an imperial decree, and one that articulated a royal certainty as to the kinship of the views of Marmontel and Gavriil. By the same token, Gavriil was being charged to preach the worldview that had exerted such an attraction on the empress. Regardless of Gavriil's personal views (and whatever else he may have been, he was no fellow-thinker of Marmontel's), he had been prescribed a program of action (which included the reading of literary works), and follow it he must.

III

Thus was created the culture of the Enlightenment in Russia, which was primarily a mythological pageant of official power. The Russian Enlightenment was a Petersburgian mirage.

Only its active agents sincerely believed in its reality; others were involuntary participants, but that did not alter its mythological essence. The

Hanging Gardens of Babylon looked down on the Neva; after solemn prayers, Minerva threw open the Temple of Enlightenment; Fonvizin unmasked vices; and the people subsisted in a state of bliss. This mirage was the prototype for the universal transformation, a backdrop against which the Russian monarch grew into a figure of cosmic significance.

In my view, the connection between that mythological structure and the mythological legacy of the new European statehood manifests clearly and particularly in its pastoral motifs, in the constantly reiterated themes of Arcadia and the Golden Age. Here, for example, is Lomonosov's description of the path along which Ioann Antonovich [the infant Ivan VI (1740-1741), under Biron's regency—Trans.] ought to direct his steps:

> *Walk in the footsteps of Peter and Anna,*
> *Trample the audacity of every foe;*
> *Truth shall show the straight way;*
> *Courage shall place you above the moon,*
> *And will cry my fame in lands*
> *Unheard of now by anyone.*
>
> [7]
> *Earth, put forth such flowers*
> *That Flora herself shall marvel;*
> *Their leaves purer than pearl*
> *And of a price higher than gold;*
> *Give them the pleasant scent of Ceylon.*
> *Nature, stand higher than laws,*
> *Give birth to that which exceeds your strength.*
> *Pluck those flowers, Nymphs, with joy*
> *And weave them with laurel into wreaths,*
> *As a sign of victories, of precious consolations.*
>
> [8]
> *Reign, gladness, thou alone*
> *Over the Might of those expansive lands.*[23]

These themes and images constantly recurred both in panegyrical poetry and in the court art of the 1740s and 1750s, but they were no less broadly exploited in Catherine's time.[24] So, for example, in Derzhavin's "Portrait of Felitsa" [*Izobrazhenie Felitsy*], we read:

As from the steep blue incline of the ether
Rays do chance to descend
From the All-Powerful of the world,
So let grace come down upon her,
And in the guise of earthly happiness
Let flowers be strewn before her,
And the golden hours of another age
Concurrently progress;
So that I may see shepherds
Calling their flocks to the meadow with sounding horns;
And in the flowering linden groves
Swarms of bees buzzing all around.[25]

One diagnostic detail of the Catherinian Arcadia that warrants particular attention is that its denizens are often found to include "savages." So, for example, in a portrayal of Catherine bestowing her *Nakaz* upon the peoples (also from the "Portrait of Felitsa"), we find:

Let her, having arisen from her throne, give
The tablet of holy commandments;
Let the universe accept
The voice of God, the voice of nature that is in them;
Let savages remote,
Covered in wool and scales,
Ornamented with the plumage of birds
And dressed in leaves and bark
Gather at her throne
And hearken to the gentle voice of the law,
And torrents of tears flow from their eyes
Down their swarthy yellow faces.

The Finn, pale and red of hair,
Would then not wreck his boats in the sea,
And the narrow-eyed Hun would reap ears of grain
Amid the gray, dry swells.[26]

As Elena Iakovlevna Dan'ko has suggested, Derzhavin's description here can be linked with a table service made by [Jean-Dominique] Rachette, also in praise of Catherine, on which figures representing the "peoples of the

East" (Finns, Kalmyks, etc.) formed an unusual retinue.[27] In both instances, the ethnographic cohort undoubtedly fulfills a panegyric function. But the appearance of these characters in the imperial Arcadia also carries a dual meaning.

First, the roster of "savage peoples" is the ethnographical equivalent of the geographical attributes of a monarch triumphant. The spread of the empire's might and good works may be represented geographically—from the waters of the Baltic, say, to the Sea of Japan—or ethnographically— from the Finns to the Huns and the Tunguz. Derzhavin's listing may be paralleled with a geographical checklist found in one of Gottlob Friedrich Wilhelm Junker's Petersburg odes (1742):

> *Dis is der Wunsch vom Belth bisz zum Iapaner-Meer,*
> *Von der Hyrcaner-See bisz, wo der weisse Bär*
> *Die Eiszberg übersteigt, am äussersten der Erden,*
> *Wo so viel Thiere grosz, die Menschen kleiner werden.*[28]

> [This is the wish, from the Baltic to the Sea of Japan,
> From the Hyrcanian Ocean to the place where the white bear
> Steps over icebergs, at the farthermost ends of the earth,
> Where so many beasts are great that men shall be the smaller.]

These "geographical fanfaronades," as Viazemskii called them, were a commonplace in the Lomonosovian tradition of the Russian ode and had, at the same time, numerous West European parallels.[29] Whereas the geographical signposts point toward the monarch's military and political might, the ethnographic tokens imply the royal progress of enlightenment: the monarch appears in the geographical space as a hypostasis of Mars, and in the ethnographic space as a hypostasis of Minerva.

The second meaning of those "savage peoples" is revealed here. They personify the ends of the earth (*am äussersten der Erden*), which are encompassed by the Arcadia that the empress has created and are the site of numerous utopias described by seventeenth-century authors. The utopia of the myth of the state inevitably subjugates those spatial coordinates and thus reveals its continuity with preceding plans for the harmonious transformation of all creation.[30]

The mythological system here described did not survive to the end of Catherine's reign. It is difficult to say exactly why and when its decline began, but the moment did come when a universal reconciliation of interests and a constant forward movement toward well-being and harmony began to be perceived as a senseless and self-compromising fiction. That perception then made steady inroads among the educated class. The Pugachev rebellion, by demonstrating how narrow the enlightened autocracy's base really was, evidently had an effect here, as, probably, did the languid pace of enlightenment.[31] Grigorii Aleksandrovich Gukovskii gave the following description of how the court literati of the 1760s had pictured this process: "All one has to do is open people's eyes, and all will go well: the wicked will swiftly reform and human life will become splendid. The results of this operation should be instantaneous. It was assumed that a few literary works could heal society."[32] The ideas of the Enlightenment acquired a mythological dimension that couched the spread of culture as the comprehensive transformation of society under the impact of that new discovery. But in the 1780s such mythological hopes became less sanguine: Aleksandr Vasil'evich Khrapovitskii had noted on 18 July 1782, "in sixty years all schisms will vanish; as soon as the public schools are established and gain purchase, ignorance will be extirpated as a matter of course; no effort will be required."[33] But only ten years later not a trace would remain of that mythology of enlightenment.

The philosophical theme of the state in Russian historico-cultural thought of the period had been depleted. The trend affected all of Europe, not Russia alone, and Russia took part in it because of its involvement in European culture. In Russia, however, European (or Europeanized) culture was a transplant, a fact that caused the traits of European development to be hypertrophied here. The culture of the Russian Enlightenment was a culture of the state, the immediate embodiment of one variant of the mythology of the state. In Russia, the Enlightenment had spliced culture, both secular and spiritual, to the state and therefore the enlightening ended with the emancipation of culture. In this, Russia was the direct obverse of France, where the emancipation of culture signaled the beginning of the Enlightenment (see above).

The rift between state and culture had numerous consequences. It had a radical impact on all three components of the Russian Enlightenment's cultural/state synthesis: spiritual culture, secular culture, and the cultural policy of the state.

By the late eighteenth century—when the dogma of enlightenment, having already compromised itself in the eyes of the government, was no longer the officially sanctioned ideology—archbishops no longer had to tailor their writings to match the Marmontelian and Voltairean spirit. Although the state's administrative oversight of the Church was only strengthening, Orthodoxy could now stop pretending and attempt to bring spiritual literature into line with the real requirements of the Orthodox population, which could well do without philosophical arguments and rhetorical flourishes. This shift was marked by a reversion to the traditional sources of Orthodox piety (translations of patristic literature, the development of ascetic theology, etc.). But the period of state-sponsored enlightenment had not left the spiritual culture untouched. Once released from compulsory unification with an alien secular culture, spiritual culture not only freed itself from that secular culture but consciously distanced itself as well. The Church's striving to isolate itself from trends in secular culture and to limit the range of its explorations and interests to prevent them from impinging on the problems of secular society became a substantial characteristic of the development of Orthodox spiritual culture up until the 1860s.[34] It was on the strength of this that Pushkin and the Venerable Moisei of Optina [Hermitage] (like many others on both sides) lived as if in mutually impermeable worlds, knowing nothing about and needing nothing from each other.

The state's cultural policy also underwent some radical changes. Previously the state had presented itself as the creator and owner of culture, which allowed the Enlightenment to become the officially sanctioned ideology. Whereas Louis XIV saw the Enlightenment as an independent system of thought rife with threats and bad omens, Catherine perceived it as one element of a mythology of the state centered on herself. Cultural and historical development therefore appeared to be controllable, lying entirely within the sphere of the Petersburg mirage; it conveyed no sense of danger. But cultural emancipation implied that cultural development had exceeded mythological bounds, become embedded in the reality of Russian life, and ceased to be controllable. In consequence, the state's cultural policy became conservative. Manifestations of the new approach were the closing of free publishing houses, increased censorship, the arrests of Novikov and Radishchev, and Fonvizin's disgrace.*

Secular culture was also experiencing profound changes. Here the emancipation of culture freed up a vast religious and mythological potential that during the Russian Enlightenment had been attributed primarily to the state and the monarch as the sponsors of cosmic harmony on earth and the creators of a new Arcadia but was now transferred to the culture itself. The poet

---

* Nikolai Novikov, Aleksandr Radishchev, and Denis Fonvizin were prominent cultural figures who flourished under Catherine's attempts to introduce the Enlightenment into Russia, only to suffer when the empress became more conservative toward the end of her reign.—Translator's note.

was granted what had previously been the emperor's charismatic authority to order the world. That development was immediately reflected in the genre characteristics of Russian poetry, where the solemn ode with its apologia for the state ceded to the philosophical lyric, dedicated to poetry itself and to the poet (from Karamzin's "Poetry" [Poeziia] to Tiutchev's "Urania" [Uraniia]) and now occupied a central place in high poetry. The poet had become a sacralized figure that mediated between divinity and mankind.[35]

> Earth, show reverence! Peoples, lend your ears!
> Immortal singers bring you tidings of God. ("Urania")

Thus, the mythology of the poet emerges from the mythology of the state. This change, in my view, is one of the chief sources of Russia's distinctive attitude toward poetry and literature, wherein the custodian of social harmony and the steward of the public good is not the political figure but the poet and writer.

But in this instance, too, a mythological continuity is clearly imprinted on the continuity of poetic motifs, a thematic transition that is particularly conspicuous in Derzhavin's poetry. So, for instance, in his "Monument" [Pamiatnik], we read:

> And word of me shall pass from the White Sea to the Black,
> Where Volga, Don, and Neva are, and the Ural flows from
> Mount Riphea.
> Each in countless tribes shall call to mind
> How from obscurity I came to fame thereby.[36]

The geographical scope of poetic fame is the same as that of the ode; poetic fame occupies exactly the same space as the might of the monarch triumphant once had and is described in the same traditional formula ("from . . . to"). The countless tribes have also transferred from the monarch (Felitsa); these are the same "savages" earlier transformed by the grace of enlightenment conferred by the state. The imperial genesis of these "savage peoples" is observed even more distinctly in Derzhavin's later "Swan" [Lebed'], where the poet also appears as the bringer of peace and harmony to a pugnacious mankind:

> From Kuril Islands to the Bug,
> From the White Sea to the Caspian,
> Peoples from half this world
> Constituents of the Russian race,

Will hear of me in time:
Slavs, Huns, Scythians, and Finns,
And others who now burn with enmity
Shall point their fingers at me and say:
"There flies one who, having tuned his lyre,
Spoke the language of the heart,
And, by preaching peace to the whole world,
Gladdened himself with the happiness of all."[37]

The same "savage peoples" living at the farthest limits of the Russian space are later picked up by Pushkin ("and Finn, and now the savage Tungus, and Kalmyk, friend to steppes" [from "Exegi monumentum"—Trans.]), because the true potentate of universal harmony is the poet, not the tsar. But Pushkin, unlike Derzhavin, openly compares poet and emperor and leaves no doubt as to the poet's supremacy:

Higher yet than Alexander's column
He raises his unruly head.[38]

Translated by Liv Bliss

NOTES

1   See Frances A. Yates, *The Rosicrucian Enlightenment* (London: Routledge and Kegan Paul, 1972).
2   Compare Frank Kermode's "Introduction," in William Shakespeare, *The Tempest* (London: Methuen, 1954), p. xlviii, with Yates, *The Rosicrucian Enlightenment,* 93-105.
3   See Yates, *The Rosicrucian Enlightenment,* 37-57.
4   L. V. Pumpianskii, "K istorii russkogo klassitsizma (poetika Lomonosova)," *Kontekst—1982* (Moscow, 1983), 316-17.
5   It may be thought that this process would result in the actual achievements of culture being understood as self-sufficient and acquiring an autonomous value. But that value is defined by the place the idea occupies in cultural development, whereas experiments in living the idea could in principle be moved outside the bounds of the actual culture and therefore bear no relation to values from the viewpoint of the culture in question. Possibly the first time that this autonomous culture, selfcontrasted with life and demonstratively refusing embodiment in life, was recognized and described was in [Denis Diderot's] *Rameau's Nephew.*
6   The view that Russia was not included in the movement of European ideas until the reign of Peter I is evidently a misapprehension. Russia was not drawn into the Thirty Years' War, but its two closest neighbors, Sweden and Poland, were highly active in that war, and it is unlikely that the new political thinking that took shape in the

course of the war would not have been accepted, at least in some measure, by Aleksei Mikhailovich (see James H. Billington, "The Great Raskol," in *Millennium of the Baptism of Russia: Second International Church Study Conference on the Theology and Spirituality of the Russian Orthodox Church, Moscow, May 11–18, 1987* [preprint]). Tsar Aleksei was in general quite attentive to the vicissitudes of European history—as is shown, for example, by his barring of English merchants from Arkhangel'sk after the execution of Charles I. I think he would not have overlooked the idea of the suprareligious police state. He was an active manager of ecclesiastical policy from the very beginning of his reign, handing off to the Monastery Chancery [*Monastyrskii prikaz*], which he had set up and which reported to him, an array of church-management functions, as well as correcting church rituals and prosecuting opponents of his innovations. Characteristically, both Archpriest Avvakum and Patriarch Nikon, from their respective sides, accused him of usurping ecclesiastical authority and pretending to be de facto head of the Church. Nikon wrote: "When is the tsar the head of the Church? Never, but the head is Christ, for thus writes the apostle. The tsar is not and cannot be the head of the Church but is as one of its parts, and for this reason may do nothing in church and is lower than the lowest lector" (N. F. Kapterev, *Patriarkh Nikon i Tsar' Aleksei Mikhailovich* [Sergiev Posad, 1909-12], vol. 2, 188). The traditional Russian mind perceived the European model, in both its Catholic and especially its Protestant variants, as the secular kingdom's sacrilegious intrusion on the clergy. It is also evident that the assimilation of the new political and culturo-historical thought was primarily reflected in ecclesiastical policy, inasmuch as the Church, as the custodian of the traditional religious consciousness, could not avoid the need to oppose innovation of that type.

7   On the concept of transplantation, see D. S. Likhachev, *Razvitie russkoi literatury X–XVII vekov: Epokhi i stili* (Leningrad, 1973), 15-23; and Iu.M. Lotman, " 'Ezda v ostrov liubvi' Trediakovskogo i funktsiia perevodnoi literatury v russkoi kul'ture pervoi poloviny XVIII v.," in *Problemy izucheniia kul'turnogo naslediia* (Moscow, 1985), 222-30.

8   Iu.M. Lotman and B. A. Uspenskii, "Otzvuki kontseptsii 'Moskva—Tretii Rim' v ideologii Petra I," in *Khudozhestvennyi iazyk srednevekov'ia* (Moscow, 1982), 240.

9   A. D. Kantemir, *Sochineniia, pis'ma i izbrannye perevody kniazia Antiokha Dmitrievicha Kantemira* (St. Petersburg, 1867-68), vol. 1, 46.

10 M. V. Lomonosov, *Sochineniia* (St. Petersburg, Moscow, and Leningrad, 1891-1948), vol. 1, 34.

11 Exact evidence of this is seen in the image of a land flowing with milk and honey, which harks back to the Bible (see Exodus 13:5: "And it shall be when the Lord shall bring thee into the land . . . which he sware unto thy fathers to give thee, a land flowing with milk and honey"; see also Exodus 3:8 and Deuteronomy 26:9). Compare L. Solosin, "Otrazhenie iazyka i obrazov Sv. Pisaniia i knig bogosluzhebnykh v stikhotvoreniiakh Lomonosova," *Izvestiia Otdeleniia russkogo iazyka i slovesnosti Akademii nauk,* vol. 18 (1913), bk. 2, 248-49.

The eschatological significance of that image is underscored by its attribution in the Orthodox tradition to the Mother of God, as the leader of mankind renewed (see, in the Akathistos to the Mother of God, "Rejoice, Thou from whom floweth milk and honey!"). This image appears repeatedly in Lomonosov: "In the Neva shall run the sweetness of honey" (Lomonosov, *Sochineniia,* vol. 1, 54), and "The rivers flow with milk and honey, / The land grows fruits of itself" (Ibid.). It later became one of the clichés of the Russian panegyrical ode.

[12]   V. M. Zhivov and B. A. Uspenskij, "Tsar and God," in this volume, 1-112.

[13]   Feofan Prokopovich, *Slova i rechi pouchitel'nye, pokhval'nye i pozdravitel'nye* (St. Petersburg, 1760-74), vol. 2, 157.

[14]   V. M. Zhivov, "Azbuchnaia reforma Petra I kak semioticheskoe preobrazovanie," in *Trudy po znakovym sistemam* (Tartu, 1986), vol. 19, 54-55.

[15]   Zhivov and Uspenskij, "Tsar and God."

[16]   See V. M. Zhivov, "Koshchunstvennaia poeziia v sisteme russkoi kul'tury kontsa XVIII-nachala XIX veka," in *Trudy po znakovym sistemam* (Tartu, 1981), pt. 13, 65-70.

[17]   There was in that end result no distinction between the cultures of Russia and Western Europe (for example, French culture during the time of Louis XIV). Western Europe, however, lacked the fundamental heterogeneity of the cultural traditions that formed this synthesis and were characteristic of Russia. In Western Europe, the spiritual and secular cultures had common traditions of long standing and absorbed the new ideology of state and polity in tandem.

[18]   Ekaterina [Catherine II], *Nakaz Ee Imperatorskogo Velichestva Ekateriny Vtoroi Samoderzhitsy Vserossiiskaia, dannyi Komissii o sochinenii proekta novogo ulozheniia* (St. Petersburg, 1770), 4, 26.

[19]   Ibid., 3, 21.

[20]   See Isabel de Madariaga, *Russia in the Age of Catherine the Great* (London: [Weidenfeld and Nicholson], 1981), 151-55.

[21]   On failed attempts to produce a legal code, see *Obozrenie istoricheskikh svedenii o svode zakonov* (St. Petersburg, 1833); and A. Lappo-Danilevskii, *Sobranie i svod zakonov Rossiiskoi Imperii, sostavlennye v tsarstvovanie imperatritsy Ekateriny II* (St. Petersburg, 1897).

[22]   Marmontel' [Jean-François Marmontel], *Velizar, sochineniia gospodina Marmontelia, chlena frantsuzskoi akademii, pereveden na Volge* (Moscow, 1768), ll. 3-4 verso.

[23]   Lomonosov, *Sochineniia*, vol. 1, 26.

[24]   Compare Lomonosov's frequent repetition of that theme in his poetry of the 1740s and 1750s (ibid., vol. 1, 54, 214-15; vol. 2, 118, 276, etc.). The combination of panegyric and pastoral, embodying the idea of the return of the Golden Age as the charismatic action of the emperor-demiurge, led to the development of a unique type of idyll, the panegyrical idyll (see Lomonsov's idyll "Polidor"). On the history of the Russian panegyrical idyll, see Joachim Klein, *Die Schäferdichtung des russischen Klassizismus: Habilitationsschrift* (Berlin, 1986).

[25]   G. R. Derzhavin, *Sochineniia*, explanatory notes by Ia. Grot, 9 vols. (St. Petersburg, 1864-1883), vol. 1, 280.

[26]   Ibid., 275.

[27]   E.Ia. Dan'ko, "Izobrazitel'noe iskusstvo v poezii Derzhavina," in *XVIII vek* 2 (Moscow and Leningrad, 1940), 242-44.

[28]   Lomonosov, *Sochineniia*, vol. 1, 82.

[29]   L. V. Pumpianskii, "Lomonosov i nemetskaia shkola razuma," in *XVIII vek* 14 (Leningrad, 1983), 23-25.

[30]   The theme of the expansion of mythological well-being to peoples inhabiting the far boundaries of the earth appeared earlier, in Lomonosov. See his ode to Elizabeth (1742): "Reports of Thee also captivated those peoples / Who wander amid wild animals / And pasture with fierce lions. / To Thine honor they shall arise with us" (Lomonosov, *Sochineniia*, vol. 1, 95). But this theme is expressed even more distinctly in the 1747 ode, in which the Russian Minerva creates a kingdom of science and poetry and dispatches

her heralds to spread that state of bliss to "unknown peoples": "That curtain of gloomy eternity / Hope flings open for us! / Where there are no rules, nor law / Wisdom there shall found a temple! / Ignorance before her pales. / There the watery wake of vessels / Gleams white as they ply eastward. / Across the waters the Russian Columbus / Hastens to the unknown peoples / To tell them of Thy munificence" (ibid., 151).

The link between ethnographical coordinates and enlightenment triumphant is also clearly seen in a speech on the opening of the public schools written by Derzhavin and delivered by Zakhar'in, a smallholder [*odnodvorets*], in 1786. This text again refers to "wild peoples" and offers a lively description of the horror of their unenlightened state. Thus, the Hottentots (*die Menschen kleiner werden*), for example: "In very truth, if the Hottentot were to be deprived of the gift of good sense and the gift of the word, what animal may be more closely compared to him than the orangutan?" Later comes an ethnographical listing: "This is the image of the Kadar, the Acridophage, the Negro, the Laplander, the Kamchadal, and other suchlike grotesqueries! This is the image of an altogether unenlightened rabble!" (Derzhavin, *Sochineniia*, vol. 7, 130-31). The public schools founded by Catherine would also initiate the transformation of those unhappy peoples, who would thus ultimately be illuminated by the Catherinian Enlightenment.

[31] See A. S. Pushkin, "Zamechaniia o bunte," in his *Polnoe sobranie sochinenii* (Moscow and Leningrad, 1937-48), vol. 9, 375.

[32] G. A. Gukovskii, *Ocherki po istorii russkoi literatury XVIII veka. Dvorianskaia fronda v literature 1750-1760-kh godov* (Moscow and Leningrad, 1936), 38.

[33] V. A. Khrapovitskii, *Dnevnik, 1782-1793* (St. Petersburg, 1874), 2.

[34] See V. M. Zhivov, "Lingvisticheskoe blagochestie v pervoi polovine XIX v.," *Wiener Slawistischer Almanach* 13 (Vienna, 1984), 363-95.

[35] See Zhivov, "Koshchunstvennaia poeziia," 70-76.

[36] Derzhavin, *Sochineniia,* vol. 1, 787.

[37] Ibid., vol. 2, 501.

[38] Additional confirmation of the legitimacy of the connection between Pushkin's ethnographic roster and the contraposition of poet and tsar comes from a comparison of [Pushkin's] "Monument" with Zhukovskii's "Recollections of the Celebration of 30 August 1834" [Vospominaniia o torzhestve 30 avgusta 1834], which describes the unveiling of the Alexander Column. In "Recollections," one of the details demonstrating the tsar's triumph is the crowd of peoples brought to stand between the monument to Peter I and the one to Alexander I: "and in that army, a hundred thousand strong, under the same eagles stood Russian and Pole and Livonian and Finn and Tatar and Kalmyk and Cherkassian and Transcaucasian warrior" (V. A. Zhukovskii, *Polnoe sobranie sochinenii* [Petrograd, 1918], vol. 3, 176; see also A. N. Shustov, "Zhukovskii i stikhotvorenie Pushkina 'Ia pamiatnik sebe vozdvig . . . ,' " in *Vremennik Pushkinskoi komissii, 1973* [Leningrad, 1975], 103-6). Another point at which Pushkin juxtaposes poet and tsar is possibly the epithet "not made by human hand" [*nerukotvornyi*], which evidently associates the "Monument" with [Vasilii Grigor'evich] Ruban's inscription for Peter's memorial (see Roman Jakobson, *Pushkin and His Sculptural Myth*[, trans. and ed. John Burbank] [The Hague: Mouton, 1975], 29; compare Rolf-Dietrich Keil, "Nerukotvornyi—Beobachtungen zur geistigen Geschichte eines Wortes," in *Studien zur Literatur und Aufklärung in Osteuropa*, ed. Hans-Bernd Harder and Hans Rothe [Giessen: Wilhelm Schmitz, 1978], 269-317). Here, too, Pushkin encroaches on the principal

myth of the Russian imperial cult—the cult of Peter as the one who brought order to the Russian tsardom. The reference to the "crowd of peoples" alongside a reference to the "monument not made by human hand" may speak to the contraposition of tsar and poet, the mirage of the imperial cult, which has no grass-roots foundation, being contrasted here with the fame of the poet as a true mediator between God and the people (see Keil, "Nerukotvornyi," 299).

The theme of propagating the poet's fame among savage peoples has a long pedigree in world literature, and innumerable parallels to both Derzhavin's "Monument" and his "Swan" and to Pushkin's "Monument" can be found in West European literature (see M. P. Alekseev, *Stikhotvorenie Pushkina "Ia pamiatnik sebe vozdvig ... "* [Leningrad, 1967], 78-82). All these undoubtedly derive from Horace's "Ode to Maecenas" (Book 2, Ode 20): "Me Colchus et qui dissimulat metum / Marsae cohortis Dacus, et ultimi / noscent Geloni, me peritus / discet Hiber Rhodanique potor." [In a 1894 translation by W. E. Gladstone, found at www.archive.org/stream/a587951400horauoft/a587951400horauoft_djvu.txt: "Dacia, that masks her fear of Rome, / Colchian, and far Gelonian home, / Who dwells in Spain, who drinks of Rhone, / Shall know me, and my fame shall own."—Trans.] The sources, however, did not ritualize this motif's semantic mission. In Russian literature, the "savage peoples" motif becomes part of another paradigm, where it simultaneously points to the contraposition of poet and monarch (compare in this connection the liturgical allusions in Derzhavin's "Swan," which radically modify the semantic mission of the Horatian lyric: Zhivov, "Koshchunstvennaia poeziia," 74 n. 33).

ABBREVIATIONS

GIM   State Historical Museum, Moscow.
RGADA Russian State Archive of Ancient Acts, Moscow.
RGB   Russian State Library. Moscow (formerly, Lenin State Library).
RNB   Russian National Library, St. Petersburg (formerly, Saltykov-Shchedrin State Public Library).

List of Original Publications

B.A. Uspenskij, V.M. Zhivov, "Tsaȓ i Bog. Semioticheskie aspekty skralizatsii monarha v Rossii," in B.A. Uspenskij, *Izbrannye raborty* in 2 vols. (Moscow: Iazyki Russkoi Kul`tury, 1996) 2, 295-337.

B.A. Uspenskij, "Tzar and Imposter," [English Translation] in Ju. Lotman, B. Uspenskij, *The Semiotics of Russian Culture*, ed. by A. Shukman (Ann Arbor, 1984), 259-292.

B.A. Uspenskij, "Postavlenie na tsarstvo v russkoi i vizantiiskoi traditsiiah," in *Pravoslavnoe Uchenie o Tserkovnyh Tainstvah* III (Moscow: Sinodal`naia Bibleisko-Bogoslovskaia Komissiia, 2009): 416-440

B.A. Uspenskij, "Evropa kak matafora i metonimiia," in his *Istoriko-filologicheskie ocherki* (Moscow: Iazyki Slavianskoi Kul`tury, 2004), 9-26.

V.M. Zhivov, "Kul`turnye reformy v sisteme preobrazovanii Petra I," in *Iz istorii Russkoi Kul`tury* III (XVII-nachalo XVIII veka) (Moscow: Iazyki Slavianskoi Kul`tury, 1996), 528-583.

Viktor M. Zhivov, "The Myth of State in the Age of Enlightenment and Its Destruction in Late Eighteenth-Century Russia," [English Translation] *Russian Studies in History* 48, 3 (Winter 2009-2010): 10-29.

Index

"deity" (epithet) 33, 36

Demidov, Mit`ka 122

Derzhavin G. R. 32, 46, 58, 68-71, 91n164, 100n265, 104n315, 107n385, 110n409, 242, 248-250, 253, 254, 257n30, 258n38; "The Drunk and Sober Philosopher" 46;"Epistle to I. I. Shuvalov" 32, 100n265; "Felitsa" 68; "Graitiude to Felitsa" 68; "Monument" 253, 258n38; "A Murza's Vision" 68; "Ode on Greatness" 71; "Ode on Nobility" 100n265; "On the Grand Princes Nikolai Pavlovich and Mikhail Pavlovich's Departure from Petersburg for the Army" 58; "Portrait of Felitsa" 248, 249; "The Russian Amphytrite's Procession Down the Volkhov [River]" 58; "Swan" 253, 258n38; "To the Tsarevich Khlor" 68; "The Voice of St. Petersburg Society" 46

devil 6, 9, 10, 26, 112n434, 118, 127, 128, 130, 131, 146n84, 148n88, 198, 204
    Peter the Great as in league with 128, 204
    See also Satan.

Diderot, Denis Rameau's Nephew 254n5

Dionisios, Constantinopolitan Patriarch 172n44

"divinity" (epithet) 2, 46, 47, 63, 64, 66, 68, 134n11

Dmitriev, M. A. 92n178

Dmitrii Ivanovich (grandson of, and co-ruler with, Grand Prince Ivan III) 115, 153, 163n1, 170n34

Dolgorukii, Ia. F. 34

Donation of Constantine 102n304, 103n304, 195-197, 202, 211n21

Dosifei (Dositheus), patriarch of Jerusalem 44, 137n38

Dostoevskii, F. M. 1, 193; Notes from the House of the Dead 1; Demons 193

"The Dream Vision That I Had on June 4, 1794" 107n396

Dye, George 240

E

"earthly god" (epithet) 3, 30-33, 47, 91n164, 92n178, 93n178, 111n431, 115, 134n11, 244

Egorov, Abram 33

Ekaterina Alekseevna — see Catherine I (p. 10), Catherine II (p. 64).

Ekaterina Pavlovna, the Grand Princess 58

elevation
    degrees of 160

Elijah, Prophet 55, 76, 116, 135n20

Elizabeth — see Elizaveta Petrovna, Empress.

Elizabeth I of England 223n50, 224n60, 225n60

Elizaveta Alekseevna, wife of Alexander I 67

Elizaveta Petrovna [Elizabeth], Empress 23, 37, 45, 55, 56, 61-64, 66, 89n140, 90n140n141, 108n404, 116, 120, 121, 134n17, 135n17, 245, 256n30

Emperor Alexander — see Alexander I.

Emperor Nicholas — see Nicholas I.

emperor's portrait as an icon — see Icon.

enthronement
    orders of enthronement 154-156, 171n40
    Formulary Edition 154, 155, 164n16, 165n17n21, 171n40, 172n44
    Chronicle Edition 154-156, 171n40
    Byzantine 155, 167n27, 171n40, 172n46

Ephrem the Syrian 90n149

Epiphany 128, 156, 166n24, 212, 222n44

Eremina Kuritsa (Oboliaev S. M.) 119

Eucharist 23, 171n40

Europeanization 17, 18, 182, 185, 186, 193, 194

Eusebius 44, 88n115; "Church History" 88n115

Evgenii (Bolkhovitinov), metropolitan 87n110

excommunication 50, 51, 59, 105n336, 159, 162, 163, 197, 198, 236n113
    of Mazepa and Stepan Glebov 105n336

Explanatory Psalter — see Psalter.

external bishop 83n56

F

faith 2, 9, 13, 15, 19, 25, 58, 70, 88n112, 149n88, 152n117, 160, 161, 165n17, 173n46, 174n57, 192-195, 199, 201, 211, 215, 219n13, 220n13, 245

Petr Fedorovich 28, 63, 64, 90n141, 108n407, 115, 120

Petr Fedorovich, the Grand Prince — *see* Peter III.

Petrine era 17, 54, 60, 86n85, 105n336, 217

Petrine innovations (refotms) 191-194, 198, 199, 207, 214, 217, 218, 230n85, 233n94, 255n6

    as a new faith 192-194

Petrov, V. P. 23, 28, 32, 33, 45, 46, 49, 58, 66, 67, 104n315, 109n408; "On Composing a New Law Code" 23, 33; "On Concluding Peace with the Ottoman Porte"; "On His Imperial Majesty Paul I's Triumphal Entry into Moscow" 45, 49; "On the Celebration of Peace" 58; "On the Triumphal Entry of His Imperial Majesty Paul I into Moscow on March 28, 1797" 28; "People's Love" 67; "Russia's Lament and Consolation, to His Imperial Majesty Paul I" 45; "To the High Title of Great Catherine, Accorded Her Majesty, Most Wise Mother of the Fatherland, in 1767" 109n408

Pimen the Black, Archbishop of Novgorod 139n59

Pishkevich, A. S. 33

Pitirim, metropolitan 50, 51, 228n77

Platon (Levshin), Moscow Metropolitan 23, 28, 29, 36, 46, 48, 49, 58, 68, 101n280, 109n407; "Speech on the Arrival of His Imperial Majesty [Alexander I] in the Reigning City of Moscow, On his Entry into the Uspenskii Sobor" 36

Pletnev, P. A. 112n434

Pobedonostsev, K. P. 37

Pogodin, M. P. 75-77, 109n407, 112n434, 165n17, 215, 216; "Peter I" 109n407

Pokrovskii, N. N. 136n24

Polotskii, Simeon 9, 134n14

pontifex, pontifex maximus 11, 28, 38, 73, 74, 85n84, 192, 203

pope 13, 30, 83n56, 102n304, 116, 145n80, 195, 202, 203, 210, 211, 221n21, 224n60, 225n60, 232n94, 235n104,

poteshnyi polk — *see* "toy soldier regiments."

pretender, pretendership 10, 11, 100n252, 113-133, 151n111, 152n122

    psychology of the pretender 114, 120

priest, priesthood 11, 14, 16, 28, 39, 41, 42, 48, 57, 80n13, 89n140, 97n231, 98n231, 99n241, 105n323, 112n434, 129, 138n55, 140n59, 146n84, 151n109, 156, 166n25, 172n46, 173n46, 174n57, 189n2, 202, 213, 219n13, 224n60, 229n78, 232n94, 235n104, 237n114

    the emperor as a priest 41, 42, 97n227, 98n231, 107n385

Prince-Caesar 39, 125, 126, 143n72, 209, 211-214, 227n72, 233n103, 234n103, 236n110

Prince-Pope 39, 54, 126, 207, 208, 209-211, 213, 226n72, 227n77, 229n78, 230n88, 233n103, 234n103, 235n104

    the mock marriage of Nikita Zotov 206, 208, 209, 213

procession on a donkey

    Peter the Great's hatred for 50-54, 103n304n308n311, 139n57, 195, 196, 209, 220n14

propaganda — *see* Semiotic propaganda.

Prozorovskii, Prince 143n72

Psalter, Explanatory (Tolkovyi Psaltyř) 6, 20, 80n30; Lectionary Psalter (Sledovannaia Psaltyř) 87n111

Pufendorf, S. von 191

Pugachev, Emel`ian 105n336, 118-121, 152n122, 171n43, 251

Pumpianskii, L. V. 242

Pushkin, A. S. 56, 109n407, 112n434, 182, 252, 254, 257n38, 258n38; "Bronze Horseman" 109n407; "Monument" 257n38, 258n38; "The Start of an Autobiography" 56

Pushkin, N. B. 122

Q

Quintilian 189n1

R

Rachette, J.-D. 249

Radishchev, A. N. 252

Razumovskii, Kirill, Hetman 31, 57, 73

CPSIA information can be obtained
at www.ICGtesting.com
Printed in the USA
BVHW03s0840130618

518949BV00006B/118/P